[redacted]

IRELAND RESTORED

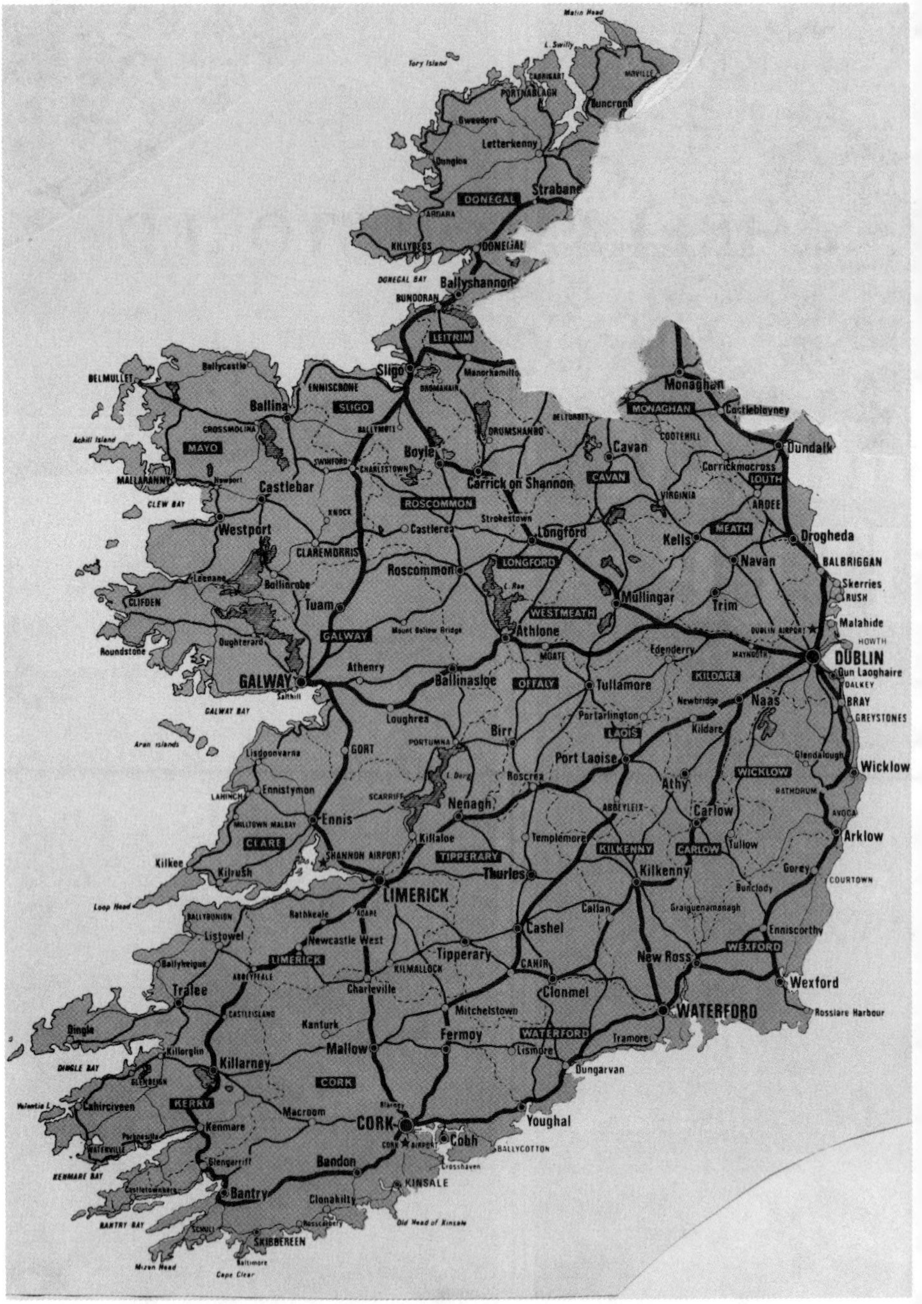

"The name of the State is Eire, or in the English Language, Ireland"
(Article 4, Constitution of Ireland, 1937).

IRELAND RESTORED

The New Self-Determination

VINCENT J. DELACY RYAN

Focus on Issues, No. 13

Freedom House

First published in 1991.

Cover design by Emerson, Wajdowicz Studios, Inc. N.Y.C.

Library of Congress Cataloging-in-Publication Data

Ryan, Vincent J. Delacy.
Ireland restored : the new self-determination / Vincent J. Delacy Ryan.
p. 457 cm. -- (Focus on issues : no. 13)
Includes bibliographical references and index.
ISBN 0-932088-60-0. -- ISBN 0-932088-59-7 (pbk.)
1. Ireland--Constitutional history. 2. Ireland--Politics and government--20th century. 3. federal government--Ireland. 4. Northern Ireland--Constitutional history. 5. Northern Ireland--Politics and government. 6. Irish reunification question. I. Title. II. Series: Focus on issues (Freedom House (U.S.)) ; no. 13.
KDK1220.R95 1991
342.417'029--dc20
[344.170229] 90-44856
CIP

Distributed by arrangement with:

University Press of America, Inc.
4720 Boston Way
Lanham, MD 20706

3 Henrietta Street
London WC2E 8LU England

IN MEMORIAM MEORUM

New Beginning

The joy in a new beginning
Is more than a heart's passion –
It's a gift of creation.

The pride in a new beginning
Is more than a life history –
It is hope, the light of the world.

The message in this beginning
Is more than a youthful cry –
It is a song of love.

Deny this birth,
And all our sons and daughters
Will face starvation.

THERESA KIKO

The Appendices to this work are published in a separate volume titled *Supplement to the Framework of the All-Ireland Republic Restored* (250 pp.). Copies can be had only on request from the publishers, or the author (P.O. Box 183, Northridge, California 91328-0183), priced $12.00 each.

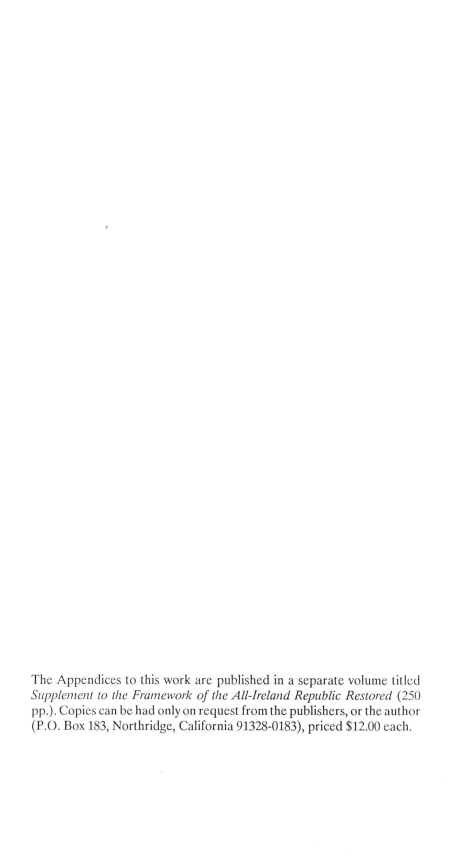

New Life

A crisp spring morning.
A bright flower blooms. A sun
Has been created.

ROSALEEN H. RYAN

TABULA GRATULATORIA

The following persons have very generously shared in the publication cost of this book.

William E., Mae and Patricia M. Barnett,
San Diego, California
Leo V. Corbett,
Garden Grove, California
Daniel Dee,
Whitestone, New York
Gerald and Pat Downey,
Santa Barbara, California
Michael Flannery,
Jackson Heights, New York
Joseph Harkey,
Granada Hills, California
Mary M. Inglis,
Manchester, New Hampshire
James Lamont,
Culver City, California
Peter and Amparo MacAnulty,
Santa Monica, California
Helen McClafferty,
Nutley, New Jersey
Tom McConville,
North Hollywood, California
Michael A. McDermott,
Newport Beach, California
Peggy Moran,
Los Angeles, California
Mary T. Muggivan,
Montebello, California
James P. Shannon,
Olivehain, California
Kathleen D. Harkey Smith,
Granada Hills, California
Jack Webb,
San Francisco, California

LIST OF ILLUSTRATIONS

CONTENTS

Part II: Reconstruction

Appendices

(The Appendices are published separately in the *Supplement*)

FOREWORD

Minority rights are rights too fundamental
– and too precious –
to be determined by majority rule.

ESCHEL RHOODIE

When Ireland shall strike her harp
to the wild notes of Erin and Liberty,
the ocean breeze will bear to her shore
the prayers of Americans
to cheer her in her glorious struggle
and hail her regenerate
in the rights of mankind.

GEORGE WASHINGTON

FOREWORD

The centuries-old tangled skein of the relationships existing between Great Britain and Ireland has surely chosen some rather strange ways through which to manifest itself in our day. The never-ending strife and violence we witness in Northern Ireland cannot be given a full explanation without a proper respect for the long-tortured history of those relationships. A respectful understanding of the complexities of the British-Irish equation is difficult to achieve, but it is possible to pinpoint a modern source period in order to better understand the present seemingly endless tragedy. Vincent Delacy Ryan does just that. He selects the era 1919 to 1925, a period that began with the adoption of the first Irish Constitution to establish a Republic for Ireland and the Irish people – for all of Ireland and all of the Irish people – and that ended with the conclusion of a Treaty of peace and friendship between Britain and Ireland.

A Treaty of peace and friendship, we say, that achieved a solution to the problem in principle. Whence, then, came the present apparently insoluble stalemate and deadlock? Can the potful of grievances stemming from this abnormal condition be met with a final satisfactory solution? True, there can be no redress of grievances in the short term without a basic reformation of the system of justice, a radical change in the security and police forces, and a fundamental restructuring of employment practices and job opportunities in the North of Ireland. Certainly the present abhorrent conditions, especially the discrimination, the oppression and all the other wrongs being committed in the six counties of the

North call for redress and reform. But this volume pleads another thesis. Grievances may easily be settled in the short term, and the latest Irish-British Agreement does serve to address them. But in the long term? For that we must go beyond the effects to the cause of the effects, beyond the symptoms of the disease to the disease itself, beyond the grievances to the reason for them.

The present study puts the finger squarely on the ultimate factor: partition – the partition of Ireland and even of the province of Ulster that was enforced against the majority popular will. With the Anglo-Irish Treaty of 1921 the Irish had wrested independence and unity from Britain in essence, not only of the territory of Ireland but, more importantly, of the people of Ireland, whether Nationalist or Unionist, Catholic or Protestant, or indeed others of different faiths or political persuasions. There seemed to be some hope that partition would not perdure, because the Treaty had provided for a Boundary Commission that hopefully would accommodate the aspirations of the parties to the dispute. Alas! It all came to naught. Misinterpretation of the Treaty requirements for the preservation of essential Irish unity, plus, it is claimed, heavy-handedness in the way that that misinterpretation was applied, rebuffed the people's aspirations and ensured the continuance of the injustice of partition.

This detailed and splendid study takes the reader through the thicket of Irish constitutional history from the Proclamation of the Republic, the Declaration of Independence, the establishment of a Constitution and Parliamentary form of Government, through the Irish Free State era of the Treaty Agreement, the Saorstat Constitution, the Boundary Commission, the more republican period of External Association, the indigenous Constitution, and the Republic of Ireland Act, to the New Ireland Forum and Irish-British Agreement of our times. Force and counterforce, intrigue and disingenuousness, deception and expectation, promises and betrayals, threats and counterthreats, move among such world-renowned names as Lloyd George and Winston Churchill, de Valera and Collins, Carson and Craig, Haughey and FitzGerald and Thatcher, and many lesser lights.

The central thesis of the work is that Ireland, if it is to be reunited, must return (or be returned) to the original status of Republic it enjoyed in the years 1919 to 1922. That all-Ireland Republic as recognized by Britain in the Treaty Settlement must be restored, not through violence or physical force, but by constitutional and legal means. By this is meant, in addition to the restoration of the Republic itself, implementation of all Anglo-Irish agreement that was entered into chiefly in that early Republican period. In this way would Britain be bound even by her own law – bound to honor her recognition of the all-Ireland nature of the Irish Republic.

But such national restoration, involving so much constitutional implementation, cannot be successfully effected without the key to its effectuation. That key is basic to founding a viable restored all-Ireland Republic. A workable foundation is the missing ingredient. As Alfred Gaston Donaldson is quoted as stating, "the core of the Irish question was not the difficulty of devising a form of Constitution: the chief difficulty was to discover a basis on which any constitutional system could be founded." Discovery of the necessary basis on which to found a 32-county constitutional system appears to be what has eluded the Irish in pursuit of a solution before.

In the present work Ryan points to this elusive basis as he puts the problem of the reunification of Ireland through restoration of the Republic and attendant constitutionalism quite pithily and clearly: "On the basis of the unitary nature of Ireland, the right of a minority to dissent (or consent) could not be admitted; on the basis of partitionism or a working pluralism, the right of a minority to consent (or dissent) could not be denied. Holding that distinction, we would proceed to restore the Provisional Republic of Ireland and, in the process, reunite Ireland territorially." Recognition of a right to consent that can simultaneously be coupled with denial of a right to dissent reflects a distinction (of jurisdiction) between territory and people that lies latent in the Republic-based Anglo-Irish constitutionalism of the past. It is in this distinction that there lies the kernel of the solutional theory Ryan has developed into what is called the doctrine of interfiliation.

Interfiliation is defined as being a framework of government within which mutually opposed and disaffected communities in a pluralistic society can achieve complete self-determination without the necessity for a territorial partitioning of their shared nation. In the Irish context, each component group could retain its proper allegiance to its own particular Government – the Unionists to the British Government and the Republicans to the Irish Government. The allegiance, it is explained, would be popularly rather than regionally based, so that territorial partition would be rendered unnecessary. It can easily be seen that if the constitutional agreement of former times is to be implemented and all-Ireland sovereignty restored, some such formula as interfiliation has to be applied as part of the solution.

In the present study Lloyd George is quoted as inviting the Irish leaders to collaborate with Britain within the Commonwealth: "Let us together rule the Empire." Britain's 'Ulster option' as it has always been interpreted has made collaboration impossible and divided Ireland and the Irish people in a way never before countenanced in their long history. Author Dorothy Macardle, in 1937, wrote with confidence and hope that ". . . a generation of Englishmen with new ideals of statecraft is taking the reins of power. Perhaps this generation may make anew the opportunity that, in 1921, was so tragically wasted, and may see an Irish Republic make, with the British Commonwealth of Nations, a compact of unity and peace." Perhaps with the advent of the Restored Republic such noble hopes may finally be made possible of fulfillment.

If the partition of Ireland were solved, the Irish and British would in the world community become and be the most mutually friendly of peoples, since they have more in common with each other than with any other people. As Eamon de Valera said in the Irish Dail in 1941, "they are certain at all times to have more interests in common than they have with other nations. Surely, then, it must be the aim of statesmen on both sides of the Irish Sea to make the relationship between the peoples of these islands that of friendly neighbors."

That ought indeed to be the aim of Irish and British statesmen (and women), and *The Framework of the All-Ireland Republic Restored* may go a long way toward setting a climate for the achievement of that aim.

BISHOP MARK J. HURLEY
SANTA ROSA, CALIFORNIA
and
ROME, ITALY

PREFACE

The independence of America
considered merely as a separation from England
would have been a matter but of little importance
had it not been accompanied by a revolution
in the principles and practise of governments.

THOMAS PAINE

Let us settle ourselves, and work and wedge our feet downward through the mud and slush of opinion, and prejudice, and tradition, and delusion, and appearance, that alluvion which covers the globe, through Paris and London, through New York and Boston and Concord, through Church and State, through poetry and philosophy and religion, till we come to a hard bottom and rocks in place, which we can call **reality**, *and say, This is, and no mistake; and then begin, having a point d'appui, below freshet and frost and fire, a place where you might found a wall or a state, or set a lamp-post safely, or perhaps a gauge, not a Nilometer, but a Realometer, that future ages might know how deep a freshet of shams and appearances had gathered from time to time. If you stand right fronting and face to face to a fact, you will see the sun glimmer on both its surfaces, as if it were a cimeter, and feel its sweet edge dividing you through the heart and marrow, and so you will happily conclude your mortal career. Be it life or death, we crave only reality. If we are really dying, let us hear the rattle in our throats and feel cold in the extremities; if we are alive, let us go about our business.*

HENRY DAVID THOREAU

PREFACE

The Chestertonian apothegm that anything worth doing is worth doing badly – but only until one can marshal the resources to do it as well as it should be done, is very applicable to the Irish constitutional situation. There is no gainsaying the fact that the Irish wresting of independence from Britain in the 1919-1921 period was something that was done badly, but it was done as well as it could be done for those times. The ensuing Anglo-Irish Treaty may have been far from perfect, but, since perfection belongs to the gods, an imperfect Treaty was better than no Treaty at all. The question now ever so many years later is: Have the Irish people by this time marshaled the resources to do the job again, but this time to do it as well as it ought to be done? Since the original job was only three-quarters (or, at most, four-fifths) done, is Ireland ready to redo the job in complete form? In other words, is the time ripe to achieve the reunification of Ireland and the Irish people once and for all?

In dealing with these and related questions, the present volume explores the many and complex implications of these questions and seeks to answer them as objectively and impartially as possible. In an attempt to fulfill the mandate of the Anglo-Irish deliberation of December 8, 1980, it explores the totality of relationships within the British-Irish islands and proposes a possible new institutional structure. Its basic thesis is that in order to achieve a solution of the problem most besetting Ireland – the mutually exclusive political positions of the communities inhabiting the island as they are concretized in partition – a certain continuity from Ireland's

Republican past must somehow and as a very first step be established. By that we mean that the Republic of Ireland that was instituted upon declaration of independence in January 1919 and that held sway for "four glorious years" must in one way or another be restored and linked up with in the present. As Sean MacEntee once said, we must "start from 'square one' " or as Sean MacBride put it, "we must go right back to the beginnings of this State."

One reason it is necessary to go back to and reconstitute the early Irish Provisional Republic is that the Republic was a Republic of ***all*** of Ireland and to restore it now would mean that a virtually united Ireland would be brought into existence as a base from which to work to achieve actual reunification. For it was while enjoying the status of 32-county Republic that Nationalist Ireland was trying to accommodate the Unionist position before and that partition was ineluctably imposed on Ireland as Britain's answer to the Irish question. And it is the unfinished work of political accommodation which that Republic represented that must now be resumed and completed.

Another and very important reason it is necessary to restore the former Irish Republic and its constitutionalism is that it was with that Republic as representing ***all*** of Ireland that the Treaty was concluded with Britain, the Loyalist community of the North the while assenting. (Any Agreement that might be entered into now with Britain would of necessity be between an Ireland that is an alien country to Northern Ireland and the United Kingdom (of Britain and Northern Ireland) and would, therefore, be of an irredentist and weak nature as far as all of Ireland would be concerned.) Which leads us to our second most important consideration, the step of going back also to, taking up and implementing the Anglo-Irish constitutionalism of the Treaty Settlement that recognized for Ireland the principle of essential unity, the different title deeds of the communities in dispute, and the nonnecessity for a balkanization of Ireland to resolve the communal problem. We feel now that all parties to an Agreement that contained seminally a solution to so intractable a problem as has existed heretofore should be compelled to fulfill what they agreed to in principle in such an Agreement and to honor their commitments to the Agreement and its concomitant Constitution and Amendments – even after so long a lapse of time.

It is necessary, then, as a means to finding a permanent solution, to return to and restore not only the original Irish Republican constitutionalism, but also and at the same time the Anglo-Irish constitutionalism of the Irish Free State that prevailed for the first 15 years of the newly independent nation's life.[1] True it may be that the remote cause of partition was the odious Government of Ireland Act that burst in on Irish independence, "that statutory abortion of December 1920, sardonically entitled 'An Act to provide for the better government of Ireland.' " This was the way George Gavan Duffy described the 'Partition Act' that unilaterally and statutorily guaranteed (in British constitutional law) the hegemony of the Loyalist/Unionist majority in the six northeastern counties of Ireland. And the less remote cause of partition was (as we shall see) the Boundary Commission's misinterpretation of a Treaty clause that was enforced in 1925. But the proximate cause of partition was Ireland's own acquiescence in it, an acquiescence that was as unnecessary as it was unsure. This occurred in 1937 with the rash abandonment of the externally associating all-Ireland Constitution of 1922 and the consequent changeover from the 32-county Saorstat Eireann Irish Free State to the 26-county Republic of Eire when a new Constitution was instituted. That is another reason it is necessary to return to the former Republican and Anglo-Irish constitutional systems to find a genesis of a solution, and in this book we examine where and how precisely Ireland acquiesced in partition, in what ways that mistake might be corrected, and what exactly the solutional genesis itself might be.

Still another reason it is necessary to return to the original Irish Republic and Free State is that the problem of reunification is not just one of conjoining two contiguous territories or parts of former Ireland into one loosely associated confederation or 'bination.' The problem is, as Eamon de Valera put it in the current Irish Constitution, one of ***reintegrating*** the national territory into an ***integrally*** united whole, either as a unitary or federal nation. Any attempts falling short of restoring the former Republic and Free State of Ireland in order to reintegrate the Irish nation, in either form, would be bound to prove self-defeating, because they would be undertaken in practice from outside of the constitutional

1 In advocating also a restoration of Anglo-Irish constitutionalism, we were prompted by the realistic procedure advised by Professor Claire Palley that any effort to find a solution to the British-Irish constitutional problem "must proceed on the basis that United Kingdom governments, as the only effective catalytic agents, will exercise their power so as to achieve their own aims in so far as they are not constrained by the effective vetoes enjoyed by both communities on new institutional arrangements" ("Ways Forward: The Constitutional Options," David Watt, ed., *The Constitution of Northern Ireland, Problems and Prospects*, p. 185).

politics of Ireland itself (32 counties). They would be undertaken from within the 'nation' which is, for all practical purposes, foreign to the larger nation. That is to say, they would be undertaken from within the ambit of the irredentist partition politics of the 26-county constitutionalism that was born of Irish acquiescence in partition back when the Free State was given up. And any move undertaken from within that kind of persuasionist politics has a history of ending up in the cul-de-sac of British umbrage-taking in the Loyalist guarantee and veto, of which rejection of the Irish Forum proposals and reimposition of British sovereignty and the Unionist stance in the most recent Anglo-Irish Agreement are prime examples. That is why the basic problem has to be tackled from within the framework of the restored Irish Republic and Free State and from within all-Ireland and Anglo-Irish constitutional politics.

Restoration of Anglo-Irish constitutionalism, in addition to the native Republican variety, is also necessary because of the fact that the Anglo-Irish Treaty of 1921-22 repealed the very Acts upon which the Partition Act depended for constitutionality (in British law), namely, the Acts of Union of 1800. And the only conditions under which a form of partition might become constitutional and be continued were laid down in that Treaty Settlement. We explain herein what those conditions were and how they were never really fulfilled, but, by the same token, how conditions agreed on for the abolition of territorial partition were never fulfilled either. The main point is that if British (and Unionist) agreement could have been obtained to abolish partition in principle, then, surely, that agreement should be exploited to the full now and Britain's cooperation should be secured to implement such agreement and to compel all-round compliance. That degree of cooperation, we feel, can only be secured by a reinstitution of the legal framework of the former Free State of Ireland, that is, of basically the Treaty Agreement and the British Irish Constitution of 1922. That form of Anglo-Irish cooperation to solve a mutual problem is, despite the 1985 Agreement bedeviling it in its aim, entirely possible of securement, because it would be worked from within the all-Ireland framework that secured such cooperation before – when the Treaty itself was negotiated and concluded and when in that instrument the essential unity of Ireland was recognized by Britain and assented to by Northern Ireland.

A final reason for the need to invoke additionally Anglo-Irish constitutionalism to settle the Irish problem is the fact that all the British-Irish agreement there ever was has also been formulated and confirmed in British statutory law; so that in invoking such constitutional law one is also and thereby compelling the United Kingdom rulers to abide by their own law. Indeed, reinstitution of Anglo-Irish constitutionalism means, to a very great extent, the reactivation for Ireland of that large corpus of British Irish constitutional law (centered on the Treaty and Free State Constitution) by which, of course, the British and the Northern Irish Unionists would be bound. And in reactivating such constitutional law one is *ipso facto* commanding implementation by the law's own subjects of what was agreed to by the formulators of that law when essentially the 1922 Irish Free State Constitution Act ratified the Treaty and the Treaty's Constitution.

At this point, it may be objected that the effort to reinstate Anglo-Irish statutory law in Ireland as a way of compelling compliance with or implementation of existing agreement would be a self-defeating undertaking, because it would necessitate resorting to the adoption of forceful constitutional law in a take-it-or-leave-it fashion. It would involve more than the usual force that Constitutions ordinarily import, and so it would be bound to be resisted with a certain counterforce. Moreover, it might be said, resorting to the imposition of a constitutional force would be a negation of the principle of unity by agreement and consent which has itself been agreed to in the same Anglo-Irish constitutionalism that one would be enforcing. Such would be unfair and unjust and would, one might say, amount to a compulsion bordering on coercion, which in Republican Ireland has ever been eschewed. If it were to be attempted, what is to prevent a revolt against such an all-compelling force this one time rather than ever in the past since partition began – especially when resistance is being evidenced against so benign and partition-favoring an Agreement as that of November 1985?

The answer to such objections is, in a word, 'interfiliation,' the term that stands for the new self-determination that, while being legally forcibly emplaced, acts additionally as a safety valve in the enjoinment of constitutional force. This principle is, ironically, contained in the very same constitutionalism that would be enforced and has, in fact, been educed from it. The principle of interfiliation is what makes an otherwise unacceptable constitutional system acceptable, and is what makes the force such a 'mixed' constitutionalism bears to be tolerable to all concerned.

Interfiliation was not hypothesized as a mechanism that might fit the complex Irish situation. Rather, with Judge John T.

Noonan's dictum in mind – "A page of history is worth a volume of logic" – interfiliation was derived entirely from the Anglo-Irish Treaty Settlement as that faced up to the complex problem and provided in 1921 and succeeding years a seminal solution. But the Treaty was treated originally as having a complex problem of its own. As we know, there was a supposed notorious ambiguity in the document, though it was an 'ambiguity' that was more apparent than real and was only raised as an issue at all to encourage its exploitation to the advantage of one side over the other. It was this exploitation that was more notorious than the alleged ambiguity itself, and this took the form of an interpretation of the text (specifically of the Boundary Commission provision – Article 12) that a close exegetical and historical inspection does not at all bear out. In other words, it was a forced and slanted interpretation, a misinterpretation, and it is what has caused the disastrous results that are so well known today.

To the extent that Article 12 admitted of more than one possible interpretation at all, the misinterpretation that was attempted was that the grievances of the communities in northern Ireland (Ulster) could be simply remedied by adjusting the glaring abnormalities that existed on either side of a partition that was imposed as a deliberate gerrymander to begin with. This was the misinterpretation that was enforced by the Boundary Commission in its adjudication more of the Government of Ireland Act, 1920 than of the Treaty Article 12 provision. But the only honest and valid interpretation that there could have been placed on the passage in question would be that it provided some sort of ***communal*** means of remedying the grievances of the populations involved. This latter interpretation is the one we argue here, and it is one for which there is ample authority (Cosgrave, O'Higgins, Laffan among others).

In our work, in fact, we have presented repeated evidence of the way the Treaty was interpreted, by more than one, to have acknowledged and guaranteed the rights and liberties of the mutually opposing traditions in Ireland. How that could be achieved, equally, for all was, we explain, through the Treaty provision for the interfiliation concept. This was not thought out or developed at the time, and because it was assumed to be an unworkable principle (because not clearly understood) its application was easily blocked in 1925 by the Boundary Commission misinterpretation and the political climate of the time. Herein is where, building on the 1985 rerecognition of the equality of communal rights, corrective action ought presently to be taken and herein is where the interfiliation principle that has lain latent so long in the Treaty ought to be solutionally applied.

Interfiliation, which we also refer to as 'people-based jurisdiction,' 'communal jurisdiction,' and 'jurisdictional identity,' is, briefly, a system of government of a pluralistic nation whereby a community inhabiting such a nation but owing allegiance to another nation may do so without impeding the sovereignty of its own nation as that is upheld by a fellow community and recognized by the host nation. The sovereignty of the home nation is unimpeded by the disaffected community being governed by and from the foreign nation on a ***personal*** rather than a territorial basis. The community (or communities) owing allegiance to its own nation is likewise governed on a personal basis. Each community is so governed only in the minor powers area of jurisdiction, however. Both (or all) are collectively responsible for the government of the home nation in the major powers area – national defense, international relations, and the like. The system works analogically to the way the government of states/provinces in a federal/confederal nation would – with one possible difference: confederation with the foreign nation would probably be entailed.

Interfiliation is somewhat akin to a system of rule recently suggested by Northern Nationalists in Ireland and reported by the writer Tom Collins. Referred to as a people-based 'Irish dimension option,' it is not a matter "of looking at territories and borders and divisions of land, but of considering the people involved – the individual human beings – and letting them decide what allegiance they prefer" (*The Centre Cannot Hold*, pp. 177-179). While this particular model would, while hoping for the respective allegiances to be institutionalized, renounce all territorial claims to the North of Ireland, the interfiliation principle more resolutely posits an all-Ireland restored Republic as the framework within which to fit the personal jurisdictions. It is, besides, what is rigorously derived from constitutional Irish history and, as such, is only what is allowed by that history and as being strictly constitutional.

Interfiliation is very akin to, though essentially distinct from, the concept of 'confiliation' newly discovered and developed by Professor Albert P. Blaustein of Rutgers University. Interfiliation can be compared broadly to confederation, while confiliation can be compared rather to federation. The rationale of this is that while the communities living under one system appertain to both their own pluralistic homeland and an alien country, the communities living under the other appertain to a distinct pluralistic country. Both systems, it will be noted, concern themselves with group rights – as distinct from individual rights, heretofore in history reflected in and protected by national Constitutions and Bills of Rights. Both systems recognize national minorities' rights to self-rule and are based on personal rather than territorial jurisdictions. The systems are described and compared in detail in the Epilogue to our book, the reason for their appearance in such a spot rather than in the text being that the system of confiliation only came to our attention after the text was written. But we are happy to have come across it at all and to learn that we were not alone in finding a similar formula by which ***mutually*** disaffected communities might severally discover satisfactory forms of self-determination and coexistent self-government.

The necessity of finding some such mutually accommodative structure as interfiliation in the Irish context, not only for solving the domestic problem but also for regularizing British-Irish constitutional relations, could hardly have been demonstrated more forcibly than in Paragraph 4.15 of the New Ireland Forum Report:

> The solution to both the historic problem and the current crisis of Northern Ireland and the continuing problem of relations between Ireland and Britain necessarily requires new structures that will accommodate together two sets of legitimate rights:
>
> – the right of nationalists to effective political, symbolic and administrative expression of their identity; and
>
> – the right of unionists to effective political, symbolic and administrative expression of their identity, their ethos and their way of life.
>
> So long as the legitimate rights of both unionists and nationalists are not accommodated together in new political structures acceptable to both, that situation will continue to give rise to conflict and instability.

Of course, it is not only in Ireland and between Ireland and Britain that interfiliation can be adopted to solve problems of common concern. Interfiliation, or confiliation, can be employed to solve the political problems of people in many areas of the world – the Kurds in Turkey, Armenia and Iran; the Greeks and Turks in Cyprus; the Basques in Spain and France; the Anglos in Argentina and the Falklands; the Palestinians in Israel, Lebanon and Jordan; the Indians in America and Canada; the Blacks in South

Africa; the 55 national minorities in China; and, of course, the Anglo-Irish and Gaelic Irish in Ireland. If the system of interfiliation can be adopted to solve the Irish problem, it will not only be because it lies latent in the existing Anglo-Irish constitutionalism and is mandated by it, but also because the 1985 Irish-British Agreement practically mandates it too. Otherwise, this Agreement has to be understood in a purely territorial sense and as such runs the risk of being declared unconstitutional – by either the British or Irish Courts, or both. The question, then, is not whether interfiliation should be put into effect, but when and how and by whom.

As for when it will be, just about all that can be said is that interfiliation will be implemented when all sides – British, Republican Irish, Unionist Irish – are ready for it. That may be a while yet, because there will surely be some who will say the innovative principle goes too far and there will surely be others who will say it doesn't go far enough. Interfiliation is not a proposal, modest or other. It is not anyone's bright idea or an invention. In the Irish context, it is only what is contained latently in existing constitutional agreement, no more and no less. Now the job is not to destroy that agreement, but to fulfill it; not to allow the Hillsborough Accord to stand in the way of that fulfillment, but to utilize this latest Anglo-Irish Agreement as the framework through which to implement all preceding bipartate and tripartate agreement. And if that is going too far for some and not far enough for others, well – that's interfiliation.

As to how the interfiliation concept might be implemented, that in effect is what this book is all about. While we do not offer a blueprint for a solution of the partition problem, we do treat the *sine qua non* conditions for putting in place the solution to the problem: restoration of the all-Ireland Republican constitutional system and its concurrent Irish Free State constitutional system. What we say needs to be done is, as Sean MacBride has again exhorted, "to go right back to Square One now." For as soon as both the native Irish and Anglo-Irish constitutional systems are restored, together with the safety valve of interfiliation, and as soon as those systems are then exploited to the utmost of their utility to Ireland, Irish reunification is virtually assured. And it is in that exploitation that we would utilize our blueprint.

Finally, as to by whom the interfiliation principle might be implemented, that is up to each reader to determine for himself and herself. We cannot go so far as to intimate, without incurring an obvious partiality, what political grouping other than one of

Republicans of the Tone-Davis-Collins-de Valera tradition might be best suited to execute the interfiliation program. That risk, however, does not deter us from presenting our constitutional message, no matter how laden with political overtones it may unavoidably be. We plead the belief of Keith Middlemas that "the position of Catholics and Protestants in Northern Ireland and the border between North and South are open issues where the historian's role can scarcely be separated from the polemics of today." While we have written as objectively and impartially as possible, and done so on a subject that is difficult to treat with complete impartiality, we trust that we will not be found guilty of more than an honest partiality. Otherwise, we will take umbrage in Chesterton's statement: "The nearest that any honest man can come to the thing called ***impartiality*** is to confess that he is partial."

But, no matter when, how and by whom interfiliation is to be inaugurated, we do not consider the system to be something fixed and unalterable as a working idea. As with Mikhail Gorbachev on the new thinking of *perestroika*, "we do not think that we have found the final truth which others merely have to accept or reject, that is, take a [contrary] position which we would call erroneous." Interfiliation as a restructuring of society is as much for us as for anyone a new process, a novel experience, in the development of which we, too, have much to learn as we participate in its unfolding.

I set out 'aeons' ago to write a constitutional history of modern Ireland, but I ended up defining a system of government designed to suit the peculiar Irish situation. In this I feel my work may not be unlike that of the artist in Thoreau's ennobling story who, in a timeless mode, fashioned a staff from a tree of the forest into something more than a mere staff. "He had made a new system in making a staff, a world with full and fair proportions," the Great Ponderer mused, "in which, though the old cities and dynasties had passed away, fairer and more glorious ones had taken their places." If the present 'staff' proves to be the means that will restore at least a corner of the world to suchlike full and fair proportions, then my original intention will have been amply fulfilled.

If mention must be made of the many who helped me make the writing of this book a possibility, pride of place must surely go to my teacher-parents, who, being steeped in Irish history themselves, gave me a deep and abiding interest in that subject. After them, an old friend, Willie Crowe of Thurles, County Tipperary, must be mentioned, for it was he who reinforced my love for Irish history in my youth by giving me Dan Breen's classic, *My Fight for Irish Freedom*. Many have helped with the composition of the material of this book, either through their works or by their personal efforts, but chief credit must be given to two notable historians: Dorothy Macardle, whose chronicling of events in her very fine work, *The Irish Republic*, was indispensable to me in treating the Republican side of Irish constitutional history; and F.S.L. Lyons, whose diligent research as reflected in his *Ireland Since the Famine* proved a veritable gold mine to me in presenting the Anglo-Irish side of the story. Several other author-historians, whose original work has been of invaluable help, deserve also to be mentioned with appreciation. Chief among these are: Lord Longford, Leo Kohn, J.L. McCracken, Thomas P. O'Neill, J.G. Swift MacNeill, John A. Murphy, Oliver McDonagh, Nicholas Mansergh, Edmund Curtis, Giovanni Costigan, Colin Cross, Alfred LeRoy Burt, D.J. Akinson, J.J. Fallin, C.H. Currey, Frank Gallagher, J.C. Beckett, T.W. Moody, F.X. Martin, Michael Laffan, John Bowman and Joseph M. Curran. Still others, whose research I have profitably availed of, but who are too numerous to mention here, are given credit by being included in the Literature Cited and Consulted.

An extra special note of thanks is due to some who collaborated with me on a more personal level. Very valuable criticism of my manuscript, particularly with regard to balancing its emphases, was offered by Judge J. Michael Byrne of Los Angeles. Joseph Drohan of Monrovia (and South Tipperary) must also be thanked for checking portions of the work. Others whose help or encouragement is also greatly appreciated are: Ailfrid Mac Lochlainn and Aidan Cullen (Dublin); Pat Goggins (San Francisco); Brian Farrell (National University of Ireland, Dublin); Gerald-A. Beaudoin (University of Ottawa); Niall O'Dowd and Sean McGeever (San Francisco and New York); Tim Pat Coogan (Dublin); Thelma Doran (San Francisco and Dublin); my ever so political family members Veronica Molloy, Bernadette Lynch and James Ryan (Ireland); and the staffs of the University of California Library (Los Angeles campus), the National Library of Ireland (Dublin), Trinity College Library (Dublin), University College Library (Dublin), the California State University Library (Northridge campus), the Los Angeles County Law Library, the Irish Government Stationery Office (Dublin), and Her Majesty's Stationery Offices (London and Belfast). The magnificent staff of the magnificent Los Angeles County Law Library must be given a special word of thanks.

The ultimate acknowledgment must perhaps be given to an extraordinarily unique political organization without whose spirit and patronage – if a time-worn cliche will be excused – this book could not have been written. The uniqueness of the U.S. Irish Forum, of which I am proud to be a charter member and as which I wrote this book, lies in the fact that it must ever be faced with a dilemma of its own purposeful creating. So open, unpartisan and noncommittal must the Forum be in seeking a solution to the Northern Ireland problem that it may not formally espouse the solution if it should find it and yet remain the Forum as we've known it. Neither, on the other hand, may it be uncommitted to the solution when it is found and continue on meaningfully in the pursuance of its declared purpose: "to explore all avenues toward a peaceful resolution of the problem of Northern Ireland" and to that end to "provide a forum for the exchange of ideas from across the spectrum of Irish, British, American and other international viewpoints." Only from within such a singular matrix of studied openness and firm impartiality could the solution to so complex a problem ever emerge, and without so truly unique an organization as the Irish Forum could the all-round acceptable solution ever be found.

Honorable mention must, too, be made of Ray Bradbury, who composed *To Ireland . . .*; Eric Wechsler of VMH, Northridge, who word processed the manuscript in thoroughgoing fashion; Elaine Holzer of Crest Secretarial Service, Northridge, who further processed the manuscript; Patricia E. Williamson of Caltrans, Los Angeles, who designed the chart on the course of British disengagement from Ireland; Joyce Celeste of Word Magic, Van Nuys, who formatted the recorded data in final form; and Dwayne Spraglin, Kathy Smith and Bobby Villapando of Dynatype, Glendale, who designed and produced the book.

Finally, my wife, Monica, and our children, Rosaleen and Fintan, must be given the credit they deserve for ungrudgingly allowing me to encroach heavily on the time that under normal circumstances I would have shared with them.

Irish Forum
Los Angeles, California

PROLOGUE

Political creativity is a moral and religious act.

ARNOLD CANTWELL SMITH

Easter 1916

MacDonagh and MacBride
And Connolly and Pearse
Now and in time to be,
Wherever green is worn,
Are changed, changed utterly:
A terrible beauty is born.

WILLIAM BUTLER YEATS, I.R.B.

PROLOGUE

The Republican Roots of a Unitary Ireland

On Easter Monday morning, 1916, a giant step forward was taken in Ireland's centuries-long struggle for freedom and independence. On that fateful morning, seven brave men, led by their Head of Government, Padraic Henry Pearse, signed and issued the Proclamation of the Republic that established the Provisional Government of Ireland.[1] In putting their signatures to that Republican document, the gallant seven realized full well that they were sealing their fate and that soon they would be called on to make the supreme sacrifice for their Ireland. For, establishment of an Irish Government, in defiance of the ruling order, was to bring about a backlash of British force and fury that transformed a bold political stroke into a war and that made of a hefty constitutional blow a revolution. The Rising of Easter Week was on.

The infant Provisional Government that Pearse and his comrades in arms established was attacked almost at once by the British forces of occupation. Within three weeks it was totally destroyed, with the court-martialing and execution by firing squad of all seven Government members and eight other leaders of the Rising. In addition, a pacifist associated with the Rebellion, two journalists, a youth, and a diplomat were executed. During the week of the Insurrection 64 other insurgents and 254 civilians, including 15 of the North King Street massacre, were killed, while 134 members

1 The seven signatories were, including Pearse, Thomas J. Clarke, Sean Mac Diarmaid (MacDermott), Thomas MacDonagh, Eamonn Ceannt (Kent), James Connolly and Joseph M. Plunkett.

of the Crown forces lost their lives. But the Republic endured, and for several glorious days the Green, White and Orange of the Irish Nation flew above the rooftops of Dublin and in the provinces of Ireland.

But whatever the military outcome of the Easter encounter was to be, the long-awaited constitutional blow for Ireland was struck. The deed was done, the old order changed. Under the Provisional Proclamation of the Republic, the Irish people were, from that springtime of the nation forth, to switch their allegiance away from the old Government of Great Britain to the new Government of all Ireland. All were summoned to the Flag of the Republic and exhorted to strike for freedom. "The Irish Republic is entitled to, and hereby claims," the Proclamation declared, "the allegiance of every Irishman and Irishwoman." Until the time that such a switch in allegiance could be made effective, the Provisional Government would administer the civil and military affairs of the Republic in trust for the people. When the destined moment arrived there would be established "a permanent National Government representative of the whole people of Ireland and elected by the suffrages of all her men and women."

By its expectation of a permanent National Government for the people of all Ireland, the Proclamation of the Republic looked to being ratified eventually in a duly elected Parliament of the Irish nation. In so doing, it anticipated and paved the way for the Declaration of Independence that was to be issued by just such a Parliament barely three years later. On January 21, 1919, the Republic that was constituted by the Proclamation of 1916 was endorsed unanimously by the elected Representatives of the Irish people assembled in Dail Eireann, the first Dail and Constituent Assembly of Ireland. Thus it was that upon ratification by a democratically elected Assembly of all Ireland, the Proclamation became the seminal constitutional instrument of the Sovereign and Republican Irish Nation.

The Proclamation of the Republic

The document the Proclamation of the Republic, chiefly the composition of Pearse and the Tipperary poet Thomas MacDonagh, is to modern Ireland what the Declaration of Independence is to the United States. By its clear and emphatic statement of purpose, by its moral elevation of tone, and by the dignity of its language, the Proclamation bears comparison with any statement of nationalism formulated in recent centuries. Noted for its brevity and conciseness, the document contains a political philosophy that at once encapsulates the history of the Irish struggle for liberation and sets forth a vision for Ireland that will endure in inspiring future generations of the Irish people. (The text of the Proclamation of the Republic is reproduced in Appendix 1, *Supplement to the Framework of the All-Ireland Republic Restored.*)

Throughout the Proclamation document the emphasis is on the sovereignty of the ***people*** of Ireland, and on the nationhood of Ireland as inhering in the inhabitants of the island. Herein is contained the basis of the doctrine of Government by consent of the governed, a doctrine that was drawn from Wolfe Tone and indeed the ancient Gaelic State and that was echoed, from the Proclamation, in the Declaration of Independence and in the first Irish Constitution. This latter declared, as we shall see, that all powers of Government were derived from the sovereign Irish people (Article 1). The doctrine of popular sovereignty was reproduced also in the second Irish Constitution, that of 1922 (Article 2). And it is stated, of course, in the third Irish Constitution, that of 1937 (Article 6).

By basing the legitimacy of the new Irish State on the historical right of the sovereignty and nationhood of the inhabitants of Ireland, the Proclamation of 1916 established the Easter Rising as the revolutionary culmination of the long process of Ireland's emergence into full nationhood and independence. Fired by a deep and abiding faith in God and in the divine will to free Ireland once a blood sacrifice was offered as a propiatory act to the Almighty, the Insurrection, that appeared a failure, proved a tremendous success. The sacrifice would bear its fruits, death would turn into life, a new beginning would be made. A New Departure would be begun.

A New Departure it was. All was changed, changed utterly. The Proclamation of the Republic, with its concomitant establishment of a Provisional Government, wafted the nation beyond the prevailing Nationalism to full-fledged Republican status. In the process, the gauntlet was thrown down to the British and the functions of Government were for once taken over from the alien ruler. Britain, in spite of having granted Home Rule to Ireland two years before, continued to deny the country its enjoyment. This Britain did in spite of the fact that Ireland was until then contributing tens of thousands of her sons yearly to the war effort of that time. A Britain who would go so far as to betray Ireland's trust in her in this way was bound to strike back in 1916 if Irish self-determination was to be wrested from her by force. This is in fact what Britain did.

Paradoxically, however, it was not so much the establishment of an independent Irish Government that Easter Week that forced the issue with Britain in the public mind. It was rather the public reaction to the executions that took place with complete absence of supposed British magnanimity that joined the issue. These executions, which were carried out so callously over a ten-day period within two weeks of the end of the Rising, evoked feelings of utter revulsion in the general public. An entire Government-in-Arms had been wiped out. The reaction and outrage gradually translated itself into a political galvanization of the people of Ireland, and this resurrection of the public was soon enough to find an effective outlet in a political action of an unprecedented kind. In the General Election of December 1918, Republican Sinn Fein and the Nationalists captured 80 percent of the Parliamentary seats in Ireland. Irish Republicanism that seemed to have died in the 'failed' Rising of 1916 arose from the ashes like a resurgent phoenix flame and spread its fire to every corner of the land in an unheard-of form of new life. Constitutional Republicanism resurgent was on its way.

The Declaration of Independence

In preparation for the 1918 General Election the Republican Movement, under the banner of Sinn Fein, issued a very special Election Manifesto to the Irish people, and in response to that Manifesto the people at the polls gave the Republicans a very special mandate. The mandate of the Irish electorate was that political and constitutional effect be given to what had been catalyzed by the setting up of the Provisional Government and the Rising of 32 months earlier. That is to say, the mandate was to establish a free and independent all-Ireland Republic, and as a means to achieving this to set up a Constituent Assembly. The elected leaders of the independence movement accordingly convened on January 21, 1919, the Parliament of all Ireland, Dail Eireann, the first elected Irish political Assembly since the demise of 'Grattan's Parliament' in 1800. Eamon de Valera was elected President of this First Dail,[2] and the Cabinet consisted additionally

2 Although he was President (*Priomh Aire*) of Dail Eireann, de Valera was not, like Padraic Pearse before him, President (*Uachtaran*) of Ireland. Denis McCullough, by virtue of his being President of the Supreme Council of the I.R.B. in 1916, was first President of the Irish Republic that Ireland was declared to be at that time. Michael Collins was, for the same reason, second President of Ireland from some time in 1918. And de Valera was third President of the Irish Republic from 1921 to 1922. (See further Appendix 2, *Supplement to the Framework of the All-Ireland Republic Restored*.)

of Arthur Griffith (Home Affairs), Michael Collins (Finance), George Noble Count Plunkett (Foreign Affairs), Cathal Brugha (Defense), Eoin MacNeill (Industries), Constance Countess de Markievicz (Labor), William Cosgrave (Local Government), and Robert Barton (Agriculture). Lawrence Ginnell became Director of Publicity and Richard Mulcahy was appointed Volunteer Chief of Staff of the Irish Republican Army (which had been the Irish Volunteers).

One of the first acts of the new Dail Eireann acting as a Constituent Assembly was to ratify in the Declaration of Independence the establishment of the Irish Republic of three years earlier. The Declaration marks accordingly not another New Departure, but rather, as F.S.L. Lyons points out (in *Ireland Since the Famine*, pp. 398-399), a reaffirmation of the establishment of the Irish Republic that occurred in 1916. "And whereas at the threshold of a new era in history the Irish electorate has in the General Election of December, 1918, seized the first occasion to declare by an overwhelming majority its firm allegiance to the Irish Republic," the Declaration states; "Now, therefore, we, the elected Representatives of the ancient Irish people in National Parliament assembled, do, in the name of the Irish nation, ratify the establishment of the Irish Republic."

As with the Proclamation of the Republic, the emphasis throughout the Declaration of Independence is on 'the Irish people,' 'the Irish electorate,' 'the Irish nation,' and 'the declared will of the people.' It is 'the Irish people' that is determined 'to secure and maintain its complete independence,' to build up and ensure the security of the nation, and 'to constitute a national policy based upon the people's will, with equal right and equal opportunity for every citizen.' Correspondingly, it is 'the elected Representatives of the Irish people alone' who have power and authorization from the people to make laws for the people of Ireland, and 'the Irish Parliament is the only Parliament to which that people will give its allegiance.'

All these expressions of the will of the people are so many reiterations of the doctrine of popular sovereignty first voiced in the Proclamation of the Republic. The medieval notion of the divine right of kings was abhorrent to the Irish people. For them, as for the inhabitants of the ancient Gaelic State, all authority came from God to the people and was delegated by them to their Representatives in Parliament. It was largely the need the Irish people felt to assert this doctrine of Government by consent of the governed that impelled them to rebel against a then-nonunderstanding British rule and to insist that the mandate they gave to their Representatives in the elections of 1918 be put fully into effect. The people's Representatives did accordingly in ratifying the Irish Republic "pledge ourselves and our people to make this declaration effective by every means at our command."

In ratifying the establishment of the Republic, what "the elected Representatives of the ancient Irish people" primarily did was to declare restored to the people the historic unitary Irish State. But, in addition, and in accordance with the principles of the Proclamation of the Republic, they declared the unitary State to be restored in multinational form. That is to say, what was declared was not a Gaelic but an Anglo-Gaelic State born of the popular will, with self-determination for the traditional communities in Ireland. True, it was Republican and Nationalist Irish who were in the vanguard of the drive for the particular form of independence Ireland needed or could achieve. But these acted as the majority of all the people – Republican, Nationalist and Unionist – as this was the only way the people could change the old order in practice. The 'General Will' of Alfred Cobban had exercised itself – which, as Cobban would say, had "to be identified with the will of the majority if it [was] to mean anything practical."

With the birth of the Multinational Irish State the dream of Tone and Davis had come true. The New United Ireland of Catholic, Protestant and Dissenter under the common name of Irishman had arrived. This the Declaration of Independence ***declared.*** It remained for the arrival to be acknowledged by Great Britain in the spirit of the post-World War times. To this end the Declaration proscribed all foreign Government in Ireland, which, insofar as it had been based on force and military occupation, was totally opposed to the traditional Irish concept of Government by the will of the sovereign Irish people. In keeping with this and the other assertions of the will of the people, the document demanded the evacuation of the country by the British garrison. It presupposed British military occupation to be a threat to the peace and security of Ireland and proclaimed Irish independence to be a necessary precondition to international peace and security.

The Declaration of Independence was unanimously adopted and promulgated as a public act by the elected Representatives of the Irish people assembled in Dail Eireann as a Constituent Assembly on January 21, 1919.

The text of the Declaration of Independence is given in Appendix 2, *Supplement.*

The First Constitution of Ireland

The Declaration of Independence issued in the first Irish Constitution, a document which was also promulgated by the elected Representatives of the Irish people on January 21, 1919. This instrument formed primarily the legal foundation on which Dail Eireann was established as the Parliament of all Ireland on that same date. Since the Declaration of Independence was regarded by the framers of the Constitution as the Preamble to the Constitution, the Constitution must be studied in conjunction with the Declaration from which it flows.

The Constitution of 1919 was intended as a fundamental law for the new State, and not, despite its title ('The Constitution of Dail Eireann'), a Constitution of the Dail alone. It is true that it left much unwritten, but then it must be remembered that it was drafted under trying and uncertain conditions, with most Sinn Fein leaders either on the run or in prison and with the drafting committee's papers seized in a police raid on Sinn Fein headquarters four days after the committee was appointed to draw up the Constitution. It was intended as well that the Constitution would be fleshed out by amendment when normal times would return – or, as Cathal Brugha put it, "when the Republic was recognised they would draw up a regular constitution."

Although presented as the Constitution of the Dail only, the Constitution actually covered two of the three branches of Government – the legislative and the executive. (The third branch, the judicial, was not treated, and this may have been because it was thought that the Republican courts which were already functioning did not need to be regulated by Constitution, and besides it was not yet known whether they would be continued or the older system would be taken over: eventually the older system was taken over.) Covering as it did the two main branches of Government, the Constitution would have to be said to be devised for the nation as any Constitution would be, although it directly and primarily concerned Dail Eireann. "The intention to provide a framework for the government of the state and not merely for the functioning of the Dail is clear throughout," Brian Farrell points out (*The Founding of Dail Eireann*, p. 63). "[This] is stated explicitly in the preamble to the original text in the [Sean T.] O Ceallaigh papers."

The Preamble that was prepared by O Ceallaigh (O'Kelly) for the Constitution, and which confirms beyond doubt the intention of the document's framers, ran as follows: "We, the people of Ireland, in order to establish justice, insure domestic tranquillity, provide for the common defence, promote the general welfare, and secure the blessings of Liberty to ourselves and our posterity, do ordain and establish this Constitution for the Irish Republic, provided that this Constitution be provisional and subject to amendment as the People of Ireland, through their elected Representatives, may consider necessary."

"The subsequent deletion of this paragraph is understandable in view of the terms of the Declaration of Independence which accompanied [the Constitution and which constituted, in effect, its Preamble], but this direct borrowing from the preamble to the Constitution of the United States is a further indication of the intention to formulate a constitution in the full sense of a fundamental law for the state," concludes Farrell. (*See also* Farrell's "A Note on the Dail Constitution, 1919," *The Irish Jurist*, Vol. IV n.s. (Summer 1969), pp. 128-138.)

The Constitution of 1919 was, then, a Constitution for the nation itself, and it is rightly termed the First Constitution of Ireland. As the fundamental law of the State, it embodies primarily the doctrine of the sovereignty of the Irish people, and stipulates that all Governmental authority derives from that very popular sovereignty. In so doing, the Constitution corroborates and gives legal effect to the self-same doctrine of popular sovereignty enshrined in the Proclamation of the Republic and the Declaration of Independence.

The Republican Constitution of Ireland was not formally repealed by its successor, the Saorstat Eireann Constitution, and must be regarded as having been held in abeyance from 1922 as an Internal Constitution of all Ireland which awaits restoration. The text of the First Irish Constitution is to be found in Appendix 3, *Supplement.*

'The Three Sisters'

The triad of constitutional instruments – the Proclamation of the Republic, the Declaration of Independence, the First Constitution of Ireland – formed the firmest foundation there could be to Constitutional Republicanism in Ireland. These three important sources were to well up together and, in a confluence not unlike that of the Barrow, the Nore and the Suir, issue in a New

Ireland that was determined to be united and free, from the center to the sea – but in a way that would satisfy the two communities concerned. Those sources, in fact, constituted the Republican roots of a ***unitary*** and ***multinational*** Ireland. But the question was, of course, given the alien medium in which the revolutionary and constitutional event occurred, how was this bold show of Irish Republicanism to sit with Crown and Empire? And, out of the confusion and turmoil to follow, would the unity of Ireland be preserved? But most importantly of all, perhaps, as regards the issue of self-determination for unitary nation-states that arose in international politics out of World War I – would Ireland have applied to her as a unit the principles and practices of the Versailles Peace Treaty equally as the other combatant nationalities and nations of Europe did?

MEMBERS OF THE FIRST DAIL EIREANN · 1919

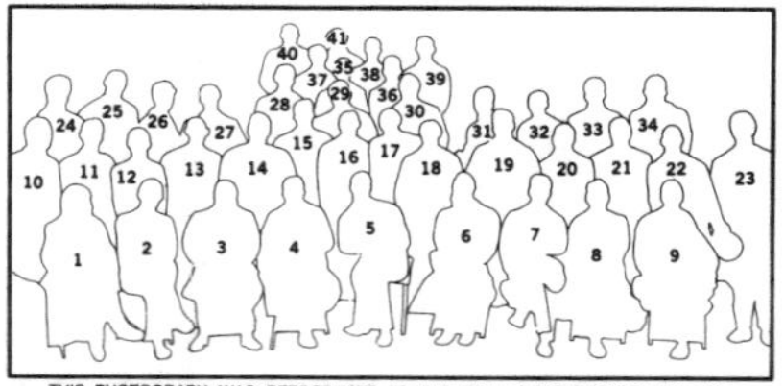

THIS PHOTOGRAPH WAS REPRODUCED IN *THE IRISH TIMES* IN FEBRUARY 1987.

1. L Ginnell, 2. M. Collins, 3. C. Brugha,
4. A Griffith, 5, É. de Valéra, 6. Count Plunkett,
7. E. McNeill, 8. W. T. Cosgrave, 9. E. Blythe,
10. P. J. Maloney, 11. T. McSwiney,
12. R. Mulcahy, 13. J. O'Doherty,
14. J. O'Mahoney, 15. J. Dolan, 16. J. McGuinness,
17. P. O'Keefe, 18. M. Staines, 19. J. McGrath,
20. B. Cusack, 21. L. de Róiste, 22. M. P. Colivet,
23. Fr. M. O'Flanagan, 24. J. P. Ward, 25. A. McCabe,
26. D. Fitzgerald, 27. J. Sweeney, 28. R. J. Hayes,
29. C. Collins, 30. P. Ó'Máille, 31. J. O'Mara,
32. B. O'Higgins, 33. J. A. Burke, 34. K. O'Higgins,
35. J. McDonagh, 36. J. McEntee, 37. P. Beasley,
38. R. C. Barton, 39. P. Galligan,
40. P. Shanahan, 41. S. Etchingham.

PART I

RESURRECTION

I found Ireland on her knees,
I watched over her with an eternal solicitude:
I have traced her progress from injuries to arms,
and from arms to liberty.
Spirit of Swift! spirit of Molyneux!
Your genius has prevailed! Ireland is now a nation!
in that new character I hail her!
and bowing to her august presence, I say,
Esto perpetua!

HENRY GRATTAN

To Ireland

I dare not go – that land has ghosts
And spectral rains along the coasts,
Such rains as weep their loss in tears
Till I am drowned in sunken years.
When last I walked a Dublin street,
My gaze was clear, my pulses fleet,
Now half a life or more is gone,
I cannot face sad Dublin's dawn.
The book clerks who once waited me
Are grey and gaunt, how can that be?
The hotel staff has up and fled,
Some stay as haunts, the rest are dead.
The candy butchers, beggars, maids,
Sleep out beyond in Maynooth's shades.
O'Connell's harpists? Gone to stay
Deep strewn along the hills at Bray,
Their happy faces smoke and stream
Across my life to shape each dream.
So, Ireland? No, I'll not return
Where ghosts in smoking rainfalls burn.
Through Dublin I'll not stroll again;
I cannot stand that haunted rain,
Where youngness melts away to sea
And kills my soul, my heart, and me.

RAY BRADBURY

CHAPTER 1

IRELAND ASSERTS HER INDEPENDENCE

The First Dail Eireann

When the enactment of the Republic of Ireland Act of 1948 was being celebrated in ceremonies at the General Post Office in Dublin on Easter Monday in 1949, de Valera and his followers in Fianna Fail absented themselves most conspicuously – and inconsistently. The reason given by de Valera was cogent and logical, even if it was at variance with his actions which led to this moment: it was the Republic of all Ireland established 30 years before that he had always stood for and he was not now recognizing the establishment of a lesser Republic. Although he had condoned the establishment of this lesser Republic of 1949, he would not display outwardly any enthusiasm for it. Speaking then in the Dail on the all-Ireland Republic, de Valera stated (somewhat inconsistently with himself): "It must be on the basis of that Republic, ***existing as a State***, that the relationship and the association, whatever it may be, whatever its form, with the states of the British Commonwealth will be founded" (*italics ours*).

Implicit in that statement must be the thought that it is solely through restoration of the Republic of all Ireland, and of the original Republican Dail Eireann, that the two parts of Ireland can be reunited and become one State or Nation. The emphasis must be, then, on restoration if national reunification is to be brought about. And the restoration must be specifically of Dail Eireann as it existed before – as the Provisional Parliament of the Republic of all Ireland. Such was de Valera's strongly held belief, and he never showed that he felt the new Republic of the 26 counties, whether associated or not, in whatever form, would avail anything towards reunification of the 26 with the six counties. Since that was, as it were, the predetermined outcome of constitutional development in the 26-county state, the break away from the Commonwealth was only to be expected.

But if de Valera in his constitutional career had by force of circumstances been incongruous with his early Sinn Fein self, there was one matter in which he strove to act most consistently. In the Republican Sinn Fein tradition the term 'Irish Republic' has a particular connotation. It does not mean any or every Republic that may be set up in Ireland or part thereof, or a Socialist, Cooperative, or any other kind of Republic, but the one, specific, original Republic of all Ireland, the Republic that was declared in 1919 and maintained for well-nigh four 'glorious' years, the Republic that ushered in the Eire Nua. De Valera rightly showed no real ardor for declaring the 26-county state, already from 1936 internally a Republic, externally a Republic also. He decried use of the word 'Republic' to describe the 26-county state, even though this is what the area was internally. In the 1937 Constitution, for instance, de Valera advisedly omitted reference throughout to the term 'Republic,' even though referring to the 26 counties in that manner would have been quite in order since that was the area to which the Constitution specifically applied. But that would not have satisfied de Valera, who understood the term exclusively in its original, 1919-1922 sense. He gave as his view that use of the designation 'Republic' could only be justified if the State had jurisdiction over the whole of Ireland. Such jurisdiction could only exist, of course, if the all-Ireland Republic of 1919-1922 were to be restored and if the all-Ireland Provisional Parliament of the Republic – Dail *Eireann* – were to be reestablished. To such a reunited State only may the term 'Irish Republic' ever be properly applied.

In other words, and to put it simply, the term 'Irish Republic' in traditional Sinn Fein usage means 'united Ireland.' It is not without significance that the term 'Irish Republic' may only be applied to a 32-county, united Ireland – which is another way of saying that it is not without significance that the term 'Irish Republic' may only be used to describe the original, all-Ireland Republic as it was declared and maintained for four years. The reason is clear: the term was used uniquely in Irish history to refer to the constitutional status the Irish nation enjoyed when independence was declared for the 32 counties of Ireland. It is almost as if the founding fathers had decreed a monopoly on the use of the term for a united Ireland, and any identical phrase used to connote an area in a divided Ireland is a pale imitation of the original appellation – not to mention an 'infringement of copyright.'

When Ireland will be reunited as a nation, it will not be by accident that it will be called the 'Irish Republic' (or 'Republic of Ireland') once again as in days of yore. Put another way, it is only through restoration of the all-Ireland Republic of the 1919-1922 period that the reunification of Ireland can be brought about. If we are to participate in this restoration, we must understand and know the nature of the early Irish Republic, but above all we must be convinced of the firm foundation upon which it was based. That foundation was the unitary nature or indivisibility of the island of Ireland.

The unitary nation

From time immemorial, Ireland has been conceived of as being a geopolitical and national unit. It has always been regarded as such by the rest of the world, and it was always treated as such by England. Even under the Union the United Kingdom treated Ireland as a single and separate nation. The three Home Rule Bills of 1886, 1893, and 1912-14 took Ireland as a unit, and the third Bill was signed into law by King George V for *all* Ireland. The sometimes mooted exclusion of Ulster or part of it was opposed by all Irish leaders from Parnell on down to de Valera – and even by such Britons as Gladstone, Winston Churchill, and (as a permanent solution) Lloyd George.

Originally nobody in Ireland, or Britain, thought of excluding Ulster from Home Rule, especially as not all Ulsterites were Unionists anyway. In the General Election of 1885, in which the Nationalists won overwhelmingly, even in Ulster the Nationalists won by a majority of one seat over the Unionists – 17 to 16. (A similar pattern of voting was to repeat itself for Sinn Fein and the Nationalists in the 1920 Local Government elections.) Thus the province was not portrayed as being homogeneously a Unionist area – nor therefore separable as a territorial unit from the rest of Ireland. As regards any possibly special treatment for Ulster, even so staunch an Orange leader as Edward Saunderson, M.P. for Cavan, speaking proudly as an Irishman indignantly rejected the idea. "On the part of Ulster and every loyal man in that province I repudiate that suggestion" [that Ulster be excluded in some way from the Home Rule Bill of 1886], he declared. "We are prepared and determined to stand or fall, for weal or woe, with every loyal man who lives in Ireland" (Hansard, *Parliamentary Debates*, April 12, 1886, Vol. 304, cols. 1395-1396). If some Unionists or Loyalists were opposed to Home Rule, they were opposed to it for all Ireland, not just for Ulster. They, too, regarded Ireland a unit.

It was Parnell who made the most effective case against a separate Home Rule legislature for Ulster or any territorial area. If a statelet were to be set up along sectarian lines, this would make no sense to him. Not only was Ulster not homogeneous religiously, but separating it from the rest of Ireland for sectarian reasons would not give 'protection' to Irish Protestants as a whole, because there would be as many as 400,000 Protestants left outside the jurisdictional area. Even if a special parliament were created simply for the concentration of Protestants in northeastern Ulster alone (the counties of Down, Antrim, and Derry), where the Protestant majority was clear, that would entail abandoning to an even greater extent those Irish Protestants on whose behalf the exclusion was invoked, for "seven-twelfths of the Protestants of Ireland live outside these three counties . . . ," said Parnell, "and the other five-twelfths . . . live inside those counties. So that, whichever way you put it you must give up the idea of protecting the Protestants either as a body or as a majority by the establishment of a separate legislature either in Ulster or any portion of Ulster."

Parnell continued, in handsome terms, to express his positive objections as an Irish Nationalist to any such measure as exclusion of territory on religious grounds. "No, sir," he exclaimed, "we cannot give up a single Irishman. We want the energy, the patriotism, the talents, and the work of every Irishman to ensure that this great experiment shall be a successful one. The best system of Government for a country I believe to be one which requires that that Government should be the resultant of all the forces within that country. We cannot give away to a second legislature the talents and influence of any portion or section of the Irish people. . . . The class of Protestants will form a most valuable element in the Irish Legislature of the future, constituting, as they will, a strong minority, and exercising . . . a moderating influence in making laws. . . . We want all creeds and classes in Ireland. . . . We cannot consent to look upon a single Irishman as not belonging to us." (Hansard, June 7, 1886, Vol. 306, col. 1180.)

It is clear from all this that, like Saunderson in Ulster, Parnell thought of Home Rule solely in terms of self-government for all

Ireland and that he treated Ireland as a practically indivisible unit. Likewise did Gladstone, and most other statesmen of that time. However, possible exclusion of Ulster, or part of it, had been 'kite-flown' by a British Minister, and it was to dispel such a notion that Parnell spoke out as he did. But the notion that Ireland might be divisible was not in the least widespread at the time.

Gladstone seemed to confirm the general idea that Ireland should be treated as one nation. Speaking on the occasion of the first Home Rule Bill, in 1886, he said: "I cannot conceal my conviction that the voice of Ireland as a whole is constitutionally spoken. I cannot say it is otherwise when five-sixths of its lawfully chosen representatives are of one mind on this matter. I cannot allow it to be said that the Protestant minority in Ulster, or elsewhere, is to rule the question at large for Ireland. I am aware of no constitutional doctrine tolerable on which such a conclusion could be adopted or justified."

Redmond, of course, was very outspoken about Ireland as a unitary nation. "Ireland is a unit," he declared. "The two-nation theory is to us an abomination and a blasphemy."

Carson himself even recognized Ireland as a unit. It is important to note that he was fighting not to exclude Ulster from Home Rule, but to make Home Rule impossible for ***all*** of Ireland, even if the majority of Irishmen desired it. "I entirely agree with you," wrote Carson's friend, Lord Arran, "that we must use all our physical and armed forces to prevent Home Rule, not only for Ulster, but for the whole of Ireland, as sworn by the Covenant." The great Carson slogan was not "We Shall Not Have Home Rule for Ulster," as has sometimes been misconceived, but rather "We Shall Not Have Home Rule for Ireland." "Ulster," swore Carson, "will ***never*** be a party to any separate treatment." True to his word, Carson did not himself vote for the separate six-county setup in 1920. "There is no one in the world," he claimed, "who would be more pleased to see an absolute unity in Ireland than I would."

Even in British *law*, as we have seen, Ireland was recognized as a single unit. The Home Rule Act of 1914, if it did nothing else, recognized the unitary nature of the island of Ireland. To disregard their own law in imposing partition on Ireland was not beyond the British to do (at a time that they were violating their own Constitution over Ireland), but the fact remains that the long-held British recognition of the oneness of Ireland received expression in their own very law. The arbitrary creation of a six-county statelet for Britain's own purposes was just that – arbitrary. At the back of it all, the British, like the people of any country of the world, recognized Ireland as the unitary nation it was. It was only natural, then, that this recognition should be reflected in their own law.[1]

Churchill, too, regarded Ireland as a unitary nation. Speaking in Parliament on the third Home Rule bill, in 1912, he said, "At one sweep of the wand, they [the Ulstermen] could sweep the Irish Question out of life and into history and free the British realm of the canker which poisoned its heart for generations. If they refuse, if they take to the boats, all we say is they shall not obstruct the work of salvage and we shall go forward at any rate to the end."

At Brandford in 1914, in what Redmond called "a superb speech," First Lord of the Admiralty Churchill flung down the gauntlet to Carson's Ulster. Speaking gravely and deliberately – in words that anticipated his mood of 1940 – he warned, "If every concession that is made is spurned and exploited, if all the loose, wanton and reckless chatter that we have been forced to listen to these many months is in the end to disclose a sinister and revolutionary purpose, then I can only say to you: 'Let us go forward together and put these grave matters to the proof.' "

Writing on another occasion, Churchill made a telling point: "Whatever Ulster's right might be, she cannot stand in the way of the whole of the rest of Ireland. Half a province cannot impose a permanent veto ***on the nation***" (*italics ours*).

In a speech on Ireland in the House of Commons on April 30, 1912, Churchill took up the cause of the Irish as "an ancient people, famous in history, influential all over the English-speaking world, whose blood has been shed on our battlefields, whose martial qualities have adorned our ensign . . ." This was two years before World War I, when another well-nigh 260,000 Irishmen marched off in the Munster Fusiliers, the Connaught Rangers, the Dublin Fusiliers, and the Ulster Thirty-Sixth Division to fight for what was to be known as 'Wilsonian self-determination' for 'the little nations of Europe' (including Ireland), some 49,400 of them

---

1 The fact that the 1914 Act was, even before it was (or could be) enacted, prevented from coming into force (by the Suspensory Act, 1914) did not militate against its being of an all-Ireland character, but Orders in Council that were unauthorizedly issued annually thereafter until a Partition Act could be enacted that would repeal the Act, did militate against its coming into force as an all-Ireland measure. (The Orders in Council were issued ***unauthorizedly,*** because what had been agreed on with Ireland in the Suspensory Act was that the Home Rule Act should come into force at no later than the end of World War I, and there was no authorizing power by which the Orders might legally be issued after 1918; see Appendix 14, *Supplement*.)

to give their lives in the cause, with 32,000 or 70 percent of those killed coming from Nationalist Ireland alone. "No words," wrote Major Willie Redmond, brother of the Irish leader and himself to be killed in 1917 in the gas-poisoned salient of Ypres, "could do justice to the splendid action of the new Irish soldiers. They have never flinched." The cause they were fighting for, the self-determination of national minorities, was aptly described by the poet and politician, Tom Kettle, a few days before he was killed at Givenchy in the Battle of the Somme:

> So here, while the mad guns curse overhead
> And tired men sigh with mud for couch and floor,
> Know that we fools, now with the foolish dead,
> Died not for Flag, nor for Emperor,
> But for a dream, born in a herdsman's shed,
> And for a secret scripture of the poor.

"Simple justice demands the recognition," the historian Giovanni Costigan has written, "that Irishmen such as these, who gave their lives believing that an Allied victory would save democracy and bring freedom to Ireland, were just as good patriots, and cared for Ireland as deeply, as those who died in Easter Week." Such recognition, we can agree with Costigan, has not always been forthcoming, although a measure of honor has been done to their memory by the erection south of the Phoenix Park in Dublin of the War Memorial Monument and by the preservation at the British Legion in Dublin of the volumes in which the names of those killed in action are inscribed.

And in World War II many more brave Irishmen and women devoted themselves to the cause – 85,000 of them in Britain's munitions factories and 80,000 in the British Army and Navy – eight of whom were to gain the Victoria Cross and 750 the Iron Cross and other awards. In the testimony of President Eisenhower, more people from Ireland contributed to the British war effort than there were from all the other states of the Commonwealth put together. How well might Churchill have again paid tribute to the many "whose martial qualities have adorned our ensign"!

All the cooperation that was offered Britain in her wartime hours of need, all the sacrifices that were made, all the blood that was shed – all was given on the basis of the belief that Ireland was an integral part of the Free West and that that was the way the Irish wanted to keep it for posterity. During World War I all was also undertaken in the firm belief that, now that Home Rule was on the Statute Book for all Ireland and would, as Britain had pledged, be applied as soon as the war was expected to be over (1915) – that freedom for Ireland as a unit would be fully purchased from a Britain that officially recognized Ireland as a unitary nation and that was, so to speak, putting partition out of its head after all.

Churchill spoke out clearly for "the great ideal of a united Ireland," and in 1924 he was to declare that what he always urged for Ireland, over all, was "an Ireland free, united, the friend of Britain and a proud co-founder and co-inheritor of the world-wide [Celto-British] Commonwealth of Nations."

The then staunchly Unionist *Irish Times* totally rejected the idea of a divided Ireland (on June 27, 1916). Unionists, it said, accepted the fact that the Home Rule Act was on the Statute Book and realized they must accept the inevitable. As patriotic Irishmen they intended to live in their country and accept self-government. But, "If we are to have self-government, Ireland must be a self-governing unit. That instinct is implanted deeply in the heart of every thougtful Irishman, Unionist or Nationalist. In the first place, the country is too small to be divided between two systems of government. In the next place, the political, social and economic qualities of North and South complement one another: one without the other must be miserably incomplete. . . . In a word, the permanent partition of our country is inconceivable."

More than three years later, on the eve of partition, the *Irish Times* summed up Lloyd George's Bill as follows:

"The principle is hateful alike to Unionist and Nationalist. They know that national ideals and the ancestral spirit of a common patriotism cannot persist in a divided country. They know that the fantastic homogeneity which the Government proposes for the Ulster Unionists would be an excrescence on the map of Ireland, and would be ruinous to the trade and industry of the Northern Protestants. . . . We yearn for peace, but in Mr. Lloyd George's proposal we see not peace but a sword."

Although he pushed his Act through, intending it to be a temporary measure, even Lloyd George admitted to the reality of the oneness of Ireland. In reply to a proposal Carson's successor Sir James Craig made for Dominion Home Rule for the six counties of northeastern Ireland, Lloyd George pointedly answered that the border on the basis of Craig's proposal would be stereotyped into an international boundary. "Partition on these lines, ***the majority of the Irish people*** will never accept, nor could we conscientiously attempt to enforce it" (*italics ours*). By using the italicized phrase 'the majority of the Irish people,' Lloyd George revealed both that he regarded the people of all Ireland as constituting the Irish nation and that the thought the wishes of the people of all Ireland, and not just of the people of six counties of Ireland, should be respected in any considerations of continuance or discontinuance of partition. His important words also show that he intended partition to be of a temporary nature.

Indeed Lloyd George is said to have been convinced by de Valera's argument for self-determination for all of the Irish people, the Ulster people included, in an integrated, federal-type Ireland. This argument was in response to Lloyd George's indirect, prior challenge to de Valera's statement on the right of Ireland to self-determination, by making a similar claim for the six-county area. "Our answer to this wholly inadmissible claim is not a mere negation," de Valera replied. "I have made it clear in public statements which reflect the views of the Irish people that Ireland, so far from disregarding the special position of the minority in north-east Ulster, would be willing to sanction any measure of local autonomy which they might desire, provided that it were just and were consistent with the unity and integrity of our island."

More convincing evidence than all of the foregoing could hardly be found, even within the broader ambient of Celto-British Isles history, in support of the argument that all Ireland is by right an indivisible and unitary nation. The 1916 Proclamation of the Republic was for all Ireland, the 1918 General Election was for all Ireland, the 1919 Declaration of Independence was for all Ireland, and the 1919-1922 Irish Republic was for all Ireland. The latter two of these developments were executed by the First Dail Eireann, the Parliament that was set up for all Ireland in response to the mandate given chiefly to Sinn Fein by the vast majority of the people of all Ireland. This mandate was confirmed in 1920 in Local Government elections and again in 1921 in a General Election, both of which elections were also held on an all-Ireland basis – under British law.

From all the arguments and the facts of history that we have presented above, it can only be deduced that Ireland has to be thought of as being a unitary nation. In fact, it is axiomatic that the island of Ireland is one indivisible nation. Any division that is attempted has to be regarded as being so unnatural and antihistorical that it would be extremely hard to believe anyone could espouse the idea as a workable hypothesis. And yet, as we know, this unfortunately is exactly what has been done. But partition has not been acquiesced in by all the Irish people or their representatives. In the Irish Republican view, to the extent that there has been deviation by political Parties from the principle that Ireland is a geographic unit and unitary nation, partition cannot be abolished by those same Parties.

Originally, espousal of an idea like partition would have been unthinkable to the Irish people. The historical fact is, indeed, that it was so unthinkable to them that the terms North and South were not even in their political vocabulary. It was on the solid basis of their concept of the unitary nature of the Irish nation that the all-Ireland Republic was founded in 1919. How this was achieved was, as we have seen, through establishment of the First Dail Eireann in response to the wishes of the Irish people. Nationalists and Republicans, who stood for a unitary Ireland, were returned 80 percent strong to the 105-seat Dail. As Dail *Eireann*, this Dail was for ***all*** Ireland, the Provisional Parliament of the all-Ireland Republic. (Further exposition of the basing of the original Irish Republic on the indivisible Irish nation is given in this author's pamphlet, *Towards the Restoration of the Republic*; see also Frank Gallagher's *The Indivisible Island.* And see the Addendum to this Part.)

The Constituent Assembly

The First Dail Eireann was, in addition to being elected a Provisional Parliament, elected also a Constituent Assembly (to adopt a Constitution for the country). The establishment of a Constituent Assembly was the mandate of the Irish people given in a national plebiscite, the General Election of 1918. The people's mandate was in response to the Election Manifesto of Sinn Fein for the occasion. The Manifesto was devised, in turn, in accordance with the Constitution of the reorganized Sinn Fein as adopted by its Ard Fheis (Convention) of October 25, 1917. That Constitution read, in part, as follows:

> 1. The name of this organisation shall be Sinn Fein.
>
> 2. Sinn Fein aims at securing the International recognition of Ireland as an independent Irish Republic.
>
> Having achieved that status, the Irish people may by referendum freely choose their own form of Government.

> 3. This object shall be attained through the Sinn Fein organisation.
>
> 4. WHEREAS no law made without the authority and consent of the Irish people is or ever can be binding on their conscience,
>
> THEREFORE, in accordance with the Resolution of Sinn Fein adopted in Convention, 1905, *a Constituent Assembly shall be convoked*, comprising persons chosen by the Irish Constituencies as the supreme national authority to speak and act in the name of the Irish people and to devise and formulate measures for the welfare of the whole people of Ireland [italics ours].

This Sinn Fein constitutional decree was translated into the Manifesto of Sinn Fein for the 1918 elections. Clause 3 of the Manifesto stated:

"Sinn Fein aims at securing the establishment of that Republic: By the establishment of a constituent assembly comprising persons chosen by Irish constituencies as the supreme national authority to speak and act in the name of the Irish people, and to develop Ireland's social, political, and industrial life for the welfare of the whole people of Ireland."

The mandate the electorate gave in the national plebiscite of 1918 was, then, that the First Dail should regard itself as having been elected not only a Provisional Parliament, but also a Constituent Assembly. Dail Eireann was fully empowered to act in a constituent manner by (1) a mandate of the people which (2) was the fulfillment of the Manifesto to the electorate that (3) was itself derived from the 1917 constitutional decree of Sinn Fein (which latter, in turn, drew its strength from a Sinn Fein Resolution of 1905). By convening when elected as a Constituent Assembly, the Dail was empowered to enact and promulgate a Constitution for Ireland, which was in fact what it did. By this means it constituted itself a *de jure* Provisional Parliament for all Ireland.

In his address to the electorate on the occasion of the General Election of May 1921, de Valera confirmed the fact that the First Dail Eireann had been elected a Constituent Assembly (as he had agreed with Arthur Griffith beforehand it should be). "By your overwhelming choice of Republican candidates in the general election of 1918," he said, "you made known your will in a manner there was no mistaking. On your suffrages the Republic of Ireland was constitutionally founded . . ."

The British spoiler Act

Since Ireland declared her independence at the first session of Dail Eireann, on January 21, 1919, and since Dail Eireann was constituted as the Parliament and Government of the all-Ireland Republic that the Irish people had willed overwhelmingly in the General Election of December 1918, it follows that the British Partition Act, the 'Government of Ireland Act' of 1920, would, in the face of Irish constitutional law then established, be absolutely invalid and null and void in every particular. "There is in Ireland at this moment only one lawful authority," declared President de Valera in a statement to the Dail on April 10, 1919, "and that authority is the elected Government of the Irish Republic. . . . Our attitude towards the powers that maintain themselves here against the expressed will of the people shall then, in a word, be this: We shall conduct ourselves towards them in such a way as will make it clear to the world that we acknowledge no right of theirs." (Dail Eireann, *Minutes of Proceedings of the First Parliament of the Republic of Ireland, 1919-1921*, Official Record, 1921, pp. 45-47.)

That partition was gone ahead with and effected – and this a full two and a half years after the all-Ireland Dail was established – would have been nothing less than a naked act of aggression as far as Ireland was concerned. As a matter of fact, the Irish Declaration of Independence had denied emphatically Britain's further right to legislate for Ireland in any way. "We ordain that the elected Representatives of the Irish people alone have power to make laws binding on the people of Ireland," ran the Declaration, and "we solemnly declare foreign government in Ireland to be an invasion of our national right . . ." Since the Declaration was promulgated as a Constituent Act of Parliament by Dail Eireann on January 21, 1919, in response to the democratically expressed wishes of the Irish electorate in what was regarded a plebiscite, Britain should have felt herself bound by it to regard Ireland a foreign nation thenceforth.

Consequently, Ireland would not have been legally or validly divided at the time the Partition Act allegedly went into effect – in mid-1921. In Irish law – the only law that counted then – Ireland remained a unitary and undivided country, and it continued to be so for another year and a half after partition was forcibly imposed. That is, Ireland was still one and undivided for as long as four years after independence had been legally and constitutionally declared. "Constitutionally" declared, we say, because, we are talking in terms of the Declaration of Independence and of the new Irish Constitution. The Declaration, which was the Preamble to the Constitution, was enacted and promulgated together with the Constitution by the Constituent Assembly as a public general act. The main point, however, is that by such legal action independence was declared for the whole of Ireland, and, incidentally, we can hardly conceive of a more forcible way of declaring a nation's independence. Recognition of such all-Ireland independence should have been willingly forthcoming from Britain, because, as we have seen, in British law Ireland was recognized as a unitary nation – in the Government of Ireland or Home Rule Act of 1914, an Act that might be regarded as being legal and valid with respect to Ireland then. (It is interesting to note here that in the Canada Act of 1982, an Act governing the newly revised Constitution of Canada, the Canadians did not need to make any big point about terminating the power of Britain to legislate for Canada. They simply had it stated: "No Act of Parliament of the United Kingdom passed after the Constitution Act, 1982 comes into force shall extend to Canada as part of its law." How would it sit with Canada if four years after April 17, 1982, Britain were to partition out Quebec or some such area from the rest of Canada?)

If Irish Republican and constitutional rule could have been maintained, partition would never have taken hold in Ireland. But even though it was not maintained, partition was not forcibly put into effect for fully four years after the all-Ireland Republic had been established. By the end of 1922 the Anglo-Irish Treaty took effect, and from then on Treaty-based Irish constitutional rule began to force out Republican constitutional rule. But up until this point, despite the Partition Act, Ireland was still a united nation. That was because the Treaty, which superseded the Act, did not afford the North of Ireland an opportunity to opt out of Ireland/the Irish Free State until December of 1922.

Actually the imposition of partition was a process that went on for a long period of time, perhaps for as long as 28 years, that is, until 1949. It was only then that partition was 'finalized' (in British law, with the Ireland Act, about which later). But as for when it began really to take hold, we would have to say it was some time in 1923. Certainly partition was firming up pretty well around the end of 1922 and during the spring and summer of 1923. It is true to say that Ireland was effectively, but not constitutionally, divided only when the Dail and Government of Ireland *acquiesced* in partition. Put another way, Ireland was effectively divided when the Dail and Government of 32-county Ireland agreed to be reduced to the Dail and Government of 26 counties of Ireland. It is our theory that that development took place during the tenure of the Third Dail, which opened on September 9, 1922, and which lasted until September of 1923, and that it is that acquiescence which must be undone if the problem of partition is to be solved. That is where a start might be made.

The lamentable acquiescence that occurred could have relatively easily been undone, because nothing of a constitutional nature happened to entrench partition at that time. Ireland could not help it, of course, that the North should choose to opt out. But since that happened, the nation was left with little choice but to accept it, especially as Dail Eireann had already agreed that Northern Ireland should have the freedom that was eventually accorded her under the Treaty. The important thing to note, however, is that the Constitution, no matter how British it was, did not of itself institute partition. It is true that the Constitution contained a provision for the holding of elections after a year from promulgation, and that in practice those elections would be confined to the jurisdictional area to which the Constitution would be restricted – 26 counties – but the Constitution did not itself say that elections should be restricted to that area. However, the first General Election held under the new Constitution, that of August 1923, was in fact confined to the 26-county area. It would be difficult to pinpoint the date that the Dail fully acquiesced in becoming the Parliament of the 26 counties, because it was a process that went on over a period of a year or so. But if we were to attempt it, we should say it was at the time that those first elections were held for 26 counties of Ireland alone. It should be noted again, however, that the Constitution ***technically*** did not induce partition, but to the extent that it was abused for the purpose of contributing to partition, it indirectly affirmed the institution of partition and left no alternative to acquiescence in it for the time being.

CHAPTER 2

IRELAND CONSOLIDATES HER INDEPENDENCE

The Second Dail Eireann

The last time Ireland was united as a single nation was, as we have seen, during the existence of the Third Dail. Obviously, if Ireland is to be reunited, we must, for starters, go back to those days of the 'Pact Dail' and see what went wrong, and determine how best that wrong might be set right. One must know what to remedy before one can decide how to remedy it. The events of the Third Dail ought, then, to be of major concern to us. We must examine them, but before we can do so we ought to take a look at what led up to the establishment of this Dail. That is, we must study the existence of the Second Dail, which had a direct bearing on the nature of the Third Dail. The exact relationship between the two Dails has been very much a point of controversy over the years. Whether was there direct continuity of one Dail from the other or not?

The Second Dail was supposed to dissolve (but did not) on June 30, 1922, and to transfer its powers to the newly elected Third Dail, which was scheduled to meet on July 1st. Since the Second Dail never formally closed, as it was decreed to do, and since it never transferred its powers to the incoming Dail, it is considered by all-Ireland Republicans to have equivalently adjourned *sine die* on June 28, 1922 (the day on which the Civil War broke out), or perhaps on September 9, 1922 (the day on which the Third Dail opened), and accordingly still to exist. However, apart from the formality of dissolution and transference of powers, the Third Dail was freely elected as Pact Dail of all Ireland (in accordance with the terms of the Constituent Pact, that is, of the 'Collins-de Valera

Pact,' about which we will have much to say in succeeding chapters treating the Third Dail proper) and it could be said to be, at least for the first few months of its tenure, the direct successor of the Second Dail. But, since it was eventually to be usurped and reinstituted under the influence of what was in effect a British Constitution as strictly a 26-county Parliament, it has not been recognized by Republicans, who prefer to acknowledge the exclusive legitimacy of the adjourned Second Dail Eireann. The present Dail of the 26-county Republic is regarded by Republicans as being constitutionally the collateral successor of the Second Dail – and, they hold, part of the problem of partition.

The First Dail Eireann had functioned until August 1921. In May 1921 a General Election had been ordered by Royal Proclamation for the return of members to serve in the Parliaments of 'Northern' and 'Southern' Ireland, as the newly enacted Partition Act had attempted to establish. "Dail Eireann decreed that these elections for north and south should be treated as elections to itself and candidates duly elected should be regarded as deputies of Dail Eireann" (Nicholas Mansergh, *The Irish Free State, Its Government and Politics*). As R.B. McDowell described it, technically "the Second Dail comprised persons elected to the house of commons of the parliaments of Northern and Southern Ireland" (Edmund Curtis and R.B. McDowell, eds., *Irish Historical Documents, 1172-1922,* p. 316). Only representatives elected to the lower house were recognized by the Republican Government, so that 'Northern' and 'Southern' Irish ***Parliaments*** (comprising the lower and upper houses) did not exist in the official view. "Elections for the Senates were not to be recognized, as . . . a certain number of Senators [were] nominated by . . . the Crown. The Representatives of all Ireland would constitute the Dail and each would be allowed to take his or her seat on subscribing to the Republican oath." (Dail Eireann, *Minutes of Proceedings . . .* , May 19, 1921, pp. 291-292; quoted from Dorothy Macardle, *The Irish Republic*, pp. 469-470.)

The Interpretation Act, 1923 (Ir.), at Section 2 (8), defined the Second Dail Eireann thus: "The expression 'the Second Dail Eireann' shall mean the assembly of members of Parliament elected for constituencies in Ireland at a Parliamentary Election held on the 13th day of May, 1921 [the day nominations were taken in all of Ireland], who met as Dail Eireann and Government of Saorstat Eireann in a Parliament held at Dublin in the Mansion House aforesaid on the 16th day of August, 1921."

The Second Dail Eireann duly assembled on August 16, 1921. The elected Deputies of *all* Ireland had received the summons to this National Assembly of Ireland. The so-called Parliaments of 'Northern' and 'Southern' Ireland were ignored by the majority of the elected Deputies, who attended the Dail instead. The roll of the Dail, which had been expanded to 180 seats, consisted of 130 Republican, 6 Nationalist, and 44 Unionist seats (but there were only 125 Republican members, due to the fact that five were returned from double constituencies).

President de Valera spoke to the Assembly of the mandate given to the Dail members by the elections of 1918 and 1921. It was not a mandate as much for a form of Government, he said, as it was "for Irish freedom and Irish independence, and it was obvious to everyone who considered the question that Irish independence could not be realised at the present time in any other way so suitably as through a Republic." He went on to say that the first duty of the Ministry was to make the *de jure* Republic a *de facto* Republic of all Ireland, and he spoke of the representatives of the Irish Republic that had been accredited to foreign countries. It was because of Ireland's inherent right that the Dail's ambassadors were listened to, he said, and that the peoples of foreign countries "recognised that the only lawful authority here in Ireland is the Government of the Republic of Ireland. In the hearts of the people of these countries, therefore, the Republic is recognised. We recognise it, and it is only on the basis of our [own] recognition of that that we deal with any foreign power whatever." (*Dail Debates*, Tuairisg Oifigiuil (Official Report), 1921 and 1922, pp. 8-10.)

The preconditions of the Treaty

The newly elected Second Dail Eireann at its first session got down to the business of discussing Anglo-Irish relations. It considered preliminary British peace proposals and rejected them (*Irish Bulletin*, August 17, 1921). De Valera had asked British Prime Minister Lloyd George's representative, Lord Derby, whether his principal would refuse to negotiate with representatives of the Dail unless the principle of complete independence were first surrendered. Lloyd George replied indirectly (through an American journalist) that he was prepared to meet the Irish leaders without preconditions on his part and without extracting promises from them in advance (Macardle, pp. 447-451). The British Prime Minister, nevertheless, subsequently refused to acknowledge, as he put it (with complete disregard for the authority of the Dail and Government of Ireland), "the right of Ireland to secede from her allegiance to the King." He also insisted that the Parliament and Government of Northern Ireland retain "all their existing powers and privileges, which cannot be abrogated without its consent." That is, separate treatment for the North, though as yet not necessarily partition, was to continue as long as Ulster willed it[1] (Macardle, pp. 466-474; Frank Pakenham, *Peace by Ordeal*, pp. 75-79 NEL Mentor paperback edition).

The two sides were obviously still far apart. De Valera proceeded, nevertheless, to communicate with Lloyd George and to express his willingness to negotiate "on the basis of the broad guiding principle of government by the consent of the governed." That is, in effect, on the basis of the recognition of Dail Eireann and the already existing all-Ireland Republic. De Valera explained his stand to the Dail: "Our position is unchanged. We cannot change our position, because it is fundamentally sound and just. And the moment we get off that fundamental rock of right and justice, we have no case whatsoever. No fight can be made except on that rock, and on that rock we shall stand." (*Dail Debates*, 1921 and 1922, p. 82.) It would remain to be seen whether this time Lloyd George could politically afford to be as openly realistic as de Valera expected him to be.

For de Valera and his Ministers the Irish Republic as then existing meant the island of Ireland, because it was for all Ireland the Republic had been declared in January 1919. When de Valera would not budge with Britain on the negotiability of the Republic, he was in effect rejecting the partition of Ireland. In probing with Lloyd George for a noncommittal position vis-a-vis the British demands, he completely ignored the so-called Government of Ireland Act of 1920. "We most earnestly desire to help in bringing about a lasting peace between the peoples of these islands," de Valera had written to Lloyd George on June 28, 1921, "but [we] see no avenue by which it can be reached if you deny Ireland's

---

1 That partition was not in fact intended by Lloyd George is clear from the fact that his insistence that the powers and privileges of the Northern Ireland Parliament not be abrogated without the consent of that Parliament could, because of the Partition Act's disabling of the Northern Government to be treatied with, only refer to the 'nonreserved powers' that were being exercised by the British and the Northern Parliament in what could become a state within a federal Ireland, whereas the existence of a partition of a unitary sovereign nation would require a reference to the 'reserved powers' that were being reserved by ***Britain*** from ***Ireland*** for a part of the latter.

essential unity and set aside the principle of national self-determination."

Frank Owen in his life of Lloyd George considers that in his letter "de Valera defined that 'Rock of the Republic,' independent and indivisible, from which he never budged throughout the Truce, the Treaty, the Peace, the Second World War, and anything that has ever happened since." In conference with some Unionists about his letter, de Valera "stressed the necessity for a settlement [at the Anglo-Irish Peace Conference of 1921] for the whole of Ireland. Any settlement based on less than this would be impermanent and cause great problems later." (Earl of Longford and Thomas P. O'Neill, *Eamon de Valera*, p. 131.) De Valera was to make sure, in fact, that the Treaty would cover all of Ireland and not just part of it – that is, that the Treaty should supersede the Partition Act.

The Irish Republic, or national sovereignty, was not negotiable, but what de Valera was willing to negotiate was the 'external association' of the Republic with Britain and the then-existing Empire (which was evolving into 'the Commonwealth'). This was a negotiating position which Lloyd George was later to appear to accept in advance. External association was a device by which for Ireland the Republic – and hence essential unity – might be preserved and for Britain the integrity of the Empire might not be impaired. "A certain treaty of free [or external] association with the British Commonwealth group, as with a partial League of Nations, we would have been ready to recommend, and as a government to negotiate and take responsibility for," de Valera wrote to Lloyd George in a letter approved by the Irish Cabinet on August 6, 1921, "had we an assurance that the entry of the nation as a whole into such association would secure for it the allegiance of the present dissenting minority, to meet whose sentiment alone this step could be contemplated."

The emphasis was still on national unity. The British Prime Minister did not actually reject unity, but he could not explicitly accept the precondition of the Republic in terms of which essential unity was being expressed. However, he was interested in the idea of external association and he hit upon a formula which opened the way for negotiations without apparent prior commitment of either side to the other's position. He sent de Valera an invitation to a conference to be held on October 11, 1921, in London, "where we can meet your delegates as spokesmen of the people whom you represent, with a view to ascertaining how the association of

Ireland with the community of nations known as the British Empire may best be reconciled with Irish national aspirations."

Replying in his capacity of President of the Irish Republic, de Valera stated, "Our respective positions have been stated and are understood ... We accept the invitation. ..." Neither in the invitation nor in the reply is there any emasculation of the status of Republic, anymore than there is that of Empire. De Valera's preconditions of external association and essential unity appear to have been accepted in principle, and the Conference was gone ahead with on that basis and in the hope of reconciling those demands with the needs of Empire. It would further be agreed towards the end of the Conference that the respective positions had in fact been accepted and adhered to throughout the Conference (see Pakenham, *op. cit.*, p. 197 paperback).

A few comments need to be made about the crucial formula in Lloyd George's invitation.

First, it was to de Valera as President of Dail Eireann that Lloyd George extended his invitation, and it was in that sense that he acknowledged de Valera as representative of the people of all Ireland.

Second, by this time – since early August to be precise – de Valera's position was made more explicit than that of President of Dail Eireann. By constitutional amendment his status was changed additionally to President of the Irish Republic, that is, of the all-Ireland Republic that was then existing. Lloyd George could not have been unaware of this fact, and it was to de Valera in this capacity that the British Prime Minister wrote about "your delegates as spokesmen of the people whom you represent." That is to say, de Valera was also addressed as representative of all the people of Ireland, North and South.

Finally, by his use of the word 'Ireland' Lloyd George had to mean the island of Ireland, the only sense in which the word was then understood – and used at other times by Lloyd George himself. He had to mean by 'Ireland' the Irish Republic, as a matter of fact, because (1) this was the only constitutional status the island of Ireland had at that time and (2) it was about the external association of the Irish Republic that de Valera had been communicating with Lloyd George as a subject of negotiation.

This, then, was the sense in which Lloyd George understood de Valera when the Prime Minister wrote about "the association of Ireland with the community of nations." That Lloyd George did not understand de Valera to speak of excluding northeastern

Ireland from external association with Britain and the Empire is clear from his not contradicting the Irish President when the latter had intimated in a letter dated July 19, 1921: "I have made it clear in public statements which reflect the views of the Irish people that Ireland, so far from disregarding the special position of the minority in north-east Ulster, would be willing to sanction any measure of local autonomy which they might desire, provided that it were just and were consistent with the unity and integrity of our island." Lloyd George appeared to accept this suggestion for separate treatment for 'Ulster' and to include the six counties in his notion of the word 'Ireland.' This is a far cry from insisting on partition *per se*, and a resultant Treaty would, in fact, supersede the Partition Act, would guarantee the national sovereignty of Ireland, and would be made with all of Ireland.

A Treaty for all Ireland

What precludes any possibility of imagining that the Treaty might not have been understood to be negotiated with ***all Ireland*** is the fact that the Irish proposals as submitted to the London Conference were designed and presented with a united Ireland in mind. The Dublin Government had its Draft Articles for a Treaty prefaced with a "Note" that read as follows: "The following proposals are put forward upon the assumption that the essential unity of Ireland is maintained." Article 10 of the proposed Articles read: "In the event of the existing legislature of the North-East of Ireland accepting its position under the National Parliament, Ireland will confirm the legislature in its existing powers and will undertake to provide the safeguards designed to secure any special interests of the area over which it functions."

It is accordingly clear that the understanding on embarking on the Conference was that the Treaty was to be made with all of Ireland, and the understanding throughout the Conference was likewise that the Treaty was being negotiated with the Irish representatives on a 32-county basis. This fact is further reinforced by the requirement of the Conference that the Treaty when finalized be approved by Dail Eireann, which was the Assembly elected by the people of all of Ireland. That the Treaty was made with all Ireland or, more specifically, with Dail Eireann representing all of Ireland – was the expressed understanding of many Irish and some British statesmen already at that time, among them Collins, Griffith, Eoin MacNeill, Lord Edward Grey, Patrick Hogan (Clare), de Valera and Cosgrave. The latter two, as Cabinet Ministers, took pains to see that the Irish negotiators to the Treaty had the proper credentials as Plenipotentiaries from Saorstat Eireann or the Republic of all of Ireland. The credentials, issued by President de Valera for Dail Eireann on October 7, 1921, and which were sealed with the Seal of Dail Eireann, read as follows:

> To all to whom these presents come, greeting. In virtue of the authority vested in me by Dail Eireann, I hereby appoint Arthur Griffith, T.D., Minister for Foreign Affairs, Chairman; Michael Collins, T.D., Minister for Finance; Robert C. Barton, T.D., Minister for Economic Affairs; Edmund J. Duggan, T.D.; and George Gavan Duffy, T.D., as envoys plenipotentiary from the elected Government of the Republic of Ireland to negotiate and conclude on behalf of Ireland, with the representatives of His Britannic Majesty George V a treaty or treaties of settlement, association and accommodation between Ireland and the community of Nations known as the British Commonwealth. In witness hereof I hereunder subscribe my name as President.
>
> [*Signed*] Eamon de Valera

That the Treaty was negotiated and concluded with all Ireland for all Ireland is clearest of all from Lloyd George's enunciation of the four main principles upon which the Treaty Conference was based. These, as listed in a letter of November 10, 1921 to Sir James Craig of Northern Ireland, were:

> (*a*) Ireland would give allegiance to the Throne and agree to enter into the partnership of free nations comprising the Commonwealth of Nations.
>
> (*b*) Provision would be made for naval bases indispensable to Britain and her overseas communication.
>
> (*c*) A federal Ireland would be established, with the Government of Northern Ireland retaining the local powers ordained by the Government of Ireland Act, 1920.
>
> (*d*) "The unity of Ireland would be recognized by the establishment of an all-Ireland Parliament, upon which would be devolved the further powers necessary to form the self-governing Irish State."

All four principles were essentially honored in the negotiations and the Agreement reached was concluded with and for all of Ireland. As if to confirm this fact, the Treaty itself was titled

'Articles of Agreement for a Treaty between Great Britain and Ireland,' an international treaty between the two island nations. And many years later even the British were to admit, officially, that the new Irish jurisdiction had extended under the Treaty to all of Ireland.

In the Ireland Act, 1949 the British sanctioned the view that the jurisdiction of Saorstat Eireann once extended to all of Ireland at least for two days – the 6th and 7th December, 1922. The Constitution of the Irish Free State came into operation on December 6, 1922, and although it was framed to apply to all of Ireland, its powers were not to become exercisable in respect of the six northeastern counties until a period of one month had elapsed and, during that month, the Parliament of Northern Ireland might have opted for exclusion from the Irish Free State. On December 7, 1922, the Northern Parliament resolved not to remain within the newly created State but to resume the status of the Government of Ireland Act, 1920, and on December 8, 1922, the King acknowledged the exercise of the North's option. In these circumstances the Republic of Ireland claimed that the jurisdiction of the Free State extended on the 6th and 7th of December to the whole of Ireland, although its powers were not actually exercisable in it all, and that it was only on the 8th of December that these powers were definitively suspended in respect of Northern Ireland. The import of this claim was that by the law of the Republic a person born anywhere in Ireland before December 6, 1922, but domiciled on the 6th and/or 7th in Northern Ireland, was a citizen of the Republic and thus, as from January 1, 1949, was denied by the British Nationality Act, 1948 the status of a British subject. Acknowledging the validity of the Irish argument, the British Government, in Section 5 of the Ireland Act, 1949, remedied the defect in the Nationality Act (in Sec. 12) and ensured that a person circumstanced as above described should not be obliged to lose his status as a British subject. Thus did Britain recognize the all-Ireland Free State's *de jure* and *de facto* existence for a brief moment in history and, by extension, the Treaty provision for the power of the Free State to extend herself to all of Ireland under the proper conditions.

It can be concluded, then, that the terms under which it had been agreed to enter into negotiations at the planned Peace Conference and under which those negotiations were actually conducted were essentially three: (1) that the Irish Plenipotentiaries be negotiated with as representatives of all of Ireland; (2) that Ireland's relationship with Britain and the then Empire be one of external association; and (3) that the essential unity of Ireland be preserved – that is, that the Partition Act in its British jurisdiction clauses be overridden. In other words, what was at most to be conceded was separate statehood for the six-county area, but under no condition should the national sovereignty of all Ireland be in any way abridged.

The self-determination option

What was also agreed on to be conceded was, as an alternative to the six-county statehood offer, a form of self-determination for each of both the Unionist and Nationalist communities in Ireland, a form in which each community could preserve its own particular way of life and identity, though at this stage nobody was saying how such self-determination forms might be given expression, nor did anybody seem to know how. The closest anyone came to explaining the self-determination in mind was de Valera, when he described to the Dail on August 17, 1921 the sense in which he understood preliminary negotiations to have been undertaken that he had had with Lloyd George (in which he rejected the partition idea), and the sense in which the Treaty negotiations were likewise about to be undertaken.

"In the same way that the people of the North of Ireland can recognise themselves if they want to," de Valera explained, "we recognise ourselves. Even on such a base there can be negotiations," he averred. That is, both identities might be equally affirmed, without the necessity for partition, on the one hand, or exclusion of the one side by the other, on the other. "But if negotiations can only be begun," de Valera continued, "when we have given up the right of this country [the Nationalists] to live its own life in its own way, there can be no negotiations at all with the North or anywhere else. If the North of Ireland – the people of the North of Ireland – are free to regard themselves from their own point of view in going into negotiations with us, they have not to give up that point of view." Then de Valera mentioned what would be expected of Nationalists in an integrated and not just united Ireland: "As far as I am concerned, I would be willing to suggest to the Irish people to give up a good deal in order to have an Ireland that could look to the future without anticipating distracting internal problems." De Valera concluded, indicating the tone that would be set for the Treaty negotiations: "That is what this negotiation has been [about] as far as I am concerned."

But whichever option might ultimately be adopted by the Northerners – separate statehood or community self-determination – in the pending Treaty negotiations essential Irish unity was in no way to be abridged. It was not abridged, of course, as things turned out. But, for all de Valera and others knew in advance, it ***could*** be – if a certain Boundary Commission idea that was to emerge during the Treaty negotiations were not carefully defined and left incapable of being interpreted to the advantage of the *force majeure*. The important point, however, is that Lloyd George and his Cabinet felt the Ulster Loyalists could live with an associated Republic, and it was as "envoys plenipotentiary from the elected Government of the ***Republic*** of Ireland" that he accepted the Irish negotiators to the Peace Conference. It can be safely concluded, then, that the British Government, notwithstanding the Partition Act, agreed in advance not to retain jurisdiction over the North of Ireland, but to treat Ireland as a unit under Irish Government jurisdiction and at most to allow separate statehood for 'Ulster.' This yielding of jurisdiction over Northern Ireland was, as we shall see in the next chapter, what was indeed going to be agreed to in the ensuing Treaty, an instrument that was designed to override the Partition Act's British jurisdiction or reserved powers clauses. In this respect the Treaty has been reinforced by Britain's repealing in its essentials the 1920 Government of Ireland Act beginning on March 30, 1972 (see Appendix 14, *Supplement*). The question now is: Did the Treaty itself exclude partition? Was the document a direct outgrowth of the 1914 All-Ireland Act of Unity that was itself described in the British Parliament as "a solemn bond . . . a treaty of peace between England and Ireland"? Was the 1920 Act a mere intervention for the introduction of federalism into Ireland? Was perhaps such a settling Act needed to prepare the North for the Treaty and Treaty acceptance?

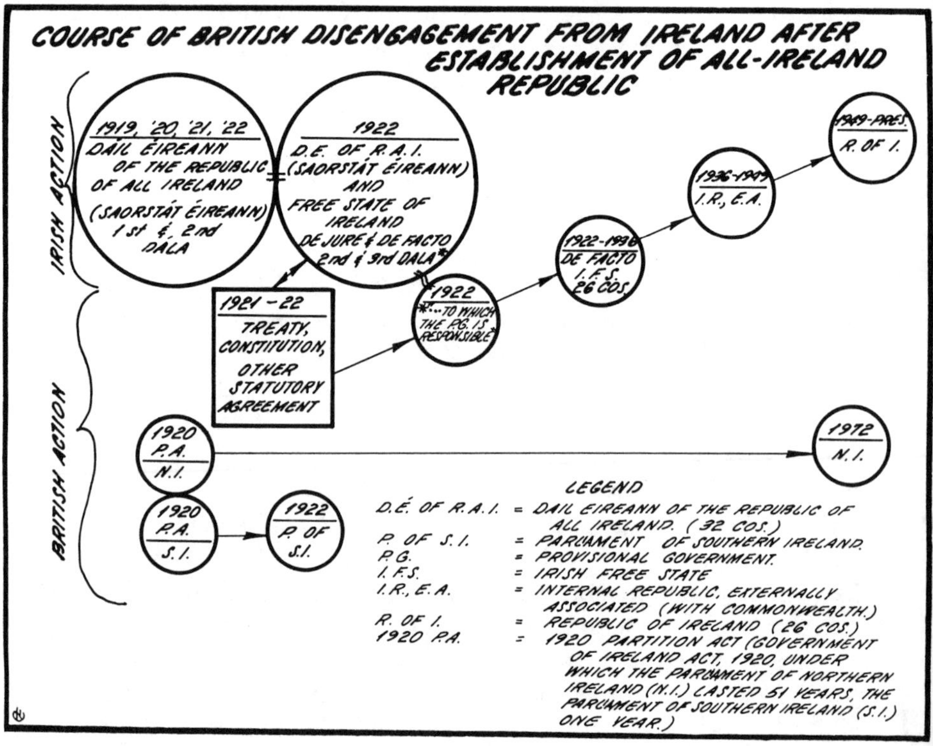
COURSE OF BRITISH DISENGAGEMENT FROM IRELAND AFTER ESTABLISHMENT OF ALL-IRELAND REPUBLIC
IRISH ACTION
BRITISH ACTION
1919, '20, '21, '22
DAIL EIREANN OF THE REPUBLIC OF ALL IRELAND (SAORSTÁT ÉIREANN) 1st & 2nd DALA
1922
D.E. OF R.A.I. (SAORSTÁT ÉIREANN) AND FREE STATE OF IRELAND DE JURE & DE FACTO 2nd & 3rd DALA*
1921-22
TREATY, CONSTITUTION, OTHER STATUTORY AGREEMENT
1922
*"...TO WHICH THE P.G. IS RESPONSIBLE"
1922-1936
DE FACTO I.F.S. 26 COS.
1936-1949
I.R., E.A.
1949-PRES.
R. OF I.
1920
P.A.
N.I.
1972
N.I.
1920
P.A.
S.I.
1922
P. OF S.I.
LEGEND
D.É. OF R.A.I. = DAIL EIREANN OF THE REPUBLIC OF ALL IRELAND. (32 COS.)
P. OF S.I. = PARLIAMENT OF SOUTHERN IRELAND.
P.G. = PROVISIONAL GOVERNMENT.
I.F.S. = IRISH FREE STATE
I.R., E.A. = INTERNAL REPUBLIC, EXTERNALLY ASSOCIATED (WITH COMMONWEALTH.)
R. OF I. = REPUBLIC OF IRELAND (26 COS.)
1920 P.A. = 1920 PARTITION ACT (GOVERNMENT OF IRELAND ACT, 1920, UNDER WHICH THE PARLIAMENT OF NORTHERN IRELAND (N.I.) LASTED 51 YEARS, THE PARLIAMENT OF SOUTHERN IRELAND (S.I.) ONE YEAR.)

CHAPTER 3

THE TREATY IMPACTS ON INDEPENDENCE

The Second Dail Eireann Preserved

The course negotiations at the London Peace Conference took is only too well known. (Readers are referred to Frank Pakenham, *Peace by Ordeal*; to Pakenham's considered second thoughts in "The Treaty Negotiations," in T. Desmond Williams, ed., *The Irish Struggle*, pp. 107-115; to Frank Gallagher, *The Anglo-Irish Treaty*; to Volume III of Thomas Jones's *Whitehall Diary*; to Lord Longford, "The Unwanted Solution, 1914-1921," in Lord Longford and Anne McHardy, *Ulster*, pp. 60-73; and to the Earl of Longford and Thomas P. O'Neill, *Eamon de Valera*, Chapters 12 and 13.) It must be held that the main preconditions the British had accepted were honored in principle at the Conference. While the national sovereignty of Ireland was basically acknowledged, the principal issue of national unity was forcibly subjected to a so-called Boundary Commission arrangement – a loophole in the Treaty for 'Ulster.' For one month after Britain's ratification of the Treaty the six-county area was to continue to be exempt from the jurisdiction of Saorstat Eireann.[1] If within that month the Northern Parliament

1 The six-county area was not expected to be exempt from Saorstat Eireann jurisdiction for longer than a few months after the signing of the Treaty. For that reason, one month's further exemption after British ratification of the Treaty was not considered excessive. While Britain regarded the Treaty as being functional in Ireland from the moment of Westminster's approval of it in December 1921 or, at the latest, Dublin's acceptance of it in January 1922, and while she proceeded on that basis to transfer power and services to the Provisional Government, nevertheless she failed to formally ratify the Treaty until a full year after signature. By so doing Britain acted quite illegally if not also invalidly, because

so requested – and it could only be *guessed* that it would – northeastern Ireland was to remain indefinitely excluded and was to enjoy the status defined in the Partition Act of 1920.

But what was that status? Obviously, Northern Ireland was not to enjoy more than the local or minor powers status defined in the Act, and Britain had limited these powers very much on her indeed. But was she also to have a say in how the major powers reserved under the Act to Westminster from all of Ireland were now to be reserved? That is, was she being given the authority to dictate to London that those reserved powers should now be divided on a North-South basis and withheld from the North but to be granted to the South? In other words, was Northern Ireland being given the right to *secede* from the rest of Ireland, and if she was would she not then be exercising that right on behalf of Britain herself? Was the so-called 'Ulster option' in reality a Westminster option? Was *partition* perchance agreed to?

If these questions can be answered in the affirmative, it can only be said that such possibilities were certainly putting a very strained interpretation on the clause stating that Northern Ireland was to enjoy the status that had been defined in the Partition Act. Could it be that the British dog would allow itself to be swung by the Northern Ireland tail like this? Hardly. Those same British who restricted Northern Ireland's scope so much were not likely to turn the 1920 Act on its head and now give the Northerners unlimited power, as it were. But anything was possible, and the more Republican members of the Irish Cabinet, including de Valera, were not taking any chances. They right away allowed for a broad interpretation to be given to the new proposals, although they realized that the proposal to allow Northern Ireland to control Westminster-reserved powers would be going beyond what had been agreed to in the preconditions.

They should also have realized then that the boundary proposals were purposely worded in unhelpful *double entendres* in order to

---

unquestionably March 2, 1922 (by de Valera's calculation), was the date beyond which it was incompetent for the King, by Order in Council, to postpone promulgation of the Treaty law. It was thought in British Government circles that the Irish Free State (Agreement) Act, which had been designed to ratify the Treaty, would be enacted by that date. When it was not (it was enacted on March 31st) it was held merely to 'legalize' the Treaty, not ratify it. By the time Britain did *ratify* the Treaty – December 5, 1922 – Northern Ireland's position was well consolidated, and the one-month period within which the Northern Parliament was to exercise its option began, in the British view, from that date.

secure Ulster's consent while evading Ireland's dissent. For, since essential unity was to be the real option for Northern Ireland, it was imperative that she be got to consent to the proposals. In the event of her consenting and exercising her option (however her option was to be understood), a Boundary Commission was to be set up ostensibly to determine the boundary between the two states of Ireland. This was to be determined "in accordance with the wishes of the inhabitants, so far as may be compatible with economic and geographic conditions," phrases that were borrowed directly from, and intended to reflect the sense of, the Treaty of Versailles in providing for plebiscites for territories around Germany's borders. That is to say, a plebiscite registering the people's preferences was to be held in Ireland also.

At first the reference to "wishes of the inhabitants" was taken to mean consulting the inhabitants on the border only, because the phrase was followed closely by a reference to "boundaries" between Northern Ireland and the rest of Ireland. But, on close inspection, determining the wishes of inhabitants on a border is, except philosophically, about as possible as counting the number of angels that might fit on the head of a pin. Obviously, the intent of the Treaty was (as was that of the Treaty of Versailles with regard to the German territories) that the inhabitants on either side of the border, in the two new Irish states, were to be consulted on their wishes regarding the territorial extent of their respective state jurisdictions, although this provision was couched in terms of determining where the border was to lie among those inhabitants. In other words, as was the way with the Treaty of Versailles, *mutatis mutandis*, a national plebiscite was called for, the outcome of which, if it were to have been held, can well be imagined, especially since the issue was whether to have a border at all or not. Little wonder that this Treaty requirement was never met and little wonder that the requirement was a proposal that was, as might have been expected, to prove none too palatable to Ulster. In fact, she was eventually to be up in arms against it. That is why extremes had to be gone to in the proposal to get her to accept it in spite of herself.

Essential Irish unity maintained

It had been a cardinal point with the Irish negotiators to insist on the essential unity of Ireland – even to the point of being willing to break off the negotiations if it would not be agreed on and to blame this on the intransigence of Ulster (whose responsibility would be Britain's, of course). By 'essential unity of Ireland' was meant national or federal unity by which there would be acknowledged separate statehood with local or minor powers for Ulster, but not British jurisdiction with reserved or major powers withheld from Ulster by Westminster. A state boundary would be compatible with essential national unity, but partition would not. The Irish delegates to the Conference wished to avoid at all costs the mistake of the Parliamentarians of five years earlier in agreeing to partition proper, no matter how hedged about with qualifications it might be. Now that partition was rearing its head again under the guise of a Boundary Commission that was first proposed in the draft of the Government of Ireland Bill back in 1919, it was only to be expected that the Irish negotiators would reject it out of hand as a firm proposal. Some might tolerate the idea only as 'a tactical maneuver,' however. When the British Draft Treaty was presented to de Valera in Dublin, he was adamant in his rejection of the terms, saying he could never put his signature to a document offering any part of Ireland an option to secede from the rest of the country.

Contrary to the sense in which all the preconditions had been accepted, the idea of separate statehood for Ulster was to all appearances widening to include a partitioned area under British jurisdiction. The so-called Ulster option was becoming, it seemed, a Westminster option. This is what de Valera was so strongly opposed to. He observed that the delegates were getting "neither this nor that," neither external association (which had been emasculated into something more like internal association) nor essential unity (which, although it held, looked capable of being gradually stolen away). He thereupon sent the reluctant delegates back to London with instructions to reject, among other things, the Boundary Commission idea and to try to put the blame on Ulster.

The Plenipotentiaries were not going to be inclined to do as de Valera instructed, however, because there was always the hope that Ulster would not exercise her option, and insofar as it was only an option the Treaty acknowledged the national sovereignty of all Ireland. Besides, they knew that without this loophole the British were not going to sign the Treaty and let Ulster down.

Back in London the Irish delegates found 'the Welsh Wizard' his old wily and unyielding self. His general attitude was as his son, Major Richard Lloyd George, described under other circumstances. "There was the hot and the cold technique. He could be infinitely patient, amiable, and amenable – until his contestant proved intractable to all these affabilities – and then an artificial storm of such terrifying suddenness that his opponent would be reduced to a state of alarm for his personal safety."

The twin problems of the Conference were Crown and Ulster. And they were inseparable. Either they were both solved together or neither one was solved. They were not to be solved, of course. Internal association and apparent partition, both, it was to be. As soon as one of the negotiators made the point that in addition to partition Ireland's difficulty was in coming into the Empire, the British negotiators found it a convenient moment to jump to their feet, shuffle their papers, and storm out of the room. The negotiations had broken down!

Lloyd George had once told his son about his dealings with Clemenceau. "I was in conference with him for about ten minutes when suddenly I appeared to take exception to a minor point of procedure. I jumped up and gave the meeting hell. A perfect blistering demonstration. Absolute apoplexy."

Something like absolute apoplexy mixed with bamboozlement and bluff seems to have occurred during the closing hours of the London Conference the evening of December 5, 1921. Lloyd George would brook no bargaining on the external association issue or the essential unity question, but forthwith issued his famous ultimatum of immediate and terrible war if the Irish Plenipotentiaries would not sign the Treaty as it stood – with the Ulster loophole. He seems to have exercised at that moment all the qualities his son has ascribed to him. "The cunning of the serpent – yes, but the courage of the lion, too. When craft failed, he was capable of taking a calculated risk and driving forward like a bulldozer." (Earl Lloyd George, *My Father, Lloyd George*, p. 161.)

The calculated risk coupled with the bulldozer technique is surely what was used in the early morning hours of December 6, 1921. The Irish negotiators were not allowed reference back to Dublin. Nor to Belfast. Not even, as a last resort, to the Commonwealth Prime Ministers.[2] Sign now or else . . . The Treaty was duly signed and brought back to Dublin, where de Valera and some of

---

2 Reference to the Commonwealth Premiers prior to signature would have been in order, since the Treaty as a Commonwealth as well as Anglo-Irish instrument committed the Commonwealth Governments as much as the British and Irish to guaranteeing Ireland's and the Dominions' new, liberated status, and such reference was in fact intended by the Irish negotiators (see Pakenham, p. 235 paperback).

his Cabinet colleagues immediately denounced it. Why had not instructions been followed that were renewed but three days earlier? What had come over the President's men? There was going to have to be some explaining to do.

De Valera, goaded by the Republican Ministers Brugha and Stack, was torn between wanting to fire the signatories and having them arrested for treason. But then there were two Republicans who had signed! And the text of the document happened to be vastly improved over the version that had just been so severely disapproved in the Dublin Cabinet. Yet it was far from being the kind of Treaty the Irish would have preferred. The President objected particularly to the apparent recognition of the right of any part of Ireland, in this case the North, to secede from the rest of the nation. He would propose an alternative solution, which in calmer moments he would set about putting on paper. In this he would be greatly aided by the constitutionalist Erskine Childers.

A mixed reception for the Treaty

Much ink has been spilled over whether and why the Irish Plenipotentiaries did not adhere to their instructions before committing their signatures to the Treaty instrument. But there is a real sense in which the instructions had, in fact, been carried out. As documented by Frank Pakenham, on pages 210, 211 and 298 of his *Peace by Ordeal* (paperback edition), the instructions were to be observed, as decided (in the Mansion House, Dublin, on December 3, 1921, three days prior to D-Day), only if: (1) the Treaty Agreement could not somehow be gotten to be accepted by Prime Minister Craig of Northern Ireland; (2) internal allegiance as dictated by the oath of allegiance in its then-constructed form could not be changed into at least internal association; and (3) the oath (therefore) could not be changed from one of being allegiance to the Crown as King of Ireland into one of being faithful recognition of the Crown as Head of the Commonwealth. All three concessions were successfully extracted by the Irish negotiators, and indeed further achievements were scored: the right for Ireland to have an army, the right to have a navy, and the right to have full fiscal autonomy. Under these circumstances, the Irish delegates had no further obligation to de Valera or to Craig not to sign, and under pressure from Lloyd George they had an obligation to the Irish people not to plunge them into war. That agreement to sign was not considered a disregarding of instructions can also be deduced from the decision of the Plenipotentiaries not to deem it necessary to check by phone with Dublin or Belfast, especially of two of them who had been so reluctant to sign as afterwards to repudiate their signatures.

The compromise de Valera proposed between pro-Treaty Free Staters and anti-Treaty Republicans was to be given expression in the celebrated Document No. 2, which he undauntedly called "a Republican document . . . as true to the Republic, every line of it, as any document that I wrote to Lloyd George" (*Dail Debates*, Priv. Sess., 17 Dec. 1921, p. 272). This proposal, introduced in an effort to head off approval of the Treaty in the Dail, would essentially make the externally associated Saorstat Eireann of that instrument to be less a part of the Commonwealth and would change the oath of allegiance into an oath of recognition. The proposal was, de Valera said (in writing to his friend Joe McGarrity in Philadelphia), "the farthest possible that Republicans could go to meet the claims of England and the North without sacrificing the Republic." Even so, this was not agreed to by Free Staters as going far enough. Republicans would be expected to go the extra mile in order to meet the farthest possible the British could come, given the Northern Irish obduracy and the adversarial climate of public opinion in Britain at the time.[3]

In Document No. 2, in its Irish unity provisions, de Valera accepted fully the Treaty's proposal for resolving the Northern Ireland problem. He went so far in a preliminary rough draft as to reproduce virtually verbatim the Treaty's clauses on Ulster in general and the Boundary Commission proposal in particular. He would go so far later as to refer to Document No. 2's unity proposal in terms of "the Treaty's Ulster clauses." But he saw no partition in the Treaty; it would not then be in Document No. 2. In this he would be supported by a Sinn Fein election leaflet for 1923 which asserted that Document No. 2 made "no recognition of the Partition of Ireland." Nevertheless, the Document did actually meet the British, and Free State, positions, as we shall see. (See John Bowman, *De Valera and the Ulster Question*, pp. 80-82.)

---

3 An index of the degree to which anti-Irish feeling rose in Britain upon the Treaty being entered into with Ireland was given in the thanksgiving message issued by the Archbishop of Canterbury: "Primate's Thanksgiving: For the success of the Devil's work in Ireland, for the murder of hundreds of Loyalists, for the sorrows of widows and orphans, for the suffering of the homeless and bereaved, for treachery to God, King and Country, *We thank Thee, O God.*" (Quoted from Edgar Holt, *Protest in Arms*, p. 275.)

All de Valera did see in the Treaty was a federal arrangement of some sort, which would not involve anything more than special treatment for Ulster. He pointed out that while partition would have represented an intrusion by Britain in Irish affairs, a federal solution, because it preserved a unitary nation, entailed no quarrel for him between the Irish Government and the North. After all, it was he who had suggested a federal solution in the first place, this to the Treaty conferees shortly after the London Peace Conference had commenced. Now he could not easily denounce a federal proposal in a Treaty that had endorsed his own suggestion.

But what if the North should reject the Treaty's federal option (as it was to do)? To meet that possibility (and eventuality) de Valera had to concede the Boundary Commission clauses of the Treaty that would provide what John Bowman has called "some variant of federalism." This alternative de Valera could readily accept, because he had already acquiesced in the way in which it was found necessary at the Treaty Conference to formulate its achievement (the Boundary Commission proposal). Now he could not easily denounce a contingency plan in a Treaty that only reflected his own acquiescence. Besides, he thought that to denounce the Boundary Commission proposal as worthless might, as Michael Laffan has suggested, "actually help to make it so and thereby play into Craig's hands" (*The Partition of Ireland*, p. 88).

However, even though de Valera could accept 'the Treaty's Ulster clauses' *in toto*, he would only do so if their underlying condition of essential Irish unity affirmed were made explicit and emphatic – which he now made it in Document No. 2. "He was willing that Dail Eireann should grant to the minority in the North-East a separate legislature which would have all the powers accorded under the Treaty. But there must be a declaration, firm and clear, which safeguarded an overriding Irish unity." (Longford and O'Neill, *Eamon de Valera*, pp. 178-179.)

It was this very proviso, however, made explicit as it had to be, that obliged de Valera paradoxically, if he were not to be ineffectually offering one federal solution for another – it was this necessary proviso that obliged him to agree with and essentially re-present the Treaty's Ulster clauses and their variant of federalism. This alternative offer, he realized, must be so structured that it would, given the *fait accompli* of Unionist entrenchment in the North already, be "tolerable both to [Republicans] and to the British government and which also could be ***imposed*** on the Ulster unionists" (Bowman, pp. 57-58; *emphasis ours*). To be imposed on Unionists the offer would have to be British backed, which only the Treaty's Ulster clauses were.

How de Valera would make his all-around acceptable offer to the Ulster Unionists was he would propose that "that portion of Ulster which is defined as Northern Ireland in the British Government of Ireland Act of 1920" be granted "privileges and safeguards not less substantial than those provided for in the 'Articles of Agreement for a Treaty.' " That is to say, in addition to the grant of the local powers of the Partition Act as listed in the Treaty for a federal setup, de Valera would also acknowledge to northeastern Ulster the rights provided in the Treaty for an alternative form of federalism that the Unionists couldn't refuse but that would still be within a unitary nation. In other words, in all he would concede the provisions of Treaty Articles 14, 15 and 16, and also, but in a nonsecessionist sense, Articles 11, 12 and 13. He would concede the provisions of the latter three Articles "in a nonsecessionist sense," we say, because he spelled out clearly in his proposal the condition that was implicit in the Treaty of an overriding Irish unity to be safeguarded, that "declaratory clause which safeguarded the supreme authority of the Dail over the whole national territory" (Longford and O'Neill, p. 172). How Unionist objection to a unitary nation might be sustained in the face of a simultaneous denial of a partitioning of Ireland was not to be made clear at this time, however (see Chapter 13).

De Valera's unity proposal was as follows: "That whilst refusing to admit the right of any part of Ireland to be excluded from the supreme authority of the Parliament of Ireland, or that the relations between the Parliament of Ireland and any subordinate legislature in Ireland can be a matter for treaty with a Government outside Ireland, nevertheless, in sincere regard for internal peace, and in order to make manifest our desire not to bring force or coercion to bear upon any substantial part of the province of Ulster, whose inhabitants may now be unwilling to accept the national authority, we are prepared to grant to that portion of Ulster which is defined as Northern Ireland in the British Government of Ireland Act of 1920, privileges and safeguards not less substantial than those provided for in the 'Articles of Agreement for a Treaty' between Great Britain and Ireland signed in London on December 6, 1921." (For the complete text of Document No. 2 see Appendix 7, *Supplement.*)

A necessary evil agreed

With the putting away (for the time being) of Document No. 2, the Treaty itself, as it had been agreed on and signed in London, was formally proposed for acceptance. The Dail debate on the document was sometimes bitter and oftentimes at cross-purposes – which is not to say that firm stands were not taken in every instance. Cardinal D'Alton quoted the *Catholic Herald* of December 24, 1921 as having reported that "some members who are for rejecting the Treaty are hoping and praying that it may pass" (*History of Ireland*, Vol. VIII, p. 334). And according to Patrick Sarsfield O'Hegarty, the entire debate was largely unreal: everyone hoped the Treaty would be passed, but by the votes of others (*The Victory of Sinn Fein*, pp. 83-84).

The vote in the Dail for acceptance of the Treaty was 64 to 57, with 54 abstentions (five Deputies representing double constituencies were not allowed to vote twice). (There were in all Ireland 175 elected Deputies, although there were 180 seats in that Second Dail; see Macardle, *The Irish Republic*, pp. 495-496.) If all of Ireland's Representatives had voted, there is no doubt that the motion to approve the Treaty would have been overwhelmingly defeated – but by different groups for different reasons. To the Unionists the phrase 'the wishes of the inhabitants' in the Boundary Commission clause was particularly offensive. "It may seem that our northern areas will be so cut up and mutilated," Captain Charles Curtis Craig, Representative for South Antrim, pointed out, "that we shall no longer be masters in our own house. The decision of that Commission may be a matter of life and death to us. I submit to the Prime Minister [Lloyd George] that he had no right to do that, and that he was in honour bound not to allow such a Commission to appear in this document by the promise he had given to the Prime Minister of Northern Ireland." (The promise Craig was referring to was the pledge Lloyd George had given to Craig's brother, Sir James Craig, at a meeting he and Lloyd George held some ten days before the Treaty was signed. Craig understood the British Prime Minister to promise that the Treaty would not be signed before the Northern Ireland Government had considered the Boundary proposals – and turned them down, as it was bound to do. About this episode, more later.)

From the reaction in Loyalist circles, it is clear that the Northerners would have voted strongly against the Treaty if they had had a chance to do so. Already a month before the Treaty was signed, Sir James Craig had rejected the Boundary Commission idea. He had gone farther, in fact, and, as we have seen, with tongue in cheek had demanded of Lloyd George that Britain confer Dominion status on the six-county area. Craig based his demand on, as he perceived it, "the just equality [between the two parts of Ireland] exhibited throughout the Government of Ireland Act" (letter to Lloyd George of July 29, 1921). But the Prime Minister rejected Craig's demand, as the 1920 Act never intended an equality of territorial jurisdictions but of territorial representation. He accordingly pointed out that the Irish people would never accept that the border should be erected into an international boundary, nor could the British in conscience attempt to enforce it (cf. SFB 27, Prime Minister to Craig, November 14, 1921, Cab. 43/2, Records of Anglo-Irish Negotiations, 1921-22).

The initial fears of the Unionists, though very real, were not, of course, to materialize. During the Treaty negotiations Craig, in replying on November 17, 1921, to Lloyd George's proposal that Unionists should come under an all-Ireland Parliament, declared that the insurmountable difficulty was the proposal to place the Unionist community under the Irish Nationalists. "To sum up," he wrote, "if you force Ulster to leave the United Kingdom against the wishes of her people, she desires to be left in a position to make her own fiscal and international policy conform as nearly as possible with the policy of the Mother Country, and to retain British traditions, British currency, British ideals, and the British language, and in this way render the disadvantages entailed by her separation from Great Britain as slight as possible."

All signs, then, are that if a full vote could have been taken on the Treaty it would have been resoundingly rejected. But the fact is that of those who did vote on it a majority favored it. This posed a very great problem for de Valera and Republicans (but not as great as it might have been if they had to have all voted along with .... Unionists!).[4] Although the Treaty was made with Ireland and imposed on all Ireland Free State status (with northeastern Ireland retaining for the time being the existing arrangement), the fact

4 When we say 'Republicans' we generally mean those hard-core Republicans of the 'New Sinn Fein' who were opposed to the Treaty Settlement. We do not intend those other Sinn Fein Republicans who accepted the Treaty and who formed themselves mainly into the 'Old I.R.A.' Least of all do we intend those Republicans of the I.R.B. movement, since the Irish Republican Brotherhood, called by Lyons "the doyen of revolutionary movements in Ireland," also supported the Treaty (as guaranteeing the Republic with Unity) and was commonly accredited with swaying the vote in favor of the Treaty Agreement both in the Dail and in the country.

remained that Ulster *was* given the choice of opting out of Irish jurisdiction, and this was interpreted by some to mean that London was given the option of holding on to a part of Ireland. There was little doubt but that Ulster would exercise this option, as she thought, for Britain, and this likelihood is mainly what made the Treaty unacceptable to Republicans. It was likewise unacceptable to Loyalists (even though they had not voted against it) but for different reasons.

To Republicans the Treaty was also unacceptable because it was, in denying them an affirmation rather than an oath of allegiance, in conflict with their oath of allegiance to the Saorstat and they justly could mount conscientious objection to such an instrument. The Republican oath, by comparison, did, as oaths usually do, allow for conscientious objection: "I, A.B., do solemnly swear (or affirm) that I do not and shall not yield a voluntary support to any pretended government, authority, or power within Ireland hostile and inimical thereto, and I do further swear (or affirm) that to the best of my knowledge and ability I will support and defend the Irish Republic and the Government of the Irish Republic, which is Dail Eireann, against all enemies, foreign and domestic, and I will bear true faith and allegiance to the same, and that I take this obligation freely and without any mental reservation or purpose of evasion, so help me, God."

For de Valera the dilemma of the Treaty was "the conflict between two principles: majority rule on the one hand and the inalienability of the national sovereignty on the other." Nevertheless, he (though not formally) proposed disapproving it, because it did not preserve the externally associated united Republic as he perceived it. Erskine Childers, who had been secretary to the Irish delegation at the London Conference, supported de Valera, saying the Plenipotentiaries had failed to bring about an acceptable and honorable association of a sovereign united State with England. Ireland under the Treaty, he held, would be "virtually a protectorate of England."

On the pro-Treaty side Collins and Griffith maintained that Irish national sovereignty had been basically preserved. For them the dilemma of the Treaty was to bring the Saorstat Republic through the hecatomb without losing the Unionists in the process – that is to say, without surrendering essential Irish unity. They did not seem to worry that the Boundary Commission loophole was a loophole. They thought it was the best that could be achieved under the circumstances. In their view they were supported by

Kevin O'Higgins, who strongly favored Commonwealth membership (which then had constitutional significance). O'Higgins held that by this means Ireland could grow into complete freedom and have her national aspirations fulfilled. He expressed his belief, in a prescient phrase, in "the evolution of this group . . . towards a condition, not merely of individual freedom but also of equality of status" (quoted from John A. Murphy, *Ireland in the Twentieth Century*, p. 40). (With a basic requirement of the Treaty being that the status of Ireland should be in conformity with the constitutional practice of Canada, it was heartening to realize that that practice was developing towards a status of equality with other Commonwealth countries, Britain included.)

The Treaty, we can see, as it came back signed from London, posed a dilemma every bit as great for its opponents to accept as it did for its proponents to defend. For the time being, all President de Valera could do in a moment of deep distress and confusion was to write an open letter to the Irish people in which he assuredly stated, among other things: "There is a definite constitutional way of resolving our political differences. . . ."

In 1921 the emphasis for Irish Republicans on the one hand, as it was for Irish Unionists on the other, was more on the "differences" than on the ways to resolve them. The imposition of 'Dominion status' on Ireland was, as we shall see, a very objectional point to Republicans. But, as with the transformable oath of allegiance, it was tolerated for the sake of securing essential Irish unity. And besides, as we shall also see, it was not as bad a status in itself as it was generally made out to be. This was because, by the Treaty itself, the status of ***Dominion*** was no longer the same as previously, only the name was. As W.K. Hancock demonstrated (in his *Survey of British Commonwealth Affairs*, Vol. I, p. 146), "[the Treaty] stretched the framework of dominion status in the attempt to make room within it for 'the national and self-derived statehood' which Ireland claimed" (which was the Saorstat).

The compatibility of 'Dominion' with Republican status had been insisted on, in fact, by the Irish Plenipotentiaries at the Peace Conference when they stated that if Commonwealth association was to be accepted for Ireland, it must "be based not on the present technical, legal status of dominions, but on the real position they claim, and have in fact secured. . . . It is essential that the present *de facto* position should be recognised *de jure*, and that all its implications as regards sovereignty, allegiance, constitutional independence of the governments should be acknowledged."

(Quoted from F.W.F. Smith, *Frederick Edwin, Earl of Birkenhead*, p. 383; D.W. Harkness, *The Restless Dominion*, p. 16.)

But it was not just the concept of Dominion status for Ireland that bothered Republicans – it was the very idea of membership within the British Commonwealth. However, this too was not to be seen in the circumstances as a really bad thing. The vehicle of Commonwealth membership with its attendant constitutional evolution would enable Ireland one day to change the external association that was controlled by the Council of the Commonwealth into the external association that would be controlled by the Government of Ireland. But in 1921 it was very difficult, if not impossible, to foretell that there could be enormous progress made in the direction of external association by constitutional means. It was particularly difficult to predict that within a mere ten years there would be such a development as the Statute of Westminster, a constitutional breakthrough that crowned Irish efforts of several years to use Commonwealth membership to broaden and strengthen the nation's constitutional status and at the same time to undo all – or almost all – the Treaty restrictions placed by Britain on Ireland. The Commonwealth constitutional development that was to favor Ireland so admirably during the Cosgrave decade of Government was not foreseen even by supporters of the Treaty themselves. De Valera too, in fact, was obliged in 1932 to admit that a lot of constitutional progress had been achieved since the Treaty. "There have been advances made," he then said, "that I did not believe would be made at the time . . . advances which I think have been made beyond what would be reasonably expected at the time" (*Seanad Debates*, Vol. 15, col. 938; cf. Edward Norman, *A History of Modern Ireland*, p. 300). And in 1935 he was able to go even farther and say: "I have admitted, and I admit now, that I anticipated even worse things from the Treaty than the things that happened [such as the Civil War].[5] I did not anticipate that the movement based on the Treaty would have gone in the direction it has taken as fully as it did. I am quite willing to admit that there is an immense difference between the powers that are possessed [now] and the powers that existed [then]. . . . I am willing

5 According to de Valera, the Civil War was fought not so much over the Treaty *per se* as over interpretation of it – in terms of "what it meant and what it would lead to." It was, he said, a case of *Beirt ag troid agus iad ar aon sgeal*, "two people quarreling over a point with both saying the same thing." One person was overstating the case, de Valera explained, while the other was doing the opposite.

to grant that there is a big difference between the present position and the position as it existed. . . ." (*Seanad Debates*, Vol. 19, cols. 1588-1589; see also cols. 1045 and 1082.)

With the hindsight of many years it may be easy to accuse de Valera and Republicans, as they have been accused, of mistaking the shadow for the substance in the Treaty, but in 1921 it was no easy matter to see what could with time be remedied and so might be submitted to for the time being, and what could not and so would have to be opposed. The tragic thing was that generally what could be, and was with time, remedied or amended – matters of a constitutional status nature as opposed to those of an essential unity nature – could only be remedied on a 26-county basis. So that the more the Treaty would be transcended or Republicanized, the more partition would be reinforced or made 'permanent.' There obviously was something lacking in the constitutional way being pursued, and perhaps it is only now, several decades later, that the "definite constitutional way" of de Valera is being found.

Addendum to Part I. Like the British Empire itself, the partition of Ireland appears to have been nothing more than an accident of history. For the British Government never seemed to have wanted aught but self-determination for the two communities in Ireland, Churchill himself saying of the new Irish rulers: "We can do our best to include the Six Counties in a larger Parliament, plus autonomy. . . . If they get unity, we could press Ulster not to object to holding autonomous powers for the Six Counties from them instead of from us." But 'Ulster' saw things differently, and forced the British to retain their *fait accompli* deed as it stood unintended – and the phlegmatic Lord Birkenhead to gasp: "Our position as to the Six Counties is an impossible one."

Moreover, when at the Treaty Conference Arthur Griffith in response to a question from Lloyd George about noncontiguous areas of the North said, "There we would have to do a deal," the Prime Minister hopped at him: "Ah-ha! That is not self-determination. That is a deal. That is what we had to do." In other words, the partition setup was not exactly something to be sworn by. Self-determination would somehow have to be applied. (See Thomas Jones, *Whitehall Diary*, Vol. III, pp. 136, 146, 148, 153, 154.)

On the other side of the coin, the Irish at the Treaty Conference never wanted aught either but genuine self-determination for both communities in Ireland. To achieve this, it was not beneath them to accept an otherwise objectionable Treaty as a steppingstone to the real thing. Even no less a personage than Padraic Pearse, as Richard Mulcahy has recorded, was later to be quoted as providing evidence that *he* would have supported the Treaty as a means to the end (Mulcahy MSS, UCD Library). Pearse, it appears, in a 1912 editorial in *An Barr Buadh (The*

Trumpet of Victory), urged acceptance of Home Rule as a weapon and means that would give Ireland ultimate freedom. Translated, the relevant portion of that editorial is as follows:

"The Gael who would take the settlement that the foreigners are now offering us as a full settlement and who, because of that settlement, would make friends with the foreigners, would surrender his honor for his advantage. But the person who would refuse the present Bill which is before the British Parliament because that Bill denies the complete supremacy of the Gael in his own territory, or because he did not think the freedom under such an Act would be sufficient for us, would in our opinion postpone unnecessarily his own advantage and the advantage of his people. . . . He would be doing as did the prisoner who refused to have one of his manacles taken from him when his oppressors would not remove the second one too. That prisoner did not understand that to remove one of the manacles would make it easier for him to escape, and perhaps it would be a weapon in his hand given him by God. It is clear to us that, not only is this a proposal to take a manacle from the Gael, but it is also putting into the hands of the Gael a weapon. Our honour and our advantage are on the same side this time." (Translation from, and reproduced with gratitude to, Ruth Dudley Edwards, *Patrick Pearse, the Triumph of Failure*, pp. 159-160, pbck. ed.)

PART II

RECONSTRUCTION

Paribus se legibus ambae
Invictae gentes aeterna in foedera mittant.

"Under equal laws may the two nations,
mutually unconquered, be partners in an eternal comity."

VIRGIL

The Signing of the Death Warrant

When you have sweated, toiled,
had mad dreams, hopeless nightmares,
you find yourself in London's streets,
cold and dank in the night air.

Think – what have I got for Ireland?
Something which she has wanted
these past seven hundred years.
Will anyone be satisfied at the bargain?
Will anyone?

MICHAEL COLLINS
(Writing to his fiancee)

CHAPTER 4

REPUBLICAN REACTION TO THE TREATY

The Third Dail Eireann and Pact Dail

To many Republicans the Treaty was unacceptable because it betrayed the Republic and the martyred dead, but primarily because it was associated with partition. The oath of allegiance was, of course, the main stumbling block, and this summed up for them everything that was odious in submission to Britain and in the internal association within the Commonwealth as then constituted that was imposed on their country. "The oath crystallised in itself the main things we objected to," wrote de Valera to Joe McGarrity, "inclusion in the Empire, the British King as King of Ireland, Chief Executive of the Irish State, and the source from which all authority in Ireland was to be derived" (quoted from P.S. O'Hegarty, *A History of Ireland under the Union, 1801-1922*; Sean Cronin, *The McGarrity Papers*, p. 109). The oath primarily involved allegiance to a British-devised Constitution, by provision of which the British Monarch would be made Head of State in Ireland. There were other reasons also for objecting to allegiance to the Constitution, as we shall see, but these were not perceivable at the time, due to the fact that the Constitution was withheld from publication until it was too late to do much about them.

But all was not lost, and it was agreed that the Second Dail, being a Republican body, was powerless to ratify the Treaty and so disestablish the Republic. It was further agreed, after months of struggle, that the Treaty should not be put before the people as an issue, since it was they only who had the power to disestablish the Republic and it was feared that this was what indeed they might do for the sake of peace. The agreement reached by opposite sides of the Treaty split concerned the forming of a pact whereby the issue of the Treaty would not have to be faced directly by the people and they would be able to vote as they pleased in the upcoming elections. By this device the Republic would be preserved – and British pressure given the slip.

What led to the formation of this pact was a move made by the Archbishop of Dublin on the political front and a concomitant move by Dan Breen of Tipperary on the military front. Towards the end of April 1922 the Archbishop, Dr. Walsh, sponsored a meeting that was attended by de Valera, Collins, Griffith, Brugha, three Labour leaders, the Lord Mayor of Dublin, and the Mayor of Limerick. Ways were discussed for preventing the Treaty from being made an issue in the elections scheduled for later that year, but the pro-Treaty side was not yet ready for compromise with the anti-Treaty forces and no agreement was reached.

However, where the Archbishop failed Dan Breen succeeded. It will be understood that, in addition to dividing the people and the politicians, the Treaty had split the Army also and given rise to mutually hostile feelings and sporadic clashes. In a way the split in the Army was the more serious of the two, especially as the Army Executive of the I.R.A. had, in March, constituted itself into a separate government determined to uphold the Republic and had set up its headquarters in the Four Courts in Dublin. This development, as might be expected, was provocative to the 'Free State' Government, and in an effort to avert impending civil war Dan Breen organized a move to close ranks on the Treaty split and to effect a compromise agreement. Breen, who was nominated for election to the Dail from both sides of the political divide, promoted his reconciliation process among leading pro- and anti-Treaty Army officers, and this initiative culminated in quite an unusual agreement. Drafted as the well-known 'Army Document,' the agreement served as a basis of discussion in the Dail, where a bipartisan committee was appointed to explore the implications of the agreement fully. Breen describes his efforts in his record of his involvement in the Revolutionary War, *My Fight for Irish Freedom* (pp. 172-173 paperback edition), wherein is given also the text of the agreement signed by the officers of opposing sides:

> I met Sean O'Hegarty (Commandant of the First Cork Brigade), Florrie O'Donoghue (Adjutant of the First Southern Division), Humphrey Murphy of Kerry, Tom Hales of Cork, and Sean Moylan, T.D., all of whom were

opposed to the Treaty. After some discussion we decided to seek out some officers on the other side in a last attempt to find a way out. We made contact with Mick Collins, Dick Mulcahy, Owen O'Duffy, Gearoid O'Sullivan and Sean Boylan.

After a long exchange of views, agreement was reached upon a certain basis of settlement. This agreement was put down in writing and all the members attached their signatures (Sean Moylan was the only one who refused to sign). This document was published in the Press on 1 May. I give it here in full:

> We, the undersigned officers of the I.R.A., realise the gravity of the position in Ireland, and appreciate the fact that, if the present drift is maintained, a conflict of comrades is inevitable; we hereby declare that this would be the greatest calamity in Irish history and would leave Ireland broken for generations.
>
> To avert this catastrophe, we believe that a closing of the ranks is necessary.
>
> We suggest to all leaders, *army and political*, and to all citizens and soldiers of Ireland, the advisability of *a union of forces on the basis of the acceptance and utilisation of our present national position* in the best interests of Ireland; we require that nothing shall be done that would prejudice our position or dissipate our forces.
>
> We feel on this basis alone can the situation best be faced, viz.:
>
> (1) The acceptance of the fact, admitted by all sides, that *the majority of the people of Ireland are willing to accept the Treaty*;
>
> (2) *An agreed election* with a view to
>
> (3) Forming a *Government which will have the confidence of the whole country*;
>
> (4) Army unification on the above basis
>
> [*italics ours*].

The agreement was signed by Tom Hales, Humphrey Murphy, Sean O'Hegarty, Florrie O'Donoghue, Sean Boylan, Dick Mulcahy, Owen O'Duffy, Gearoid O'Sullivan, Mick Collins and myself. Five of the signatories opposed the Treaty [Hales, Murphy, O'Hegarty,

> O'Donoghue, and Breen] and five favoured it [Boylan, Mulcahy, O'Duffy, O'Sullivan, and Collins]. . . .
>
> On 3 May the signatories of this document were received by the Dail, and Sean O'Hegarty addressed the House. A Committee representing both sides of the Dail was appointed to discuss the proposals.
>
> (See also Joseph M. Curran, *The Birth of the Irish Free State, 1921-1923*, pp. 186-187.)

The Republican, anti-Treaty forces had every reason to fear that in the upcoming General Election the electorate would approve the Treaty and disestablish the Republic, and so strenuous efforts had to be made to translate the bipartisan Army Document of May 1922 into a similar bipartisan political agreement. This had to be done in order to give the electorate an alternative to the Treaty to vote for and is, in fact, what happened eventually.[1] The several discussions held in the Dail led to the idea of a 'Panel' Election, with a Coalition Government to follow. In this way was the famous 'Collins-de Valera Pact' born. The essence of this seven-point Pact was that there would be a national coalition slate or panel of candidates to be drawn from both sections of opinion in the Dail and in Sinn Fein. All Panel candidates would stand as a United Sinn Fein, and the number allowed to each side would be the same as its existing strength in the Dail. After the election a Coalition Government would be formed with an elected President (possibly a Republican), a Minister of Defense representing the Army (probably a Republican), and nine other Ministers, five from the pro-Treaty side, four from the anti-Treaty side. These would constitute the Government of the Third Dail Eireann.

1 Bowman is of the opinion that it was awareness of the ill effects which the pro-Treaty/anti-Treaty split would have on the North – entrenchment of the Government there, partition being made permanent, exposure of Nationalists to those "only thirsting to proceed with [their] extermination" – that it was this realization that proved to be the catalyst for the *rapprochement* between Collins and de Valera. These grave consequences of a Sinn Fein split were impressed by Frank Aiken and other Northern I.R.A. leaders on Griffith, de Valera, Collins, Brugha, Richard Mulcahy, Rory O'Connor, Liam Lynch and Eoin O'Duffy at a pre-election meeting. " 'Emphasizing the dangers, the northern delegation helped to close Sinn Fein's ranks through the Collins-de Valera pact" (*De Valera and the Ulster Question*, pp. 72-73; Mulcahy Papers, P 7/A/145, Archives Dept., UCD).

The Collins-de Valera Pact

The story of the Collins-de Valera Pact is perhaps best told in its fullness by Dorothy Macardle in her classic, *The Irish Republic* (pp. 710-727).

"During the meeting of the Dail on Saturday afternoon, May 20th [1922], it was announced that Eamon de Valera and Michael Collins had agreed upon a settlement and signed a pact. The news was received with an outburst of applause.

"The Pact was an agreement by which the forthcoming elections should not be taken as deciding the issue of the Treaty, but as creating a government to preserve peace. It provided for a National Coalition Government. Sinn Fein was to put forward a panel of candidates, sixty-six nominated by the Treaty Party and fifty-eight by the Republicans, each party keeping its present strength 'without prejudice to their present respective positions.' [2]

"Proportional Representation was the method which would be used [in the General Election about to be held].

"The expectation of the supporters of the Pact was that each voter, having given votes to the Panel candidates of his own [pro- or anti-Treaty] party, would give the rest of his votes to the Panel candidates of the opposition party, pro-Treaty or anti-Treaty. Thus the men and women who had represented the nation throughout its recent struggle would be returned . . . [and from these reelected Deputies a Coalition Government designed to sidestep the Treaty issue would be formed]."

The following were the terms of the Collins-de Valera Pact for a National Sinn Fein Panel.

We are agreed:

(1) That a National Coalition panel for this Third Dail, representing both parties in the Dail and in the Sinn Fein Organisation,

2 As far as I can ascertain at this point in my research, 59 candidates were actually nominated by Republicans to make a total of 125 candidates for the Sinn Fein Panel. Macardle omits to count Sean O'Mahony, a Republican Deputy elected from within the six-county area. (It was probably because he was already elected that she overlooked him.) If O'Mahony was counted in, although he was not to have to submit to any election in his constituency, the fact of his inclusion in the Panel would indicate that Sinn Fein regarded the forthcoming election as being equivalently held for all of Ireland, a point that would be consistent with the nature of the Pact itself. See Brian M. Walker's *Parliamentary Election Results in Ireland, 1921-1976* (Royal Irish Academy, Dublin) for possible further clarification of this matter.

be sent forward, on the ground that the national position requires the entrusting of the Government of the country into the joint hands of those who have been the strength of the national situation during the last few years, without prejudice to their present respective positions.

(2) That this Coalition panel be sent forward as from the Sinn Fein Organisation, the number for each party being their present strength in the Dail.

(3) That the candidates be nominated through each of the existing party Executives.

(4) That every and any interest is free to go up and contest the election equally with the National Sinn Fein panel. (A clause such as this one was included to make the election be as free and democratic as possible and to demonstrate that Sinn Fein did not seek to monopolize the election. Unfortunately, this clause was to provide Collins and other politicians with the means to circumvent the basic objectives of the Pact. They did not break the Pact, however, as has been widely alleged; they merely exploited Clause 4 to the full, as any red-blooded politician would do. See Michael Gallagher, "The Pact General Election of 1922," *Irish Historical Studies*, Vol. XXI, No. 84 (Sept. 1979), pp. 404-421.)

(5) That constituencies where an election is not held shall continue to be represented by their present Deputies. (Clause 5 was intended to meet the situation in the six occupied counties in which the General Election was not to be held in June 1922. (It was held in constituencies in those counties in the following November.) In the meantime five of the 52 Deputies from those constituencies were reelected from constituencies in which the General Election was held (that is, in the 26 counties), and the remaining 47 could, under the terms of the Pact, consider themselves free to attend the Dail as if they had been newly elected. In this way the resultant Dail would be a 32-county Assembly, which was in accord with the terms of the Treaty, and the 32-county Republic would be preserved.)

(6) That after the election the Executive shall consist of the President, elected as formerly; the Minister for Defence, representing the army; and nine other Ministers – five from the majority party and four from the minority, each party to choose its own nominees. The allocation will be in the hands of the President.

(7) That in the event of the Coalition Government finding it necessary to dissolve, a general election will be held as soon as possible on adult suffrage.

The Pact was ratified unanimously by Dail Eireann on May 20, 1922.

"Arthur Griffith . . . amended his motion [of two days previously, May 18th] for an election in June, making it subject to the terms of the Pact. The motion thus amended was seconded by de Valera and unanimously approved. This, constituting a decree of the Second Dail for an election for the Third Dail, made the Pact part of the law of the Republic . . .

"It was understood that the Treaty was not to be an issue in the elections decreed for June. Instead of being faced with the necessity of recording an immediate decision on this overwhelming question, the people were offered a chance to postpone their decision until the matter could be clarified and understood. [For the time being] they were offered an opportunity of returning a coalition government pledged to peaceful conservation of the present national strength. Should the differences between the two parties in the Government later oblige it to dissolve, the issue of the Treaty was to be put before the people at a General Election. By that time, the Treaty-Constitution would have been published and examined, adult suffrage established, and the electoral register properly revised. Thus an ultimate peaceful solution was provided for.

"No Pact could place the Republic beyond danger, but any further attempts to weaken the Republican position in advance of a decision of the people could be forestalled. For the new Parliament was to be the Third Dail. It was to be the heir and successor of the First and Second Dail Eireann, not a 'Provisional Parliament' for the Twenty-Six Counties, creature of an English Act. . . .

"Every member of Sinn Fein became committed [to the Collins-de Valera Pact] on May 23rd [1922], when the Pact was ratified, with only one dissentient [vote], by a great Ard-Fheis.

"Speaking to that assembly, de Valera said that those who made the Pact and those who approved it looked upon it not as a triumph for one section or the other, but as a great triumph for the Irish nation.

"Michael Collins made a speech which was regarded as signifying a determination to sacrifice even the Treaty if necessary to this reconciliation among Republicans; it would, he said, bring stable conditions to the country, and if those stable conditions were not more valuable than any other agreement, well, then, they must face what those stable conditions would enable them to face. His words were received with tremendous applause." (Macardle.)

The Third Dail elected

The situation up to now was that the Republican Dail Eireann had approved the Treaty in response, as it was pointed out (chiefly by Liam Mellowes), more to the fear of the people than to the will of the people; but it had not ratified the Treaty. Republican Deputies held, and all agreed, that a Republican Dail could not ratify a Treaty that purported to disestablish what that Dail itself embodied, namely the Republic, and that it was only the people who could disestablish the Republic they had created by their own free votes. If, then, it were not for an instrument such as the Collins-de Valera Pact, the Irish people were to be faced with a dilemma in the forthcoming elections. A vote for the Treaty, while being a vote for peace and placation of the British, could be construed as a vote for the disestablishment of their cherished Republic – and possibly also for the dismemberment of Ireland, depending on how the Boundary Commission act was going to play. A vote for the Republic, on the other hand, would be a vote cast for the risk of a Falklands-type war and possibly for the loss of a once-in-the-history-of-a-nation opportunity of getting the British out of Ireland. The dilemma facing the Irish people was enunciated succinctly by de Valera as the conflict between what the majority of the people wanted, on the one hand, and the inalienability of the national sovereignty, on the other. (De Valera ***presumed*** to know how the Boundary Commission act was eventually going to play; yet, technically, all he had to base his political position on was a presumption.) The overriding consideration for the people was how to extricate the nation's hand from the British lion's paw without being mauled and savaged irreparably and yet in the process not disestablish the Republic. The Collins-de Valera Pact with its acceptance essentially of Document No. 2 offered an admirable way out of the dilemma.

By the elections held under the Pact neither was the Treaty ratified nor the Republic disestablished. These elections were held on June 16, 1922. The Second Dail had adjourned on June 8th after decreeing that it would reconvene on June 30th to dissolve and transfer its powers to the incoming Dail. The new Parliament was to meet on July 1st. Of the 180 seats in the Assembly, 128 were electable and 52 nonelectable for the time being (elections were not held for these 52 seats in the occupied six counties for another five months). Members who held 47 of these latter seats from the all-Ireland election of a year before were eligible to sit in the new Dail without reelection (as per Clause 5 of the Pact); members who held the remaining 5 seats did, in fact, sit in the new Dail (since they were also elected from constituencies in the South anyway). Of the 128 electable seats, 93 went to Panel candidates (of whom 58 were pro-Treaty, 36 anti-Treaty), 17 were won by the Labour Party (which had declared its support of the Pact), 7 seats went to the Farmers' Party, 6 went to Independents, and there were 4 Unionists (who were returned automatically from Dublin University). Of the 52 nonelectable seats, 5 were simultaneously held by Panel candidates reelected from constituencies in which the elections were held, and at least 7 others (1 Sinn Fein and 6 Nationalists) could be said to have been Panel candidates. (It is not known how many of the remaining 40 Deputies would have been willing to join the Panel had elections been held in their constituencies as well.) Of course, this situation held only until November of 1922, when what could be considered as the remainder of the General Election was held (in the North).

As far as the voters of Ireland were concerned, what had been elected was the Third Dail Eireann, which was, of course, to be the successor to the Second Dail and to assemble as soon as the Second Dail could reconvene and transmit its powers. Before the Second Dail could reconvene for this purpose, however, the whole political situation, due to external pressures, became transformed. The main source of pressure was the 'Monarchical' Constitution Britain was attempting to impose upon Ireland. But there were also threats of a resumption of war coming from the British, who disliked the whole idea of the Pact and denounced it vehemently as being a violation of the Treaty.

No one summed up the Pact's likely consequences for Britain better than Churchill: "It prevented an expression of opinion on the Treaty; it gave the Provisional Government no further representation of strength or authority from the Irish people; it left the Government in its present weak and helpless position; it ruptured Article 17 of the Treaty" (quoted from Calton Younger, *Ireland's Civil War*, pp. 285-286). The reference to Article 17 of the Treaty was inspired by the assumption that if four (or five) Republicans were to sit in the Coalition Government they would refuse to fulfill the obligation imposed on Ministers of signifying in writing their acceptance of the Treaty. But strictly, the obligation of Article 17 applied to members of the Provisional Government alone and for a further six months only.

However, more than Article 17 was at stake. The whole Treaty settlement hung in the balance, and this situation was soon to be underlined by the presentation in London of the Draft Constitution of Ireland which departed in important particulars from the terms of that settlement. The Provisional Government went as far as they could in drafting their Constitution along the lines of external association of an internal united Republic. Their dilemma was real enough. Either they formulated a Constitution that conformed with the Treaty and quarreled with de Valera; or they produced a Constitution that amended the Treaty in a Republican sense and risked an open break with Lloyd George.[3]

In the event, Lloyd George proved that he could exert more pressure than de Valera, and he succeeded to make the Irish leaders knuckle under and accept amendments which brought the Constitution squarely within the confines of the Treaty and the Empire.

Ironically, the Constitution did not legally have to be submitted to the British Government at all, as there was nothing on the face of the Treaty which said that the Irish leaders were under an obligation to submit their Constitution to the British for approval. But the existence of the Collins-de Valera Pact so alarmed the British that they demanded to see the Constitution. They feared, rightly, that a Coalition Government in Ireland might retain the Republic in defiance of the Treaty, a situation that would have been none too palatable to the Loyalists anymore than to the British themselves. Northern Ireland Prime Minister Craig, in fact, seized the opportunity to denounce the whole idea of the Boundary Commission, and thought that if it were to be enforced in those

3 It should be noted that the front presented by having the so-called Provisional Government draft the Constitution was intended for British acceptability. In reality there was some Republican input too. As Bowman regards it, "the subsequent attempts ***by both factions in Sinn Fein*** to draft a constitution somehow compatible with the Treaty and with external association proved abortive. In their ***joint*** draft they excluded the Oath, went beyond the already agreed Dominion status, and sought to undermine Northern Ireland's constitutional position." (*De Valera and the Ulster Question*, p. 73 (emphasis ours); see also Thomas Jones, *Whitehall Diary*, Vol. III, pp. 198-199; Collins to Duggan memo of May 4, 1922, Hugh Kennedy Papers, P 4/E/1, Archives Dept., UCD.)

circumstances it would lead to civil war with Britain. A Republic at their doorstep was perceived by the British to be a menace to their Empire. Bellowed Churchill about the Republic: "We should no more recognize it than the Northern States of America recognized secession" (quoted from Robert Kee, *The Green Flag*, Vol. 3, *Ourselves Alone*, p. 163).

The British were at this time, too, stung by the assassination of Sir Henry Wilson, for which they (wrongly) blamed the anti-Treatyites who were holding out in arms against the progressive usurpation of the Republic. In addition, there were pogroms being held against the North of Ireland Nationalists, who were being held virtually as hostages by the British army and the newly formed Ulster Special Constabulary. All this was done in order to force 'Southern' Ireland to submit to a humiliating Treaty and, worse, to a British-devised Constitution of which the Treaty would be made to form a part and be enacted as the law of the land. Inevitably feelings ran high on opposing political sides, and civil war broke out on June 28, 1922.

The upshot of all this was that the Second Dail Eireann did not reconvene on June 30th for formal dissolution and transference of powers as it had decreed to do. Some Republicans consider this Dail to have equivalently adjourned *sine die* as of the day the Civil War broke out or as of June 30th, the day it was scheduled to reconvene for dissolution but was prevented by the war from doing. Technically, the Second Dail would be said to exist until the Ceann Comhairle (Speaker) would have been elected by the incoming Dail and taken his seat in it. This did not take place until September 9, 1922, but it was not performed in the prescribed manner nor in accordance with the Dail decree of June 8th.

Meanwhile, and more significantly, the Supreme Court showed that it regarded the Second Dail to be still existing. For example, on August 11th the Court issued an Absolute Order to the Ceann Comhairle, Eoin MacNeill, directing him to show cause why he had been failing to summon the outgoing Dail and fix the place and hour of its meeting for formal closure. Also, the Second Dail's own Ministry acted in certain instances on the authority of that Dail after the June 30th date for its dissolution, a fact that would indicate that it, too, regarded the Second Dail as being still in existence.

A Pact Coalition Government made unlikely

The refusal to close out the Second Dail was disappointing enough to Republicans and all those concerned with maintaining continuity of the 32-county National Parliament or Dail Eireann, but there was also making its presence felt at this time the new British-revised Constitution that had been accepted by the electorate. This was threatening to strain the Collins-de Valera Pact to the limit and to make the prospect of a Coalition Government extremely dim. If there were to be imposed on Ireland a Constitution that, for example, went *ultra vires* as regards the Treaty in making obligatory on Dail Deputies an oath of allegiance – and Article 17 stated that it did: "Such oath shall be taken and subscribed by every member of the Parliament (Oireachtas) before taking his seat therein before the Representative of the Crown or some person authorised by him" – then it was extremely unlikely that even a semi-Republican Coalition Government was going to be established. Worst of all, if, as was to be the case, the Constitution was going to restrict the jurisdiction of the Dail from 32 counties to 26 counties, then the formation of a Coalition Government was absolutely out of the question, as for Republicans there could be no question of their being forced to accept partition.

The improbability – or even impossibility – of a Coalition Government *per se* was not going to bother the principals of the Pact much, however. What was important for them was that the Republic not be disestablished by the people, and that the electorate, despite British pressure, be provided with a way of voting for the candidates of their choice without at the same time causing the national sovereignty to be infringed on or putting the nation into submission to the Empire. This national objective the people achieved by voting for a Pact Dail and not saying yea nor nay to the Treaty. Thus, as far as the nation was concerned, continuity of the all-Ireland Republic was preserved, no matter what action the Dail might be forced to take.

But was continuity of the all-Ireland ***Dail*** preserved as well? The answer is a qualified Yes: because it was a Pact Dail that was elected, and in accordance with Clause 5 this was elected for all Ireland as any Dail Eireann heretofore had been and the six-county Deputies were welcome to attend. But, due to the pressure exerted by the Westminster Irish Free State (Agreement) Act, which had been enacted the previous March 31st – which pressure was exerted through the Act's creature, the Provisional Government – the new Dail's membership was being made to realize that their jurisdiction no longer extended to 32 counties of Ireland, but was to be restricted to 26. This may have been in accordance with the Treaty's suspensive provision (Article 11), but it clearly prejudged the Boundary Commission's outcome and would to that extent have been an illegal constraint.

However, although Dail Eireann was being obliged to become the Dail of the 26-county area alone, there would have had to be continuity preserved. A Pact Dail Eireann had been elected and the Members returned were elected as a Panel for a National Coalition Government. No Coalition Government came into being, however, but this fact would not militate against the Third Dail's continuity of succession nor its qualifying to be the Parliament of all Ireland. But there was one ominous note sounded – and this was something that bothered de Valera – although it was of no constitutional significance. The newly elected Dail had not been summoned, at least not openly, as the Third Dail Eireann. It was the Provisional Government that convened the new Parliament, although this could be explained by pointing out that the Provisional Government often covered for the Second Dail Government, it being almost identical in personnel, and it could be that the Irish rulers wanted to give the British the impression of continuity from the Treaty. Even Lord FitzAlan, "Governor General of Ireland," acting in accordance with the pertinent provision of the Partition Act, heightened the fiction by declaring: "The Provisional Government having so advised, I hereby call a Parliament to be known as and styled the Provisional Parliament." Thus, in British eyes, a continuity of sorts even from the 1920 Government of Ireland Act was preserved! The reality was, of course, quite otherwise.

By the Interpretation Act, 1923, the Third Dail was to assert its own succession from the Second all-Ireland Dail Eireann. In Section 2 (9) of the Act it defined the Third Dail Eireann thus: "The expression 'the Third Dail Eireann' shall mean the assembly of members of Parliament elected by an Election held pursuant to a Resolution of the Second Dail Eireann passed on the 20th day of May, 1922, and in manner particularly mentioned in an Act of the United Kingdom Parliament entitled 'the Irish Free State (Agreement) Act, 1922,' in which Act the said Dail Eireann is referred to as the House of Parliament to which the Provisional Government shall be responsible, being the Constituent Assembly which enacted the Constitution." (The United Kingdom Parliament was defined in this Act as "the late United Kingdom Parliament of Great Britain and Ireland.")

On June 27, 1922, the official gazette of the Government, *Iris Oifigiuil*, contained the following notice: "The House of Parliament to which the Provisional Government is to be responsible will assemble at the Theatre of the Royal Dublin Society, Leinster Lawn, Kildare Street, Dublin, on Saturday, the 1st day of July, 1922, at the hour of 11 o'clock in the forenoon, for the purpose of answering the Roll, after which the House will proceed to the election of a Speaker, and to the discharge of such other business as may be decided."

The notice was signed by Diarmuid O'Hegarty, Secretary of the Provisional Government, and it was issued in the name of the Irish Provisional Government. It was addressed to members for constituencies in 'Southern' Ireland only. The origin and manner of the issuance of the notice could be construed as window dressing to placate British pressure, but the fact that the notice of the meeting was not addressed, as it should have been, in accordance with Clause 5 of the Pact, to Members from the six counties was an indication that the new Assembly was not going to be regarded as the Third Dail Eireann, as had originally been intended. While it is true that the mere issuance of a notice could not be taken as the determiner of the constitutional nature of a Dail, the non-invitation of six-county Deputies helped clear the way for the British to steamroll their way in with a Constituent Act that would set up the new Dail as strictly a 26-county Assembly.

That the Pact was not being scrupulously upheld by the members of the Provisional Government did not cause widespread concern among the Irish leaders, however, Republicans included. What mattered most was that the Dail as *elected* was the Dail of the whole of Ireland. The main objective of the Pact had been achieved – the preservation of the Irish Republic. By electing a Pact Dail and endorsing thereby Document No. 2 an admirable constitutional way was found of surmounting the obstacle of the Treaty, as de Valera ever since the signing of the Treaty had hoped there would be. The Republic (for all Ireland) did not have to be disestablished, submission (for all Ireland) did not have to be made to the British Empire, and continuity of the all-Ireland Republic and possibly also of the all-Ireland Dail could be preserved. And most importantly for future Irish unity, Document No. 2 was preserved – even if the Collins-de Valera Pact wasn't.

But if the principals of the Pact were not so worried about its discontinuance, other people were. One Deputy, Donal O'Rourke, was to resign from the Provisional Parliament or Third Dail. In a letter to the press dated November 29, 1922, he wrote: "As far as I know the views of my constituents, they were wholly in favour of the Collins-de Valera Pact, and while I was elected as pro-Treaty representative for this constituency, it was distinctly on the understanding that a Coalition Government would follow the election that I was returned. The terms of this Pact whose ratification was the last solemn act of an All-Ireland Dail have not been carried out and consequently I have no option but to resign. . . ."

What was to make the Pact impossible of fulfillment after the Dail convened was the 'Imperial' Constitution that Britain was at the time imposing on Ireland. However, something like a Pact did have to be devised as a way of holding elections under the near-impossible conditions Britain had been placing then upon Ireland. Even such staunch supporters of the Treaty as Collins and Griffith, Cosgrave and O'Higgins defended the Pact and explained to the British Government that it was only by means of the Pact that elections could be held at that time in Ireland at all. And even Churchill agreed when he understood the Irishmen's intentions. "They have argued vehemently that the course they are taking," he declared in a heated Parliamentary debate on the possible violation of the Treaty by the Pact, "that the course is the surest way, and indeed the only way open to them of bringing the Treaty into permanent effect" (quoted from Macardle, pp. 715-716). Thereupon the British Government supported the Pact Election, with all that that implied in terms of a resultant all-Ireland Dail Eireann.

However, what bothered most people about the nonimplementation of the Pact, the noninvitation to elected Representatives in the six-county area, and the nonformation of the Coalition Government was that, outwardly at least, the Third Dail was gradually being restricted under British pressure to the 26-county area. The Irish leaders hoped with time to remedy what could be remedied of the facets of Irish Free State Government that they were being forced to accept, even if these were of a constitutional nature. But, in submitting to one thing after another, there was the danger of not being able to avoid the pitfall of the 32-county Dail becoming a 26-county Dail. If the Dail were going to be ***constituted*** a 26-county Dail, then that was going to be a real danger indeed.

Eamon de Valera unveils a statue of Robert Emmet in San Francisco's Golden Gate Park on July 20, 1919.
(Courtesy Timothy Sarbaugh, San Jose, California)

CHAPTER 5

THE CONSTITUTION IMPACTS ON THE PACT DAIL

The Third Dail Eireann Restricted

The new Constitution for Ireland would soon be wending its way through both the British and Irish Parliaments. The Constitution was to be made an Act of the British Parliament whether the Irish people had approved it or not. As long as it met with the approval of the British Government their Parliament would make it law – in Britain, of course, although the British would hold that they were making it law for Ireland as well. However, that was something that would not faze the Irish. "Let them pass their Dominion Act," declared Eoin MacNeill. "We don't care a fig for their Dominion Act," he said, believing that a Republican Constitution could yet be achieved in Ireland by the Provisional Government independently of Britain.

It remained to be seen whether the British would relinquish control of Irish affairs as easily as some Irish Government officials wished. If Churchill's words were any indication, the British intended to hold a tight rein until the 26-county Dail was established and partition became an accomplished fact. "The Constitution will be submitted by and with the authority of the Provisional Government," he announced emphatically in the House of Commons on February 27, 1922, "and not by and with the authority of Dail Eireann. The Provisional Government recognise that they will have to take steps to satisfy themselves that the Constitution so framed is of a character that the British Government can accept as fulfilling the Treaty." If by that Churchill meant that the Constitution would have to be of a character that the British could accept as enforcing partition, then to achieve that the Constitution would have had to fall short of the Treaty and to that extent could not possibly be said to be fulfilling the Treaty. For until the Ulster option were exercised, the Treaty had to be regarded as being an Agreement covering all Ireland. And if the British were insisting in advance that the Constitution be enacted for the 26 counties only, they were wanting that the Constitution not be in accord with the Treaty right from the start. At the very least, they were prejudging the outcome of the Treaty's provisions as they related to Northern Ireland.

At the time that the Constitution would be discussed and enacted in the Dail, enormous pressure was going to be brought to bear upon the Irish leaders to pass a Constitution that would be in accord with the peculiar British interpretation of the Treaty. This pressure would come from the British Government mainly through the Irish Free State (Agreement) Act on March 31, 1922, an Act that ratified the Treaty in British law and made it part of the municipal law of Great Britain. In prejudging the Ulster option outcome the British Government would want the Constitution to be restricted to 26 of the 32 counties. We reproduce here the relevant Sections of the I.F.S. (Agreement) Act so that the reader may see for himself or herself how this statute was intended to have the Third Dail restrict its jurisdiction to 'Southern Ireland' and regard the Constitution as if it had been meant for 26 counties alone. Bear in mind that the Dail was convened in accordance with this Act, that it proceeded in its business by virtue of this Act, and that the Constitution was not allowed to be repugnant to the Treaty as 'legalized' by this Act.

The Irish Free State (Agreement) Act, 1922

(12 & 13 Geo. 5, c. 4)

An Act to give the force of Law to certain Articles of Agreement for a Treaty between Great Britain and Ireland, and to enable effect to be given thereto, and for other purposes incidental thereto or consequential thereon.

(1) The Articles of Agreement for a Treaty between Great Britain and Ireland set forth in the Schedule to this Act shall have the force of law as from the date of the passing of this Act.

(2) For the purpose of giving effect to Article 17 of the said Agreement, Orders in Council may be made transferring to the Provisional Government established under

> that Article the powers and machinery therein referred to, and as soon as may be and not later than four months after the passing of this Act the Parliament of Southern Ireland [*sic*] shall be dissolved and such steps shall be taken as may be necessary for holding, in accordance with the law now in force with respect to the franchise number of members and method of election and holding of elections to that Parliament, an election of members for the constituencies which would have been entitled to elect members to that Parliament, and the members so elected shall constitute the House of Parliament to which the Provisional Government shall be responsible, and that Parliament shall, as respects matters within the jurisdiction of the Provisional Government, have power to make laws in like manner as the Parliament of the Irish Free State when constituted. Any Order in Council under this Section may contain such incidental, consequential, or supplemental provisions as may appear to be necessary or proper for the purpose of giving effect to the foregoing provisions of this Section.
>
> (4) No writ shall be issued after the passing of this Act for the election of a member to serve in the Commons House of Parliament for a constituency in Ireland other than a constituency in Northern Ireland.

This last provision, decreeing nine months before the Ulster option would be exercised that no writs should be issued for the election of members to the U.K. House of Commons from constituencies in Ireland other than those in Northern Ireland, clearly prejudged the outcome of the option and prejudiced unfairly its exercise. The provision further, since it concerned itself with the major powers area of jurisdiction, left the Irish Government with little choice but to concentrate on the rest of Ireland, 'Southern Ireland.'

At this point in our account it might perhaps be appropriate to indicate that the predominant feature characterizing Irish constitutional history of the 1921-1931 period, the main period under study in this work, is what might conveniently be described as 'parallel duality.' The period in question is bounded at the one end by perhaps the most historical and yet most controversial Treaty ever known in history, and at the other by another great Commonwealth Treaty, what William Manchester has called (in his biography of Churchill *The Last Lion*) "perhaps the vastest piece of legislation ever to pass through this [Westminister Parliament] or any other legislative body," the Statute of Westminster. The parallel duality of the period is a parallelism of dual Irish and British, Republican and Commonwealth constitutional authority and origins that is in addition judicially delineated and defined. Such dual sources of action are perhaps appropriately described 'parallel duality,' even though, as we have seen, their 'rails' or modes of procedure sometimes so closely coincided that it is extremely difficult to ascertain to which source some particular line or lines of action must be attributed, and to which another or others.

The dual sources of action are oftentimes referred to as 'views,' they being 'the Irish view' and 'the British view.' Both views touch on the legal foundation of or authority for the Saorstat Eireann Constitution of 1922, and were until 1931 what Kenneth Wheare termed matters of "irreconcilable dispute." Both views found basic judicial determination in the cases *The State (Ryan and Others)* v. *Lennon and Others* (Irish) and *Moore* v. *The Attorney-General for the Irish Free State* (British), both of which decisions were rendered in 1935, respectively by the Supreme Court of Ireland and the Judicial Committee of the Privy Council of Great Britain.

For our purposes here it is not necessary to portray the struggle for predominance that the British view waged over the Irish view from the drafting of the Irish Free State Constitution on out. That struggle will be described as our story unfolds, but those who desire a summary might consult V. T. H. Delany's essay "The Constitution of Ireland: Its Origins and Development" (*University of Toronto Law Journal*, Vol. XII, No. 1 (1957), pp. 3-6) or the first two sections of Kenneth C. Wheare's chapter 'Autochthony' in his *Constitutional Structure of the Commonwealth.* Suffice it to say here that it was not just the struggle over Irish or British authority for the Saorstat Constitution that was so much the issue. More importantly, it was the struggle to resist the British pressure to confine the new Constitution to 26 counties that counted most for Ireland and the effort exerted to succeed in this imposition that counted most for Britain. In comparison with the struggle over jurisdiction, the struggle over origins or authority was quite unimportant and might indeed have been waged largely as a smokescreen. The Irish view might be welcome (by Britain) to prevail eventually over the British – so long as it was held of a jurisdiction restricted to a part of Ireland and not the whole of it.

For all the pressure exerted on the Irish rulers, we have to say that they would succeed in establishing a Constitution for all Ireland, and further that it would as such be in keeping with the Treaty. But where the British scored was in forcing the Dail to keep the application of that Constitution restricted to 26 counties and to hold future elections to the Dail for the 26-county area alone. In that way, the Constitution, although theoretically applicable to all of Ireland, would be restricted in practice to 26 counties.

An all-Ireland but non-Republican Constitution

But what of the Irish hopes for making the Constitution a Republican one? It is possible that de Valera had access to the text of the Constitution when it was being formulated by the Collins Committee and that he may indeed have collaborated with Collins on the final draft of the Constitution. (See D.H. Akinson and J. F. Fallin, "The Irish Civil War and the Drafting of the Free State Constitution," Parts I, II, and III, *Eire-Ireland* (St. Paul, Minn.), Vol. V, Nos. 1, 2, and 4 (Spring, Summer, and Winter, 1970), pp. 10-26, 42-93, and 28-70 respectively.) If that be so – and de Valera's hand is certainly evident throughout the finished work – then, upon the Constitution being radically revised by the British Government, de Valera would have realized the futility of further resistance. This theory would explain why, upon no requests being forthcoming from Collins to form a Coalition Government after the Pact Election, de Valera did not bestir himself to enquire the reason why nor to forward on his own initiative the names selected by his Party to form the Coalition Cabinet.

With the capitulation of de Valera there was little likelihood the new Dail was going to be recognized as the Assembly of all-Ireland, as the First and Second Dails had been. But there was still hope. Perhaps the Treaty could be favorably amended before it would be, in effect, incorporated in the new Constitution. In that way the area of jurisdiction of the Constitution would not be restricted to the 26 counties when the Constitution would come into effect, because the Treaty (which was to be scheduled to the Constitution) would have been amended to exclude any possibility that it, the Treaty, might not apply to the entire 32-county area. That is, the Ulster option would, hopefully, be rescinded.

It will be remembered that the British in inspecting and revising the new Constitution imposed upon the charter a Preamble that was designed to make the Constitution subject to the Treaty and interpretable only in terms of the Treaty. This Preamble would form part of the Constituent Acts of both the British and Irish Parliaments that enacted the Constitution and ratified the Treaty. The Preamble (Section 2 of the Constituent Act) ran as follows: "These presents (or "The said Constitution") shall be construed with reference to the Articles of Agreement for a Treaty between Great Britain and Ireland . . . which are hereby given the force of law, and if any provision of this Constitution or of any amendment thereof or of any law made thereunder is in any respect repugnant to any of the provisions of the Scheduled Treaty, it shall, to the extent only of such repugnancy, be absolutely void and inoperative and the Parliament and the Executive Council of the Irish Free State shall respectively pass such further legislation and do all such other things as may be necessary to implement the Scheduled Treaty."

This Preamble, to become the much-disputed Repugnancy Clause which was not to be deleted from the Constitution Act until 1933, invested the Treaty with the highest legal status in Ireland. Henceforth the Treaty's provisions would override both the Constitution and all subsequent legislation. An international Agreement was thereby dragged down to the level of national law and invested with the force of municipal law of the State. The intention was humiliatingly to maintain that the basis of the partitioned all-Ireland Free State rested on the Treaty and that this was indeed the instrument which called partition into being. It was of the utmost importance, therefore, that de Valera should try to get the Treaty amended if at all possible so as to head off the likelihood of partition becoming a constitutionally established fact. At least, it was feared at the time that the Treaty did have that dangerous capability. But de Valera was not to succeed in his efforts. (However, with the Removal of Oath Act of 1933, which was to delete from the Constitution Act of 1922 the Repugnancy Clause and from the Constitution itself (Article 50) the requirement that amendments be "within the terms of the Scheduled Treaty," the Treaty was 'liberated' from Irish municipal law and accorded its rightful place of international Agreement. And the Constitution was released from the requirement that it be interpreted in terms of the Treaty. All of this rejection of British law for Ireland was achieved by virtue of the Statute of Westminster of 1931.)

Before the Third Dail was due to assemble, de Valera succeeded to have a meeting with General Richard Mulcahy, Commander-in-Chief of the Irish Free State Army and soon to become Minister of Defense in the Irish Government. At the meeting de Valera made a final – and vain – attempt to have the Treaty amended. For him, Article 12, the Ulster option provision, was the central vitiating clause of the entire Treaty. With that clause, as well as the (remediable) oath of allegiance clause, the Treaty could not be accepted by de Valera and Republicans. (Without it, however, as Lord Birkenhead (F.E. Smith) had said, the Treaty would never have been signed – by anyone. "All those concerned in the signing of the Treaty," said F.E., "knew that in Article 12 . . . there lurked the elements of dynamite. The clause was forced upon them in the sense that the Treaty never could have been signed and never would have been signed without it.")

But Mulcahy was standing pat. The Free State side could have no second thoughts. For de Valera his mission was futile. His own description of the meeting gives the impression that he was beginning to realize he was fighting a lost cause. "Couldn't find a basis," he wrote in his diary for September 6, 1922. "Mulcahy was looking for a basis in acceptance of the Treaty – we in revision of the Treaty" (quoted from Longford and O'Neill, p. 199).

It was probably the failure of the meeting with Mulcahy that caused de Valera to look so negatively on the nature of the Third Dail when it finally convened on September 9, 1922. Certainly if the Treaty could not be amended in advance to remove the oath of allegiance and to close the loophole on Ulster, then the Constitution that was imminent could easily be regarded not only as an instrument setting the all-Ireland Free State down smack within the confines of the Empire, but it could also be misconstrued as being the Constitution of a truncated State, one bereft of six of its northern counties. This misconception of the true nature of the Constitution as an all-Ireland charter would be quite unjustified, because until after enactment it could only be *presumed* that Ulster was going to opt out of Free State jurisdiction. The likelihood that the Constitution would be forced to be regarded a 26-county instrument was no pleasing prospect to Republicans certainly, and they were none too inclined in the midst of a raging Civil War, with their opponents grieved over the deaths of Griffith and Collins, to enter the newly convened Dail and run the risk of being dubbed collaborationists.

The Third Dail convened

When the new Dail did finally convene, there was some confusion as to whether it might after all constitute the Third Dail Eireann as elected. After the vain attempt de Valera made to have the Treaty amended, he tried to clarify the situation as he saw it. He sent a memorandum to the Republican Party in which his view of the Dail was explained. This was letter 13 of *Correspondence of Mr. Eamon de Valera and Others*, published as a pamphlet by the

Provisional Government and quoted in the press of October 16, 1922. De Valera looked quite pessimistically on the new developments and pointed out that the Second Dail Eireann had not been formally dissolved. The Parliament summoned to meet on September 9th was going to be the Provisional Parliament, he held, because it had not been summoned by the Government of the Second Dail. Nor were the Second Dail's powers going to be handed on to the new Dail. Also, since the question of the oath of allegiance to the Irish Republic and Dail Eireann would have to be brought up, the presence of Republicans, de Valera thought, would retard rather than promote peace. Hence he was in favor of abstention.

The new Assembly, which was not constituted in accordance with the Collins-de Valera Pact, was referred to in the House as the 'Dail' (the 'Assembly' or 'Parliament'), not as 'Dail Eireann' (the 'all-Ireland Assembly' or 'all-Ireland Parliament'). When questioned on the nature of the Assembly, President Cosgrave categorically stated that the new Assembly was "the Dail," no more (*Dail Debates*, Vol. 1, col. 193). Officially it was called the 'House of Parliament to which the Provisional Government is to be responsible,' a title that echoed British terminology. (The Provisional Government was still in existence, it not being due to expire until December 6, 1922. Technically it needed a Parliament to be responsible to, and as long as the Second Dail Eireann lasted the Provisional Government was responsible to it and was treated as an agency of the Dail for the transmission of the machinery of Government. But for three months of mid-1922 there was no Parliament in session to which it could be responsible, and it acted on no authority save that of a British Act.) The new Dail was called by the British Government the 'Provisional Parliament' of the twenty-six counties as 'decreed' by their Irish Free State (Agreement) Act of 1922. Another sign that the Dail was not going to be the Third Dail Eireann was that the obligatory Republican oath was not taken by the new Deputies. (Although this fact influenced Republicans like de Valera a lot, the mere absence of an oath could not be taken as the determiner of the nature of the new Assembly.)

But all of these outward appearances may have been cases of bending to superior British force. It could be held that there was continuity of authority directly from the Second Dail to the Third Dail, the absence of the formalities of dissolution and powers transference from the Second Dail notwithstanding. There certainly was direct continuity of succession for the Third Dail from the Second insofar as the Third was *elected* as a Third Dail, which it was because of the Pact. But whether such continuity was disrupted and authority from the Second Dail usurped is a question that remains to be examined (see Chapter 7). The point here, however, is that de Valera, for one, was not taking any chances as to the outcome of events. He had pinned his hopes on having the Treaty amended and in circumventing the British pressure in that way. He foresaw that when the British Constitution would come into existence, if it did so without being changed back into Republican form by the Irish (which it was not going to be, of course), then the 32-county jurisdiction of the Third Dail was irrevocably going to be reduced to a 26-county one.

It could be, then, that out of despair de Valera took such a negative view as he did of the manner in which Irish constitutional continuity of the Dail was being handled. Why was the first Irish Constitution, that of 1919, being cast aside, and the Dail taking its being from the Treaty, or, more correctly, from a prejudiced British interpretation of the Treaty? De Valera was of the opinion, for example, that the new Dail did not pretend to be the Third Dail Eireann, because it had not been summoned by the proper authority. But the fact that it was ostensibly summoned by the Provisional Government instead of the Dail Government would not of itself be sufficient to interrupt continuity, because these two bodies were practically identical in their personnel and the same people could justifiably act as one authority at any time while outwardly appearing to act as the other. There existed, as George Gavan Duffy pointed out, 'an interlocking directorate,' which meant that one and the same authority had to act in various capacities as the need arose. However, all of this rolling with the punches was to serve little to preserve 32-county national sovereignty if the Treaty could not be amended and the injurious parts of the new Constitution thus rendered harmless. But such was not to be the way. There could be no roadblocks put in the way of the British bulldozer. Disengagement would be on their terms, and on their terms alone – the oath and partition.

A polemic pamphlet published by Frank Gallagher in London during the Civil War, *By What Authority?* reflects the despair and pessimism experienced by Republicans at the turn of events in the Dail of 1922. The relevant section is quoted from Tim Pat Coogan's *The I.R.A.*, Seventh Fontana Impression, page 290.

> Before the Treaty was signed, Civil War in Ireland was impossible. What made it possible?

> For five terrible years the nation had remained united on three great principles:
>
> 1. The existence of the Republic founded in Easter Week, and confirmed by national plebiscite in 1918;
>
> 2. The sanctity of our national independence declared by the Sovereign National Assembly in January, 1919; and
>
> 3. The territorial integrity of Ireland, which had outlasted history itself.
>
> The Treaty violated these three fundamental principles, destroying the Republic, surrendering our national independence, partitioning our ancient nation.

(Actually these three fundamental principles were not violated by the Treaty *per se*, but by the incorrect, British interpretation of the Treaty as reflected in the forcibly imposed Imperial Constitution of 1922 and the accompanying actions of the Provisional Government mandated to it by the British Free State Agreement Act, which actions were in distinct violation themselves of the Collins-de Valera Pact (especially, e.g., the failure positively to invite to attend the Dail the six-county elected Deputies). However, the violations of principles 1 and 2 above were eventually remedied, by constitutional amendment; the violation of principle 3 remains to be remedied. But if the British could not have gotten their way to violate principle 3, there would have been no Treaty. In which case, all three principles would have been permanently violated under another form of force.)

Republican preoccupation with whether the Third Dail would continue as the Third Dail or be usurped as a 'First Dail,' as the British wanted it to be, was amply justified, but a question equally important with continuity was whether the 'First Dail-to-be' would be strictly the Dail of the 26 counties or not. If it would be – and all indications were that it was going to be – then the preoccupation of the Republicans was doubly justified.

The de facto *Irish Free State of 26 counties is begun*

Nobody realistically believed that the 'Northern' Ireland Parliamentarians were not going to exercise their option of 'contracting' out of Free State jurisdiction as soon as the Treaty would be finally ratified, and it was on the basis of the presumption – and it was only a presumption – that they would opt out that the British had hitherto taken steps to ensure that the Irish Ministers and Deputies understood that their jurisdiction was going to be restricted to 26 counties. These steps were taken in violation of the terms of the Treaty strictly understood, it could be said. But it was necessary to take them if the British were to have a smooth steamroller ride into the Dail and impose a Constitution on that Assembly for 26 counties alone. This they did through the influence of their Irish Free State (Agreement) Act and, as we shall see in Chapters 7 and 8, by having enacted their version of the Irish Constitution and making sure that the new Dail, whatever it called itself and however it regarded its succession, would be strictly a 26-county Assembly and would itself contribute to the permanence of partition. And, as we saw at the beginning of this chapter, by legislating and establishing partition as they did, the British Government prejudged and determined the entire Boundary Commission outcome and left the Northerners with no choice but to go through the motions of exercising an empty option.

We set out in this chapter to describe the impact enactment of an effectively British Constitution had on the Pact Dail. Whatever *technical* effect the imposition of the Constitution had on the Dail, the *practical* effect was that the Third Dail as *elected* – the Pact Dail for all Ireland – became an Assembly for 26 counties, as it was *not* elected. As the product of British pressure and what was in effect British legislation (the Constitution), the post-Constitution Dail would have to be regarded as a First Dail (of 26 counties), and significantly – though wrongly – 1922 is taken widely as a starting point in modern Irish history.[1] But as the product of Irish legislation (to the extent that that is what the Constitution was), the Dail could continue at least to be regarded as the Third Dail Eireann, although with the application of its jurisdiction so greatly reduced it would hardly merit the designation Dail ***Eireann***. Whether it was entitled *technically* to claim this appellation we shall have to leave to later chapters for consideration, when we will examine the all-important question of continuity.

1 Leo Kohn stands out conspicuously among historians in holding that it is from the January 21, 1919, meeting of Dail Eireann "that Irish constitutional theory dates the establishment of the new Irish State. (Cf. s. 7 of the Indemnity Act (No. 40 of 1924).)" (*The Constitution of the Irish Free State*, p. 36.) (Section 7 of the Indemnity Act reads: "For the purposes of this Act, no authority conferred by or derived from the First Dail Eireann or the Second Dail Eireann shall be considered to have been terminated . . . by the election of the Third Dail Eireann.")

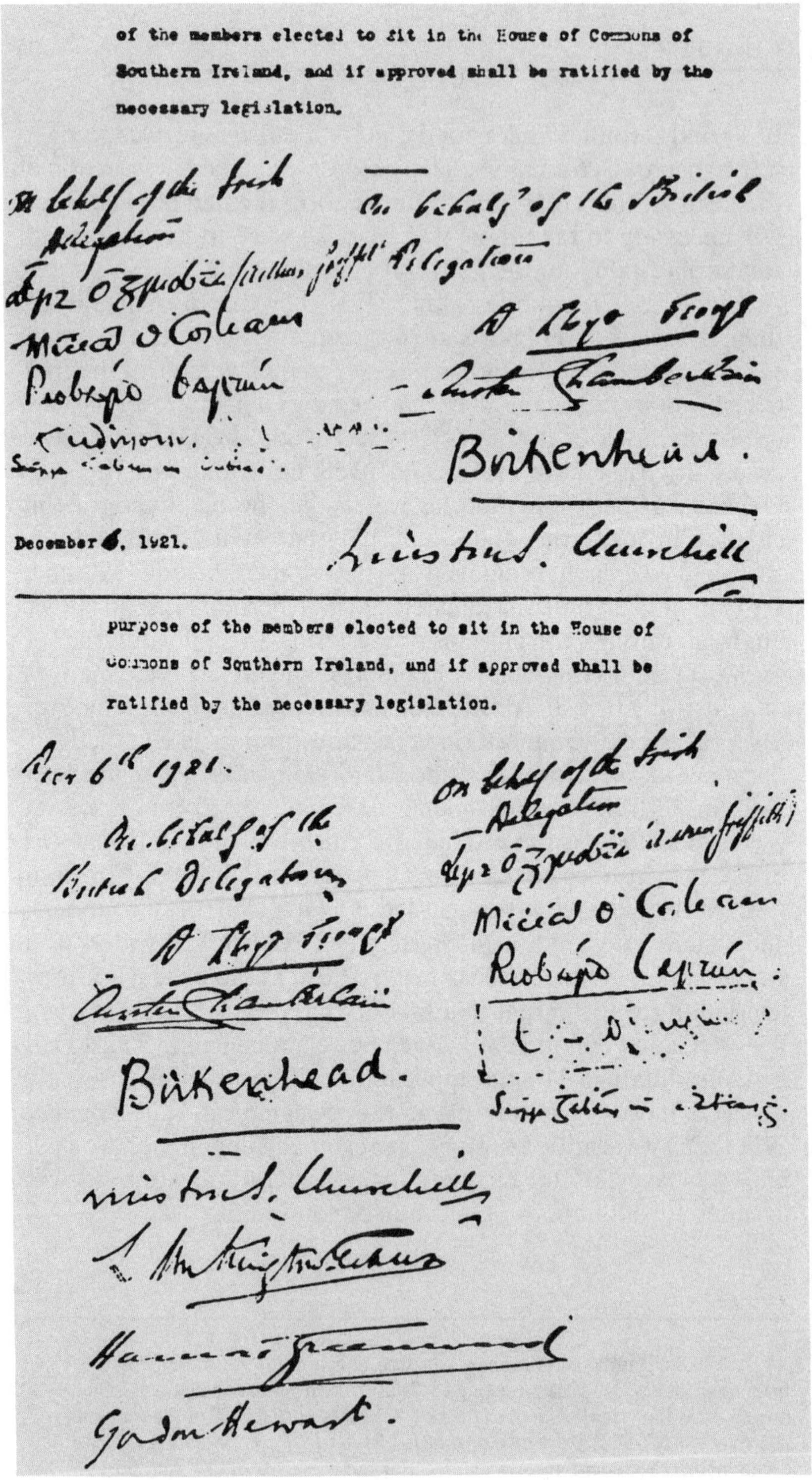

of the members elected to sit in the House of Commons of Southern Ireland, and if approved shall be ratified by the necessary legislation.

December 6, 1921.

purpose of the members elected to sit in the House of Commons of Southern Ireland, and if approved shall be ratified by the necessary legislation.

Signatures of the Irish and British Government representatives appended to the Irish (above) and British (below) versions of the Anglo-Irish Treaty of 1921.

CHAPTER 6

THE BIFURCATION OF IRISH POLITICS

Republican Sinn Fein Upholds the Second Dail

The question of continuity of succession from the Republican all-Ireland First and Second Dails is an extremely important one for many reasons, but especially for finding a solution to the problem of reunification. In his Inauguration Address on January 20, 1981, President Ronald Reagan called continuity in the American constitutional system "the bulwark of our Republic." For the Irish people, likewise, constitutional continuity is absolutely essential if they are to maintain what they achieved in 1919 after centuries of struggle – the united Irish Republic. After all, what they fought for for years was the independence of all Ireland, not just part of it. It was all or nothing. If, then, continuity from the centuries of struggle was disrupted somewhere along the line, the Irish could be on the wrong track the way they are pursuing reunification. It is crucial, therefore, to ascertain, if partition is ever going to be resolved, whether continuity from the all-Ireland Second Dail was preserved or not in the Irish constitutional system.

It is our opinion that direct lineal succession was preserved up to a point. With the Collins-de Valera Pact, the Third Dail was elected as an all-Ireland Dail and as the direct successor to the Second Dail. But it was not to continue as such for long. Where exactly the frayed thread of continuity was snapped we shall examine in the next two chapters. For now we will take a look at what de Valera and Republicans thought about the nature of the Third Dail, and at their attitude towards what it was likely to become as they saw it being gradually based on the Treaty ***law*** (as the Treaty was made to be) and on what George Gavan Duffy was to call "a British Act of Parliament," the new Irish Constitution.

If, as we have seen, the Collins-de Valera Pact had not been devised, a General Election would not have been possible in the Ireland of 1922. At the same time, however, the existence of such a Pact, designed as it was to preserve the Republic in Ireland in spite of the Treaty (or, more properly, Britain's interpretation of the Treaty), evoked the wrong kind of response from the British. They immediately demanded, quite illegally, to see the draft of the new Irish Constitution, which was, understandably, very Republican in form at that point. The horrified British overhauled the draft completely in the determination that by imposing their interpretation of the Treaty – and theirs alone – upon Ireland in the form of a Monarchical Constitution they would smash the resurgent Republic. As soon as the Constitution was published (on June 16, 1922) it was clear to Republicans that the Pact could not be implemented and that a Coalition Government could not be formed.

With the failure to convene the Coalition Government prescribed by the Pact, the Treaty split was complete. With this development and the outbreak of Civil War, there ensued a bifurcation of Irish politics. On the one side were the Dail-abstentionist Republicans, on the other the pro-Treaty Dail attendees. The following is the sequence of events surrounding that political and constitutional bifurcation as related mainly by Dorothy Macardle.

"On September 9th [1922], when the Assembly in Dublin was shown definitely to be the Provisional Parliament [of the 26 counties, as opposed to the all-Ireland Parliament of the Republic], Republicans found themselves debarred from all channels of democratic action and without programme or policy other than a military one. It was a situation which called for a declaratory act by the Republican Party – an act which would not only register their protest against this repudiation of Dail Eireann but would create a political position that the Republican Party would be able to maintain.

"The position in which Republicans found themselves was, in a measure, a revolutionary one, for, although they were fighting to maintain a Republic democratically established, they were without a functioning government and their army was under no civil control. The Pact election, while it had given no mandate to the Treaty Party to function as the Provisional Government, had not, on the other hand, given authority to Republicans to resist such usurpation with arms. Their armed struggle was not now, therefore, endorsed by the votes of the people. The army was, at the same time, in absolute control of Republican policy: the Republican Party was without power."

Reaction to the Third Dail's going factually Free State

De Valera fully appreciated the predicament of the Republican politicians. On September 13th, four days after the opening of the new Parliament, he addressed a letter to the Republican Party in which, among other alternatives, he urged that the Army Executive take control and assume responsibility for Republican political as well as military policy. Although he was convinced that constitutionally the political arm of the Republican Movement should be the one to exercise control over political affairs, nevertheless he felt that, in view principally of the unlikelihood of the Army to render unconditional allegiance to a civilian Government, formation of a Republican Government by the Party alone would be a practical impossibility. For that reason de Valera proposed, against his better judgment, that the Army assume responsibility.

"The Army Executive must publicly accept responsibility," he wrote. "There must be no doubt in the minds of anybody on the matter. This pretence from the pro-Treaty Party that we are inciting the army must be ended by a declaration from the army itself that this is not so. The natural corollary to this is that we, as a political party, should cease to operate in any public way – resign in fact. This is the course I have long been tempted to take myself, and were it not that my action might prejudice the cause of the Republic, I'd have taken it long since. Our position as public representatives is impossible." (Letter 20 of *Correspondence of Mr. Eamon de Valera and Others*, dated September 13, 1922.)

However, one month later de Valera came out strongly in favor of the Party being the body to assume responsibility for Republican policy, and he proposed as much to the I.R.A. Army Executive. He thought that the political arm of the Movement should go ahead and form a Republican Government in order to preserve the Republic, maintain continuity, and prevent the majority in the Third Dail from establishing that Assembly as the sole successor to the Second Dail.

After giving concentrated consideration to de Valera's proposals, the Republican Army Executive declared itself willing to give allegiance to a Republican Government under the presidency of Eamon de Valera. It would reserve to itself, however, certain powers in the matter of peace and war. The Executive called upon de Valera to bring into being an Emergency Government and to form a Council of State, and declared that such Government as might be appointed by that Council would be "temporarily the Supreme Executive of the Republic and the State, until such time as the elected Parliament of the Republic can freely assemble, or the people being rid of external aggression are at liberty to decide freely how they are to be governed and what shall be their political relations with other countries" (Sean Cronin, *The McGarrity Papers*, pp. 193-196; Florence O'Donoghue, *No Other Law*, pp. 270-277).

The Army declaration continued: "On behalf of the army, we pledge to that Executive our allegiance and our support in all its legitimate efforts to maintain and defend the Republic, and we call upon all our comrades and loyal fellow-citizens, and upon our kin throughout the world, to join with us in reasserting our ancient right to be a free people and a free nation, owing allegiance to no foreign authority whatever." In calling on de Valera to set up a Council and Government, the Army Executive was authorized to act, as Dorothy Macardle tells us, "in accordance with a Resolution of Dail Eireann which provided that if at any time all democratic means of securing a Republican Government should be prevented by enemy action the army should have power to proclaim an emergency government" (*The Irish Republic*, pp. 807-808).

The declaration was signed on behalf of the Army of the Republic by thirteen senior officers, all members of the Executive of the I.R.A. These were: Liam Lynch, Chief of Staff; Liam Deasy, Deputy Chief of Staff; Earnan O'Malley, Assistant Chief of Staff; Con Moloney, Adjutant-General; Tom Derrig, Assistant Adjutant-General; Sean Lehane, O.C. 1st and 2nd Northern Divisions; Frank Aiken, O.C. 4th Northern Division; Frank Barrett, O.C. 1st Western Division; Seamus Robinson, O.C. 2nd Southern Division; Tom Barry, Operations Staff; Sean Moylan, O.C. Cork No. 3 Brigade; Pax Whelan, O.C. Waterford Brigade; and Joe O'Connor, O.C. 3rd Battalion, Dublin 1st Brigade.

As a result of this decision by the I.R.A., Republican Deputies held a meeting in Dublin on October 25, 1922, the fifth anniversary of the famed Sinn Fein Ard Fheis and the very day on which the Constituent Assembly of the Dail adopted the Constitution of the Irish Free State (Saorstat Eireann) Act, an Act which also ratified the Treaty and was to establish the Dail embryonically a partition

Parliament (in accordance with the provisions of the Treaty as they were being interpreted under duress from the British who *presumed* to know the outcome of these provisions, and in accordance with the misinterpreted provisions of the Westminster Irish Free State (Agreement) Act of 1922 and the Government of Ireland Act of 1920). The Deputies in attendance, men and women who had remained faithful to the Republic and the Republican oath, styled themselves Members of the Second Dail Eireann, which, as we know, had never been brought to a formal conclusion. (It is hard to see why the Irish leaders felt impelled not to close formally the Second Dail and to transfer its powers in the usual way – unless it was that they knew the Third Dail was going to be strictly a 26-county Assembly and they left the Second Dail suspended to be reconvened an all-Ireland Assembly a better day.)

Since they regarded themselves as members of the Second Dail, which remained the *de jure* Government of Ireland, the Republican Deputies meeting in Dublin made no pretense to representing or constituting the Third Dail, to which they had in fact been elected and which they could easily have set up as a rival Parliament. They called instead upon de Valera "in the name of all loyal citizens of the Republic and by the express wish of the soldiers fighting in its defence" to resume the Presidency of the Republic and to nominate a Council of State and Executive Ministers to assist him in carrying on a Government until such time as the Parliament of the Republic was allowed to assemble or the people were permitted by free elections to decide whether they should be governed as a Republic or not.

Institutionalizing the repository of Constitutional Republicanism

De Valera, appointed by unanimous resolution as "President of the Republic and Chief Executive of the State," nominated twelve Members present to act as the Council of State: Austin Stack, Robert Barton, Count Plunkett, J.J. O'Kelly, Lawrence Ginnell, Sean T. O'Kelly, Mrs. Michael O'Callaghan, Mary MacSwiney, P.J. Ruttledge, Sean Moylan, M.P. Colivet, and Sean O'Mahony.

An Emergency Government consisting of seven Ministers, including de Valera as President, was appointed by the Council. In this Government Austin Stack became Minister for Finance, P.J. Ruttledge Minister for Home Affairs, Fr. Michael O'Flanagan (with linguist Eugene Fitzgerald as Assistant) Minister for Foreign Affairs, Sean T. O'Kelly Minister for Local Government, Robert

Barton Minister for Economic Affairs, and Liam Mellowes Minister for Defense.[1] Pending the next meeting of an elected Dail which would be free to honor the mandate of the people expressed in the Pact Election of June 1922, the Council of State was empowered to sanction such Ministers and Executive Officers as the President might nominate (*Poblacht na hEireann: War News*, No. 78, October 26, 1922; *Dail Debates*, Vol. 44, cols. 224-227).

The decisions taken at this meeting of October 25th were published on the following day in the form of Resolutions passed by "Dail Eireann, the Parliament and Government of the Republic of Ireland." A few days later the I.R.A. Army Executive pledged its allegiance to the new Government. A Proclamation was issued, signed by the Chief of Staff and twelve other officers. It read: "We, on behalf of the soldiers of the Republic, acting in the spirit of our oath as the final custodians of the Republic and interpreting the desire of all true citizens of the Republic, have called upon the former President, Eamon de Valera, and the faithful members of Dail Eireann, to form a Government, which they have done."

The Proclamation named the members of the new Council of State and continued: "We declare such Cabinet as they shall appoint to be temporarily the Supreme Executive of the Republic and the State, until such time as the elected Parliament of the Republic can freely assemble, or the people being rid of external aggression are at liberty to decide freely how they are to be governed and what shall be their political relations with other countries." Unfortunately, the intentions expressed in this statement have not as yet, of course, been fulfilled on an all-Ireland basis.

Dorothy Macardle concludes: "The re-constituted Republican Government was not able to function. Although regarded by a large portion of the population as the only *de jure* government, it could do little more than represent the protest against the seizure of power by the pro-Treaty Party and place the logical and constitutional facts of the situation on record by means of statements and proclamations issued from time to time [and published in the Supplement to *Eire* for February 24, 1923]." (*The Irish Republic*, pp. 805 ff.; O'Donoghue, pp. 342-343.)

1 In a second Emergency Government formed in August 1924, de Valera became President and Minister for Foreign Affairs, Stack Minister for Home Affairs and Finance, Art O'Connor Minister for Economic Affairs and Local Government, Frank Aiken Minister for Defense, and Ruttledge and Barton Ministers without Portfolio. In February 1925 Sean Lemass succeeded Aiken as Minister for Defense, and in March 1926 O'Connor succeeded de Valera as President.

There was a very positive side to the Emergency Government, however, that Macardle's low-key description fails to record. The Government was, of course, the repository of Constitutional Republicanism of 32-county Ireland, and as such it was intended to be preserved until the day would dawn when it would be the effective means of restoring the all-Ireland Republic to the Irish people. On the practical side and for the time being, however, the Emergency Government had the good effect of placing the army under civilian control, chiefly through the agency of the budding Minister for Defense, Sean Lemass, and the Chief of Staff, Frank Aiken. It also had the benefit of providing authorized representatives with whom the Free State Government could deal in winding down the Civil War and eventually bringing it to a close.

The communique of Eamon de Valera accompanying the Cease Fire Order of May 24, 1923, is a masterpiece and fairly describes the situation 18 turbulent months after the Treaty made its appearance on the scene.

> SOLDIERS OF THE REPUBLIC,
> LEGION OF THE REARGUARD:
>
> The Republic can no longer be defended successfully by your arms. Further sacrifice of life would now be [in] vain and continuance of the struggle in arms unwise in the national interest and prejudicial to the future of our cause. Military victory must be allowed to rest for the moment with those who have [attemptedly] destroyed the Republic. Other means must be sought to safeguard the nation's right.
>
> Do not let sorrow overwhelm you. Your efforts and the sacrifices of your dead comrades in this forlorn hope will surely bear fruit. They have even already borne fruit. Much that you set out to accomplish is achieved. You have saved the nation's honour, preserved the sacred national tradition, and kept open the road of independence. You have demonstrated in a way there is no mistaking that we are not a nation of willing bondslaves.
>
> Seven years of intense effort have exhausted our people. Their sacrifices and their sorrows have been many. If they have turned aside and have not given you the active support which alone could bring you victory in this last year, it is because they saw overwhelming forces against them, and they are weary and need a rest. A little time and you will see them recover and rally again to the standard. They will then quickly discover who have been

> selfless and who selfish – who have spoken truth and who falsehood. When they are ready, you will be, and your place will be again as of old with the vanguard.
>
> The sufferings which you must now face unarmed you will bear in a manner worthy of men who were ready to give their lives for their cause. The thought that you have still to suffer for your devotion will lighten your present sorrow and what you endure will keep you in communication with your dead comrades who gave their lives, and all these lives promised for Ireland.
>
> May God guard every one of you and give to our country in all times of need sons who will love her as dearly and devotedly as you.

One of the main purposes in instituting the Council of State was not so much to set up a rival 'Government in Exile' as to keep the idea of the Republic alive in the minds of the people and one day, hopefully, to restore it by reconvening the Second Dail Eireann. The purpose of the Council as recorded in the minutes of a Council meeting held on August 7th and 8th, 1924, was stated as follows: "The President declared that our policy was to preserve, as far as we can, the Republic – to keep it continually before the minds of the people. . . ." (Quoted from Longford and O'Neill, p. 236.)

Truly de Valera never ceased to keep the idea of the all-Ireland Republic before the minds of the people. He fought doggedly on in his public reeducation effort to attain the twin goals of reemergence of the Republic and restoration of national unity. Speaking at Ennis, County Clare, from where he had been arrested a year before during the 1923 General Election campaign, he began: "I am afraid I would disappoint a number here if I were not to start by saying, 'Well, as I was saying to you when we were interrupted . . .' " He continued:

"The sovereignty of Ireland . . . cannot possibly be given away by Irish Republicans. We can never give allegiance to any foreign power or to any foreign people. These are the basic principles on which we stand. Things may be forced upon us, we may have temporarily to submit to certain things, but our assent they can never have. . . . Don't forget for a moment that there is a vast difference between patiently submitting, when you have to, for a time and putting your signature to a consent or assent to these conditions."

For de Valera, the aim of Sinn Fein still held good: "To secure international recognition of an Irish Republic, it being understood that, having achieved that status, the Irish people may, by referendum, freely choose their own form of government." The way of 1917 was still considered the best way to go in 1924, as indeed it would ever be the best way.[2] "We realize the difficulties of uniting in the cause of freedom," de Valera declared. "We know that in such a fight there has to be a vanguard, and we know that very often it is only a few choice spirits who can form that vanguard."

The Republic that had been created would have to be held in abeyance until the people could freely vote to restore it. De Valera continued: "When you are free to determine [the form of Government or freedom the Irish people want], without any pressure from England, or from any outside power, when the form you choose will be the expression truly of your own free will, then we are certainly ready to bow down our heads before it" (taken from a typescript of a speech delivered at Ennis on August 15, 1924). For de Valera personally that day never came, not in 1949 nor later. That day would only come when the people of all Ireland, acting within the framework of a 32-county restored Republic, would freely choose a form of Government not incompatible with that Republic, their own form of Government, and bow down their heads before it. "I for one," de Valera was later to state, ". . . stood by the flag of the Republic, and I will do it again. As long as there was a hope . . . of getting the people of this country to vote again for the Republic, I stood for it."

Fianna Fail recognizes the factually lawfully existing I.F.S.

A prime advantage of having a Council of State and Emergency Government was that its presence kept thoughts like the foregoing continually in the minds of the people. The main purpose for the existence of such a Republican Government was, of course, to preserve continuity from the Second Dail. The hope was that some day the opportunity would arise, by reconvening this Dail as the Parliament of the all-Ireland Republic, to restore Irish unity. This hope received a setback, however, when in November of 1925 the Republican Army withdrew its support from de Valera and his Sinn Fein colleagues. Rumor had it that de Valera and some of his

2 The way of 1917 was also, incidentally, considered the best way to go in 1921 – by the Treaty's Article 12 ordering that a referendum/plebiscite be held which would, in effect, enable the Irish people to freely choose the form of government that would render partition obsolete. But this referendum has not yet, as we shall explain later, been held.

closest followers were thinking of entering the Free State Dail with a view to becoming part of it, and the Army felt disenchanted by this possibility. Soon enough – within a few months, in fact – these rumors became a reality and there was a second split in the Sinn Fein organization, when de Valera and his followers left to form the Fianna Fail organization, "The Republican Party."

In March of 1926, at an Ard Fheis of Republican Sinn Fein in the Rotunda, Dublin, President de Valera moved to resolve: "That once the admission oath of the 26-County and Six-County assemblies is removed, it becomes a question not of principle but of policy whether or not Republican representatives should attend these assemblies." But Fr. Michael O'Flanagan, Vice President of Sinn Fein, opposed him and moved an amendment to the effect that, apparently regardless of whether there were an oath of allegiance or not, it was incompatible with the fundamental principles of Sinn Fein "to send representatives into any usurping legislature set up by English law in Ireland." The amendment carried by 223 votes to 218. Whereupon, de Valera resigned from the presidency of Sinn Fein and went on to found the Party that would deanglicize constitutionally the 26 counties and that would, through steps of external association and a new Constitution, see the area through to being a republic eventually. De Valera at this stage could afford to break with Sinn Fein without hurting the future chances of the Republic and Irish reunification, because he had ensured these by, six months previously, in November 1925, having succeeded to have Document No. 2 endorsed by the Sinn Fein Ard Fheis of that year. (See Bowman, *De Valera and the Ulster Question*, pp. 86-88.)

The Republican Second Dail and its Government Executive survived this split in the Sinn Fein organization and have remained in existence ever since (cf. J. L. McCracken, *Representative Government in Ireland, A Study of Dail Eireann, 1919-48*, p. 62; Tim Pat Coogan, *The I.R.A.*, pp. 75, 159, 285). Art O'Connor, who had succeeded de Valera as President of the Second Dail, resigned in December 1927, and the Dail thereupon named an Executive of five persons: Count Plunkett, Mary MacSwiney, Daithi Ceannt, Brian O'Higgins, and Cathal O Murchadha. J.J. O'Kelly ('Sceilg') remained Ceann Comhairle or Speaker.

On December 8th, 1938, the Executive Council of the Dail, which consisted of Plunkett, O'Kelly, MacSwiney, O'Higgins, O Murchadha, Tom Maguire and Professor William F.P. Stockley, acting in accordance with the contingency Resolution made by the First Dail during the War of Independence (which was also endorsed by the Second Dail), transferred the Government of the Republic to the I.R.A., or, as it was put, "delegates the authority reposed in us to the Army Council" to be held in trust for the Irish nation. "Confident in delegating this sacred trust to the Army of the Republic," the instrument of transference stated, "that, in their every action towards its consummation, they will be inspired by the high ideals and the chivalry of our martyred comrades, we, as Executive Council of Dail Eireann, Government of the Republic, append our names." In so reposing their powers of Government in the Army Council, the members of the Dail Executive demanded no guarantees for the powers' safekeeping other than that the Council should assume the Dail members' trust as they themselves had kept it over the years. This the members of the Council unanimously agreed to do. (The text of the instrument of transference is to be found in the *Wolfe Tone Weekly* of December 17, 1938.)

Since that day in December of 1938 the position has been, as stated by J.J. O'Kelly, until then President of the Council of State, that "though the Executive Council has since held few meetings and its membership has been considerably reduced by death, both the Army and Sinn Fein as military and constitutional arms continue to give their allegiance to the Second Dail" (*Dail Debates*, Vol. 44, cols. 224-229; J.L. McCracken, p. 62; Sean Cronin, *Irish Nationalism*, p. 161).

Upon hearing the news of the transference of the Second Dail to the I.R.A. Army Council, Joe McGarrity wrote to Sean Russell, Head of the Army Council: "My dear Chief, The transfer of the Government of the Republic into the hands of your Army Executive was both dignified and impressive. It showed that the custodians of the Government who never yielded to any kind of pressure had sufficient confidence in the Army, and in the Army alone, to consider it the only body worthy of making that Government function and keeping it unsullied until such times as they by their acts of sacrifice would make it again capable of functioning as the Government of the Irish people. . . ." (Letter dated February 5, 1939; quoted from Sean Cronin, *The McGarrity Papers*, p. 169.)

To the members of the Army Council and Sinn Fein, the military and constitutional arms of the Republican Movement, and to all their Republican followers, the Treaty Dail has always been a usurping body. De Valera himself held this view, too, for he once admitted in the 26-county Dail that "the real authority lies outside this House," that the *de jure* authority of Government in Ireland rests in the Second Dail. Ruairi Brugha (son of Cathal Brugha) has stated that for Republicans to turn their back on this teaching would have been seen as an abandonment of principle. "To do so would have been as impossible as changing one's religion" (Tim Pat Coogan, pp. 285-286). The concern of Republicans, before and now, to base their legitimacy on the Second Dail is, in itself, a tribute to the strength of the Parliamentary tradition and constitutional politics in Ireland, it might be observed in passing, and if Irish reunification is to be brought about only by constitutional politics, the necessary strength will not be lacking in the Republican Movement. (Note, however, that when Republicans speak about 'constitutional' politics they are talking in terms of the first all-Ireland Constitution, that of 1919; while all others are, of necessity, talking in terms of the 26-county Constitution, that of 1937.)

The decision of a minority in the anti-Treaty Sinn Fein organization to form the new Fianna Fail Party and to abandon abstentionism did not mean that they fully accepted the Free State Dail as a constitutional or political, as opposed to socially legislative, Assembly. Both Sean Lemass and de Valera made it clear that the group's reason for entering the Dail was mainly a matter of practical politics and for the purpose of preserving law and order. "Before anything we are a Republican party," stated Lemass in his "We are a slightly constitutional Party" speech of 1928. "We have adopted the method of political agitation to achieve our end, because we believe, in the present circumstances, [that] that method is best in the interests of the nation and of the Republican Movement, and for no other reason. . . ."

"Five years ago," he continued, "we were on the defensive, and perhaps in time we may recoup our strength sufficiently to go on the offensive. Our object is to establish a Republican Government in Ireland. If that can be done by the present methods we have, we will be very pleased; but, ***if not, we would not confine ourselves to them.***" (*Dail Debates*, Vol. 22, col. 1615; *italics ours*.) After he had become Minister for Industry and Commerce in the first Fianna Fail Government, Lemass said further: "The title of this Dail to legislate for this country is faulty, and it is faulty because of this reason, that it is not open to every section of our people to get representation here" (*Dail Debates*, Vol. 41, col. 217). The Dail was, of course, closed to Deputies from northeastern Ireland, though that is not what Lemass had particularly in mind.

"*We* came in here because we thought that a practical rule could be evolved in which order could be maintained," explained de Valera; "and we said that it was necessary to have some assembly in which the representatives of the people by a majority vote should be able to decide national policy. . . . As a practical rule, and not because there is anything sacred in it, I am prepared to accept majority rule as settling matters of national policy, and therefore as deciding who it is that shall be in charge of order. . . .

"My proposition that the representatives of the people should come in here and unify control so that we would have one Government and one Army was defeated, and for that reason I resigned," declared de Valera. Then he stated, significantly: "Those who continued on in that organisation which we have left claim exactly the same continuity that we claimed up to 1925. They can do it. . . ." (*Dail Debates*, Vol. 28, col. 1398.) (See further Jeffrey Prager's *Building Democracy in Ireland*, pp. 175 ff., for the account of Fianna Fail's necessary ambivalence towards partition in Ireland – being in the Free State Dail but not of it – in order to procure a republic in Ireland.)

The attitude of de Valera, Lemass, and other Fianna Fail leaders to the 26-county Dail had been strengthened by the decision of the New York State Supreme Court in May 1927. The Court, in denying the Irish Free State Government title to the Dail Eireann funds that had been lodged in the United States in 1919-20, ruled that the First Dail Eireann was a revolutionary, Republican body existing as a Provisional Parliament and that the Free State Government was not its direct successor.

The First Dail Eireann, the Court ruled, was engaged in a revolt against British rule in Ireland. England had failed to crush the rebellion with military force, "but set up, with the consent of the governed, a *new* Government to take the place of the existing Government in Ireland." The means by which this was done was primarily by the British instituting the Constitution of Ireland themselves even after they had acknowledged Ireland as a sovereign nation in the Treaty just concluded and thus qualified to adopt her own Constitution. In so reneging on the Treaty Dail Eireann was held to have been ignored and bypassed, and as a result the Irish Free State Government was taken to be the succesor to the then Government existing in Ireland under the Act of Union.[3]

As far as a constitutional status for Ireland was concerned, the proclaiming of an Irish Constitution by a British King changed the entire character of the Dail and Government of Ireland. "On December 5th of the same year [1922] the British Parliament enacted the Irish Free State Constitution Act," the Court declared, "thus creating plaintiff, the Irish Free State, which is now a Government consisting of the King, an Irish Parliament called the 'Oireachtas'... and a ministry called the Executive Council. On December 6, 1922, the Constitution of the Irish Free State was declared to be in operation by a proclamation by the King made pursuant to the Irish Free State Constitution Act [i.e., the Constitution itself]." This Free State Government was, therefore, the Court ruled, "set up by the English Government with the consent of the people of Southern Ireland," and in the opinion of the Court that constituted a break with the earlier Irish Government, the all-Ireland body, Dail Eireann.

The Irish Free State Government had no title to the funds, the Court concluded, because it was not the direct successor to the revolutionary, Republican organization, Dail Eireann, which had

3 Although the New York State Supreme Court in *Irish Free State* v. *Guaranty Safe Deposit Company* held (correctly) that the Free State Government did not succeed from the Dail Eireann of the Republic, its argumentation in support of its conclusion was not altogether sound. The Court held that "the so-called Irish Republic never existed as a *de facto* Government" and that it accordingly never succeeded to displace the *de jure* Government existing until then in Ireland, "which was the Government of Great Britain and Ireland formed under the Act of 1800, as modified by the Government of Ireland Act in 1920 . . . " It follows, therefore, the Court concluded, "that the Irish Free State succeeded the only Government in existence in Ireland at the time it came into being, to wit, the *de jure* Government of Great Britain and Ireland." The Court's reasoning was to this extent faulty, because the Republican Dail Eireann was indeed the *de facto* Government of Ireland and was indeed recognized as such by Great Britain in concluding the Treaty with it. However, the only reason the Free State Government did not succeed from the *de facto* Irish Government was that the British, acting *ultra vires* the Treaty, withdrew in the Constitution the recognition they had accorded in the Treaty and forced their newly created Irish Government to regard itself as succeeding from the Government they had created under the Act of 1800, which was modified by the Government of Ireland Act of 1914, which in turn was modified by the Government of Ireland Act of 1920 (and as such, of course, never existed as a *de facto* Government itself).

been a Provisional, all-Ireland Parliament. The Free State Government's claim was dismissed, and the funds were ordered returned to the subscribers.

De Valera could not agree with the Court more. "I still hold," he stated in the Dail in 1929, "that your right to be regarded as the legitimate Government of this country is faulty, that this House itself is faulty. You have secured a *de facto* position. Very well. There must be somebody in charge, to keep order in the community, and by virtue of your *de facto* position you are the only people who are in a position to do it. But as to whether you have come by that position legitimately or not, I say you have not come by that position legitimately. You brought off a *coup d'etat* in the summer of 1922. . . ."

Whether such was actually the case or not, and, if it was, whether it was responsible in part for the institution of partition, we shall see in the next two chapters, but certainly these words constituted a strong statement from de Valera. How, in view of his convictions, he could bend principle sufficiently to enable him to throw in his lot with such a Government as he condemned will always be hard to understand. "Clearly majority rule *de facto* he was accepting, but he would not admit the *de jure* origin of the Government," Lord Longford and Thomas P. O'Neill explain in their biography, *Eamon de Valera*. "De Valera felt that the policy [of repression towards the I.R.A.] adopted by the Free State Government had never been based on charity and understanding in regard to those who had maintained their Republican ideals consistently since 1920. The weapon of force neither changed people's principles nor their policies. 'If you deny people who are animated with honest motives peaceful ways of doing it,' [he warned,] 'you are throwing them back upon violent ways of doing it. Once they are denied the peaceful way they will get support for the violent way that they would never get otherwise.' "(Longford and O'Neill, pp. 263-264.)

"You have achieved a certain *de facto* position," de Valera continued to explain in the Dail, "and the proper thing for you to do with those who do not agree that this State was established legitimately, and who believe that, as a matter of fact, there was a definite betrayal of everything that was aimed at from 1916 to 1922, is to give those people the opportunity of working, and without in any way forswearing their views, to get the Irish people as a whole again behind them. They have the right to do it. You have no right to debar them from going to the Irish people and asking them to support the re-establishment, or if they so wish to put it, to support the continuance of the Republic. . . ."

De Valera himself, however, entered the Dail in spite of his conscientious objections to the demand of allegiance to the British King, because he wanted to get rid of the basis of that very demand, the oath of allegiance. He wanted, in the process, to remove the Treaty from being the constitutional base of the country, and to restore it to its rightful place of international Agreement. He wanted also to 'dismantle' or republicanize the Treaty in its more objectionable aspects, to abolish the office of Governor General, to reacquire the ports and reassert Irish sovereignty, to externally associate the 26 counties with Britain, to get the State out of the British Commonwealth, and to give the country a new, republican Constitution. This latter he insisted on, because "no matter how republican the Free State Constitution was made by amendment, it could never escape its basis in British law," he felt (Longford and O'Neill, p. 290).

De Valera could and did achieve all these and other great accomplishments for Ireland in a lifetime, but as far as securing the reunification of the country was concerned – which he seriously desired – his entering the Dail appeared to avail him absolutely nothing. That was because he had put himself in a weak, if not impossible, position vis-a-vis reunification: his accepting the 26-county Dail implied actual acceptance of the six-county setup. He, in fact, had said explicitly – and logically – to Sinn Fein as its President that once the admission oath of the six-county Parliament was removed it would become a question merely of policy whether Republican Deputies might even attend that Assembly!

Having indirectly accepted partition by entering the 26-county Dail, de Valera and his followers severed their continuity from the past and found themselves helpless to do anything about the problem of Irish reunification. De Valera admitted their condition when he said that the Sinn Fein organization which they had left "can claim exactly the same continuity that we claimed up to 1925." Just as the new Fianna Fail Party could do nothing, of course, to restore succession to the Second Dail, so it could do nothing to reunite the six counties with the rest of Ireland. Little wonder that de Valera at one point felt forced in exasperation to put the blame entirely on Britain. "The British Government alone have the power to remove this obstacle [of partition]," he wrote to his friend and model, President Franklin D. Roosevelt, in a letter dated January 25, 1938. The Chief and his Party were brought face to face with the stalemate that was to haunt Irish Governments for many years to come.

CHAPTER 7

AN ALL-IRELAND CONSTITUTION IS ROYALLY PROMULGATED

The Third Dail's Republican Continuity Broken

Back at the newly elected Pact Dail of September 1922, to pick up the side of the story representing the pro-Treaty prong of the bifurcation, Government Ministers were putting the British-devised Constitution through its paces for enactment amidst fairly stiff opposition. At first there was some question about the exact nature of the Assembly in which the Deputies were sitting, with one Representative being of the firm opinion that it was a partition Parliament. But the official line given out was that it was the Third Dail, the continuation from the Second. When challenged, however, Government spokesmen admitted that by the terms of the British Act, the Irish Free State (Agreement) Act, they were bound to enact the Constitution before considering any general legislation. (*Dail Debates*, Vol. 1, cols. 424-437, 2040.) In other words, they allowed the British Act to prevent the Dail from acting as a Legislative Assembly. On the other hand, the Dail was only acting as it had been elected, that is, as a Constituent Assembly, and significantly it did not perform a single act of ordinary legislation until after the Provisional Government had disappeared from the scene and the Assembly had been constituted a Parliament. By so not legislating, the Dail emphasized the fact that it was a Constituent Assembly enacting but a Constitution as mandated so to do by the people and that it had not yet metamorphosed itself into an Oireachtas. (Cf. Nicholas Mansergh, *The Irish Free State, Its Government and Politics*, pp. 48-49.)

But if under the restrictive forces of the British Act the Dail did not yet act as a Legislative Assembly, but did as a Constituent Assembly for the purpose of enacting the Constitution, it nevertheless and rightly regarded itself as the Third Dail and legitimate heir of the Republican Second Dail. As a matter of fact, in the very Act to enact the Constitution, the Constituent Act of the Irish Free State Constitution, the Government declared its sovereignty and continuity clearly: "Dail Eireann, sitting as a Constituent Assembly in this Provisional Parliament, acknowledging that all lawful authority comes from God to the people and ***in the confidence that the National life and unity of Ireland shall thus be restored***, hereby proclaims the establishment of The Irish Free State (otherwise called Saorstat Eireann) and in the exercise of undoubted right, decrees and enacts . . . 1. The Constitution set forth in the First Schedule hereto annexed shall be the Constitution of The Irish Free State (Saorstat Eireann)" (the Constitution of the Irish Free State (Saorstat Eireann) Act, 1922 (*the emphasis of what would be prophetic words is ours*); cf. J.G. Swift MacNeill, *Studies in the Constitution of the Irish Free State*, pp. 1-6). As Leo Kohn rightly remarked, "the sovereignty as well as the continuity of the native Parliament could not have been expressed more emphatically" (*The Constitution of the Irish Free State*, p. 97).

So far, so good. Were the sovereignty and continuity of the native Parliament also to be *permanently preserved*? The answer is the sovereignty hardly, but continuity no. The sovereignty was to be chipped away at by the Government's insisting – and succeeding in insisting – that the revisions made by the British to the Constitution erecting the King as King of Ireland be approved by the Dail; and continuity was to be abruptly disrupted mainly by the last revision of all: the Article of the Constitution governing the promulgation of the Constitution itself. This Article, as we shall see, touched on the very validity of the Constitution, and if by virtue of that Article the Constitution derived its validity from a British Order of Promulgation, then the Dail itself, constituted though it was to be by the Constituent Act embodying the Constitution, would from that point on be a British creation. As such it would derive its jurisdictional authority from Britain alone – a fact that would mark a break for it in continuity from its Republican antecedents. And if that jurisdiction was to be restricted to 26 counties, as at least it appears to have been beginning to be, then there was a further breach of continuity with a Dail that up to the point of promulgation of the Constitution enjoyed a 32-county jurisdiction.

What the Constitution of 1922 was and what it was not

When the Constituent Act of the Saorstat Eireann Constitution was presented to the Dail as a Bill for enactment, the Government declared that it was prepared to stand or fall by the revisions the British had introduced into the text. These, as we know, had formally transformed the document from being a Republican Constitution to being a Monarchical one. The King was ensconced as Head of State in Ireland and Head of the Judiciary. Kevin O'Higgins, who guided the Constitution through the Dail, admitted that the Government had not gotten all it sought in the original draft by way of national sovereignty. But if the Constitution was a strict interpretation of the Treaty, it was also a fair one, he claimed, and it gave the Irish people more than ever they had before – real freedom, with a possibility of growth. The trouble was it was more than a strict interpretation.

George Gavan Duffy, one of the signatories of the Treaty, seemed to be the Deputy most disenchanted with the Constitution as it stood revised. The Constitution may have claimed popular sovereignty at the outset (Article 2), but, with royal allegiance imposed on it, at best it could be said to be looking in two opposite directions at the same time. Gavan Duffy deplored the increasing abridgment of national sovereignty with every revision that came up for a vote, and he protested, from a legal point of view, one after another against the changes imposed by the British on the Irish Draft Constitution. But one after another his protests, in the form of amendments, were voted down. Writing in *L'annuaire de legislation comparee* for 1922, Gavan Duffy summarized the history of the draft, recapitulated the changes insisted upon by the British Ministers, and showed to what an inferior instrument the Constitution had been reduced.

"In February, 1922," he wrote, "the Irish Provisional Government set up a committee to undertake the drafting of a Constitution for the Free State, on the basis of the Treaty. . . . It is to be noted that the committee was unanimous on the issues as to the principles of construction of the Anglo-Irish Treaty, which were to provoke such violent protests in England.

"In May, 1922, before convening the constituent assembly, the Provisional Government communicated its draft Constitution to the British Cabinet; Mr. Lloyd George and his colleagues, having examined the text, denounced it with such indignation that the Treaty itself seemed to be in jeopardy, and gave the Provisional Government to understand that its draft amounted to a violation of the Treaty. The Crown figured only in a single article which provided for the nomination of a Commissioner to represent the British Commonwealth of Nations in Ireland. . . . The British Government vehemently insisted on the insertion in the text of the traditional formalism which had been deliberately left out of the Irish draft with a view to facilitating the acceptance in Ireland of the new regime; thus King George was to be invested, as a formality (!), with the executive power; the judges were to be nominated by his viceroy; the King and the two chambers were together to constitute the legislature; the right of veto was to be acknowledged; the article of the Treaty which prescribed the form of parliamentary oath was to be remodelled in the Constitution so as to leave no loophole; and the Anglo-Irish Treaty was to be recognised as the sole foundation of Irish autonomy." (Quoted from Macardle, pp. 724-725; see also D. H. Akinson and J. F. Fallin, "The Irish Civil War and the Drafting of the Free State Constitution," Part III, *Eire-Ireland* (St. Paul, Minn.), Vol. V, No. 4 (Winter, 1970), pp. 28-70.)

Gavan Duffy's pessimism had been shared earlier by de Valera, who held that the Constitution as it was revised would exclude from public service and disfranchise every honest Republican. The *Republic of Ireland* called the charter "a shameful document" and "an abject surrender to England," while Rory O'Connor angrily declared: "The thing is too rotten to talk about." Griffith, however, hailed the document as the Constitution of a free and democratic State which gave Ireland the power to control its own destiny. In Britain, as might be expected, the Constitution was lauded as a triumph for British diplomacy. "The English victory is plain," declared the London *Sunday Times* proudly.

Nevertheless, in the long term, the British victory was more apparent than real on the score of Irish sovereignty. "As with the Treaty, both Britain and Ireland paid a price for peace, and – once again – the British paid more," writes Joseph M. Curran (*The Birth of the Irish Free State, 1921-1923*, pp. 217-218). "Doctrinaire assertions of democratic authority and fundamental rights . . . had strong support from the Irish government and people and, reinforced by Canadian constitutional practice, they made monarchical forms more a mockery than a splendid show."

The Constitution of Saorstat Ireland as drafted was intended to be as Republican in nature and tone as the 1919 Constitution of the Irish Republic. But, even with its British alterations and additions it was no less Republican essentially. As a renowned constitutionalist, Barra O Briain, was to judge it, it was "monarchical in external form, republican in substance and, withal, essentially democratic" (*The Irish Constitution*, p. 71). It "embodied the most revolutionary constitutional project in the political history of the two islands since the instruments of government of the Cromwellian period," wrote Leo Kohn (*op. cit.*, p. 80). "It represented . . . a most comprehensive and, in spirit, essentially republican constitution on most advanced Continental lines. It had the characteristic dogmatic ring of all constitutions which embody not the legislative crystallisation of an organic development, but the theoretical postulates of a revolutionary upheaval. It mocked the time-honoured empiricism of the British Constitution by the enunciation of basic principles and the formulation of dogmatic definitions. It postulated fundamental rights. It defined in detail the scope and the functions of the several constitutional powers. It reduced to precise terms the conventional rules of the British Constitution. Its archaic symbols had to be introduced, but their meaninglessness for Ireland was writ large on every page. The monarchical forms paled into insignificance in the light of the formal enunciation and the consistent application of the principle of the sovereignty of the people as the fundamental and the exclusive source of all political authority."

The oath of allegiance, too – rather, of *faithfulness* – was not the bitter pill it was at first imagined to be. It was taken only in virtue of the common British-Irish citizenship that then existed and of Ireland's association with the British Commonwealth nations. It was *not* taken in virtue of any allegiance that might have existed. Leo Kohn explained this convention as being what actually *gave* Ireland her freedom in British eyes. "Paradoxical as it might seem," he wrote, "it was the expression of the Irish Free State's adherence to the British Commonwealth in the feudal rite of an oath of fidelity to a sovereign liege which symbolised the full measure of its freedom in the new bond of association" (*op. cit.*, p. 56).

Similarly, all other Monarchical symbols imposed on Ireland were not as unpalatable in reality as they had at first appeared. With the Irish tie-in with Commonwealth constitutional development that was proceeding apace, Ireland was equipped with the power of rendering all restrictions and limitations placed on her status nothing more than empty symbols and bothersome nuisances. As a matter of fact, the King was also claimed by Kohn and others to be acting in some such capacity as that of External President of Ireland, since he was the promulgator of what was for Ireland in all but "name the Republican Constitution which *de facto* she actually [possessed]" (A. Berriedale Keith, *Letters on Imperial Relations*, p. 135). Summing up, Kohn stated: "The formal dualism which characterises the Irish Constitution is most evident in the structure of the Executive. Its framework is that of a constitutional monarchy, its substance that of a republic. Executive authority is 'derived' from the people; it is 'vested' in the King. It is 'exercisable' by the Representative of the Crown; it is in fact exercised by an Executive Council . . . which 'aids and advises' [i.e., apprises] him" (*The Constitution of the Irish Free State*, p. 263; see also *Dail Debates*, Vol. 1, col. 2154).

A non-Republican but a more-than-a-Dominion Constitution

Already in 1922 some astute British observers perceived that the Irish were the real victors in the struggle over the Constitution, particularly concerning sovereignty. The Constitution's assertion of democratic sovereignty in Article 2 ("All power of government and all authority, legislative, executive, and judicial in Ireland, are derived from the people of Ireland"), together with Irish citizenship (Article 3), was the one principle that undermined and rendered meaningless all claims of internal royal allegiance and adherence to the total constitutional practice of Commonwealth countries, whose inhabitants were still British citizens. Unquestionably, "popular sovereignty dominated the life of the Free State from the very beginning," wrote W.K. Hancock (*Survey of British Commonwealth Affairs*, Vol. I, *Problems of Nationality, 1918-1936*, p. 158). Arthur Berriedale Keith, an authority on Commonwealth constitutional law, declared that the Irish Constitution unquestionably recognized the sovereignty of the people and left the Treaty obligation of Ireland to adhere to Commonwealth constitutional practice entirely vague. Thus, even as Keith agrees, Eoin MacNeill was fully vindicated in having proposed already on January 7, 1922, the resolution that "Dail Eireann affirms that Ireland is a sovereign nation deriving its sovereignty in all respects from the will of the people of Ireland." (See letter by Keith to *The Times* (London), June 19, 1922; reproduced in his *Letters on Imperial Relations*, pp. 34-36.)

Even if Ireland did have to adhere to the constitutional practice of the Commonwealth, such practice was far and away ahead of the corresponding constitutional theory. Canadian constitutional usage had already, to take one instance, nullified royal veto power, so that Irish legislation would, to use Keith's phrase, be 'utterly unfettered' by the British Government or Parliament. In fact, the right of royal veto, one of Gavan Duffy's fears, did not in reality exist over Ireland, because Article 41 of the Constitution prescribed, in effect, that the royal veto was not to be used in practice just as it was never being used in Canada. As Leo Kohn described Article 41, "that compound formula was nothing short of a declaration of nullity" (pp. 204-205). Besides, it was to have been written into the Treaty proper because it was agreed on, but was somehow overlooked, that the Crown should not act in Ireland except on the advice of the Irish Government and that the authority of the Crown in Ireland was to be no more in practice than it was in Canada or any other of the Dominions – that is, that it was to be purely symbolic and never observed in practice. (See Frank Pakenham, *Peace by Ordeal*, pp. 195-197 paperback. Note that the Imperial Conference of 1930 repealed the power of royal veto. – Personal communication, Professor Gerald-A. Beaudoin of the University of Ottawa.) The lacuna in the Treaty was remedied, however, by a provision of the British Act of reratification that has been taken to be restrictive of Ireland's position but that really was restrictive of Britain's. That Act enjoined that the exercise of Westminster's power should be restricted to "any case where, in accordance with constitutional practice, Parliament would make laws affecting self-governing Dominions" (the Irish Free State Constitution Act, 1922, Sec. 4). Such exercise of 'supremacy' was, in the case of the Dominions, hardly ever and would, in the case of Ireland, be never. (Cf. Keith, *Responsible Government*, p. 42.)

In view of Ireland's need to have the Treaty accepted by Northern Ireland, it is understandable that the authority of the Crown in Ireland should not be shown for what it was, a purported authority, and that the rendering nugatory of the King's power in Ireland as had been agreed on for inclusion in the Treaty could not be actually shown in the document. The Treaty had to be presented to the North in such a way as that it would be acceptable to the Northerners and this was best achieved by making an apparent provision in the instrument for the King's control over internal Irish affairs and the negating and rendering meaningless of this had to await the Westminster Constitution Act for documentation and had at that to be translated into equivalent language in this instrument as well. In such a way was the Treaty Agreement made palatable to intransigent Ulster and so there could be extracted from her, by acceptance of the Treaty itself, agreement on essential Irish unity. Hence the *appearance* of Irish surrender in the Treaty document to royal rule in Ireland and the clothing of recognition of the Saorstat Eireann of the Declaration of Independence in the language of conformance with a restricted Commonwealth constitutional practice.

The constitutional practice envisaged for Ireland would go even still beyond that of Commonwealth countries and would be forcing the pace of constitutional development in those nations now that what appeared to be a Monarchical Constitution was being thrust upon Ireland. One area for Ireland to surpass its partners in was the one in which the Governor General of the Free State was not granted any discretionary power with respect to the dissolution of Parliament, and herein a notable discrepancy existed with typical Dominion practice. The Governor General's powers were to be whittled gradually away in practice by the Cosgrave Government until by 1932 the old chap was doing merely the Government's bidding – at a time when the King himself could not legally "give a single instruction to his representative" (Keith, *Letters on Imperial Relations*, p. 141). In this the Irish practice was greatly distinguished from that of the Commonwealth nations, especially for those Imperialist days.

Another area of distinction was that concerning attempts to safeguard appeals from the Irish Supreme Court to the Judicial Committee of the Privy Council. These attempts in the Constitution were feeble at best, and did not recognize any right of direct appeal as the Constitutions of the Dominions, except South Africa, did. All the Irish Constitution said (Article 66) was that the right of any person to petition the King for 'special leave' to appeal to the Privy Council should not be impaired. Which special leave, as Hector Hughes pointed out, might not be granted, and was only expressed as a saving clause in the Constitution. All this amounted to was that, as with the nonexistent royal veto, the Irish Free State should be made to look as much as possible like a Dominion. The also nonexistent right of appeal marked for Ireland another notable advance on Dominion practice – with the possible exception of South Africa, whose constitutional practice Ireland was going to follow until such time as it would abolish the limited appeal altogether. (Canada abrogated the right of appeal completely in December 1949 and Australia in 1986.[1])

The nonexistence for Saorstat Eireann of the right of appeal to the Privy Council was made clear by Hector Hughes when he pointed out that "the Judicial Committee Act, 1833, did not and, from its terms could not apply, to either Ireland or the Irish Free State." This Act, which created the Judicial Committee of the Privy Council, confined the jurisdiction of the Court to appeals from the Courts in India "and in the plantations, colonies and other Dominions of His Majesty abroad." The Act did not apply even to Great Britain, and final appeals continued to lie from there to the House of Lords of the United Kingdom, as they do to the present day from Northern Ireland. That the system of appeals as it was inserted in the Free State Constitution had no roots in the Treaty is evident from the explanation Kevin O'Higgins gave that, as an inducement to the Irish authorities to admit the system, "the British Government gave an assurance that its force would be theoretical rather than practical." (See Hector Hughes, *National Sovereignty and Judicial Autonomy in the British Commonwealth of Nations*, pp. 35-38, 56-58 and 112; Kenneth C. Wheare, *Constitutional Structure of the Commonwealth*, pp. 45-54; also *Attorney-General of Ontario and Others* v. *Attorney-General of Canada and Others*, [1947] A.C. 127 and 1 All E.R. 137.)

There were at least three other areas in which the Irish constitutional position was ahead of that in Commonwealth countries, but perhaps the most important area in which the Irish position was technically ahead of Canadian law and practice lay in the power that Ireland had to amend the Constitution virtually as she saw fit – within the limits of the Treaty law (although a literal adherence to the terms of the Treaty was not insisted upon by the British). The Canadian Constitution, by contrast – since, like the other Dominion Constitutions, it was passed and adopted as a Statute of the British Parliament – could only be amended in Britain by an

1 By a Proclamation signed March 2, 1986 by Queen Elizabeth II, an Australian Constitutional Act abolishing the remaining constitutional links between Australia and the United Kingdom was activated. The Australia Act 1986 provided for the following changes: Appeals from the High Court of Australia would no longer be made to the Privy Council; the British Parliament would no longer have power to enact legislation affecting Australian law; and U.K. law could no longer restrict the legislative power of the Australian states to repeal or update outdated Imperial laws.

Act of the Imperial Parliament. By its power of amendment of its own Constitution, Ireland as a member of the Commonwealth led the way in Commonwealth constitutional development and burst the bonds of British control over constitutional and legislative action outside the borders of Britain itself.

But even if the Irish Constitution was not formally made a Republican charter, it was still more than a Dominion Constitution, much more in fact. It may be right away objected that it could not have been anything of the kind when it had to be subject to a Treaty that stipulated that Ireland should have the same constitutional status as that of the Dominion of Canada. How then, it might be asked, could Ireland at the same time be anything more than a Dominion? The answer has to be, of course, that it could, and it was. As a matter of fact, in view of the Treaty equation (of particularly Article 1), the question might just as validly be asked: How could Canada (or South Africa or Australia or New Zealand) at the same time be anything less than a Free State? The truth is that the theory that the Treaty left Ireland a Dominion was never actually anything more than a myth. But unfortunately it is a myth that has been believed widely over the years. And it is a myth that needs badly, of course, to be exploded.

The litmus test of whether Ireland was subjected by her acceptance of the Treaty to Dominion status is the question: 'Was the law governing Colonies and developing Dominions, the law that distinguished pre-1922 Dominions from Free States, the Colonial Laws Validity Act of 1865 – was that law made by the Treaty to apply to Ireland, as Justice Kingsmill Moore of the Irish Supreme Court thought it did and as Lord Sankey of the Judicial Committee of the Privy Council declared it did'?[2] Actually, it didn't. This is an important point to be certain about, because if it can be demonstrated (1) that Ireland was not reduced to the status of a Dominion by the Treaty, and further (2) that the Free State instituted by the instrument was not incompatible with the Saorstat/Republic established, then it can be incontrovertibly declared that the approval of the Treaty by the Dail in 1922 or acceptance of it by the people that same year did not cause the

2 For the opinion of Justice T.C. Kingsmill Moore see *In the Matter of the Irish Employers Mutual Insurance Association Limited*, [1955] I.R. 1976, p. 218; for the opinion of Lord John Sankey, L.C., see *Moore* v. *Attorney-General for The Irish Free State*, [1935] I.R. 472 and [1935] A.C. 484, p. 494; see also *Byrne* v. *Ireland*, [1972] I.R. 241, p. 273, and Appendices 6 and 9, *Supplement*.

Republic to be disestablished, that the Treaty itself was more in appearances than reality a Dominion-instituting charter and was not then ***really*** dismantled in the 1930s, and that even now the Treaty could be accepted without any diminution of the Republic-to-be-restored or any loss of national pride.[3]

But was Ireland by the Treaty made a Dominion subject to the Colonial Laws Validity Act of 1865? The answer is an emphatic No. The reason for this is that, even if she was to be referred to loosely as a Dominion, Ireland was not subject interpretatively to the Colonial Laws Validity Act. The CLVA governed all British possessions beyond the seas, including in the post-WWI years all Colonies become Dominions. These were, in fact, by this (to them) obnoxious law kept being deprived of full nationhood and denied their newly earned complete autonomy. They were, as it was put by Sankey, fettered by the law. Overall, the CLVA maintained the supremacy of the Westminster Parliament, and this it did in many ways, most of which we have just seen. These ways may be called the hallmarks of a Dominion and may be summarized as follows:

(1) The Westminster Parliament could legislate for a Dominion; (2) the Dominion Legislature could not pass laws having extraterritorial effect; (3) decisions of a Dominion's Supreme Court could be appealed to the Privy Council at Westminster; (4) the Governor General, who represented the King, took his instructions from the King, but those instructions would have been dictated to the King by the British Government; (5) the Governor General could refuse assent to a Bill and reserve it for the King's consideration, and the King in giving or refusing his assent would be dictated to by his Government; (6) the King might, with the permission of the Government, disallow a law to which the Governor General had already given consent; and (7) the local Legislature had to be opened every session by a 'Speech from the Throne,' given on behalf of the King, and sometimes the Legislature would have to be opened by the King himself.

3 The Treaty did not disestablish the Republic, because it did not constitute Ireland a Dominion, but gave it the status of a Dominion or Free State, this being the translation of Ireland's "Saorstat" (i.e., "Republic"). That the Treaty did not constitute Ireland a Dominion was made clear by Stanley Baldwin in November 1926 when he said: "Although the Irish Free State has a dominion status, Ireland, which includes Northern Ireland, is not a dominion." (Quoted from Isaiah Bowman, *The New World, Problems in Political Geography*, p. 53.)

In the Irish situation, the Treaty ensured that the Irish Free State was not subjected to any of the foregoing CLVA restrictions and deprivations of a Dominion. This was not achieved by the Treaty alone, but by a special interpretative law that was, precisely because of Ireland becoming a Free State in the Commonwealth, provided for by Section 6 of the Irish Free State (Consequential Provisions) Act, 1922, an Act that had in any case in some of its parts been authorized by the Treaty in order to meet that instrument's requirement of modification of the Government of Ireland Act, 1920. That interpretative law was the Statutory Rule and Order, the Irish Free State (Consequential Adaptation of Enactments) Order, 1923, No. 405, 1923. By this first Adaptation Order issued as authorized by Section 6 (1) (a) of the Consequential Provisions Act, the King proceeded to do as he had been empowered to do by the Act, which was to adapt enactments relating to Dominions other than the Irish Free State in a way that might be "necessary or proper" for those Dominions – for instance, in beginning to be treated as Free States – "as a consequence of the establishment of the Irish Free State," and further to make any such adaptation to take effect retroactively from the date the Consequential Provisions Act was promulgated, December 6, 1922 (two days before the North of Ireland provisionally opted out of the Free State).

Acknowledging his empowerment under Section 6 of the CPA, King George V adapted in Section 3 of the Order all existing Commonwealth enactments, including the CLVA, that had references in them to 'the United Kingdom,' 'the United Kingdom of Great Britain and Ireland,' and the like (as did the CLVA) in such a way that the Irish Free State would not be included among the British Dominions, but would be set apart in a class along with the United Kingdom and understood in somewhat the same sense as the United Kingdom itself. The upshot of this move by the King was that the Irish Free State, being excluded from (among other Commonwealth laws) the CLVA, and thus not fettered with the hallmarks of a Dominion, was not to be considered a Dominion in the then accepted sense of the term.

That the enactments to be adapted were laws that did not apply to Ireland, or to Britain, but only to Commonwealth countries was clear to British Court of Appeal Judge T.E. Scrutton, who, in *Rex* v. *Secretary of State for Home Affairs*, ex parte *O'Brien* ([1923] 2 K.B. 361, p. 388), held that no empowerment was given "to adapt enactments so far as they relate to the territory of the Irish Free

State; their effect can only be altered so far as they relate to dominions other than the Irish Free State, and, if it may be necessary, to alter their application in other dominions, because of the establishment of the Irish Free State. . . . The alteration is only to be made in the application of the statutes to dominions other than Ireland." This opinion, incidentally, is often cited as an interpretation of the intent of the Consequential Provisions Act not to classify Ireland/the Irish Free State among the overseas Dominions. The opinion may also be viewed as being counteractive of the assertion that, as we shall see later, the Adaptation Order applied to Ireland-related laws as well and that it did so in such a way as to have Ireland in those laws to be reconstrued to mean only a part of the whole.

A strong confirmatory opinion that the Colonial Laws Validity Act never did apply to Ireland was that voiced by E.C.S. Wade in his Introduction to Dicey's *Introduction to the Study of the Law and the Constitution* (p. lxxxiv) when he said: "The Act never applied to Ireland under the Union and therefore had no application to the Irish Free State." It was, in fact, precisely because the Commonwealth (and the world) had to be notified that Ireland had changed from being a kingdom to being a Free State, and not a Dominion, that it was thought necessary to have adapted all Commonwealth legislation having references to the Union. The status Ireland acquired, we know, under the Treaty was not one that was the ***same*** as that which Canada and the rest of the Commonwealth enjoyed prior to 1921, but, as has been well said, one that was ***similar*** to that which Canada and the others until that time ***had***. The status was the same as that which Canada and its fellow Dominions themselves ***then acquired*** by the Commonwealth-Irish Treaty. (See further Chapter 11 wherein is explained the later British doctrine of 'Ministerial Responsibility to Commonwealth Parliaments' that was devised to accommodate sovereignties within the Commonwealth.)

The relevant all-important, but seldom-or-never-cited, Section 3 of the Adaptation Order No. 405 is so substantiative of our argument about the non-Dominion status of Ireland that it bears being reproduced here:

> Subject as aforesaid (i.e., to the provisions of this Order and of any subsequent Order in Council made under section six of the Irish Free State (Consequential Provisions) Act, 1922 (**b**)), references to "the United Kingdom" or "the United Kingdom of Great Britain and

> Ireland," or "Great Britain and Ireland," or "Great Britain or Ireland," or "the British Islands" or "Ireland," in any enactment passed before the establishment of the Irish Free State which applies to parts of His Majesty's Dominions outside the United Kingdom, or outside the British Islands, as the case may be, shall, in the application of the enactment to any such part, be construed as references both –
>
> (*a*) to Great Britain and Ireland or the British Islands exclusive of the Irish Free State . . . ;
>
> and
>
> (*b*) to the Irish Free State.

The footnote (**b**) to which we are cued refers us to an official interpretation of 'United Kingdom' in a later Adaptation Order, No. 453 of 1923. In that Order, at Section 5 (*f*), we are told "the expression ' United Kingdom' . . . shall, notwithstanding anything in the Irish Free State (Consequential Adaptation of Enactments) Order, 1923, be construed . . . as including the Irish Free State." And the Interpretation Act 1978 at Schedule 2, Paragraph 4 (2) provides that "the definition of 'British Islands,' in its application to Acts passed after the establishment of the Irish Free State [per S.R. & O. 1353, 1922: December 6, 1922], but before the commencement of this Act [January 1, 1979], includes the Republic of Ireland [Irish Free State]." These are interpretations that certainly confirm our conclusion of above that Ireland by the Treaty was not constituted an overseas Dominion. On the contrary, it had to be that by the Treaty equation it was Canada and the other Dominions that were beginning to be recognized as Free States, that is, as freely associated members of the Commonwealth, autonomous, and equal in status with one another and even with Britain itself. Even on a strict interpretation, if Ireland was to have a status the same as that of the Dominion of Canada, what would have been intended would have been a status the same as the status-to-bc of Canada (which was soon to be the same as that of Britain itself). So that what was in actuality recognized and acknowledged for Ireland was its sovereignty and independence of nationhood, a status virtually of Saorstat/Republic already declared.

One reason the Treaty was not in conflict with the Saorstat or Republic was that the Treaty had to do with status, while the Republic had to do with form. Status gave Ireland a legal character, an international point of reference; form meant that the Republic could go on proclaiming the sovereignty and autonomy of the Irish people. "Status is not form," declared Kingsmill Moore (*c. cit.*, p. 217). "Status is a matter of international relations; it is the position of a State as viewed from outside by other States, not as viewed from inside by its citizens." On that score alone the Treaty could not be in conflict with the established Republic, no matter how that Republic was to be referred to (Free State, Dominion, etc.), and that is why *Halsbury's Statutes of England* in explaining the Treaty Article 1 could accurately say that Ireland retained from the British point of view until 1949 the status it had been assigned in 1921 for the purposes of the Statute of Westminster, 1931, "though its actual status was that of a state organised on republican lines nominally associated with an Empire" (Vol. 4, 3rd ed., p. 637). It might be added that Ireland's decision in 1937 to adopt a republican Constitution, or her decision in 1948 to belong no longer to the Commonwealth, was not regarded by Britain as having made Ireland any more republican than the Treaty Settlement had already made her (Ireland Act, 1949, Sec. 3 (1) (*a*) and (2) (*a*); see further Appendix 6, Note 14, *Supplement*).

The imposition of 'Dominion' status on Ireland was also under another aspect not really as bad as it sounded. By the end of World War I the term 'Dominion' began to connote Home Rule – 'Dominion Home Rule,' as it was called in Britain, and, whereas in earlier times Dominionship meant entrapment in the Commonwealth and subjection to the United Kingdom, now the concept began to mean freedom to depart at will from what was becoming a voluntary Association. In fact, the conferral of Dominion status had, in postwar British constitutional politics, come to indicate Britain's (face-saving) way of recognizing a former subject nation's newfound independence and sovereignty. Even as early as 1920 Acting Prime Minister Bonar Law conceded that this was already official policy. And since this policy was pretty well formulated by 1921, its provisions would have been the terms under which Ireland was prepared to accept Britain's valued recognition of the Irish Republic in the Treaty. These terms were, as enunciated by Bonar Law in the House of Commons: "If the self-governing Dominions . . . chose tomorrow to say 'We will no longer make a part of the British Empire', we would not try to force them. Dominion Home Rule means the right to decide their own destinies." (127 H.C. Official Report (1920), col. 1125.) A Dominion's "very conception was, in 1921, still in its infancy," writes Charles Mowat (*Britain Between the Wars*, p. 91), and would more correctly have been referred to as Free State or virtual Republic. Now, as far as Ireland is concerned, several years later, the question rather is, would reassociation with the Commonwealth facilitate the reïntegration of that part of Ireland that is still within the Commonwealth? And the answer is, according to Sir William Leonard Dale and Arnold Smith, probably yes.[4] (See Dale's *The Modern Commonwealth*, page 63, and Smith's *Stitches in Time*, page 158.)

But, if England gave in one way with the Treaty she imposed, she took in another way with the Constitution she bestowed. Although the Constitution Ireland got in 1922 was the best of the Commonwealth Constitutions, it was not the Republican charter the Government had wanted or had devised. When the Free State Constitution was thrust upon Ireland it was only to be expected that she should have acted like the proverbial bull in a china shop, since she was from the beginning interiorly a Republic upon whom an ill-fitting Commonwealth cloak had been cast. Indeed she might without much British loss of face have been outwardly recognized as a Republic too. Anticipating the developments of 1926 (the Balfour Definition of the Commonwealth[5]) and of 1931 (the Statute of Westminster[5]), Keith asked as early as 1922 whether the

4 In 1968, Arnold Cantwell Smith, then Secretary General of the Commonwealth, was approached by the Irish Government about the possibility of Ireland's applying for Commonwealth association. Some top Government officials, Smith reports, favored such a move, thinking it would make it easier for Britain to be conciliatory over Northern Ireland. Others, like Sean MacBride, believed "it would help Ireland to be more outward looking." But the then Taoiseach, Jack Lynch, held that an application for reassociation would be too controversial in the current state of Irish-British relations, "but that the time might well come when Commonwealth membership could help the evolution of either a united Ireland or a separate country of Ulster [?], and reconciliation between Protestants and Catholics there." (Ireland's withdrawal from the Commonwealth was in accordance with the practice of members who would declare themselves republics (or separate monarchies or otherwise independent states). But unlike those countries who would thereupon apply for reassociation under their new status, Ireland has not so applied since 1948.)

5 The 1926 Balfour Definition of the Commonwealth was that Britain and the then Dominions were "autonomous communities within the British Empire, equal in status, in no way subordinate to one another in any aspect of their domestic or external affairs, though united by a common allegiance to the Crown, and freely associated as members of the British Commonwealth of Nations." The 1931 Statute of Westminster gave legal effect and development to this Definition. It laid down, among other things, that henceforth legislation of the U.K. Parliament would not extend to any Dominion and that the Dominions

then-existing Constitution of the Commonwealth (which has since been superseded) were not becoming flexible enough to include a Republic. This was in his letter published June 19, 1922, in the London *Times*: "Is not the Constitution of the British Commonwealth of Nations elastic enough to include a Republic?" (Cf. W.K. Hancock, *Problems of Nationality*, p. 165 n. 1; J.H. Bettey, ed., *English Historical Documents, 1906-1939*, pp. 164-166.) And in 1932 Kohn thought that the Irish Republic could have been incorporated in the British Empire at the Treaty Conference, just as, for instance, the three city republics of Hamburg, Bremen and Lubeck had found a place in the Monarchical Constitution of Imperial Germany (Kohn, p. 51). Keith, too, in 1933 was able to point to the 'colonies' of Connecticut and Rhode Island as having received from Charles II republican Constitutions within the British Empire in 1662 and 1663, respectively. Indeed during the Cosgrave and early de Valera administrations the learned constitutionalist had pleaded repeatedly in his writings for inclusion of the Irish Republic in the Commonwealth and berated Britain for her "inability to surmount a rigid legalism and to apply constructive imagination to refashioning Imperial relations." This inability was, he held, the type of mentality that lost America to the British Commonwealth. (*Letters on Imperial Relations*, pp. 134-147. See also Kenneth C. Wheare, *The Statute of Westminster and Dominion Status*, pp. 272-273, and Roger H. Hull, *The Irish Triangle*, pp. 101-102 n., for support of the view that even the present-day 26-county Republic could, more especially because of Article 29 (4) (ii) of the 1937 Constitution, enjoy membership of the Commonwealth as this is now constituted.)

Keith's and Kohn's previsions of the possibilities for Ireland were to be demonstrated capable of fulfillment within a scant fifteen years of adoption of the Constitution. That would be when, with adoption of a new Constitution, part of Ireland was to become a virtually declared Republic and yet remain within the Commonwealth. There is no reason to believe the same could not have been the way in 1922. "The imposition of British constitutional law on the Irish was a futile gesture," concludes Curran (*op. cit.*, p. 218),

---

would have power to repeal existing legislation by that Parliament in matters affecting them. The Statute of Westminster was a landmark piece of legislation, enabling as it did the Dominions and Ireland to legislate themselves out of repressive Westminster laws and into full coequality with Britain and one another.

"when they were given Dominion constitutional practice as well. Persistently and skillfully, the Free State exploited its own powers and the awakened nationalism of its fellow Dominions to secure abolition of the symbols of British rule. In the process, the Irish weakened British dominance in the Commonwealth and loosened its ties, repaying in kind those who forced Crown and Empire on Ireland."[6]

A British-devised but Irish-amendable Constitution

How the Irish were to score ultimately on the democratic sovereignty issue in the Constitution was by having available to them the capability to amend their own Constitution. If Irish popular sovereignty was to be chipped away at and curtailed by the repeated acceptance of British revisions, the power of amendment if used with patience would eventually restore that lost sovereignty. Britain's agreeing to Ireland's having the power to amend her Constitution was quite a departure from and innovative development in the constitutional practice of the Commonwealth community. Canada, for example, only acquired authority to amend her Constitution quite recently and after fifty years of sovereign independence. While Ireland could not only amend her Constitution from the beginning, but she could amend it in practically any way she liked – always with reference to the terms of the Treaty, however. But even with this restriction, the power of amendment that Ireland enjoyed was completely at odds with former Canadian constitutional practice, to which, according to the terms of the Treaty, the Saorstat was supposed to conform.

Herein lay a major advancement for Ireland indeed on Canadian law and practice, and if wisely used and at the same time advantage taken of the powers acquired through Commonwealth constitutional development, this power of amendment could go a long way to undoing the Monarchical formalism imposed on the Irish Constitution. Such a major concession by Britain can only be understood as having been made in a moment of nodding or as a

6 Actually Ireland, in being given Dominion constitutional practice, was recognized as a sovereign autonomous nation, since by Article 1 of the Constitution she was made a coequal member with Britain herself in the Commonwealth of Nations, as were all the other Dominions, and thus would have been impliedly regarded as much a Republic as Britain was a Monarchy (although the distinction with Britain did not have to be, and was not, drawn, the form of Government of such a sovereign and independent nation not requiring to be described).

compensatory or offsetting factor to the more offensive characteristics of the Constitution which the Irish had willy-nilly to accept.

The act of allowing Ireland to amend what was in reality a British and Imperial Constitution amounted to no less than a *patriation* by Britain to Ireland of the Constitution itself. The British, it could be said, patriated what was, as we have called it, although amendable, a British-devised Constitution (even though the impression they gave was that it was an Irish-devised Constitution). Patriation and promulgation of an essentially amendable Monarchical Constitution were, in effect, performed by Britain in one and the same act. This was governed by the Constitution itself, in Article 83.

What enabled the British Government to give the Irish rulers the impression that it was an Irish-devised Constitution that was in the course of being adopted was the fact that they, the British, acknowledged that the Constitution was being processed and passed by a Constituent Assembly (as opposed to possibly a Constitutional Convention). The Constitutions of Canada, Australia, and South Africa, for example, were each drawn up by *ad hoc* Constitutional Conventions in their own countries. But by the theory prevalent at the time that within the British Empire there was only one sovereign assembly, the Parliament at Westminster, none of these peoples were competent to confer their Constitutions upon themselves. They were not, that is to say, really sovereign, for the acid test of sovereignty is the power of a nation to confer a Constitution on itself. Before the Constitutions these Commonwealth countries devised could come into force, therefore, they had to be passed as Imperial Statutes by the British Parliament.[7] (Cf. Darrell Figgis, *The Irish Constitution Explained*, pp. 15-19; Barra O Briain, *The Irish Constitution*, pp. 56-57.)

7 The overseas Commonwealth countries, or Dominions, not being sovereign in the early days, were unable to enact Constitutions for themselves. The Canadian Constitution was enacted in 1867 by the British Parliament in the "British North America Act, 1867" (30 Vict., c. 3); an Elective Legislature was bestowed on New Zealand by an Act of the Westminster Parliament in 1852 (15 & 16 Vict., c. 72); the "Commonwealth of Australia Constitution Act" (63 & 64 Vict., c. 12) was passed for Australia by the British Parliament in 1900; and the "South Africa Act, 1909" (9 Edw. VII, c. 9) was enacted by the Parliament at Westminster for South Africa in 1909. The Irish Constituent Assembly of 1922, on the other hand, acting as a sovereign and Republican body, decreed and enacted itself the Saorstat Constitution for Ireland, although it was not in a position to promulgate it. Also, the instruments by which the Dominions came into being were Imperial *Statutes*, unrepealable in those nations. Whereas the instrument by which the Irish Free State came into being was a Treaty ratified by

The Provisional Parliament that devised the Irish Constitution, by comparison, was a Constituent Assembly. It was, in fact, like the First Dail, elected as a Constituent Assembly (and Pact Dail). It did have, then, by definition, the competence to enact a Constitution, and that is in fact what it said it was going to do: the Constituent Act itself began by stating that the Act was "an Act to enact a Constitution." But by a provision of the very Constitution the Assembly enacted, for the Constitution to come into force enactment alone was not enough. It had also to be promulgated. We shall see later ***how*** the highest expression of sovereignty – the act of conferral of a Constitution on one's country – was to be denied to the Irish Free State and how that act of denial resulted in the Constitution being a thoroughly British charter having as effect a British creation, the post-Constitution, 26-county Dail.

It is true that the British Parliament passed and enacted the Irish Constitution as well (which issued in the Irish Free State Constitution Act, 1922), but that process was merely an echo of the Dail operation and had no legal significance for Ireland whatsoever. It made the Constitution neither more British nor less Irish, and could not be regarded in the least as being a determinant of the nature of the Constitution. It was the 'Dominion Act' that Eoin MacNeill did not care a fig about, and we are not concerned with it here. What we are concerned with is whether the Constitution Act passed in the Dail confirmed partition or not, whether it was for 32 counties or 26 counties, and whether it was really a British charter in Irish dress.

Adoption by the Dail certainly gave the impression the instrument was an Irish one. The feature of amending power the Constitution enjoyed was another factor that enabled the British to give the impression that the Constitution was an Irish charter – although potentially that is what it was. If the Constitution could be amended in Ireland itself, the illusion of it being an all-Irish Constitution could easily be created. The British, at the same time, would not be worried by their (to them) magnanimous concession, because as far as they were concerned the trick was completed when the Constitution was promulgated as a Constitution that was

---

an Imperial *Act*, repealable in the State. The Statutory Instruments recognized a stage in the evolution of colonial autonomy under 'responsible government'; the Treaty was concluded with a Provisional Republic and mother country itself. (Cf. Sir William R. Anson, *The Law and Custom of the Constitution*, Vol. II (4th ed.), Part II, p. 99.)

encumbered with exclusion of application to a certain area, and that was something that would never be likely to be undone by amendment. Their hand was played, they thought.

The power of amendment was even expanded before it was ever to be availed of. As the Constitution was wending its way through the Dail for passage Kevin O'Higgins proposed that additions be made to the Article involving amendment power, Article 50. This Article as it stood read: "Amendments of this Constitution within the terms of the Scheduled Treaty may be made by the Parliament/Oireachtas, but every such amendment must be submitted to a Referendum of the people and shall not be passed unless a majority of the voters . . . are in favour of the amendment." O'Higgins moved that this Article be amended itself to permit amendments to the Constitution (within the terms of the Treaty) to be made by ordinary legislation alone for a period of eight years from the Constitution's coming into operation (since it was thought that the Referendum system was too cumbersome to operate with a new Constitution that might need frequent amendment). Even this the British Government subsequently agreed to, and one cannot help getting the feeling that they were perfectly willing to concede to the Irish the freedom to revel to their hearts' delight in amendments that could never exceed the bounds of the limited, 26-county jurisdiction the British had succeeded in imposing on them. And revel they were to in restrictive amendments when the Republican era arrived – even to the point of acknowledging, ***in a Constitution***, their limited jurisdiction. Good though the power of amendment was, then, as used it led in the wrong direction.

If not formally a Republican, at least substantively a Sovereign Constitution

How the Irish Constitution of 1922 emerged as the sovereign instrument it was, was due to the Treaty recognizing for Ireland a higher status than had heretofore been acknowledged for any of the Commonwealth countries. Soon after Dail Eireann was established and independence declared, in the Union of South Africa the Transvaal and Orange Free State began pressing for the restoration of their independence as logically following on the right of national self-determination just then acknowledged in the Treaty of Versailles. To appease their demands the Government of South Africa declared that all the Dominions, South Africa included, had by the Peace Settlement and membership of the

League of Nations won complete sovereignty and independent nationhood, and that they were associated with Britain and one another only through possession of a common Head of Commonwealth. Such heady doctrine was not, of course, accommodated by the current legal structure of the Commonwealth, and South Africa accordingly began to push for an updating of imperial relations. Success was had eventually in the most unlikely of places – the Anglo-Irish Treaty of 1921. As put by Keith, a redefinition of Commonwealth relations "was furthered in the highest degree by the creation in 1921-1922 of the Irish Free State" (*The Constitutional Law of the British Dominions*, p. 11).

The redefinition of Commonwealth relations that the Treaty and Irish Constitution contained meant in practice that, with the sovereignty and independence of the Dominions and the Free State acknowledged, all Commonwealth countries, Ireland included, were free as far as the United Kingdom was concerned to conduct their own internal affairs as they saw fit and to conduct their external affairs under the watchful eye of the British Monarch. With such acknowledgment of sovereignty and nationhood granted, it would have had to be lame of Britain to, at the same time, impose upon Ireland the King as Head of State and of the Judiciary in the new Constitution. Such imposition was undoubtedly a mistake for Britain to make, as it fulfilled de Valera's worst fears of what the oath of allegiance to the Constitution would entail. Had it not been for this enforced out-of-class role for the King, the oath would not have been an oath of allegiance but merely of fealty to the King as Commonwealth Ruler. As such it would not have amounted to anything more than a pledge to acknowledge the King as Head of the newly emerging free partnership of nations.

But it was not just the oath of the Treaty that was fouled up by the excessive British action: it was also the Treaty itself. For if by the Treaty Settlement the King was to be recognized as sovereign only in the external affairs of Commonwealth nations, here was one such nation, Ireland, in which the King was being required by the Constitution – anomalously – to be regarded as the Irish Chief Executive. This was a British move that was clearly *ultra vires* the Treaty – and, needless to say, very unsettling to Republicans in Ireland. And to South Africa also. Were all the preachments about South African sovereignty not going to be backed up in London after all? If they were not, of course, with Ireland having to conform with South African constitutional practice, that was not going to help Ireland either.

Urged on by South Africa, the Irish fought back against such infringement of sovereign rights just accorded to them, an infringement that might have adverse effects in South Africa too. The fear in Ireland was that internal control by the King would imply the right at Westminster to continue to legislate for Ireland, a right that was presumed to have gone out with the Treaty entree. But not so, really. 'Irish' legislation had continued right on at Westminster, where the many Acts enacted were considered the pillar and ground of the Irish constitutional position. (The corresponding Acts of the Dail were regarded, in the Keithian phrase, as just so many lucubrations of the loquacious Irish.) And since the bad habit of Westminster had not been broken with the Treaty, it was quite possible it might not be broken with the Constitution either. That being so, the battle was on to oust the King. With the Trojan efforts of such stalwarts as Patrick McGilligan, Desmond FitzGerald and John A. Costello abroad, aided and abetted by Canadian symphathizers like Mackenzie King and South Africans like General Smuts, in and out of Commonwealth Conferences, and with the Cosgrave Government obliterating wholeheartedly the symbols of royal and imperial power at home, the way was paved for the one constitutional law that would do away with the trappings and trimmings of royal power in Ireland forever – and much more besides. That law was the Statute of Westminster of 1931, the inauguration of which Ireland gladly requested and gleefully consented to as a Commonwealth partner.

With the approach of the Statute of Westminster the British had to back down and allow the King to be disregarded in Ireland as far as interference with the Irish Government was concerned. At the same time the habit of legislating for Ireland at Westminster gave way under pressure to engaging in bilateral agreements ratified by mutual legislation.[8] The last of Britain's implementa-

8 The habit was only barely broken, for right up to the moment of passage of the Statute of Westminster Churchill was pushing for specific prohibition, in the Statute, of Ireland from repealing, amending or altering the Westminster constitutional legislation of the 1920-1929 period relating to the Irish Free State. It was feared in particular that under the powers granted by the Statute "the Free State might repeal the Government of Ireland Act, 1920, and thus destroy the northern government and legislature, and might render illegal any acts done in the Free State by British officers in repressing violation of the Treaty" (Keith, *Speeches and Documents, 1918-1931*, p. 303). It was at that auspicious moment that President Willie T. Cosgrave wrote his memorable letter to Prime Minister Ramsay MacDonald asserting the extraparliamentary and mutually binding nature of the Treaty, an effort for which all Ireland is indebted to him ever since. The day was saved, the proposal to amend the Statute in Ireland's disfavor was rejected by 360 votes to 50. (For the relevant portion of Cosgrave's letter, see Chapter 10 herein, Note 1.)

tions of her obligations towards Ireland in both internal and external government were slow acoming and not expected to come at all. Yet, they came about fully five years before the corresponding moves were made in Ireland itself. In 1936, by Amendment No. 27 to the Constitution, the King was removed from all authority in all internal affairs – executive, legislative and judicial – and restricted to purely external affairs. Thus did Ireland at last emerge totally independent of the United Kingdom in internal government affairs.

In external Irish affairs, too, the pace had been quickened by Britain in acknowledging the sovereignty and independence of Ireland as the King became relegated, even in external relations, to a role that was purely passive. That is, the King became an instrument to be employed by a sovereign power rather than a sovereign to be sworn allegiance to (even through external relations). This development was produced, at McGilligan's instigation, by a twofold decision made in London in 1931. There was, for one thing, to be thenceforward only direct communication between the King and Dublin in dealing with matters of external relations. That decision was arrived at, explained Keith, "in order to make it clear that the King in the Free State was not in organic union with the Sovereign of the United Kingdom" (*The Dominions as Sovereign States*, p. 109). Hand in hand with that decision went the decision of the British Government in the same year to sanction the creation of a Great Seal for Ireland to replace the Great Seal of the Realm that was used in the instruments required for international intercourse between sovereign Heads of State. "The handing over to the Free State of its new Great Seal by the King . . . ," commented Keith at the time, "marks the final establishment of the complete international sovereignty of the Free State and the elimination of any British control" (*Letters on Imperial Relations*, p. 115).

With all of the foregoing actions, which returned the Anglo-Irish relationship of the Constitution back to what it was intended to be by the Treaty, the King was obliged to adopt a role of passive cooperation with Ireland. "His majesty must act absolutely on the advice of the Irish Free State, British Ministers being debarred from advice," concluded Keith, "and he cannot, if he wishes, refuse to accept the advice tendered, for he cannot dismiss the [Irish] Ministry, and he cannot act without its advice" (*op. cit.*, p. 141). Thus was the Treaty enabled to reassert itself as it had been negotiated and agreed on ten years before and thus was the constitutional relationship brought more closely into line with the Treaty with which it was supposed not to be repugnant. (See John A. Costello, "Ireland in International Affairs," *The Canadian Bar Review*, Vol. XXVI (1948), pp. 1195-1211.)

By such extraordinary ways, that even preceded the Statute of Westminster, was it made possible for Ireland to revert to such external association as had been allowed by the Treaty with the British Crown, and this was achieved solely through possession of the same Head of the Association as the United Kingdom had, all entirely on the basis of the Treaty. By such extraordinary ways was Ireland enabled indeed to be the Ireland that had, under the Treaty, "subordinated her external relations [not to Britain, but] to the judgment of the General Council [of the Commonwealth]," as Lloyd George had explained it during the Treaty debate. And by such extraordinary ways did de Valera see come true an interpretation of the Treaty that would practically coincide with the meaning he had originally intended for it when he proposed a compromise external relations allegiance formula: "that for purposes of the association [of the Free State with the United Kingdom and the other States of the Commonwealth] Ireland shall recognize His Britannic Majesty as head of the Association."[9] (See Appendix 7, *Supplement*; Robert B. Stewart, *Treaty Relations of the British Commonwealth*, pp. 191 ff.; and Keith, *Responsible Government*, pp. 117-128, 157.)

All of these exceptional developments were events that anticipated and even rendered superfluous the Irish establishment, benefitted by the Statute of Westminster, of a formalized external

9 It will be remembered that the Treaty, before it was (unauthorizedly) exceeded by the Constitution, had in fact provided a form of external association that made the settlement obtained to be in compliance with the status of Republic that Ireland already enjoyed, that is, with the Saorstat Eireann of the Declaration of Independence. How this would be worked was explained by Arthur Griffith at the London Peace Conference when he had external association go into the Treaty: " 'For external affairs, such as peace and war and defence [language from the Irish Memorandum of November 22, 1921], Ireland will recognise the British Crown in the way we have explained, while for internal affairs she will retain the Republic,' " as it was related by Frank Pakenham. "A fragment of dialogue that followed was destined to make history," Pakenham continued. "Griffith: 'You may prefer to translate "Saorstat Eireann" by "Free State" (instead of Republic). We shall not quarrel with your translation.' Lord Birkenhead: 'The title, Free State, can go into the Treaty.' " (*Peace by Ordeal*, hardcover p. 244, paperback p. 197.)

association five years later by appropriate amendment of the Constitution (in Article 51) and passage of the External Relations Act, 1936.[10] But, it must be remembered, none of these developments, in either the area of internal affairs or the area of external relations, could have come about if the Constitution Ireland got was not capable of being amended in Ireland. And so long as the Constitution had that power of self-amendment at home, it should not matter that it was from Britain Ireland got it.

. . . and yet, and yet a British Constitution

The Constitution of 1922, it might confidently be concluded, was the most powerful Constitution in Commonwealth countries. It was ahead of other Commonwealth Constitutions in several respects – the popular sovereignty it admitted, the Westminster supremacy it negated, the royal veto power it denied, the limited latitude it allowed the Governor General, the restrictions it imposed on appeals to the Judicial Committee of the Privy Council, and, above all, the power of self-amendment it enjoyed.

But there was still another area in which the Constitution scored – the plane to which, through subjection to the Treaty, it elevated the Treaty and imparted to that instrument the power of bringing about a coequality of Ireland and the Dominions with the United Kingdom itself. In so doing it brought about nothing less than a confederation between Ireland and Britain, which is what Arthur Griffith said the Treaty had achieved for Ireland and which is what Thomas Davis had sincerely willed for Ireland. The Treaty, being infused with so special a Constitution, was, in the words of Chief Justice Hugh Kennedy, "the whole basis and framework of what may be called the External Constitution of the Free State" (*In re Reade*, [1927] *Irish Reports* 31, pp. 47-51). Such an External Constitution, that permitted the Republican Internal Constitution of 1919 to survive, contained, said Kennedy, "the constitutional status and relationships assumed by Saorstat Eireann upon enter-

10 Although by amendment of Article 51 (Amendment No. 27) Ireland became independent in external affairs, her independence in this area was theoretically not quite so complete as that effected by South Africa more than two years earlier where, by providing for an override of a refusal by the King to cooperate (similar to the American Congressional override of a Presidential veto), the complete exercise of royal power in external affairs was vested in the South African Government. In late 1936 Ireland could have asserted the same authority and yet, because of the South African constitutional development, stayed within the terms of the Treaty.

ing as a political unit, under the Treaty of 1921, into the Community of Nations known as the British Commonwealth of Nations as one equal member thereof." (*The State (Ryan and Others)* v. *Lennon and Others*, [1935] *Irish Reports* 74, p. 206; see also Appendix 14, *Supplement*, for a report of the learned Justice's discussion of this all-important consideration of the Treaty.)

The reason the Treaty effected a confederation between Britain and Ireland was that, although the instrument recognized a ***secession*** of Ireland from the United Kingdom, it did not acknowledge a ***cession*** on Britain's part and so did not designate Ireland a foreign country. This arrangement was arrived at by retaining Ireland (howbeit against Ireland's will) within the Celto-British Commonwealth. The agreement governing such an arrangement was in marked contrast with the way the United States' departure from the Commonwealth was effected. In the Treaty of Paris of 1783 there was, as Judge Singleton stated in a British law case, a "cession of territory by the Crown to the United States." The "Definitive Treaty between Great Britain and the Thirteen United States of America" recognized the American States "to be free, sovereign, and independent states; that he [the King] treats with them as such, and for himself, his heirs and successors, relinquishes all claims to the government, propriety, and territorial rights of the same, and every part thereof." (See *Murray* v. *Parkes*, [1942] 2 K.B. 123, p. 128; All England Law Reports Annotated, [1942] 558, p. 563.) But the Irish Treaty contained no such cession. In the wake of that kind of Treaty there followed, as might be expected, a Constitution that was confederal (and hence sovereign) too.

But for all the Irish Constitution's sovereignty, amendability and Commonwealth respectability, it remained branded with one major flaw – its pedigree. As long as it was a Constitution, whether amendable or not, that had been ***promulgated*** by the British Crown, it was a British Monarchical and Imperial Constitution. It did not matter that the Constitution had been originally devised in Ireland, that the Constituent Act containing it had been enacted by an Irish Constituent Assembly, that it contained spectacular assertions of Irish national sovereignty – as long as it was promulgated by Britain it was a British Constitution. When the Constituent Assembly came to examine the Article of promulgation in the Constitution, Article 83, George Gavan Duffy strove gallantly to avert the inexorable danger. He pointed out that the words of the Article as they stood were a surrender of the whole national stand. "Are we taking the position," he asked, "that the foundation of our authority lies in a British Act of Parliament?" (It was not from "a British Act of Parliament" that the Irish Constitution would be derived, of course, and this would have had to be Gavan Duffy's way of referring to the ratification of the instrument by the British Monarch, the Order in Council of promulgation.)

Perhaps it was not clear to all concerned the effect promulgation would have on the Constitution, but to have allowed the Irish Constitution to be promulgated by the King of England was nothing short of a national disaster for the Republic. For it is a fundamental principle of jurisprudence that the promulgation of a positive law is of the very essence of that law. In other words, a positive law is not a law unless and until it is promulgated. The Irish Constitution, then, was not a Constitution – no matter whether it was passed, adopted, or enacted by the Constituent Assembly of the Dail (anymore than it was passed, adopted, or enacted by the Parliament of Westminster) – unless and until it was a promulgated in accordance with the decree it laid down for itself, that is, by the King of England himself. "The very fact that the Constitution was brought into operation not by an Act of the British Parliament, as were the Dominion Constitutions," wrote Leo Kohn (p. 89), "but by a Proclamation prescribed in the body of the Irish Statute, would seem to indicate that it is from the latter that the legal authority of the Constitution is basically derived."

Article 83 – the last Article of the Constitution – stipulated: "The passing and adoption of this Constitution by the Constituent Assembly and the British Parliament shall be announced as soon as may be, and not later than the sixth day of December, Nineteen hundred and twenty-two, by Proclamation of His Majesty ***and this Constitution shall come into operation on the issue of such Proclamation***" (*italics ours*). The Constitution would come into force only upon the issue of the Proclamation of the King. Without such promulgation the Constitution would be absolutely devoid of all force and effect. It would be merely a Constituent Act that contained a budding Constitution. It would not be a consummated Constitution.

The British themselves were cognizant of this basic principle of jurisprudence. Interpreting the Article of the Constitution in question and applying the principle to the Irish situation, the Judicial Committee of the Privy Council issued a ruling (in *Moore* v. *Attorney-General for the Irish Free State*, [1935] A.C. 484, p. 497; [1935] *Irish Reports* 472, p. 485) to the effect that the Constitution of the Free State established that it, the Constitution, "should come into operation upon being proclaimed by His Majesty, as was done on December 6, 1922. The action of the [Irish] House of Parliament was thereby ratified; apart from such ratification that body had no authority to make a Constitution." (Although the main argument of the Case was that the Irish Constitution derived its validity from a British Act of Parliament, the reference here to ratification cannot be taken as having been used by the Court directly in support of that argument. The reference, as 'an argument within an argument,' is specific of the proclamation by the King of the Constitution proper on December 6th of 1922, not to his assent given the embodying Act on December 5th. As such the reference concerns itself exclusively with the action of the British Monarch in fulfilling the prescription of the Constitution's Article 83. See also the quotation from Kohn above.)

The decision of the Privy Council can with extreme difficulty be disagreed with in view of the basic principle in law that it is the promulgation of a law that makes a law to be a law. The King promulgated the Irish Constitution and made that charter to be law as the Constitution itself said would be the way. If the Constitution had not made itself dependent on the Royal Proclamation for coming into force, then perhaps a case might be made (as there has been) for the Constitution to have derived its validity from the will of the Irish people as expressed by their Deputies in the Dail through the Constituent Act alone. But the fact remains that in that Constituent Act the Constitution did say that it would be promulgated only by an act of Proclamation of His Majesty. The Constitution was, then, amendable though it may have been, signed, sealed and delivered to Ireland as a British, Monarchical and Imperial Constitution.

The royal promulgation that interrupted Dail continuity

The manner in which the Royal Assent was given to the Constitution Act and in which the Royal Proclamation of the Constitution was issued was reported briefly and without fanfare in the press of December 6 and 7, 1922. The Lord Chancellor took his seat on the Woolsack in the House of Lords, we are told, at a quarter past 4 o'clock on the afternoon of the 5th. Discussion on reform of the House followed. Shortly before 6 o'clock a Royal Commission meeting was held in the House for the purpose of declaring the Royal Assent to the Irish Free State Constitution Act. This Royal Assent also ratified the Treaty, which, like the Constitution itself, was scheduled to this Act.

"The Lords Commissioners, who wore their scarlet and white robes, and sat on a bench beneath the Throne, were the Lord Chancellor, Viscount Novar (Secretary for Scotland), and Lord Somerreyton (Lord in Waiting). Among the few peers to be seen on the benches were Viscount FitzAlan (Lord Lieutenant of Ireland), the Earl of Denbigh, and Lord MacDonnell. The Speaker came in response to the summons of Black Rod, and standing at the Bar with him were Mr. Bonar Law, Mr. Lloyd George, Mr. T.P. O'Connor, Sir J. Simon, and other members. The Royal Assent was given in the usual form. The title of [the] Act was read by the Clerk of the Crown, and the Clerk of the Parliaments gave the King's answer in Norman French – *Le roy le veult*. Mr. J. Jones, Labour member for Silvertown, who was in the group at the Bar, called out: 'God save Ireland.'

"The House adjourned at five minutes past 6 o'clock." (London *Times*, December 6, 1922.)

On December 6th "the King held a Council at Buckingham Palace, at which he signed the Proclamation declaring the passing and adoption of the Irish Free State Constitution by the British Parliament and the Irish Provisional Parliament," the press of December 7, 1922, reported.

It is not clear from the first of these reports that the King was not assenting to the Constituent Act that was passed in the Irish Parliament as well as to its counterpart the Constitution Act that was passed in the British Parliament. The Irish Act was probably not included in the assent, however, because the Act was an *Act* of an independent Assembly that was recognized as such by Britain. But with regard to promulgation of the ***Constitution***, the announcement of the Royal Proclamation left no doubt that the Irish Act was involved in that. The official announcement of the ratification distinctly stated that it was the Proclamation of the Irish Free State Constitution as passed and adopted by the Dublin Constituent Assembly as well as by the London Parliament that the King had signed and issued. So that it does not seem to have mattered, as far as Britishness was concerned, that the Constituent Act was not assented to by the King but that its Constitution was proclaimed by him. In that case, the passing and adopting of the Constitution in the Irish Assembly would have availed nothing – in a legal or statutory sense – except that such passage had the advantage of having the document improved as it was processed through the House. All the statutory passing *per se* – as opposed to the drafting and revising – of the Constitution through the Dail and the clothing of it in a Constituent Act gave the impression that the end result was going to be a Constitution and that it was going to be an ***Irish*** Constitution. But the fact remained that it was the King of England that was to promulgate it.

The following is the text of King George V's Proclamation, dated December 6, 1922, declaring "that the Constitution of the Irish Free State has been passed and adopted [by, as Article 83 prescribed, the Irish Constituent Assembly and] by the British Parliament and bringing that Constitution into operation" (1922; S.R. & O. No. 1353).

BY THE KING

GEORGE R.I.

[The King's signature]

A PROCLAMATION

> Whereas the House of the Parliament constituted pursuant to the Irish Free State (Agreement) Act, 1922, sitting as a Constituent Assembly for the settlement of the Constitution of the Irish Free State, have passed a Measure (hereinafter referred to as "the Constituent Act" [the Irish Free State (Saorstat Eireann) Constitution Act, 1922]) whereby the Constitution appearing as the First Schedule to the Constituent Act is declared to be the Constitution of the Irish Free State:
>
> And whereas by the Constituent Act the said Constitution is made subject to the following provisions, namely: –
>
> [There follows a recital of the 'Repugnancy Clause' of the Irish Constituent Act.]
>
> And whereas by Article 83 of the said Constitution it is provided that the passing and adoption of the said Constitution by the Constituent Assembly and Parliament shall be announced as soon as may be, and not later than the Sixth day of December, 1922, by Our Royal Proclamation:
>
> And whereas by the Irish Free State Constitution Act, 1922 [British], it is enacted that the said Constitution shall, subject to the provisions to which the same is by the Constituent Act so made subject as aforesaid, be the Constitution of the Irish Free State, and shall come into

> operation on the same being proclaimed by Us in accordance with the said Article 83 of the said Constitution:
>
> Now, therefore, We, to the intent that the said Constitution shall come into operation forthwith, do hereby announce and proclaim that the Constitution of the Irish Free State as the same was passed and adopted by the said Constituent Assembly has been passed and adopted by Parliament.
>
> Given at Our Court at Buckingham Palace, this Sixth
> day of December, in the year of our Lord
> One thousand nine hundred, and twenty-two,
> and in the Thirteenth year of Our Reign.
>
> [The King's initials]
>
> God save the King.
>
> Published by authority in the *London Gazette*, No. 32775, December 8, 1922; also published in *Iris Oifigiuil*, December 6, 1922.

There is no denying the thoroughly British origin and character of the Irish Constitution of 1922. And there is no escaping the fact that installation of a British Constitution in Ireland irrevocably interrupted continuity with the Republican past. The only way out of this imbroglio might be to hold that under the 'Dual Monarchy' system which enactment of the Saorstat Eireann Constitution would have set up on October 25, 1922, the King was made a creation of the Constitution (by virtue of Article 12), that he was no longer the Absolute Monarch of Ireland he was under the Union of 1800, and that when he engaged in the act of promulgation it was in his capacity of 'Constitutional Monarch' and 'Executive Head' of the Free State of All Ireland that he assented to and promulgated the Irish Constitution.

This line of argument was taken by some authors, in particular by E.J. Phelan in an article entitled "The Sovereignty of the Irish Free State" (in *The Review of Nations*, published in Geneva) and by Darrell Figgis in his otherwise fine work, *The Irish Constitution Explained* (pp. 17-18). But it is a weak and wishful thinking line of argument. It assumes three things: (1) that the Constitution had been in force before it was promulgated (a contention that is contradicted by the Constitution itself, in Article 83); (2) that the sovereign Irish people conferred the Constitution on themselves, which was not the case (stout assertions of popular sovereignty were indeed made, but the Constitution was conferred, as we have seen, by Royal Proclamation); and (3) that the King would be committed or even sworn to uphold the Constitution, which was not at all the case (the contrary was, in fact, true: under Article 17 an oath of allegiance had to be taken to the King).

The fact is that before the Irish Constitution was adopted and promulgated (on December 5 and 6, 1922) the British Crown was not in any way erected into a Dual Monarchy – not by a Republican constitutionalism, because to Republicanism the British King was a foreign King; and not by Anglo-Irish constitutionalism, because the Treaty Settlement was not as yet complete. The new Constitution, although enacted by the Constituent Assembly of the Dail (on October 25, 1922), could not, did not, make the King of England a Dual Monarch, a Constitutional Monarch, or any other kind of Monarch. It lacked the power to perform such a feat as change the status of a ruling Monarch, and to constitute anything in fact it would have had to wait until it was brought into force – by the British King no less, as the Constitution itself had precisely prescribed.

The situation prior to promulgation was that the Free State of Ireland would, by virtue of the entire Treaty Settlement – the Treaty itself and the Constitution which interpreted and implemented it – have become a duly constituted member of the then constitutionally organized Commonwealth as soon as the Treaty would be ratified by Britain (which it was on December 6th). The Constitution in its first Article characteristically went beyond the definition of Irish constitutional status that the Treaty contained, and in stating that Ireland should be a coequal member (with Britain and the other countries) of the Commonwealth the Constitution that was so Republican in substance virtually declared the Dominions to be sovereign nations in partnership with Ireland and with Britain herself and paved the way for the Statute of Westminster of ten years later. This major development was a technicality that would at the moment of proclamation of the Irish Constitution ***begin*** to change the relationship of the King towards Ireland. But until such time as the Treaty was ratified (as per its Article 18) and the Constitution promulgated (as per its Article 83), the King would be recognized in Ireland as the kind of Monarch he theretofore had been under the Union of 1800: 'King of the United Kingdom of Great Britain and Ireland and of the

British Dominions beyond the Seas.'[11] And it was in that capacity that he consummated enactment of the Irish Constitution.

However, as we said, by the same stroke of the pen as he promulgated the Constitution and destroyed the form of kingship he had enjoyed until then in Ireland the King incipiently made himself Dual Monarch of Britain and Ireland. In fact, he began from this moment to make himself 'Multiple Monarch' of Commonwealth countries, although he was not yet fully such because he was not sworn to uphold the Constitutions of those countries. Up until then the Dominions shared a common single King with England, but this situation was not acceptable to Ireland. By virtue of the Free State status Ireland enjoyed under the Treaty Settlement the British Crown could enter into a Multiple Monarchy relationship with Ireland, however, and this it could do before it could do so with the Dominions beyond the Seas or even with Britain herself. It was the King's act of promulgation of the Irish Constitution, in fact, that led to the formal institution some years later of the 'Divisible Monarchy' – the 'sevenfold monarchy' of Kohn – whereby the King was individually to become King of the United Kingdom, Canada, Newfoundland, Ireland, Australia, New Zealand and South Africa. The Commonwealth Conferences of 1926 and 1930, in defining the constitutional status that Commonwealth countries had reached at that time, divided the British Crown into seven separate entities and settled the relationship the member states would thenceforth have individually towards the King. In 1931 the status and relationship were fully clarified and equalized for all Commonwealth countries, Britain included.

The argument that the British King somehow became Constitutional Monarch of Ireland *before* the proclamation of the Constitution is an argument that was undertaken in an attempt to demonstrate that, if the King could be shown to be a Constitutional King of Ireland, then his promulgation of the Constitution would not have made that charter a British Constitution but an Irish-derived one and would not have interrupted Republican con-

11 In May 1927, in deference to Irish susceptibilities, the official title of the King of England was changed to 'George V, by the Grace of God, of Great Britain, Ireland, and the British Dominions beyond the Seas, King, Defender of the Faith, Emperor of India.' By 1936 the form became 'George VI, by the Grace of God, of the United Kingdom of Great Britain and Northern Ireland and of the British Dominions beyond the Seas, King, Defender of the Faith, [and until 1948] Emperor of India.' This latter form was as the title was intended by Parliament to be already in 1927 and before the King changed it to reflect more closely the true Irish situation.

tinuity. But the King did not – could not – beat his own proclamation. As soon as the ink was dry on the parchment, but no sooner, the King had by his action begun to become a sort of Commonwealth King and functional Monarch of Ireland. As Leo Kohn put it, "the monarchical head of the Association into which the Free State had entered had, under the terms of the Treaty, to be introduced into the framework of the Constitution, but it was as a functionary of the Irish people that he appeared therein, almost as the permanent President of an Irish Republic. There is a King; there is no Royal Prerogative" (p. 114). The King as Commonwealth Head ***might*** have become a creation of the Irish Constitution, but he did not – because the Constitution wasn't created yet, by the King. By the time he became 'President' of Ireland the harm was done; Republican continuity had been breached. What might have later been done to heal the rupture would have been, in taking full advantage of the Commonwealth constitutional development Ireland shared, to amend the Constitution in its Article of promulgation and make it a totally Irish-derived charter (by declaring it to have actually been promulgated by the Multiple Monarch of the Commonwealth and therefore of the included Irish Free State).

There seems to be no getting away from the fact, then, that the Irish Constitution as the British Constitution it was interrupted continuity of the Dail with its Republican antecedents. "There is no constitutional continuity between the revolutionary Dails and the Free State," wrote Richard Latham (*The Law and the Commonwealth*, p. 536).[12] The manner in which the Canadian Constitution was in recent years enacted and promulgated throws much light on the way the Irish Constitution of 1922 was enacted and

---

12 It has been argued, however, that the King, by promulgating what was at once both a Republican and a New Commonwealth Constitution, and by thus virtually declaring the overseas Dominions sovereign independent nations, *ipso facto* preserved the Irish Republic and Republican continuity – albeit in a very strained form. As already seen, this interpretation postulates the King as President of the Irish Republic, which is incidentally what Kohn claims the unique Irish Constitution actually did. But we are not too eager to accept unqualifiedly this argument at the present – even though supporting evidence is rather strong (e.g. that already at the Treaty negotiations the Irish delegates expressed a willingness to recognize the King as some kind of President of Ireland: see Thomas Jones, *Whitehall Diary*, Vol. III, p. 144). On the other hand, the King *may* have, by the same stroke of the pen as he promulgated a Republican Constitution, made himself 'President' of the Irish Republic, just as King Edward VIII did, by signing His Majesty's Declaration of Abdication Act, 1936 as King of England, cause himself *ipso facto* to be something other than that same King.

promulgated. The Canadian was enacted as a British Act of Parliament (in the Canada Act 1982) and is in fact called 'the Constitution *Act*, 1982' rather than 'the Constitution.' The Irish was enacted within an Irish Act of Dail Eireann, despite which it was called by Britain 'the Constitution' and never referred to as 'the Constituent Act.' This was because the embodying Act was not enacted by Westminster: it was merely scheduled as the Irish Act it was to a British Act, the I.F.S. Constitution Act, 1922.

But, although the Constitution of the Free State was enacted independently of Westminster, it was promulgated no more independently than was that of Canada. In their actual promulgations, in fact, the Canadian and Irish Constitutions do not differ from each other at all (from the point of view of imparted validity). The Canadian *Act* (which was enacted in the Westminster Parliament because the British North America Act could not be amended in the Ottawa Parliament) was promulgated by the Queen as Queen of the United Kingdom, Canada, etc., while the Irish ***Constitution*** (which was enacted in the Dublin Dail existing as a recognized independent Constituent Assembly) was promulgated by the King as King of the United Kingdom of Great Britain and Ireland, etc. The Irish charter was thereby made no less British than was the Canadian, its prior Irish enactment making no difference at all. As far as promulgation was concerned, there is no difference between the two Constitutions whatsoever (from the point of view of imparted validity). To this, alas, they had been 'fated' by the prescriptions in their respective Constitution texts.

Article 83 of the Irish Constitution, the Article governing promulgation, has its counterpart in Section 58 of the Canadian Constitution. Section 58 states: "Subject to section 59 [which concerns the date when recognition of minority language educational rights is to commence], this Act shall come into force on a day to be fixed by proclamation issued by the Queen or the Governor General under the Great Seal of Canada." The Irish Constitution's Article 83 had used similar language: "The passing and adoption of this Constitution . . . shall be announced . . . not later than the sixth day of December, Nineteen hundred and twenty-two, by Proclamation of His Majesty, and this Constitution shall come into operation on the issue of such Proclamation."

The Proclamation mentioned in Section 58 was duly issued by the Queen of England and the Constitution of Canada was accordingly brought into force on the appointed day. The Proclamation was signed by the Queen, the Prime Minister, the Attorney-

General and the Registrar-General. The initial address and other parts of the Proclamation of interest in the Irish historical context read as follows:

ELIZABETH THE SECOND

by the Grace of God of the United Kingdom, Canada and Her other Realms and Territories Queen, Head of the Commonwealth, Defender of the Faith.[13]

To All To Whom these Presents shall come or whom the same may in any way concern.

GREETING:

ELIZABETH R

[The Queen's signature]

A PROCLAMATION

WHEREAS in the past certain amendments to the Constitution of Canada have been made by the Parliament of the United Kingdom at the request and with the consent of Canada;

AND WHEREAS it is in accord with the status of Canada as an independent state that Canadians be able to amend their Constitution in Canada in all respects;

. . . .

AND WHEREAS Section 58 of the Constitution Act, 1982, set out in Schedule B to the Canada Act, provides that the Constitution Act, 1982, shall, subject to Section 59 thereof, come into force on a day to be fixed by proclamation issued under the Great Seal of Canada:

NOW KNOW You that We, by and with the advice of Our Privy Council for Canada, do by this our Proclama-

13 Since 1953 the Queen's official title in the United Kingdom has been 'Elizabeth II, by the Grace of God of the United Kingdom of Great Britain and Northern Ireland and of Her other Realms and Territories Queen, Head of the Commonwealth, Defender of the Faith.' In the Canadian, Australian and New Zealand versions, the United Kingdom is referred to as in the Proclamation above, that is, as not being necessarily inclusive of Northern Ireland. It was, of course, because of the adoption, in 1952, of the concept of divisible monarchy that the title could be varied as done outside of the United Kingdom.

tion declare that the Constitution Act, 1982, shall, subject to Section 59 thereof, come into force on the Seventeenth day of April, in the Year of Our Lord One Thousand Nine Hundred and Eighty-Two.

OF ALL WHICH Our Loving Subjects and all others whom these Presents may concern are hereby required to take notice and to govern themselves accordingly.

IN TESTIMONY WHEREOF We have caused these Our Letters to be made Patent and the Great Seal of Canada to be hereunto affixed.

At Our City of Ottawa, this Seventeenth day of April in the Year of Our Lord One Thousand Nine Hundred and Eighty-Two and in the Thirty-first Year of Our Reign.

By Her Majesty's Command

[Signatures]

GOD SAVE THE QUEEN

Published in *Canada Weekly*, Volume 10, No. 17 (April 28, 1982), p. 2.

From the foregoing it can be seen that there was at most only a difference of degree, as far as legal status is concerned, between the promulgations of the Irish and Canadian Constitutions. But this would not have been enough for a "mother-country" and ancient European nation like Ireland that asserted its independence based on the principle of national identity. Canada, on the other hand, was an overseas colony populated largely by British citizens and had no national aspirations in former times. Indeed it then aspired to developing no more than having the needs of its inhabitants satisfied in a home-from-home way.

Britain, nevertheless, apart from the condescending way in which she agreed to the Constitution arm of the Treaty Settlement, did not treat Ireland in exactly the same way as she treated Canada or any other of the extra-European Dominions. Back in 1922 Britain regarded Ireland more as a partner with her in the Commonwealth than a Dominion in the usual sense: she certainly did not regard the I.F.S. a 'British Dominion beyond the Seas.' To describe the status Ireland would have in Anglo-Irish constitutionalism, Britain coined the phrase 'Free State,' a term that was borrowed from the name of the South African republic, the Orange Free State. In imparting Free State status to Ireland, she did not, contrary to what might be expected for a Commonwealth member, seek to control the nation's foreign policy, to represent Ireland abroad as a subordinate country, or to subject the nation in any way to the Westminster Government. As a matter of fact, the initial invitation extended by Lloyd George to the Irish Treaty negotiators was, "Come, let us rule the Empire together," and it was the spirit of this generous invitation that inspired and guided the entire course the Treaty and Constitution negotiations took. In this spirit Britain has not to this day regarded Ireland a foreign country (see Appendix 13, *Supplement*), and would gladly, we think, make her a coequal partner in leading the greatest family of interdependent nations the world has ever known.[14]

14 That is, if Britain herself manages to remain in the Commonwealth. American journalist Gene H. Hogberg has warned: "Do not be surprised if, at some future Commonwealth meeting, demands are made to enact sanctions against Britain, complete with threats to expel her from the very organization she founded" ("Britain: Trouble Within and Without!" *The Plain Truth* (Pasadena), Vol. 51, No. 3 (March 1986) pp. 2-4). As regards adoption of the term 'Free State' to describe Ireland, cf. Note 9, this chapter.

Laughing Boy

'Twas on an August morning, all in the morning hours,
I went to take the warming air all in the month of flowers,
And there I saw a maiden and heard her mournful cry,
Oh, what will mend my broken heart, I've lost my Laughing Boy.

So strong, so wide, so brave he was, I'll mourn his loss too sore
When thinking that we'll hear the laugh or springing step no more.
Ah, curse the time, and sad the loss my heart to crucify,
That an Irish son, with a rebel gun, shot down my Laughing Boy.

Oh, had he died by Pearse's side, or in the GPO,
Killed by an English bullet from the rifle of the foe,
Or forcibly fed while Ashe lay in the dungeons of Mountjoy,
I'd have cried with pride at the way he died, my own dear Laughing Boy.

BRENDAN BEHAN
The Hostage

CHAPTER 8

THE CONSTITUTION IS ENCUMBERED BY PARTITION

The Republican Dail Eireann Usurped

The conclusion that so far we have demonstrated as being inescapable – namely, that the Parliament constituted by a British and Imperial Constitution disrupted irrevocably the continuity of the Republican nature of the Third Dail – has been, nevertheless, disputed and disagreed with. This was done by the Free State Supreme Court in 1935 in a decision rendered by Chief Justice Hugh Kennedy, who had been a legal adviser to the Provisional Government and a drafter of the 1922 Constitution. The case was that of *The State (Ryan and Others)* v. *Lennon and Others*, [1935] *Irish Reports* 170, p. 203.

The Court's view was essentially that the validity of the Constitution derived from the Constituent Act of the Dail that approved it. The constitutional theory behind this thinking was that the Constituent Act, in turn, derived its validity from the will of the Irish people as expressed through their mandate given in the General Election and, in turn, through their Deputies in the Dail. We have seen that this will was frustrated completely by the Dail's surrender to Britain on (1) the final form of the Constitution and (2) making the Treaty to be the law of the land and to govern the Constitution. And the Constituent Act, on its part, not only did not produce the kind of Constitution it would have produced if it had not been fettered as it was, but also it produced, as we have seen, a Constitution that needed to be promulgated by a foreign agent to be brought into existence at all.

Since, as we have demonstrated, the Constitution depended essentially for validity on its promulgation (as per Article 83 of the

Constitution itself), we fail to see how the Constitution could at the same time have derived its validity from any Constituent Act. Without royal promulgation the Dail had no authority to enact a Constituent Act that would produce the specific kind of Constitution the Dail's Constituent Act had as object – a Constitution with a provision like that of Article 83 in it. The verdict of the Supreme Court would have had to be conditioned by the will of the many who wished to ignore the Catch-22 nature of Article 83 and were trying desperately to preserve the unpreservable – Republican continuity in the Dail, or at least the appearance of it.

Although Republican-rooted, not a Republican-instituted Constitution

The situation up to 1922-23 was that the Third Dail, sitting as a Constituent Assembly for all Ireland, enacted and adopted on October 25, 1922, the new Irish Constitution which was promulgated by Royal Proclamation on the following December 6th. With the promulgation of the Constitution, the Dail ceased to be a Constituent Assembly – because it had nothing more to constitute – but continued as a Legislative Assembly in a bicameral Parliament. Such a bicameral Parliament was constituted by the new Constitution as an entirely new institution – the Oireachtas – although the Lower House remained composed, of course, of the same elected personnel. (The Oireachtas was actually an outgrowth of the first Irish Constitution, as it had been intended by the First and Second Dails that it should be instituted as soon as practicable.) There was, then, a change from a Constituent to a Legislative Assembly, and from a unicameral to a bicameral Parliament.

Most significantly of all, because of the particular nature of the instrument by which this new Parliament was constituted, the post-Constitution Dail arm of the Oireachtas represented a complete break with its antecedent Pact Dail. In fact, insofar as the newly instituted Dail was forcibly constituted by an alien and objectionable Constitution – a Constitution that was neither requested nor consented to by even the Provisional Parliament, as it should have been if conventional Commonwealth practice had been observed – the new Dail represented a usurpation of the pre-Constitution all-Ireland, Pact Dail, which had been elected for an entirely different purpose. There had taken place, as de Valera put it, a *coup d'etat* of one Assembly by another, even though the later Assembly continued under the name of Third Dail and gave the impression of unbroken continuity from its forerunner.

Usurpation of itself was bad enough, but if it involved the effecting, under foreign pressure, of a 26-county out of a 32-county Dail, then that usurpation was doubly disastrous. If the Dail members bent to the *force majeure* only sufficiently to ensure survival, as had been commonplace in Irish history, but in the process preserved the 32-county Dail (as they were entitled to do under the Treaty), then one might understand. But if they went farther than they needed to – if they did not stick more courageously to the Treaty and the new Constitution, but submitted beyond what both the Treaty and the Constitution required of them – then history would surely condemn them. But history has not condemned them, and is not likely to, because the Irish leaders, if they went too far, did so in a trusting spirit. They trusted in the goodwill of Britain to make the Constitution active again in all of Ireland within a short time. It is true to say, then, that they were eased out rather than forced out of a 32-county Ireland, but the effect was just the same as if they had been ejected more violently and had formally or consciously surrendered.

At any rate, in his judicial opinion Chief Justice Kennedy did not see the Irish Dail leaders as going too far. His opinion read: "The Constitution, or Bunreacht, is the fundamental structure upon which the State was set up by the Third Dail Eireann sitting as a Constituent Assembly. The Dail thereby formulated the system or principles, and created the organs, of Government of the State." Kennedy's opinion failed completely to take into account the fact of promulgation of the Constitution. This, since it was by Royal Proclamation, would be sufficient alone to damn the document. But the opinion also fails to note that the Dail, although sitting as a Constituent Assembly, sat also as a Provisional Parliament (as the Constituent Act itself admits) and acted by virtue of the Westminster Irish Free State (Agreement) Act of 1922, and not exclusively in its capacity of Republican or Pact Dail. Although the Dail, as all-Ireland, Pact Dail, could have amended, or even repudiated, the promulgation Article of the Constitution (as Gavan Duffy wanted it to do), by acting as the creature of the British Free State Agreement Act it usurped the Pact Dail and bowed submissively to British pressure in adopting what was to be, if not essentially a British Act of Parliament, then an Act dependent on a British Royal Order. The opinion of the Kennedy Court, besides, leaves unanswered the questions: Why, if the Constitution was enacted by the Third Dail Eireann, sitting as a Constituent Assembly, on October 25, 1922, was not the Provisional Government disbanded there and then? Why was not legislation, under the Constitution, proceeded with right away? And why did there have to be a wait of six weeks – until December 6th – for the Irish Free State officially to begin?

Trying to put a good face on the situation, a pro-Treaty member of the Dail stated forcibly in the debate on the removal of the oath of allegiance in 1933: "On this side of the House . . . we never pretended that the authority of this Oireachtas was derived from any Act in Westminster. We held that it was derived from the decision of the Irish people of this country." (*Dail Debates*, Vol. 40, col. 727.) We have seen how the decision of the Irish people in electing the Pact Dail was utterly thwarted when it came to proclaiming the Constitution. The well-intentioned but misguided opinion of the Deputy in question brings us face to face with the realities of Article 83. By British proclamation of the Constitution the decision of the Irish people was completely negated and rendered valueless. The question George Gavan Duffy had asked in striving valiantly to stave off an abject surrender to Britain on the central issue of royal promulgation put the reality for all in its starkest terms. Are we taking the position, he had asked, that the foundation of our authority lies in a British Act of Proclamation? Unfortunately, yes. If it were otherwise, there would have been no new Constitution introduced in 1922 at all. Only a British-oriented and, more so, a British-promulgated Constitution was seen capable of fulfilling the Treaty and giving the Oireachtas any authority it would have.

Although non-Republican, not a partition Constitution

The big question, however, and one most pertinent to our thesis, is: In addition to the Constitution of 1922 disrupting the Republican continuity of the Third Dail by being British in origin and Monarchical in nature, as well as by being made subject to the Treaty fundamental law, did it also ***constitute*** the 26 counties as being the area of jurisdiction to which the Constitution was exclusively to apply and the Oireachtas to restrict itself? Fortunately, but surprisingly, the answer can be No. If the Constitution were to have formally delineated the area of Parliamentary jurisdiction, the Irish would have had a very dangerous situation indeed. For then if one were to amend the Constitution in order to correct the situation, one could not have done so without confronting the problem head-on. Fortunately, however, this was not the case. For when the Constitution came into force it did not confine itself to 26 counties of Ireland (which is more than can be said for the present Constitution), but applied to the entire island.

Just as the Irish people had an all-Ireland Constituent Assembly, that had been elected as an all-Ireland Pact Dail, so they had, too, an all-Ireland Constitution that was adopted, enacted, and promulgated *as* an all-Ireland Constitution – all of which was perfectly justified by the Treaty as well and was even dictated by the Treaty. Nobody on either side of the Irish Sea denied that the Irish had instituted the system and organs of Government of an all-Ireland State. That the Irish Free State, in fact, originally comprised all 32 counties of Ireland was as much as vouched for by, as we shall see, the Westminster Interpretation Act of 1978. And as early as 1933 it was held by an Irish lower court that the area of jurisdiction of the Irish Free State as of December 6, 1922, comprehended the whole island of Ireland (*In re Logue*, [1933] *Irish Law Times Reports* 67, p. 253).

The Constitution did not, then, directly or formally delimit the 26-county area of jurisdiction and thereby of itself reinforce partition. But did it perchance do so indirectly or informally? We're afraid the answer has to be Yes. Unfortunately, not only did the Irish allow Republican continuity to be abruptly terminated and a British-originated Dail to take root instead, but they allowed that Dail and its successors to be confined to the 26 counties alone. Where the Irish went off the track was in submitting ***unnecessarily*** to the pressures of London's Irish Free State (Consequential Provisions) Act, an Act that, when taken in combination with the 1923 Consequential Adaptation of Enactments Order, and to the extent that that Order was constitutional, railroaded partition into Ireland and enforced the effect of the 'Ulster option' (to contract out of the Irish Free State) ***before*** the option was actually exercised! How that submission exactly took place was in Ireland's allowing the first I.F.S. General Election, that of August 1923, to be confined to a portion of Ireland, even though the provision of the Constitution governing such elections did not contain that requirement at all. The Article of the Constitution governing elections, Article 81, applied to all Ireland, yet the Republican-boycotted Dail of the day quite needlessly permitted the first General Election to be held in and for the Southern part of Ireland only. In that way, conditioned as the Irish people had been by all of Ireland being treated as if the North had exercised her option already, they allowed themselves to be corralled into 26 counties and thus to be browbeaten into accepting partition.

Article 81 read as follows: "After the date on which this Constitution comes into operation the House of Parliament elected in pursuance of the Irish Free State (Agreement) Act, 1922 (being the Constituent Assembly for the Settlement of this Constitution), may, for a period not exceeding one year from that date, but subject to compliance by the Members thereof with the provisions of Article 17 of this Constitution [the taking of the oath], exercise all the powers and authorities conferred on Dail Eireann by this Constitution, and the first election for Dail Eireann under Articles 26, 27 and 28 hereof shall take place as soon as possible after the expiration of such period."

The Article in its British-revised version is somewhat confused. It assumes that the Constituent Dail was "the House of Parliament elected in pursuance of the Irish Free State (Agreement) Act, 1922," which was not the Irish view: the Assembly was the Dail elected in pursuance of the Collins-de Valera Pact as approved unanimously by the Second Dail Eireann on May 20, 1922.[1] The Article does, however, concede that the body in question was "the Constituent Assembly for the ***Settlement*** of this Constitution" (*italics ours*). Apart from the initial confusion, what the Article says is that the Dail may, for a period of one year from the date on which the Constitution is proclaimed to be in force – which would be to December 6, 1923 – act as the Dail authorized by the Constitution (for 32 counties), and that as soon as possible after the expiration of such period elections must be held for that same Dail Eireann (of, presumably, 32 counties). Whatever elections would be held under the Irish Free State Constitution, whether they might be the General Election of 1923 or later ones, all would as by constitutional right be holdable for a 32-county Dail. But the regrettable fact is that Article 81, affected as it was by the Consequential Provisions Act and Northern Ireland's exercising of the Ulster option, was not interpreted in the strictly legal and favorable sense in which it might have been. There is little doubt but that the Article involved, misread as it was in its contemporary setting, shunted the Irish off to the 26-county sideline and made them

1 The Irish Free State (Agreement) Act even went so far as to 'decree' elections for Ireland in early 1922. But this was not necessary, as the Second Dail decreed them anyway (for a different date, however, which caused the British to scurry to amend their Act).

accept partition in actual practice if not in legal theory. There was no constitutional acceptance of partition on the Irish people's part, there was no *de jure* subjection to it, but there was a *de facto* imposition of it.

The reason we've said above that the Irish people submitted "unnecessarily" to the pressures of the Consequential Provisions Act as coupled with the Consequential Adaptation of Enactments Order is that at the time that these pressures were being exerted, 1922-23, and for a while thereafter, Britain did not claim formally that partition existed, she did not ***specifically*** amend any pre-Treaty legislation (to bring it into line with the supposed post-Treaty condition), and even up to 1927 she was not openly claiming that Northern Ireland was part of the United Kingdom. In 1978 it became clear that the particular pre-Free State enactments which as 'amended' were used in the pressures would have been, even in British law, invalidly and unconstitutionally treated as amended.

It was not the Consequential Provisions Act alone that was responsible for the institution of Irish partition, because that Act only ***optionally*** provided for the 26 counties of Ireland to become a *de facto* Irish Free State. (The Act dealt primarily with Commonwealth constitutional law.) Most constitutional authorities – Quekett, Calvert, Wolf-Phillips and, especially, the latest (fourth) edition of *Halsbury's Statutes of England and Wales* (Vol. 7) – point to the I.F.S. (Consequential Adaptation of Enactments) Order, No. 405 of 1923, as being the initiator of partition and the one enactment most responsible for exerting the pressures. But, strangely, Order No. 405, to the extent that it construed 'Ireland' in the pre-Treaty legislation as now being, in effect, 'Northern Ireland,' was not a valid or constitutional enactment at all, even by British law. This admission was made by Britain in 1978 in the Interpretation Act, which precluded the term 'United Kingdom' in the 1923 Adaptation Order from applying to Ireland, the I.F.S. ***or*** Northern Ireland. (The Order had said, by exclusion, that Northern Ireland belonged to the United Kingdom.)

How the Interpretation Act precluded the United Kingdom from application to Ireland or any part thereof in the years before 1927 was by Schedule 2, paragraph 6 of the Act stating: "Sections 4 (*a*), 9 and 19 (1), and so much of Schedule 1 as defines the following expressions, namely – . . . United Kingdom . . . apply to subordinate legislation [i.e., per Sec. 21 (1), Orders in Council] made at any time before the commencement of this Act [January 1, 1979] as they [the above-referenced Sections and Schedule] apply to Acts passed at that time." Since no Acts of Parliament applied the United Kingdom as defined in this Act to Northern Ireland before April 12, 1927, no Adaptation Orders so applied it either. April 12, 1927, was the earliest date by which the Interpretation Act allowed 'United Kingdom' to be defined as including Northern Ireland (per Schedule 1, *Definitions*, and Schedule 2, Paragraph 4 (1) (*a*)). The Adaptation Order No. 405 was, of course, a 1923 Order and would not, therefore, contain the 'United Kingdom' in the sense in which this term was come to be defined in the Interpretation Act. That is to say, before April 12, 1927, 'United Kingdom' would, by definition, be Great Britain alone (to which limits the Treaty had restored it) and, accordingly, the Interpretation Act would, in this context, render the I.F.S. Adaptation Order of 1923, particularly in Section 2, to be indefinable of Ireland, the Irish Free State or Northern Ireland in any but a Treaty-established sense. In this connection it might be noted also that the Interpretation Act, according to *Halsbury's Annual Abridgment* for 1978 (Para. 2756), so governs the Adaptation Order that it repealed it in almost all but this very point, thus ridding the meddlesome Order of any partition-initiating pretenses it might have had back in 1923.

The Constitution is allowed to be used to compel submission to partition

There is no doubt but that the manifold legislative manipulation of Ireland by Britain, whether wholly or dividedly done, ineluctably imposed partition early on and that the Constitution of Ireland was sufficiently bent to ensure Irish submission to such a fate. But the paradoxical thing is that it was this same Constitution that, if used imaginatively, could have empowered Ireland to fight back and reject partition altogether. The Irish Constitution of 1922 in its British revisions and additions may have been offensive and humiliating, and in its promulgation by Royal Proclamation may even have been devastating to the Irish, but the indisputable fact about it remains that it was an all-Ireland Constitution. That was the one redeeming feature of an otherwise unacceptable national charter. It would appear, then, that the way to prevent it from being used as a vehicle for indirectly imposing partition would have been to amend it appropriately and to preserve for it its original field of jurisdiction. Such amendment could have quite easily been induced and would not have involved a head-on confrontation with the essential problem, because the Constitution in any of its provisions did not directly impose partition. All the Dail would have had to do would have been, already in 1922, to invoke the prevalent Commonwealth convention of denying the right of the Imperial Parliament to legislate for a Dominion or Free State without the latter's consent or to dictate to it which Articles of a Constitution it should adopt and which it should not. But the Dail, unfortunately and unnecessarily, applied Article 81 in all its contemporary context, wherein lurked provision for the Ulster option to work in time against the Dail itself and to reduce its jurisdiction to 26 counties of Ireland.

However, all need not have been lost. The Dail could have remedied the situation some years later. It could have amended Article 81 retroactively to state that the elections for Dail Eireann therein stated, and all subsequent elections, should be held for Dail Eireann in its all-Ireland jurisdiction. The fact that elections would not be allowed to extend to Northern Ireland in practice would only serve to highlight the injustice of partition.

The greatest and most ironic aspect of the tragedy of the 1922 Constitution was, however, that the situation could have been remedied with regard to Article 83 also but was not. Given the great advantage of the possibility of amendment at all, the entire Constitution could have been made self-derived. All that would have been necessary to do would be to amend the Article in question to make the Constitution to be Irish-promulgated and so to be a wholly Irish Constitution. If the Dail had done that, the Kennedy Supreme Court decision (*The State* v. *Lennon*) would have been wholly correct. "In a written Constitution," Leo Kohn states (*op. cit.*, p. 251), "the provisions governing its amendment constitute the acid test of its legal status" – if that power is used.

The Irish failed, inexplicably, to do for their Constitution what South Africa, for example, did for its Constitution. That country, by its Status of the Union Act of 1934, made its Constitution of 1909 to be self-derived. In quite firm though unprovocative language, the Preamble to the 1934 Act laid it all out clear. "And whereas it is expedient that the status of the Union of South Africa as a sovereign independent state as hereinbefore defined [namely, that Great Britain and the Dominions are autonomous communities within the British Commonwealth, that they are equal in status with one another and masters in their own house, and that they are all united by a common allegiance to the Crown and freely associated as Commonwealth Members] shall be adopted and declared by the Parliament of the Union and that the South Africa

Act 1909 (9. Edw. 7. c. 9) be amended accordingly." Section 2 of the Act declared the Parliament of South Africa to be "the sovereign legislative power in and over the Union" of South Africa and Section 3 provided that the Statute of Westminster "shall be deemed to be an Act of the Parliament of the Union, and shall be construed accordingly." By such subtle revolutionary moves was it made possible to establish a native root of title for a South African Constitution by either reenacting in Parliament the 1909 South Africa Act or submitting it to the people in a referendum on the authority of the Parliament. (See *Seanad Debates*, Vol. 19, cols. 1052-1054; also Latham, *The Law and the Commonwealth*, pp. 530-534; Wheare, *Constitutional Structure*, p. 110; and Alfred LeRoy Burt, *The Evolution of the British Empire and Commonwealth, From the American Revolution*, p. 765.) The Irish could have very easily followed South Africa's lead, and given themselves an all-Irish Constitution for all of Ireland. Instead they chose humbly to operate from within their confined, 26-county area and to adopt a wholly new Constitution for that area with a weak ***claim*** only to the six northeastern counties (a claim that at best is merely a pious hope and at worst is a case of irredentism).

If by the Treaty (in Article 1) Ireland was bound to observe the status of South Africa as one of the Commonwealth models, then already by 1934 it was a sovereign and independent State, since that is what South Africa declared itself to be in the Preamble to its new Constitution. Certainly by 1936, with the purging of the King from the Constitution and the erecting of the country into an externally associated republic, Ireland was just such a sovereign and independent State, yet "within the terms of the Scheduled Treaty." The Irish wanted more than that, however. But they ended up with less. In declaring their country to be "a sovereign, independent, democratic state" (but not a "republic"), as they did by Article 5 of the de Valera Constitution in 1937, they made Ireland, as was pointed out by Keith, no more sovereign and independent than it had been already 12 months before. And to compound their mistake they repealed (by Article 48) the 32-county Irish Free State Constitution in 26 counties of the land.

CHAPTER 9

IRELAND'S JURISDICTION IS SUSPENDED IN SIX COUNTIES

The Ulster Option

It will be remembered that in the Treaty negotiations the Irish delegation insisted, and the British agreed, that the Treaty should be stretched to include the area called 'Northern Ireland' in the Partition Act as an integral part of the Irish Free State and in this way to nullify the hated and unwanted partition. (The Treaty was intended, in fact, to supersede the Partition Act, and was concluded with Dail Eireann representing the whole of Ireland.) At the same time the British insisted, and the Irish negotiators conditionally agreed, ostensibly that Northern Ireland should not be bound to remain in the Free State if the Parliament in Belfast so chose – provided that if it did choose to opt out its action would be subject to the workings of a Boundary Commission later to be held.[1]

The Irish delegation's condition was that this proposal be signified as being acceptable to the Northerners before the Treaty would be signed. This condition was agreed to by the British negotiators, and presumably the proposal involved was acceptable to the Craig Government in Ireland, too, for the Treaty was gone ahead with and signed at the insistence of Lloyd George (who had been in communication with Belfast and held an unconditional

1 The Irish had no problem with the British demand in a 'people' sense, because of Ireland's longstanding policy of noncoercion of the Ulster Anglo-Irish community. At the same time, they had a problem with a territorial partition of their land. Hence the compromising on a Boundary Commission to delineate communal jurisdictions.

conference with Craig 10 days before the Treaty was signed). It turned out eventually that the Northern Parliament had, in fact, accepted the proposal – had, in fact, accepted the entire Treaty – *and* the all-Ireland Constitution – because on the day after that these instruments were ratified in the I.F.S. Constitution Act, both the Senate and the Commons in Belfast agreed unanimously to exercise their option of contracting out of the Free State. (By the terms of the Treaty, Parliament was to signify its mind within one month of ratification.) The option was exercised in the form of "an Humble Address" contained in a memorial to King George V which in the Commons had been resolved *nemine contradicente* "as followeth":

> *MOST GRACIOUS SOVEREIGN*,
>
> We, your Majesty's most dutiful and loyal subjects, the [Senators and] Commons of Northern Ireland in Parliament assembled, having learnt of the passing of the Irish Free State Constitution Act, 1922, being an Act of Parliament for the ratification of the Articles of Agreement for a Treaty between Great Britain and Ireland, do, by this humble Address, pray your Majesty that the powers of the Parliament and Government of the Irish Free State shall no longer extend to Northern Ireland.

In the Senate the same had been agreed to *nemine dissentiente*. The account of the contracting out by the Northern Parliament was reported officially in the Northern Ireland *Parliamentary Debates,* House of Commons, Volume 2 (1922), columns 1146a-1150, and the Senate, Volume 2 (1922), columns 227-228. It was also reported in the London *Times* of December 7, 1922, in the following manner:

> ULSTER IN THE FREE STATE
>
> Voting-Out To-day
>
> Memorial to the King
>
> Since midnight [of December 6, 1922] Belfast and the Six Counties have been part of the Free State of Ireland.
>
> There has not, one need hardly say, been any visible expression of the fact, and this curiosity of the Constitutional situation will not continue for more than another day at most. At 3 o'clock this afternoon Parliament's sole business will be to exercise the option provided for in the Treaty by which the Northern Parliament, acting

> for the Six Counties area, may vote itself out of the Free State....
>
> The passing of the resolution to adopt an address to the King notifying him of the desire to exercise the Treaty option . . . is regarded as a foregone conclusion, as it is intended that the memorial to the King embodying the address shall be in the hands of Sir James Craig in time for him to leave for London by the night boat [tonight, December 7th].

On December 8th the King got around to treating the Ulster address and in accepting it as he did on that day the Ulster option was consummated. The King's acknowledgment of receipt, reported in the Northern Ireland *Parliamentary Debates,* House of Commons, Volume 2 (1922), column 1191, and the Senate, Volume 2 (1922), columns 279-280, was as follows:

> I have received the Address presented to me by both Houses of the Parliament of Northern Ireland in pursuance of Article 12 of the Articles of Agreement set forth in the Schedule to the Irish Free State (Agreement) Act, 1922, and of Section 5 of the Irish Free State Constitution Act, 1922, and I have caused my Ministers and the Irish Free State Government to be so informed.

The Boundary Commission forfeit that the Ulster option entailed

By exercising the option at their disposition, the Loyalists of northeastern Ireland signified their acceptance of the Treaty terms as these applied to the six counties and bound themselves by the proviso of Article 12 of the Treaty, the whole of which for them was supplementary to and amendatory of their charter, the Government of Ireland Act of 1920 (though it was such in the tenor of the Council of Ireland provision of the 1920 Act). This proviso read: "Provided that if such an address is so presented a Commission consisting of three persons, one to be appointed by the Government of the Irish Free State, one to be appointed by the Government of Northern Ireland, and one who shall be Chairman to be appointed by the British Government, shall determine in accordance with the wishes of the inhabitants, so far as may be compatible with economic and geographic conditions, the boundaries between Northern Ireland and the rest of Ireland, and for the purposes of the Government of Ireland Act, 1920, and of this instrument, the boundary of Northern Ireland shall be such as may be determined by such Commission." No appeal against the

Boundary Commission's decision was contemplated. The boundary "shall be such as may be determined by such Commission," the Treaty had decreed. (See Macardle, *The Irish Republic*, Chapters 57-60.)

De Valera, emulating Abraham Lincoln who on no condition would stand for seccession of the Southern states, was strongly opposed to the possibility of any part of Ireland seceding from the rest. Understanding the Boundary Commission provisions in a partitionist sense, he used to speak about being "up against the realities of Article 12" and directed the full force of his authority against the Ulster option clause as if that were the one Article of the Treaty that thwarted the existence of the Republic, disrupted essential Irish unity, and contradicted the entire tenor of the Treaty insofar as this was contracted with Ireland as a whole.

Yet without that clause, according to British Government spokesmen and particularly Lord Birkenhead ('Galloper' F. E. Smith), the Treaty would never have been signed. But with it, the Treaty could not be accepted by de Valera and Sinn Fein Republicans. This, for them, was the central vitiating clause of the entire Treaty. Michael Collins, though, was convinced by Lloyd George "that the Boundary Commission clause would save Ireland from Partition" (Macardle, p. 583). The pro-Treaty side as a whole, in fact, "vigorously contested the view that the Treaty did mean partition and held, on the contrary, that the Treaty would result in bringing partition to an end." So wrote de Valera himself (in the Preface to Macardle's work), obviously with a great degree of skepticism. Such an outcome as the Treatyites prophesied was certainly an extremely dim prospect back in the 1920's.

But did the prospect need to remain always dim? To answer that question, and to understand the peculiar nature of the Boundary Commission offer, we need to digress briefly into some background considerations of what exactly the Treaty Conference in London achieved.[2] In the relationship of Britain to Ireland under the Treaty, it was not stated that Ireland was to be called a Dominion. All that was said was that the country was to have a status ***not less*** than that of a Dominion (Pakenham, *Peace by Ordeal*, p. 184 paperback). Already, for example, in the counterproposals to the Draft Treaty presented by the Irish

2 Anything other than the sketchiest consideration of what was accomplished by the Treaty would be outside the scope of this work here and in Chapter 3. A full exposition of what was achieved would fittingly constitute the subject of another book, which is, in fact, in preparation.

delegates to the Peace Conference on December 4, 1921, it was stated that the constitutional status of Ireland should in no respect be less than that enjoyed by any of the component States of the Commonwealth. In other words, Dominion status would be settled for, but more was demanded and expected. More, in fact, was achieved. By the terms of the Agreement the Anglo-Irish relationship would be "as nearly as may be" (see Pakenham, p. 195 paperback) the same as the relationship existing between Britain and the overseas Dominions. As regards the latter, their collective foreign policy was, for example, controlled by Westminster. But with Ireland the sovereignty of the London Parliament was not to be upheld. The 'sovereignty' of the Commonwealth Council (in foreign affairs) would instead be recognized, and this was an advancement in Dominion constitutional development that would extend to the entire Commonwealth – thanks to Ireland's Treaty. The sovereignty of the King in Ireland, however, would be maintained – and this symbolism was, of course, irksome if not downright unacceptable to the Irish people, who had their own Republican symbolism. And there were other important differences between the Dominions and Ireland that we have already considered (Chapter 7).

At any rate, contrary to widespread opinion, the Treaty did not impose Dominion status on Ireland, but a unique 'Free State' status, which was something more akin to 'the King, Lords, and Commons' constitutional status of 1782 (the King being, of course, the commonly shared King of England, and the Lords and Commons being, equivalently, the Senate and Dail of Ireland). Under this arrangement, dear to the heart of the early Arthur Griffith, Ireland would actually be a Monarchy (as Canada, Australia, and New Zealand have been since the King became 'divisible'), sharing a common King with Great Britain – and "Master A.G." would, as Michael Collins feared, have succeeded "to turn us all into eighty-twoites." (See Robert Kee, *Ourselves Alone,* p. 25.)

Free State status was, then, something much more than Dominion status. In Commonwealth constitutionalism it was well ahead of the stage of development the then Dominions were at. These, under Irish and South African pressure, were soon to attain absolute equality with one another and with Britain, and the British Monarch became divisible. But Ireland, by the Free State status she enjoyed, was already a coequal partner with Britain. Free State status was one, it was claimed, that virtually preserved the Republic in the Treaty, that preserved it in all but name. (It would have preserved the Republic in name if the word 'Saorstat' had been used in the Treaty, as it was to be in the Constitution, instead of the mistranslation, but etymologically correct, 'Free State.') In any case, it was the externally associated Republic that was argued for in the Treaty negotiations, not the 'isolated Republic,' and when Griffith wrote to de Valera, "I said, 'Provided we came to an agreement on other points, I would accept inclusion in the Empire on the basis of the Free State,' " de Valera did not demur (de Valera-Griffith correspondence, State Paper Office, DE 2/304/1). In fact, de Valera was later to admit himself that there was only "a slight change of form" between his conception of the externally associated Republic (as expressed in 'Document No. 2' and later in the External Relations Act) and the constitutional status that had been achieved by the Treaty. (The difference probably lay in the degree of recognition that was to be accorded the Crown.)

In the broader, Commonwealth context Ireland was recognized under the Treaty as something less than the externally associated Republic that was desired, but something more than a Dominion – a status into which the overseas Dominions were quickly evolving, if they had not already reached it. Ireland was in 1921 recognized as a free and equal partner with Britain over the other nations of the Commonwealth community – as, in other words, a quasi-externally associated self-governing country, sharing with the other Commonwealth members the common bond of allegiance to the British Crown (which for the Commonwealth countries was "the symbol of their free association" and, particularly for Ireland, "a mystic term which . . . in the British Commonwealth simply stood for the power of the people"[3]). Thus by the Treaty, Ireland and Great Britain were the first freely associated 'autonomous communities' that were 'equal in status, in no way subordinate to one another in any aspect of their domestic or external affairs,' as the Balfour Definition was shortly to acknowledge, and together led the way to the fullness of Commonwealth constitutional development that came expressly to be acknowledged in the Statute of Westminster of 1931.

Although the status Ireland in 1921 succeeded to have acknowledged was that of something more than a Dominion, it is true that

3 So said Lloyd George, at the Treaty negotiations (see Thomas Jones, *Whitehall Diary*, Vol. III, p. 207). Compare W.K. Hancock's observation: "Freedom would [only be won] by that familiar transformation of [the Crown] which filled the channels of monarchical authority with the strong current of popular will" (*Survey of British Commonwealth Affairs*, Vol. 3, p. 133).

that status was referred to in the Treaty document by the term 'Dominion.' But it is necessary to understand the sense in which this term is to be interpreted. Duncan Hall has related how Taoiseach John A. Costello informed him that it was only on the understanding that 'Dominion' was to be interpreted and used in its broadest meaning that the Irish Government had agreed to enter into Treaty negotiations as these were going to be conducted. "The Irish leaders, in their discussions in London, negotiated on the basis of a maximum interpretation of Dominion status," wrote Hall, "not the limited interpretations that still coloured British thinking." Furthermore, it had been agreed with de Valera as the Cabinet President that they should do so upon his having been so convinced by South Africa's General Jan Smuts during the latter's pre-Treaty consultations with the Irish Government in Dublin. (See Duncan Hall's *Commonwealth*, pp. 198 ff.)

It might be remembered at this point that it was not so much the constitutional status the Treaty recognized for Ireland that Irish Republicans were opposed to. It was rather the Treaty itself, not as an international Treaty – which it was not allowed to be until 1933 – but as the fundamental law to which it was reduced and made part of the Irish Constitution. The Irish, with their newly declared independent Republic, were not so disposed to accept from Britain the kind of arranging of their Constitution that the British were in the habit of undertaking for the Constitutions of the extra-European Dominions. Republicans were opposed, rightly, to this kind of treatment being dealt them and they particularly resented the Treaty being used as a big stick to keep the Irish in line instead of its proper character of international Agreement being recognized. Dorothy Macardle refers typically to the inaccuracy of the description 'Treaty' given to the Treaty as it was unilaterally applied (*op. cit.*, p. 651 n.). Nevertheless, the British, in putting the Treaty on a par with the Constitution and making it the law of the land, did perhaps no worse than would Americans, who are bound under Article VI of the U.S. Constitution to hold that "all treaties made, or which shall be made, under the authority of the United States shall be the supreme law of the land," though such a provision is, we understand, unique among the world's Constitutions.

Constitutional Republicans were also opposed to the Treaty being used to impose apparent or even symbolic allegiance on them, when strictly it did not. It must also be remembered, however, that the million or so British citizens living in Ireland would on no account have nonallegiance thrust upon them, and if the Treaty were to apply to them, as it did, it would at least have to be made ***capable*** of the interpretation that it made royal allegiance mandatory. As we have seen, the outward expression of this allegiance, the oath, was not mandatory in the ***Treaty***, but was allowed to be understood as being so. It was, of course, made mandatory, *ultra vires*, in the Constitution.[4]

The oath was allowed to be understood to be mandatory for all classes, which by right it was not, of course. For one class of persons, conscientious objectors, the oath was not mandatory (by reason of Article 16 of the Treaty). A strict reading of the Treaty's Article 2, which held that the relationship of the Crown to Ireland should be the same as that between the Crown and Canada, wherein an oath of allegiance existed, would tend to indicate that the oath was without a doubt mandatory on all other classes. During the debate on the removal of the oath, de Valera held that the oath was indeed mandatory per se: "Article II being assumed to imply an imposition of an oath of some kind, Article IV indicated what the form of the oath was to be. It was not to be the form used in Canada; it was to be another form." (*Dail Debates*, Vol. 41, cols. 927 and 1090.)

The difficulty at the Treaty negotiations for Ireland of Empire being gotten over (in the somewhat ambiguous form of an external association with the other States associated internally within the Commonwealth), there remained the all-important problem of allegiance. This, too, might have been overcome were it not mostly for Northern Ireland intransigence. Allegiance could have been changed into 'external recognition,' as was mooted at the Conference, but the British could not yield not only for reasons of their own, but also and mainly because the Ulster Loyalists would have absolutely nothing to do with having to give up their allegiance.

---

4 The curious and ironic thing about the Treaty was that the British were probably not in the position of enforcing it at any time – simply because their document of the Agreement was lost and nowhere to be found! What they had to rely on in their (much delayed) ratification process and periodic threats of enforcement was a reconstructed, discrepant, and unsigned version of the Treaty, which Asquith referred to as 'a book' and Lloyd George 'a copy.' The Treaty that, as the Prime Minister's son tells us, took so much blood, sweat, toil, and tears to achieve, was lost! And it was not to be found for a full twenty years! Upon inventory being taken of Lloyd George's papers, the Treaty turned up folded neatly in a book and tucked away on a shelf. It appears that using important Government documents as book markers had been the Welshman's wont for years, and not even the Treaty escaped being given the same casual treatment.

That is what they feared would happen to them if they were to agree to come under an all-Ireland Parliament and that was the main reason they were so bitterly opposed to coming under any such Parliament. Their only choice, they thought, would be for them to retain the autonomy of the northeastern part of the country, coupled with the partition they had by now pretty well secured, so that they would never have to fear that they would be subjected to nonallegiance.

The Boundary Commission offer that was gambled on all round

At the same time Lloyd George could not see allegiance as being in those days a real problem for the people of Ireland in general. Neither was he in favor of a permanent partition of Ireland. He did not see the sense to legalizing and stereotyping partition just to satisfy an allegiance-nonallegiance opposition. If only the Irish delegates could be induced to make concessions on allegiance. That way the Loyalists might reasonably be expected to accept, if not direct submission to an all-Ireland Parliament, then a formula whereby they could live in a united Ireland and yet enjoy allegiance to their Crown. In other words, a substitute to direct submission to Dublin would have to be provided. That substitute was the Boundary Commission proposal with its implied principle of essential Irish unity. That was something it was thought the Loyalists could not refuse. It was, too, the form in which Lloyd George offered to Griffith an all-Ireland Parliament and Irish unity in exchange for allegiance to the King. (See Macardle, p. 574.) Griffith and his colleagues acquiesced in making this trade-off and essential unity was secured. The Irish delegates could not have driven a harder bargain, because they were pledged not to break off talks on the issue of the Crown, but – if a break were inevitable – to make the break on Ulster, that is, on partition. But this they did not have to do, as it was insisted on with them that the Boundary Commission compromise practically abolished partition.

The possible hitch in the deal for the Irish negotiators was that unless and until a firm commitment were received from Prime Minister Craig to the Boundary Commission proposals to be contained in Article 12 of the Treaty, the Northern Ireland Government could reject the whole idea at any time. Still, there was a chance that the Loyalists, now that they were endowed with their very own Parliament and Government, would (as they were being exhorted by their leaders) "hold their hands" during the Treaty negotiations and possibly even accept the outcome therefrom insofar as that might affect themselves. The Loyalists were, in fact, well disposed towards the negotiations and the likelihood that they would indeed accept the outcome can be derived from a letter that Craig had written to Lloyd George as early as July 29, 1921 (but which was not read to Parliament until September 20, 1921). That letter, with Craig's own comments thereon, is mainly as follows:

> My dear Prime Minister,
>
> Your proposals for an Irish settlement have now been exhaustively examined by my Cabinet and myself. . . .
>
> In order that you may correctly understand the attitude we propose to adopt, it is necessary that I should call to your mind the sacrifices we have so recently made in agreeing to self-government and consenting to the establishment of a Parliament for Northern Ireland. Much against our wish, but in the interests of peace, we accept this as a *final settlement* of the long outstanding difficulty with which Great Britain had been confronted. . . .
>
> In the further interest of peace we therefore respectfully decline to determine, or interfere with, the terms of any settlement between Great Britain and Ireland. It cannot then be said that "Ulster blocks the way.". . .

In a paragraph faintly distrustful of the British Government, a paragraph describing how, as Craig himself explained it, the Northerners "go beyond the Prime Minister of England, beyond the Cabinet, and beyond the Parliament: we go to the British people," the letter continued:

> In adopting this course we rely on the British people, who charged us with the responsibility of undertaking our own Parliamentary institutions to safeguard the ties that bind us to Great Britain and the Empire, to ensure that we are not prejudiced by any terms entered into between them and Mr. de Valera. . . .

That is, that the people of Great Britain, with whom the Treaty Agreement would be made, were charged with the responsibility of ensuring that nothing in that Agreement would be prejudicial to the rights of the Loyalist minority in Ireland.

Then starkly indicating that the Ulsterites were willing to accept any federal-type provisions the Treaty might contain in a united Ireland (such as Articles 14 and 15 were to throw up), the letter concluded:

> Let me assure you that peace is as earnestly desired by my Government and myself as by you, and that we are prepared, when you and the British Government arrive at a satisfactory settlement, to cooperate with Southern Ireland on equal terms (as do American States) for the future welfare of our common country.

Such a reference as this latter to a "common country" showed that the Northern leader and his hearers took the Treaty to be negotiated with all of Ireland and that it was as such, if the Ulsterites were to utilize proposals contained in the instrument, that they would, for that purpose, be accepting it. Commenting on the expression in his letter of Loyalist willingness to accept the Treaty Agreement when concluded, Prime Minister Craig told Parliament: "Once having clearly fixed in our minds this determination to stand aside while the other two [Governments] were endeavoring to come to some settlement – once having come to that decision, we have most loyally adhered to the principles that it lays down. . . . It is sometimes much easier to be in the fighting line than to be lurking far behind, but I feel we would not have been interpreting properly the soul of the Ulster people if, having declined to mix ourselves in any way with the negotiations going on, we had come out in the open and laid down terms or ventured to dictate in any way to the Imperial Government." (N.I. *Parliamentary Debates* (House), Vol. 1 (1921), cols. 48-50.)

The signs were, then, that the Northern Parliament and Government were predisposed to accept the Treaty upon conclusion, and the negotiators could go confidently ahead with the improvisation of provisions that would affect the Loyalists intimately. These provisions, duly called "proposals," would not depend on Belfast's approval for acceptance. Indeed they would not be presented to the North as separate and possibly rejectable items at all, but would be made an integral part of the Treaty which itself would be presented as a package deal. This is what was now being given the all clear in the Northern Parliament, and there is good reason to believe that the ulterior motive Lloyd George had in creating a partitioned Ireland in the first place was to make possible the securing later on of some such positive cooperation from Loyalist Ulster for an agreeable settlement to be reached with Ireland at all (as we shall see further on when we treat the Lloyd Georgian policy of the segmental approach).

But apart from any human sentiment or personal reaction there might be, the Ulsterites had no technical grounds for rejecting anything the Treaty Agreement might contain. The Northern Parliament was not, and could not be, officially invited to accept (or reject) the Boundary Commission proposals – although they were apprised of what was going on – because by its charter (the Government of Ireland Act, 1920) it had no competency to deal with such major or reserved powers items as international treaties (which were reserved to the Westminster Parliament), but only with minor or local powers matters. For that reason representatives of the Northern Government were not invited to attend the Treaty Conference, for example, nor were they invited to be a party to the Treaty Settlement.

Nor could the Northern Parliament, per se, approve (or disapprove) the Treaty itself. Not even was the 'Parliament of Southern Ireland,' by the terms of the Treaty, required to approve (or disapprove) the instrument – only "the members elected to" this 'Parliament' were so required. These convened on January 14, 1922, for the sole purpose of approving the Treaty and establishing the Provisional Government. But the Northern Parliament had no such enabling commission from the Treaty.

Incidentally, the convening of the 'Southern Parliamentary' members was not necessary, because Dail Eireann, with which the Treaty was concluded to begin with, was, as a National Parliament and Government, competent to approve the Treaty for all of Ireland, which it did – barely – on January 7, 1922. But, in order to conform outwardly with British requirements, the Treaty was reapproved, unanimously, the following week mainly by those who had voted for it already.

Although it was out of the realm of competency of the Northern Ireland Parliament to accept or reject any of the Treaty terms, its Ministers were approached by Lloyd George as a courtesy just the same and the Boundary Commission proposals were broached. The British Government, like the Irish, was not inclined, in accordance with longstanding policy, to impose upon the Northerners anything of an unpalatable nature. Nobody wanted to 'coerce Ulster,' as the phrase had it. On November 25, 1921, Lloyd George met the Northern Ireland Prime Minister in a conference free of preconditions, and there the British ruler informed Craig that the Boundary Commission proposals would as a minimum have to go into the Treaty (since prior to this time Craig and his Cabinet had flatly and repeatedly refused to come directly under an all-Ireland Parliament). Although Craig was not, as expected, openly amenable to the idea, technically he was not in a position to refuse to agree with it. His agreeing to confer with Lloyd George and to discuss, as he did, the proposals as Lloyd George had them typed out was as good as assenting to them – just as Griffith's earlier reading of the typed proposals without positively rejecting them was construed as equivalently approving and supporting them.[5]

The Boundary Commission proposals as they had initially been formulated and put down on paper ran as follows: "If Ulster did not see her way to accept immediately the principle of a Parliament of all Ireland – coupled with the retention by the Parliament of Northern Ireland of the powers conferred upon it by the Act of 1920 and such other safeguards as have already been suggested in my letter of the 10th November – we should then propose to create such a Parliament for all Ireland, but to allow Ulster the right within a specified time on an address to the Throne carried in both Houses of the Ulster Parliament, to elect to remain subject to the Imperial Parliament for all the reserved services. In this case she would continue to exercise through her own Parliament all her present rights; she would continue to be represented in the British Parliament and she would continue subject to British taxation, except in so far as already modified by the Act of 1920. In this case, however, it would be necessary to revise the boundary of Northern Ireland. This might be done by a Boundary Commission which would be directed to adjust the line both by inclusion and exclusion so as to make the boundary conform as closely as possible to the wishes of the population." The Prime Minister's proposals have, of course, to be understood in the light of the general tenor of the Treaty as it modifies the 1920 Act.

Craig, no more than Griffith, with the survival of his political career in mind, could outwardly assent to these terms. But there is reason to believe that each man did in his own way indicate his assent to them – although Craig of necessity did so in a subordinate capacity to Griffith, and technically, as we have seen, his assent was not even required. The British Prime Minister had assured Griffith that if these terms were all right with him (Griffith), Lloyd George would put them over formally on the Prime Minister from Ulster. "Lloyd George intimated that this would be

5 The piece of paper on which the boundary proposals were typed out was most unfortunately lost soon after it was shown to Griffith and Craig. However, it luckily turned up in the waning hours of the Treaty Conference after a frantic and comical search through the pockets of all Lloyd George's suits in his clothes closets. It was well that it did turn up, as, deprived of it as an instrument to brandish before Griffith, Lloyd George would not have succeeded to get the Treaty signed in London or assented to in Belfast.

their last word to Ulster," wrote Griffith to de Valera. "If Ulster refused, as he believed she would, he would fight, summon Parliament, appeal to it against Ulster, dissolve, or pass an Act establishing the all-Ireland Parliament." In other words, as Frank Pakenham points out (*Peace by Ordeal*, p. 175 paperback), if Ulster refused, "Lloyd George would proceed without the consent of Ulster to set up an all-Ireland Parliament, option out of which, on Ulster's part, would involve a Boundary Commission delimiting her area." All of which is, in fact, what Lloyd George did – in the Treaty.[6]

At the November 25th unconditional conference with Craig, Lloyd George promised the Northern Ireland Prime Minister to let him have by December 6th at the latest the Boundary Commission proposal drawn up in finalized form in the Treaty and also, according to Dorothy Macardle (p. 607), "to delay the signing of any such Agreement until the Belfast Ministers could be consulted again." It is possible that this latter part of the promise was more an impression Craig gained from Lloyd George's words than an explicit expression on the British Prime Minister's part, because four days later all Craig was claiming in the Ulster Parliament was that "by Tuesday next [December 6th] either negotiations will have broken down or the Prime Minister will send me new proposals for consideration by the Cabinet" (Pakenham, p. 203 paperback). Prime Minister Craig, persisting with the fallacious reasoning, continued to announce: "Now that means that Sinn Fein, fully alive as it is now to our unflinching determination not to go into an all-Ireland Parliament, has either got to say by Tuesday next that she will still work for a settlement or else all negotiations are broken off" (Macardle, p. 574; Northern Ireland *Parliamentary Debates*, (House), Vol. 1 (1921), col. 299; (Senate), Vol. 1 (1921), col. 114.)

Lloyd George, true to his word, did manage to send the finalized Treaty to Craig by December 6th – all fine and signed. A settlement had been reached. Lloyd George had, shall we say, rushed

6 This interpretation coincides with Pakenham's understanding of Lloyd George's pledge. Pakenham states, and we agree, that the context does not render likely the interpretation that if Ulster refused the Boundary Commission offer then the all-Ireland Parliament with no option out would be imposed on her. Such an interpretation is tempting to make, but we cannot understand Lloyd George to mean to do anything more than he actually did in the Treaty. See also John Bowman, *De Valera and the Ulster Question*, pp. 63-64, for an account of that author's understanding of de Valera's acceptance of the Boundary Commission proposal.

things a little at the final stage. He had stated bluntly, according to Winston Churchill, "the British could concede no more and debate no further. The Irish Delegates must settle now. They must sign the agreement for a Treaty or else quit." It had been insisted on all day that Geoffrey Shakespeare "must leave that night for Belfast if Sir James Craig was to know the result of the negotiations in accordance with the Prime Minister's promise" (Pakenham, p. 238 paperback). A train with steam up and a destroyer were held at the ready to speed Shakespeare and the Treaty to Belfast, where they were eagerly awaited. (Shakespeare was decked out in Lloyd George's best fur coat and cheerfully assured that if anything should happen to him he would have a grave in Westminster Abbey.) Before the last night of negotiations would be out Lloyd George would have managed to fire off a bland covering letter to go with the Treaty to Craig. In it the Welshman would faintly explain the option the Northerners would find available to them when the Agreement would be received in Belfast. The choice was between accepting the Northern state as it stood and accepting it as it might not stand, but was to – always, however, as a state that would be temporarily extraterritorial. Lloyd George's letter ran as follows:

> My dear Prime Minister,
>
> I enclose Articles of Agreement for an Irish settlement which have been signed on behalf of HM Government and of the Irish Delegation. You will observe that there are two alternatives between which the Government of Northern Ireland is invited to choose. Under the first, retaining all her existing powers, she will enter the Irish Free State with such additional guarantees as may be arranged in conference. Under the second alternative, she will retain her present powers, but in respect of all matters not already delegated to her will share the rights and obligations of Great Britain. In the latter case, however, we should feel unable to defend the existing boundary, which must be subject to revision on one side and the other by a Boundary Commission under the terms of the Instrument.
>
> Ever sincerely,
>
> [Signed] D. Lloyd George

In other words, there wasn't to be a choice between apples and oranges really, only between apples and apples. That is, between a federal Ireland (directly achieved) and a federal Ireland (indirectly achieved). Such was the choice the Ulsterites were just about to be faced with in no uncertain manner.

Late on the afternoon of December 6th – 'the longest day' – the Treaty packet, sealed and transported in the British destroyer, was delivered to Prime Minister Craig and the Government in Belfast. The blase character of Craig's report of receipt of the as yet unopened packet betrayed the Ulster Government's shocked resignation towards acceptance of the "proposals" they guessed were fatefully signed. The story of the packet's delivery, told – one would have to say – somewhat ceremoniously by Sir James himself in his report to Parliament, was nothing short of a piece of comic opera, and is reproduced below with the hope that the 'gentle reader' can follow the sequence of events therein contained. The report, as found in the Northern Ireland *Parliamentary Debates* (House), Volume 1 (1921), column 428, is as follows:

> In accordance with the principle I have frequently laid down, and which I intend to continue, I think it is only right to inform the House that I received intimation early this morning that a special messenger was proceeding from London with new proposals to be placed before my colleagues and myself. I summoned a meeting of our Cabinet, and we awaited these new proposals practically all morning till the House met. They did not reach me. Since the House has met I have received a message to say that one of His Majesty's vessels has sailed up the Lough and has brought these proposals. I have not yet even broken the seal of the envelope owing to the necessity I felt to be here to-day. I can only say that the Cabinet will now proceed to peruse these new proposals, and we will take what action we think is in the best interests of the people whom we represent, and needless to say this House will be informed at the earliest possible moment consistent with what we consider is the best procedure in the matter of the proposals and of our reply to them. I cannot say any more to-day. This has only just reached me, but I propose to keep the House fully informed of all that takes place.

On the morning of the 7th things were eerily calm in the Northern Ireland Parliament. It was business as usual for the first few hours, and only on the adjournment did Prime Minister Craig proceed to unburden his fellow parliamentarians' minds. With the shock now over and the seal broken on the packet, it could not exactly be said that all hell broke loose when the signatures were verified on the contents. Counseling the continued holding of (one's own) hands and the exercise of the utmost self-restraint, Craig proceeded to explain matters thus (N.I. *Parliamentary Debates* (House), Vol. 1, col. 443):

> First of all, there is ambiguity in the document.[7] (Hon. Members: Hear, hear.) Secondly, there is a considerable amount of further information that we must be placed in possession of before we can come to a right conclusion. (Hon. Members: Hear, hear.) And, thirdly, I do not believe that a settlement and peace will be furthered in any way by rushing at it, or by tumbling over one another at the moment. (Hon. Members: Hear, hear.)

With that exhortation delivered, the Prime Minister effectively placed a gag on any discussion of the document until he had had an opportunity to repair to London and there demand and get an explanation of the implications of the proposals. The burden of his injunctions seemed to be that pending his return all should stand fast, grit their teeth and let the wave wash over them. Privately, nevertheless, Craig and his colleagues were, understandably, taken aback at the settlement – which is not the same as saying that they wished they had been consulted further. But, not practicing what he preached, Craig gave way to outbursts of anger. Chamberlain was called "a coward," and Lloyd George "a mass of corruption." The faithful public, however, was not impressed. It bore the Treaty with a great deal of equanimity. "Most of the Irish on both sides of the Border, and in both communities, accepted it with relief," Paul Johnson tells us (*Ireland: Land of Troubles*, pp. 166-167).

---

7 The "dangerous ambiguity" alleged to exist in the Treaty document was really a false fear on the part of the Ulster Loyalists and the British, since they held that the Treaty could be amended and modified by unilateral legislation (in Westminster, of course). When the Statute of Westminster came around, in 1931, they even thought that that could be repealed by unilateral legislation (this time, in the Dail). Speaking on the Statute as a Bill, Churchill, for example, opined: "I am advised on high technical authority that this Bill confers upon the Irish Free State full legal power to abolish the Irish Treaty at any time when the Irish Legislature may think fit." But Arthur Berriedale Keith quickly pointed out that this contention rested on a confusion between the repeal of an Act and the repudiation of a Treaty, and that the Anglo-Irish Treaty could only be modified or repealed by mutual agreement. (See the political commentator's *Speeches and Documents*, p. 279 n.)

Perhaps the leaders' rejection of the novel instrument could be ascribed alone to public posturing.

The Boundary Commission condition that was logically and legally justified

Over against the Northern reaction, however, it has to be understood that Lloyd George had already secured the substantial agreement of the Ulster Prime Minister and that besides he (Lloyd George) was within his rights in proceeding as he did. He acted within his rights for two reasons: (1) interpretative (of his promise to Craig); (2) constitutional (area of powers within which he acted in terms of the Government of Ireland Act of 1920).

1. ***Interpretative.*** The promise made by Lloyd George to Craig was in the form of a communique they agreed to issue in their respective Parliaments at a fixed time. The Belfast version ran as follows: "By Tuesday next either negotiations will have broken down or the Prime Minister will send me new proposals for consideration by the Cabinet. In the meantime the rights of Ulster will be in no way sacrificed or compromised." (Northern Ireland *Parliamentary Debates*, Vol. 1 (1921), col. 299.)

The promise was fulfilled, because: (*a*) new proposals, albeit signed, were sent; (*b*) the rights of Ulster were not sacrificed or compromised (by the manner in which the proposals were formulated and sent).

(*a*) The new proposals were formulated mainly in Articles 14 and 12 of the Treaty. Article 14, which should be taken together with Article 11, consisted of an offer to Ulster of the possibility of coming ***directly*** under an all-Ireland Parliament. If the Northern Ireland Cabinet should reject that offer, the alternative was to go the route of Article 12 and the Boundary Commission. That meant, in reality, that Northern Ireland should come ***indirectly*** into a united Ireland, but that in that case her border as it existed could not be guaranteed to remain intact. Moreover, Lloyd George strictly did not promise that the proposals he would send would actually be unsigned: it would not be necessary to withhold signature in order to have such proposals considered. He did go so far, on the contrary, as to pledge that the rights of Ulster would not in any way be sacrificed or compromised. He would have thought that that would be sufficient guarantee for the Ulsterites, and to his way of thinking there would be no reason for them to decline the proposals upon consideration of them. The fact that they were already settled and signed in London would in no way inhibit their acceptability in Belfast. Signature was irrelevant.

(*b*) Ulster's rights were not sacrificed or compromised, because, whichever route the Northern Ireland Government chose to go, its basic jurisdictional extent was guaranteed (under either Article of the Treaty) to be preserved either as a state or a communality with a distinct identity of its own in a united Ireland.

Craig, however, did not see things this way. He thought, or wanted to think, that the 1920 Act was permanent, and he hoped against hope that the Act would sooner or later be worked in Ireland and on that basis that a separate Ulster would mean an Ulster within the United Kingdom. But Lloyd George and the British Government had other ideas for Ireland. They were committed to a separated, unitary Irish nation – they had legislated it in their 1914 Home Rule Act – and dividing up the nation was merely Lloyd George's pet approach to a way of disengaging from Ireland without precipitating civil war there or unnecessarily risking the condemnation of his own Unionist-dominated Cabinet or for that matter of the House. Lloyd George, his son tells us, had declared confidently that he would succeed where all his predecessors had failed. The failure of the 1914 Act to achieve its purpose convinced him of the futility of the global approach to the British-Irish disengagement problem. He would try the segmental approach. He would divide Ireland in order to free it and then reunite it – although his colleagues were not so sure.

At any rate, as we know, the Partition Act was intended only as a temporary measure. Lloyd George had intimated as much to Craig when he, Craig, thought that, since the two parts of Ireland were given equal weighting, the country might as well be erected into a two-Dominion island – comparable to the two-nation land masses of the U.S. and Canada on the North American Continent or Spain and Portugal on the Iberian Peninsula. It was clear that Craig had taken the Partition Act out of its proper context altogether. Lloyd George, acting on his intention of treating the 1920 Act purely as a device to divide Ireland in order gradually to unite it, quickly disabused Craig of his perspicacious notions, and let him know clearly what Britain's long-term intentions for Ireland were. On the basis of its commitment to eventual Irish unity, then, the British Government proceeded to conclude with Dail Eireann and the Government of Ireland a Treaty for the whole of Ireland.

This would be an Agreement amending the 1920 Government of Ireland Act and providing for the eventual unification of Ireland.

But Craig persisted in misunderstanding. One reason he could do so and get away with it was that the 1920 Partition Act was of such 'fantastic complexity'[8] that he could latch on to any aspect of it to Northern Ireland's advantage, and his stand could not readily be challenged by the British without their being inconsistent with themselves. He insisted, for example, that the Treaty was concluded between Britain and the representatives of Southern Ireland for Southern Ireland, just as many Northerners then held – and many Anglophilic historians and constitutionalists still hold – that the Second Dail Eireann was but the Dail of Southern Ireland, that the 1920 Act was already so authoritative and effective and valid, in 1921, that it crowded out from the North of Ireland, and confined to the South, all candidates who were not for election to the Northern Ireland Parliament. That is, that the non-Northern Ireland Parliament candidates were, due to the Act, of necessity Southern Ireland Parliament candidates exclusively – a theory that is historically incorrect, as we saw at the outset of this book. The 1920 Act of itself allowed this interpretation – allowed any number of interpretations – but the historical context of the Act demanded quite another.

Craig was one of those who subscribed to this mistaken theory, because he believed, of course, that the Partition Act was sacrosanct and all-powerful – and that it would exclude from the North and bottle up in the South all of Sinn Fein eternally. As a corollary to this, he believed – or gave the impression he believed – that the Treaty negotiations were conducted with and for Southern Ireland alone, and that because the Northerners were not invited to sign the Treaty they were not included in the Treaty! When it came time to receive the signed Treaty he met it with a great deal of alarm and feeling of crisis. "Never before has the situation been so complicated as that which has been created by the signatures attached to what is called a Treaty between the British representatives on the one hand and the Sinn Fein representatives on the other," he complained in the Northern Ireland Parliament on December 12, 1921. Noting that his Government

8 A.J.P. Taylor writes of Lloyd George's Government of Ireland Act: "He devised an arrangement of fantastic complexity. . . : the United Kingdom, united Ireland, a separate Ulster, all mixed together. . . . Most of this ingenuity was dead from the start" (*English History, 1914-1945*, p. 156). Lloyd George redeemed himself, however, with a Treaty not of fantastic complexity.

was not invited to sign the Treaty, he said that "we refused to either interfere with or attempt to determine the terms of any settlement which might be reached between those two parties, but we reserved to ourselves the right to go into conference with British Ministers when Ulster's rights and privileges became affected. On that clear and distinct understanding," Craig stated, "the Prime Minister of England assured me – assured this House by the statement he permitted me to read at this Table – that by last Tuesday either the negotiations would have broken down or that fresh proposals would be submitted, and that, in the meantime, the rights of Ulster would neither be sacrificed nor prejudiced. I think those were the exact words." (Northern Ireland *Parliamentary Debates*, Vol. 1 (1921), col. 543.)

If Craig understood by what he stated – namely, that in the event of the negotiations not breaking down fresh proposals would be submitted for consideration by his Cabinet – if he understood by that, as he wrote to Lloyd George he did (Macardle, p. 607), that Lloyd George had promised "to delay the signing of any such Agreement until the Belfast Ministers could be consulted again," then we can only say that that was a construction he, Craig, put on Lloyd George's words. For our part, we do not read in Lloyd George's promise a pledge to send ***unsigned*** proposals. Either negotiations would have broken down or they would not. If they would, that would be that. If they would not, a settlement would have been reached, and there would have been no new proposals to send! Neither would there be any reason why negotiators as plenipotentiaries should not all sign the old proposals on the spot. (It is true that de Valera, who could sympathize with Craig in his predicament, criticized the Irish Plenipotentiaries for not sticking by their instructions not to sign on their own authority, but the Irish President should have remembered with Elizabeth I that instructions given to generals do, with time, wear thin – and the Treaty negotiators were truly of the general class. Besides, as we saw in Chapter 3, instructions were not really disregarded, but mainly the Irish signed because they were forced to – see Appendix 9, *Supplement*.)

It fell to Austen Chamberlain's lot to explain, mainly for Craig's benefit, how the Belfast Ministers, who were not in London but in Belfast, could not have been consulted before the signatures were appended to the Treaty. He did not explain why the telephone to Belfast was not used. Perhaps it was because of the lateness of the hour. "Sympathising with the indignation of Sir James Craig's party at the signing of the Articles without further conference with them, Austen Chamberlain explained on December 16th: 'To have held up at that last moment for further consultation with Cabinet Ministers, who were not here but were in Belfast, the Articles of Agreement which were then ready for signature and which the Irish Representatives were prepared to sign would have been to jeopardise, and in my opinion to destroy, all chance of an agreement' " (Macardle, pp. 606-607).

2. ***Constitutional.*** To take the second reason Lloyd George acted correctly with Craig, the rights of Ulster were in no way sacrificed or compromised by the proposals as they were submitted to Craig, that is, in the form specifically of Articles 11, 12, 14 and 15 of the Treaty together with signatures. Lloyd George acted within his constitutional rights in having the proposals signed, because these as made, even if they had not been signed, did not hinge on the local jurisdictional powers of the six-county Government, but came, along with the whole Treaty Agreement, within the ambit of the major powers area of Government (especially with reference to the 1920 Act) and could therefore be concluded by representatives of National Governments without prior securement of formal or anything more than substantial agreement from a state Government. It was, in fact, on this basis that Lloyd George had all along intended to proceed. He had made the Unionists an offer of an all-Ireland Parliament, which they refused, and thereupon he offered them the same with option out subject to a Boundary Commission's adjusting the Northern-Southern boundary, as closely as possible in accordance with the wishes of the inhabitants. "If they refused both, nevertheless he would proceed with the second," recounted Austen Chamberlain to Frank Pakenham (Pakenham, p. 177 paperback).

At the actual signing of the Treaty, Lloyd George was more specific about jurisdictional authority. He pointed out that if the Irish did not sign and negotiations broke down Craig would have no proposals to be faced with, but that if he did he could only do one of two things. "He could either accept the Parliament subordinate to Dublin or he could refuse. In the latter case the British would proceed, whether Craig liked it or not, with the Boundary Commission" (Pakenham, p. 232 paperback). Despite intense British pressure, coupled with threats of renewed war, the Irish delegates were prepared at the last minute to break off negotiations pending a commitment by Craig to the Boundary Commission proposals. Griffith, although he was not in a strong position to do so (having indicated his agreement with the proposals already), made one last, valiant effort to give Craig a chance to make his intentions known. But "the British said that, with or without Craig's approval, their Ulster proposal remained" (Macardle, p. 582). With that Collins went to bat for Craig with an effort of his own. But "the Englishmen maintained that, as they were going forward with their Ulster proposal irrespective of Craig, there was no ground for contention here," that Craig's intentions were irrelevant at this stage (Macardle, p. 584). No further approval from Belfast was required.

In formulating the Boundary Commission proposals with Griffith and Craig, Lloyd George acted as he had done on an earlier occasion with Redmond and Carson. He assured the one that the Boundary Commission did not mean partition, while he gave the other to understand, at least in his public self, that it did.[9] If it did not, as we know it did not, then it would not matter much whether the border was to be adjusted somewhat 'by inclusion or exclusion' and one could afford to have all the work of the Boundary Commission itself come to nothing; if, as some were to believe, it did, one could take precautions (by, e.g., a last-minute insertion of the phrase, 'so far as may be compatible with economic and geographic conditions') and go to other pains to ensure that the work of the Commission would come to naught also. Craig, above all people, would have known that Lloyd George did not have partition in mind ever since the British Prime Minister rejected the Northern leader's idea of a two-Dominion Ireland. "Partition on these lines," Lloyd George had written at that time, "the majority of the Irish people will never accept, nor could we conscientiously attempt to enforce it." The 'partition' Lloyd George had in mind was something more in the nature of a provision for gradual and ultimate Irish unity, as had been contained in the Partition Act. By insertion in the Treaty of the Boundary Commission clauses, then, the British Government meant in the only way possible in the

9 For example, in his proposals on the Boundary Commission to Craig, Lloyd George stated that Ulster should be allowed the right "to elect to remain subject to the Imperial Parliament for all the reserved services." If by this the Northerners understood an offer of permanent partition to be made and an assurance that the six-county area would form part of the U.K., we would have to say they were mistaken, because such an interpretation could not be put on the Treaty's provisions, as we shall see in the next chapter. Since the reserved services were restored by the Treaty to Ireland as a whole, Lloyd George's offer could only mean that Britain would for the time being exercise these services or major powers of jurisdiction for Northern Ireland on behalf of the Irish Free State.

circumstances of the time to ensure the essential unity of Ireland in principle, and this was agreed on all round.

To conclude, Ulster's rights were not in the least infringed upon or compromised by Lloyd George's dispatching the signed Treaty in the form in which it was to the Northern Ireland Government. Her rights were not compromised and the Prime Minister had no need to fear, because (1) all Craig had demanded of the Treaty (in an open letter he wrote to Lloyd George during the preliminary negotiations of July 1921) was that it observe "the sanctity of the powers and privileges of the Northern Ireland parliament"; (2) the Dail had conceded, and in fact proposed, to Britain that the six-county state might be preserved, together with any "measure of local autonomy which they might desire" (as de Valera put it), as long as the area was placed under the jurisdiction of Dail Eireann in the major powers area (i.e., as long as partition might not be imposed); (3) the British, for their part, agreed to the Dail's proposals (and Craig's), provided Ireland stayed within the Empire, owed allegiance to the King, yielded naval bases and the use of air bases to Britain, and, finally, agreed to the Ulster option of "states' rights" involving establishment of a Boundary Commission to determine the line of demarcation between the Northern and Southern states; and (4) Ireland, in turn, agreed to these conditions and, with Craig's intentions surmised, the Treaty was ready for signature. Thus, everyone's conditions being met all round, the Treaty was signed and sealed, partition was avoided, and Lord Birkenhead lost his bet with Lloyd George.[10] Ulster quickly enough got over her initial alarm and agreed to the Treaty conditions. She confirmed her agreement by accepting and exercising her option, but she vowed at the same time not to abide by the Treaty lest it somehow cause her to lose the very parliament and privileges it secured to her.

---

10 When the Treaty of Treaties was signed, and it came time to pass out the drinks, Birkenhead, who had laid a bet with Lloyd George to the equivalent of $10,000 that he would imbibe no more before the end of 1921, ordered a scotch and soda.

"What's the matter, Smith?" asked a surprised Prime Minister. "Remember your bet that you wouldn't touch a drop of drink before the year was out, and you have only a few weeks to go."

"I know, I know," protested the Galloper, "but don't you realize we've just signed a Treaty?"

"You may lose your thousand quid," said Lloyd George.

"Make it a double," said F.E.

Three days after the signing of the Treaty, Lloyd George met with Sir James Craig to explain what the Boundary Commission clauses of the Treaty involved. According to Craig's understanding of their discussions, the clauses were intended, in the words of Lloyd George, merely to make "a slight adjustment" of the boundary line so as to bring into Northern Ireland those Loyalists who were now outside that area "and to transfer an equivalent number of those having Sinn Fein sympathies to the area of ***the Irish Free State***" (Macardle, p. 600). Here is the first record of the term "Irish Free State" having been used to refer to the 26 counties of Ireland, a usage that was a distinct departure from the then common practice of using the term in an exclusively *de jure* sense and applying it to all of Ireland. The loose usage could only be justified if, as was going to happen, it were based on a misinterpretation of the Treaty Article 12 and consequently of the entire Treaty. Worse, the peculiar reference adopted was a clear message to Craig that he, too, if he wanted, could give a new twist to Article 12 and read the Treaty wrong.

But Craig was not at all disposed to read the Treaty wrong. Not for him to gamble with the "grave and dangerous ambiguity" of Article 12 and trust to a favorable outcome. He would not exactly be the Orange Card the British took him to be. On the other hand, he was not going to be fazed by the Article's vague and adumbrative language either. Reading through to the main principle involved, Craig had ample reason to feel concerned. Although he knew full well that the Boundary Commission proposals implied more than what the British Prime Minister had superficially averred, he nevertheless concentrated his attention on the stateline adjustments involved when discussing the problem with his colleagues. But it was their deeper meaning that disturbed him. He felt, he told the Northern Ireland Parliament, such "grave dissatisfaction and alarm" that he would write soon to Lloyd George and tell him that the Ulster Government reserved the right to dissent from the appointment of a representative from Northern Ireland to the Boundary Commission as the Treaty mandated. The stage was being set for a showdown with Britain on the Boundary.

Padraic H. Pearse.

CHAPTER 10

SUSPENDED SOVEREIGNTY OR RESOLUTE PARTITION?

The Boundary Agreement

Opposition to the Treaty settlement in general and the Boundary Commission proposal in particular mounted in the Northern Ireland Parliament, but attention was focused on the possible amounts of territory that would be lost or gained and not on any essential unity principle the proposal might have entailed. The Northern Parliament's intention seemed to be that it should do no more than block, if it could, restrictions from being placed on the option it believed itself to be offered of seceding from the Free State of Ireland and going into the United Kingdom. But, on a correct interpretation of the Treaty, this was really a possibility that had eluded the Ulster Assembly.

Northern opposition to the Treaty persisted in many forms for more than two years after settlement of the instrument. When on April 26, 1924, the Saorstat Government finally requested that, in conformity with Article 12 of the Treaty, the Boundary Commission be set up, the British Government formally requested the Government of Northern Ireland to appoint its representative to the Commission. But the Northern Government, acting in accordance with the reiterated statements of its leader, Craig, and other spokesmen, "respectfully declined."

The British Government was now in a position of being unable to fulfill the terms of its Agreement. The quandary the British found themselves in, however, was not as great as was originally imagined, because the Ulster Government's attempt to render the Treaty's Boundary Commission provisions inoperative was utterly incapable of harming the principle of essential Irish unity that was enshrined in the Treaty and the working out of the Boundary Commission's actions was destined to be a huge exercise in futility anyway. But the operation had to be proceeded with, because everybody was committed to it, although those involved must have felt somehow they were allowing themselves to be led up a creek. The Saorstat Government was, however, in a strong position at this turn of events to press for a revision of the Treaty, to demand a rescission of the Ulster option clauses, or to insist, in accordance with the pledge of Lloyd George, that Britain pass an Act to provide for an all-Ireland Parliament (Macardle, p. 871). But this was not as golden an opportunity for the Irish as was supposed, because, as we have seen, Lloyd George's pledge could not be interpreted literally or in a manner favorable to Ireland – that is, it could not be taken to mean establishment of an all-Ireland Parliament with no option out. There was nothing really to revise the Treaty on.

But if the Saorstat Government failed to capitalize on its presumed opportunities, it at least was unwilling to bail the British Government out of its latest dilemma. Tim Healy, Governor General of the Irish Free State, in a dispatch to the British Secretary for the Colonies, expressed in unequivocal terms the refusal of his Government to cooperate with Britain in disregard of the Treaty requirements. For this is precisely what the British Government was proposing to do. Still imagining itself to be 'legislating' for Ireland, it embarked, in violation of its own law (the Irish Free State Constitution Act, 1922 (Sec. 4)), on what would have to be called a new act of aggression. It planned to bring in fresh legislation in the form of a Bill to amend the Treaty, unilaterally, thus enabling itself to appoint the representative of Northern Ireland on the Commission. It would also appoint the Chairman, of course. The British were, in short, to appoint the majority of two who would report out from the Commission and whose report was to be binding on the Free State regardless of any objection which the Saorstat's single representative might make.

Britain's proposed action would have been clearly illegal. Her Treaty Agreement with Ireland, like any contractual agreement, could only be amended by mutual agreement of the parties concerned, as President Cosgrave was later to point out on more than one occasion. The Treaty was law in Ireland, in the British view, from the moment of its ratification, and in accordance with practiced constitutional convention in the Commonwealth, of which Ireland was then a member (albeit an unwilling one), it could only be changed 'at the request and with the consent' of the member country at least, or by mutual consent at most. Yet, here was Britain taking an unprecedented unilateral action in treating the Treaty as a mere, amendable law. That such could be done was never the Irish view. "Contract, not statute," said Donaldson, "was the basis of the Irish Free State's claim." [1]

Moreover, when, in the course of the debate on the Irish Free State (Agreement) Bill in the House of Commons, Carson pressed for definitions of the Ulster clauses, Churchill replied that "as to the amendments made to the Bill in the Lords, the Government could not consent to any alteration of the Treaty, however small. . . ." (Cf. U.K. *Parliamentary Debates*, Fifth Series, Vol. 152, col. 1709.) Yet, here was that same Government, more than two years later, arrogating to itself the power to amend the Treaty in an important essential. But, before worst could come to worst for Britain, the Judicial Committee of the Privy Council came out with a decision that was in keeping with the stance the Irish Governor General had taken and that did little to ease the British Government's worries. It ruled that the Boundary Commission could not be proceeded with if Northern Ireland did not cooperate in the manner the Treaty specified. If the Northerners refused to appoint a representative, a Commission would not be properly constituted nor competent to determine the boundary in compliance with Article 12 of the Treaty. But, the Committee deigned to advise, there was something Westminster could do about it. Legislation involving agreement could be passed to amend the Treaty in its weak spot. And, the Committee conveniently added, once the third Commissioner was appointed, a simple majority of two would be sufficient for

---

1 In a letter dated November 21, 1931, Cosgrave wrote to his opposite number at Westminster (in response to Churchill's proposal that the Statute of Westminster explicitly restrict the power of Ireland under it): "I need scarcely impress upon you that the maintenance of the happy relations which now exist between our two countries is absolutely dependent upon the continued acceptance by each of us of the good faith of the other. This situation has been constantly present to our minds, and we have re-iterated time and again that the Treaty is an agreement which can only be altered by [mutual] consent." (Quoted from Keith, *Speeches and Documents, 1918-1931*, p. 302; cf. Alfred G. Donaldson, *Comparative Aspects*, p. 84, and David Harkness, *The Restless Dominion*, pp. 244-245.) Richard Latham has held that the Treaty was recognized as a contract between two countries by no less august a body than the Judicial Committee of the Privy Council: "But the Board desire to add that they are expressing no opinion upon any contractual obligation under which, regard being had to the terms of the Treaty, the Irish Free State lay" (*Moore* v. *Att.-Gen. for the I.F.S.*, [1935] A.C. 484, p. 499).

decisions to be made, fateful advice indeed that was soon enough to be taken seriously to heart.

The heretofore baffled British accordingly had a change of mind. Instead of proceeding as planned, they resorted to applying pressure to the Irish Government to help them out. And the Irish Government that at first refused to cooperate and that might have demanded that Lloyd George's pledge[2] given for such circumstances now be fulfilled, at this time suspiciously relented and allowed itself to be drawn into an agreement with Britain amending the Treaty. Prime Minister Ramsay MacDonald and President Willie T. Cosgrave drew up a so-called Supplemental Agreement that left Britain free to appoint the missing representative for Northern Ireland (see Appendix 10, *Supplement*). The bugbear phrase of the Treaty "a Commission consisting of three persons, one to be appointed by the Government of the Irish Free State, one to be appointed by the Government of Northern Ireland, and one who shall be the Chairman to be appointed by the British Government" would have to be amended to read, in effect, "a Commission consisting of three persons, one to be appointed by the Government of the Irish Free State and two, including the Chairman, to be appointed by the British Government"!

It might be observed here that the American patriot John Jay, who drafted the 1795 Treaty between the U.S.A. and Great Britain, would not have approved of this particular composition of the Boundary Commission. In his Draft Treaty, Jay proposed that boundary disputes should be settled by a commission of three persons, one each from the respective countries and a third chosen by the two. Even those who spoke for their own countries should take an oath (or affirmation) of disinterestedness and impartiality in their survey work, a far cry from the prejudice and callousness that was to invest the British-Irish affair.

But one would not have to cross the Atlantic to find condemnation of the heavy-handedness that went on. Dorothy Macardle termed the action of the British 'the Treaty broken.' Craig, naturally, blasted it as well. He dared the British to bring an Amending Bill through a House of Commons in which Ulster had a majority of support. He boasted confidently that since Northern Ireland refused to appoint its representative to the Boundary Commission

2 Lloyd George's pledge was, as shown in the previous chapter, that if Ulster refused to cooperate, as he believed she would, he "would fight, summon Parliament, appeal to it against Ulster, dissolve, or pass an Act establishing the all-Ireland Parliament."

and since the British Government would be unable to amend the Treaty to have a substitute appointed, "therefore, a deadlock has been reached" (N.I. *Parliamentary Debates*, Vol. 2 (1922), col. 1153).

No deadlock ensued, however. Britain got her way. With a Treaty-amending (but not Constitution-amending) Agreement having been foisted onto Ireland, confirmatory legislation was quickly passed and the way was cleared for Britain to appoint her second member. This was not entirely to Ireland's disadvantage, it could be said, because it meant that if the Treaty was to be saved the essential Irish unity the Treaty guaranteed would be preserved as well. The Boundary Commission was duly set up. All of its motions were shrouded in secrecy, but it is known that for a large part of a year, 1925, it held roving perambulations along the border with a picnic basket, while it spent most of the year sitting in London. For all the general public knew, it might have been functioning seriously. Then it suddenly hit a rough spot. Upon learning of the Commission Chairman's prepared misinterpretation of the Treaty Article 12, the representative for the Saorstat, Eoin MacNeill, resigned. The resignation, it was hoped, would have the effect of blocking publication of the Commission's Report and promulgation of its 'Award.' This, under the terms of the Treaty, would be legal and final, and so it was imperative that it be headed off.

Furthermore, because the Award-to-Be was known to be based on a misinterpretation of Article 12, with a consequent misrepresentation of the entire Treaty, it was not going to be acceptable to the Irish Government. Such revisionism would destroy the Treaty content of essential Irish unity, and this naturally concerned the Government greatly. The border was not an issue. But, taken as the terms in which the real issue (essential unity) was expressed, the Commission's determination was going to prove unfavorable to the area of *de facto* jurisdiction of the Irish Free State. And this also, since it was based on a misapplication of Article 12, concerned the Dublin Government.

But, to compound matters, MacNeill's resignation did not have the desired effect of blocking promulgation of the Commission's Award, as the remaining two members of the Commission went ahead with their work as a majority. This the Privy Council had said could be done for validity. The Award might be issued any moment. A quick decision was made in Dublin and London, and a hasty Agreement was finalized between the Governments of the Free

State and Britain, with Northern Ireland subscribing. This situation-saving Agreement, which was to amend further the Treaty Agreement, was negotiated at Chequers and signed in London, on December 3, 1925. The powers of the Boundary Commission were revoked and the boundary was left to coincide with where the outer countyline now become a stateline lay between the six and the 26 counties – and with where the border had been set up in 1920 under the Partition Act.

Scope of the Boundary Agreement

Since the Boundary Agreement is considered a main stumbling block to Irish reunification, it bears some looking at. It is often cited as the ultimate confirmation of partition and as a slamming of the door in the faces of Republicans (Lyons, *Ireland Since the Famine*, pp. 487-488 hardcover, p. 493 paperback). We do not agree. We feel that this Treaty-amending Agreement dealt merely with the state [3] borders and the minor powers of Government that the Treaty concerned itself with (in phrases such as "the provisions of the Government of Ireland Act, 1920, so far as they relate to Northern Ireland").

An indication that it was a stateline, understood literally or in equivalent terms, that was intended by the Agreement was the presence of Sir James Craig and his Cabinet's Secretary at the Agreement Conference, plus the fact that they appended their signatures. Their presence would not necessarily imply that major jurisdictional powers were involved. In a matter concerning state borders and states' powers, it is only natural that the state Governments would be consulted and involved. The representatives of the Saorstat Government would have to be said to have been present in a dual capacity – that is, as representing both the major and the minor levels of jurisdiction, since Southern Ireland has never had a separate state Government anyway, the one Dail taking care of both orders of powers.

The import of the Boundary Agreement, which was called euphemistically the Financial Agreement, 1925 (because it also settled financial questions in the Treaty), was to define the border between the Northern and Southern states of Ireland. It defined

3 When we use the term 'state' here, we intend it (as do the 1922 and 1937 Irish Constitutions) in the sense both of a geographic area and of a juristic person (cf. *Comyn* v. *The Attorney General*, [1950] I.R., 142; *Commissioners of Public Works* v. *Kavanagh*, [1962] I.R., 216; *Macauley* v. *Minister for Posts and Telegraphs*, [1966] I.R., 345).

the border by leaving it unaltered and standing exactly as it had been tentatively set already. The first Article of the Agreement is the only one that concerns us here. It was agreed "in a spirit of neighbourly comradeship" that "the powers conferred by the proviso to Article 12 of the said Articles of Agreement on the Commission therein mentioned are hereby revoked, and the extent of Northern Ireland for the purposes of the Government of Ireland Act, 1920, and of the said Articles of Agreement, shall be such as was fixed by sub-section (2) of Section one of that Act." That is, that the Northern Ireland state should consist of "the Parliamentary counties of Antrim, Armagh, Down, Fermanagh, Londonderry, and Tyrone," as they are listed in the 1920 Act, and that Northern Ireland should be deemed to enjoy this territorial extent for the purposes of both the Act and the Treaty. (The Act *and* the Treaty were mentioned, because the Act was allowed by the Treaty to continue when modified to apply in certain situations to Northern Ireland.)

What were these purposes? They were, including those of the Treaty-referenced 1920 Act in its special applications to Northern Ireland, what the ***Treaty*** stated they were in reference both to Ireland in general and to Northern Ireland in particular. First, in reference to Ireland in general, the Treaty purposes were as follows: Ireland should be virtually an independent, self-governing, and unitary sovereign nation that would have a Parliament and Government equipped with powers to make laws for the peace, order, and good government of Ireland.[4] While provision would be made for the erection of Ireland into two states on one jurisdictional level, the essential unity and sovereignty of the nation would be preserved on another.

Spelled out, the purposes were:

> 1. *Ireland* should be virtually an independent, self-governing, and sovereign nation – that is, all Ireland, 32 counties.
>
> 2. Ireland should be *virtually* an independent, self-governing, and sovereign nation – that is, as a member of

4 With partition as its object, the 1920 Act stated (Section 4, subsection (1)) that "the parliament of Southern Ireland and the parliament of Northern Ireland shall respectively have power to make laws for the peace, order, and good government of Southern Ireland and Northern Ireland" (at the minor powers level). But with essential unity in mind, the Treaty consolidated these assemblies in one and stated (Article 1) that "Ireland shall have . . . a Parliament having powers to make laws for the peace, order, and good government of Ireland" (at the major powers level).

> a constitutionally organized Commonwealth Ireland's independence, self-governing power, and sovereignty would be somewhat impaired (but with Commonwealth constitutional development she would be capable of evolving into an actually independent, self-governing, and sovereign nation).
>
> 3. Ireland should have a Parliament and Government enjoying *powers* to make laws for the peace, order, and good government of Ireland – that is, that the major as well as minor powers of Government would be yielded up by the British to the Irish Parliament and Government to be used by it to make laws for the peace, order, and good government of all Ireland.
>
> 4. Ireland would, in effect, be erected on the option of Ulster into two states enjoying minor powers of jurisdiction. But the essential unity of Ireland would be acknowledged on the major powers level of jurisdiction, and this would be expressed in the institution to be called 'the Irish Free State.' However, the jurisdiction of the Free State was to be suspended indefinitely in the six-county area of the North, though that would not detract from the Treaty's main provision of a *unitary* Irish sovereignty.

Second, in reference to Northern Ireland in particular, the purposes of the Treaty were simply to ensure that the provisions of the Government of Ireland Act, 1920, would, insofar as they related to Northern Ireland, be preserved, and the Agreement of 1925 did no more than guarantee that the area of application of those provisions would be such as was fixed by the 1920 Act. It must, then, be asked, what were the provisions of the 1920 Act, as they related to Northern Ireland? We shall endeavor to answer that question momentarily, but first we must point out that regardless of what those provisions were, they were, under the Treaty, intended to last only as long as the 1920 Act itself would last, of which, of course, they were a part. This particular view is strengthened if we take into consideration the Report of the Boundary Commission which determined that the phrase "this instrument" at its first mention in Article 12 of the Treaty referred exclusively to the Treaty itself. That is, that the instrument that was to be "subject to the necessary modifications" was not the 1920 Act mentioned in that same Article. It was the Treaty itself that would be modified – rather, would modify itself. It would not be the Act at all. In other words, according to this 'theory,' the Treaty in dealing with the 1920 Act would have decreed that it was the provisions of that Act as it stood frozen in the Treaty – as unmodified and unmodifiable – that would ever apply to Northern Ireland. Consequently, the particular jurisdiction that flowed from those provisions would only last for the duration of the bare Act itself. And it was this decree of the Treaty, expressed in terms of the extent of such jurisdiction, that the 1925 Agreement would have now confirmed.

It is important, then, to see, in determining how long partition is supposed to last, whether the purposes of the Treaty as they related to Northern Ireland (the provisions of the bare 1920 Act) included partition. Much depends on interpretation, obviously, and if the Boundary Commission's interpretation of the Treaty Article 12 were correct, partition would have been ended as from New Year's Day of 1974. But, alas, partition is not that easily got rid of, because, unfortunately, the B.C. interpretation was *not* correct, as we shall later demonstrate. So that it remains imperative that we ascertain the purposes of the Act as contained in the Treaty and of the Treaty as confirmed by the Agreement. Otherwise, one would be unable to refute the British-Loyalist argument that those purposes included establishment of *de jure* partition. We therefore explain further the powers of jurisdiction to be exercised in Ireland and the states of Ireland under the Treaty and the extent of the application of those powers as decreed by the Treaty and agreed on in the Boundary Agreement.

What the Treaty and Boundary Agreements guaranteed to Ireland more specifically

A favorite claim of Irish Loyalists – and Anglophilic Irish historians – is that in and of the 1925 Agreement the dissolution of the Council of Ireland and the confirmation of the North-South border together formed "the keystone of Northern Ireland's constitutional structure" and that this "was confirmed in the Ireland Act of 1949" (Harkness). The fact is that whatever the Ireland Act confirmed, it was no valid claim to the maintenance of partition when partition even was not in the Boundary Agreement. Really the more things changed in 1925, the more they remained the same. Let us try to explain.

As a state within Ireland, Northern Ireland would have no jurisdiction in *major powers* whatsoever. Just as under the 1920 Act the authority of the Westminster Parliament was to be held supreme, so under the Treaty the authority of the Saorstat Oireachtas was to be supreme in Ireland and in all parts thereof.

That is to say, with the exception of some safeguards and privileges listed in Article 15 of the Treaty, Northern Ireland would have no power to legislate in the following areas as listed in the 1920 Act: peace and war, foreign policy, navy, armed forces, treaties with foreign countries, conferring of titles of honor, treason, deportation, naturalization, trade agreements with Southern Ireland or any foreign country, postal services, cables and radio, air navigation, lighthouses, coining of money, weights and measures, trademarks, copyright, patents, customs and excise duties, income tax and surtax, sales tax, corporate profits taxes, and any other taxes on profits. And in the area of the Judiciary, Northern Ireland could not have a Supreme Court.

This is such a formidable list that the 1920 Act, to the extent that it was authorized by the Treaty to apply to the North of Ireland at all, left hardly any ***minor powers*** in which the state legislature ***could*** legislate. The Northern Ireland state was much more restricted than the usual state in a federation, but it did have some areas left to it in which it had jurisdiction. Notable among these local powers areas were education, agriculture, industry, commerce, health, community relations, and a few powers largely taken over from local authorities: police, fire, electricity, telegraphs, water, housing, public transport, and limited taxation. In this latter area the Government could do no more than collect motor vehicle taxes, death duties, stamp duties, and a few excise duties (although with time these would have been expanded, as the Treaty's Article 15 guaranteed). Judiciarywise, Northern Ireland could only have lower courts.

With the passage of the Treaty and the amending thereby of the 1920 Government of Ireland Act, Articles 11 to 15 of the Treaty introduced a division of the application of the minor powers along the lines of the division of the Act. That is, they would be applied separately to Northern and to Southern Ireland. But there was no division of the major powers, of course. (After all, how would one divide a nation's foreign policy, for example?) The major powers were to apply *en bloc* to all of Ireland – just as they would have been reserved *en bloc* from all of Ireland if the 1920 Act had been worked in its totality. However, an exception was introduced with the inclusion of Article 12. If the Ulster option out were exercised, the major powers, now enjoyed by the Irish Free State, were to be suspended in the six counties of Northern Ireland. But the minor powers were to be applied in that state – and in the Southern state – as they would have been under the Act or under the Treaty anyway, that is, if the Ulster option were not exercised. (There is no 'Southern state' in Ireland, of course, because there is no distinction made between the major and minor powers as they are exercised in the present Republic – and this is certainly a feature that does not help us to understand the kind of constitutional Ireland that might have emerged if the Treaty Settlement had not first been misinterpreted and then put clumsily into effect.)

Put in its simplest terms, under the Treaty and ultimate Boundary Agreement plan, Irish minor powers of Government were to be applied statelike on the basis of a North-South division (Article 14), while the major powers would be enjoyed by the Irish Free State in the whole of Ireland. Should Northern Ireland, however, object to this arrangement, she would have to live with it for a period of one month maximum (Article 11), after which time she would be free to contract out, under certain conditions, if she so chose (Article 12). If she did choose to opt out, she would continue to exercise her minor powers alone. That is, the Irish Free State's major powers would not be exercised in the Northern Ireland area for an indefinite period of time. (It was not stated how long the period of suspension of the Free State's powers would have to be, but it was implied that it was not to last longer than the 1920 Act and its minor powers would.)

However, *prima facie* the size of both Northern Ireland's area and Southern Ireland's area would if the Northern state opted out be subject to the scrutiny of a Boundary Commission (proviso to Article 12), which might go so far as to abolish the North-South border altogether. In fact, it was believed by the Irish negotiators at the Treaty Conference that the Boundary Commission if set up ***would*** go so far as to abolish the border altogether, and in that belief they accepted Britain's proposal. "A threat of renewed war, on the one hand, and a promise to revise the boundaries between the two parts of Ireland," wrote Berriedale Keith, "which the Irish negotiators interpreted with some warrant as meaning the bringing of pressure to bear on Northern Ireland to accept inclusion in the new Irish Free State, induced the Irish negotiators to give way. . ." (*Responsible Government*, pp. 40-41; cf. Cmd. Pprs. 1539 and 1688). (See also Thomas E. Hachey, *Britain and Irish Separatism*, p. 187.) The belief that essential Irish unity was secured by the Boundary Commission principle was held by more than the Irish negotiators indeed. The conservative *Irish Independent* at the time had declared that were it not for the assurance that Irish unity was by that principle secured the Treaty "would never have received five minutes' consideration in this country."

In the event, however, the Boundary Commission, acting in an unprecedented manner, did not abolish the northern border. The border was left as it already was. This was what the Boundary Agreement confirmed. But this must be understood in its historico-Treaty context.

What the Treaty guaranteed through the Article 12 that was invoked was that Ireland should be in effect a unitary state, but what the Boundary Agreement effected was that Ireland would have some sort of federal setup. Two 'states' would each have a Parliament and Government exercising minor powers of jurisdiction *de facto* and, in effect, a ***separate***, overall Central Parliament and Government enjoying major powers of jurisdiction *de jure*. But these major powers would as yet be suspended in part.

To explain the anomaly further, the Agreement first revoked the powers of the Boundary Commission and then it established the stateline between Northern and Southern Ireland. In so doing it approved the separate functionings of the minor powers of Government in the jurisdictions of the Northern and Southern states. As far as major powers of jurisdiction were concerned, the Agreement did not change the Treaty arrangement. Major jurisdiction was still reserved to the Irish Free State. But in the North of Ireland its application continued to be suspended from an all-Ireland Government. This sovereign jurisdiction the Boundary Agreement did not destroy, but preserved. However, the rub was it also preserved *de facto* partition.

The foregoing might be the way to describe the Treaty and Boundary Agreement for Ireland by, as we said, putting it in its simplest terms. But the Northern Ireland problem was never one that could be dealt with in simple terms. In what sense the Agreement affirmed the functionings of the minor powers of jurisdiction and in what sense it understood the states to exist was no minor part of the problem. President William T. Cosgrave described the nature of the problem in all its complexity when he said in the Dail: "Article 12 . . . was a formula designed in the event . . . the minority in the Northeast opted to retain their existing relation with the Parliament of Great Britain . . . to prevent the coercion of a minority within that minority" (*Dail Debates*, Vol. 13, col. 1302). How boundaries were to be drawn to achieve that aim would have been nothing short of the divine deed it was described to be in the Dail. Obviously something entirely other than territorial division was envisioned by the Article 12 formula. What that was we shall soon begin to see.

In terms that might be regarded as being descriptive of this other-than-partition division that the Treaty seemed to enjoin, President Cosgrave went on to explain the complex Northern problem in considerable detail in the light of Article 12. "The Irish people agreed to recognise the constitution of a province of northern Ireland, even if it would detach itself from the country to which by nature it belonged and become a province of Britain, ***on condition that*** [some] people who had been swept into it should in their turn have effect given to their wish not to be so detached, but to remain part of their native land, sharing its destiny. That is to say, while the Irish people . . . made a Treaty whereby they forbade themselves coercion over the people in the Northeastern corner who might elect to stand aloof from the National Government, they at the same time stipulated that the Nationalist population should not be coerced to quit their own nation or to denationalise themselves. . . .

"The Northern politicians claim the right under the Treaty to determine for themselves that they shall be governed from Westminster. – Conceded. We insist on the condition that the people who likewise claim the right under the Treaty to determine for themselves that they shall be governed by an Irish Government shall have that right made effective. We do not seek to coerce anyone – but we say that the principle of no coercion shall be applied fairly and impartially." (Cols. 2410 and 2413.)

The President further explained, on the occasion of the blundering of the Boundary Commission being brazened out, the lines along which divisions, if any, were to be drawn. In his Emyvale, Monaghan speech, he said: "The Treaty settlement was intended by all parties to mark the end of coercion in Ireland and to substitute the principle of democratic government based on the consent of the governed. No other interpretation of Article 12 could possibly accord with the general spirit of the Treaty. [Article 12] was clearly intended, in the event of Northern Ireland deciding to secede from the Irish Free State, to bring relief to the Nationalist inhabitants of the Six Counties, who would otherwise be held under a Government not acceptable to them." (*The Irish Times*, November 23, 1925, pp. 5-6; quoted from Jeffrey Prager, *Building Democracy in Ireland*, p. 148.)

What Cosgrave was indicating was that there was more to Article 12 than the 'Loyalist guarantee,' that there was also the 'Nationalist guarantee.' How those guarantees were to be accommodated in the concrete, however – that is, where, if anywhere, agreed-upon boundaries were to be set down – Cosgrave did not say. Nor did anyone else, before or since. The only valuable insight offered on the subject was that contributed by Sean Milroy, T.D., who stated, correctly, that Article 12 did not have to do with boundaries at all. And another Dail Deputy, Tom Johnson, elaborated by emphasizing that what Article 12 really made provision for was the right of minorities in each Irish jurisdiction to the essential unity of Ireland, whether those minorities might be Nationalists in the Glens of Antrim or Loyalists on the Ring of Kerry. "Anyone who confuses rectification of boundary with securing for the Irish Nation such a share of territorial integrity as is consistent with the agreement to provide certain safeguards for a minority of settlers and their descendants in the North-Eastern corner," declared the Labor leader, "are thinking of something else than mere rectification of boundaries.... We still adhere to what we have never abandoned – the claim that Ireland shall one day be a unit State." (Vol. 7, cols. 2361 and 2836-2838.)

It appeared that ever after the failed Buckingham Palace Conference of 1914 boundaries were being given up on as a way to satisfy in the concrete people's right to self-determination. And it did appear indeed that boundaries were not really contemplated in the Treaty Article 12, and that phrases like "the boundaries between Northern Ireland and the rest of Ireland," if they were not to have been used recklessly and totally meaninglessly, would have had to be intended in some sort of metonymical sense or other. President Cosgrave summed it all up by saying: "That the Act of dismemberment [of 1920]... was an Act to which the consent of the Irish people had yet to be given was clearly recognised in the Treaty of December, 1921.... The Treaty gave effect by Article 12 to the principle which had been proclaimed fundamental in the European War and embodied in the Treaty of Versailles whose very terms are invoked in prescribing that a boundary shall be fixed... according to the wishes of the inhabitants subject only to the limitations of economic and geographic conditions.... That principle, which emerged on a war-cry throughout the world in the European War, was crystallised in the Treaty of Versailles in a formula which fell naturally into its proper place in the Treaty of 1921." (Vol. 8, cols. 2409-2414.)

The Versailles perspective

President Cosgrave's particular interpretation of Treaty Article 12 introduced an essential aspect of the partition problem, that of plebiscites being held in the context of the Treaty of Versailles to determine the possible boundaries of states or the limits of state jurisdictions. This essential aspect, particularly in its form of limits of jurisdictions, brought up in turn the distinction between people and states that it was necessary to hold if the findings of plebiscites in some instances (for example, the Irish one) could be put into workable order.

Here we shall examine briefly the provisions of plebiscites in Article 12 as being intended in terms of the Versailles Treaty and then we shall proceed to consider at greater length the distinction between People and State that the Anglo-Irish Treaty introduced to give effect in the Irish case to the Versailles-type requirement for plebiscites. Our treatment of the People-State distinction will, in turn, bring up a necessary digression into considering how the 1937 Constitution, which also adopted this distinction, is unable nevertheless to deliver on the benefits of the Versailles Treaty to Ireland.

The benefits the Versailles Treaty imported were, of course, plebiscites, and there is no telling what beneficial results these might have had, if applied, for the traditional communities in Ireland. They were not applied, because they were read out of the Irish Treaty. This was not hard to do with impunity, since the Treaty, being particularly brief and preparatory in nature – it comprised Articles of Agreement *for* a Treaty – did not make detailed and explicit mention of plebiscites. They were, rather, referred to obliquely and were very definitely intended. In fact, the entire Anglo-Irish Treaty was devised in the context of the Treaty of Versailles (cf., e.g., Article 8, with its observance of "the principle of international limitation of armaments") and it was devised at a time that, as Geoffrey J. Hand has noted, plebiscites were very much on people's minds – and at a time that, as Michael Laffan has noted, the Report of the Council of the League of Nations on the Silesian plebiscite was published. As a matter of fact, a Treaty of Versailles rather than Commonwealth type of solution was suggested (by Michael Collins) at the London Conference as being more pertinent to the Irish problem and Lloyd George indicated that the whole purpose of the negotiations was to satisfy self-determination (see Thomas Jones, *Whitehall Diary*, Vol. III, pp. 131 and 136).

That the Anglo-Irish Treaty, with its provision for plebiscites, was devised within the context of and was intended to be an extension of the Treaty of Versailles, with its similar provisions and language, can more assuredly be ascertained from the Resolutions of the United States Congress of March 4 and June 6, 1919. These constrained President Woodrow Wilson, who had prescribed self-determination for the little nations of Europe as one of America's conditions for entering World War I, to demand of Lloyd George and the British Peace Commission that the Prime Minister and the Commission enable Ireland's right to freedom, independence and self-determination to be heard by the Peace Conference and recognized in the Peace Treaty then being negotiated by the Allied and Associated Powers at Versailles.

The Resolution of March 4, 1919 was House Concurrent Resolution No. 357 and ran as follows: "*Resolved by the House of Representatives (the Senate concurring)*, That it is the earnest hope of the Congress of the United States of America that the peace conference, now sitting in Paris, in passing upon the rights of various peoples, will favorably consider the claims of Ireland to the right of self-determination." (See *U.S. Congressional Record*, 65 Cong., 3 Sess., 1919, Vol. 57, pp. 5026-5027, 5033-5035, 5042-5051 and 5057.)

The Senate Resolution, that of June 6, 1919, No. 48, was somewhat more pointedly worded and was passed by a vote of 60 to 1. This Resolution ran as follows: "*Resolved*, That the Senate of the United States earnestly requests the American peace commission at Versailles to endeavor to secure for Edward De Valera, Arthur Griffiths, and Count George Noble Plunkett a hearing before said peace conference in order that they may present the cause of Ireland." (See *U.S. Congressional Record*, 66 Cong., 1 Sess., 1919, Vol. 58, pp. 728-733.)

Such strong pressure that was exerted by the U.S. Congress in Ireland's behalf on President Wilson could not but have been translated into action by him at Versailles, and indeed he wrote at the time himself that he was "diligently trying to render [assistance] in the matter of bringing the Irish aspirations to the attention of the Peace Conference" and that by his "unofficial activity in the matter we had practically cleared the way for the coming of the Irish representatives to Paris" (quoted from Alan J. Ward, *Ireland and Anglo-American Relations*, p. 183). Wilson did not do so wholeheartedly, as history records, but he at least succeeded to persuade Lloyd George that the latter take Ireland into his postwar European reconstruction calculations. As Thomas Hachey has recorded, Wilson "repeatedly impressed upon Lloyd George the need for some kind of Irish settlement agreeable to American opinion." And Wilson himself assured a deputation of Irish-

Americans in Paris that he had "the deepest sympathy for Ireland and her people and her cause. I know I speak for the others [of the Treaty Conference 'Big Four'] when I say that all we could do unofficially we have been doing and will do." [5] In addition, Wilson was not unmindful, as he said himself, of the Senate Resolution supporting Ireland's representation at the Paris Conference. Whatever about pressure from the House of Representatives, not to mention that of several state legislatures and of numerous civic organizations, the President could not afford to buck a Senate that supported Ireland so overwhelmingly when he depended on that same Senate for American ratification of the Treaty of Versailles and his League of Nations. In the event, however, the Senate rejected the Treaty – and the League of Nations. (See Thomas E. Hachey, *op. cit.*, pp. 212, 215-216 and 228-229.)

But in what sense exactly, it may be asked, was self-determination to have been applied in Ireland? One of the concepts ever present to the minds of the Irish people, and put into constitutional effect in 1919, 1921-22 and 1937, was the distinction between People and State that we referred to. In the 1921-22 Treaty Settlement this distinction could be said to have been formulated as a refinement of the Versailles Treaty's pioneer effort to provide self-determination for national minorities. The People, through enacting a Constitution, created the State, and this they so much did that they imparted a 'juristic personality' to the State, a personality that was not enjoyed by, for example, Monarchical States wherein the King/Queen would be the personification of the State and above the law. The People in the Irish sense is the Nation, the 'Poblacht,' the Saorstat or Republic (as explained by Justice F. G. O. Budd). But what of the State? All that can safely be said is that, apart from being the juristic person that is suable by the People and not above the law, the State in the 1919 and 1922 Constitutions is without doubt the 32-county territory of Ireland; but in the 1937 Constitution, because of the rather enigmatic 'Nation' and 'State' Articles 2 and 3 that have to be taken in conjunction with the other 'State' Articles of the rest of the document (notably the Preamble and Articles 30.3, 46 and 47), the State is the Southern territorial area, but it is not certain that the State does not also mean some sort of nonterritorial, juristic person extending to Northern

5 *Treaty of Peace with Germany*, Hearings before the Committee on Foreign Relations, U.S. Senate, 66th Congress, First Session, *Senate Documents*, Vol. 10, No. 106 (Aug. 30, 1919), pp. 837-838; Macardle, *The Irish Republic*, pp. 296-297.

Ireland out of the 26-county territory of Ireland. Which may be what caused Justice George D. Murnaghan once to complain that the expression 'the State' and the word 'Ireland' are something "which everybody understands but which is difficult to define precisely." (See *Byrne* v. *Ireland*, [1972] *Irish Reports* 241, pp. 245, 261 and 296.)

Expanding on the People-State distinction, the Irish Supreme Court, in alluding to the 1937 Constitution's 32-county juristic-person State (in *In the Matter of Article 26 of the Constitution and in the Matter of The Criminal Law (Jurisdiction) Bill, 1975*), declared: "One of the theories held in 1937 by a substantial number of citizens was that a Nation, as distinct from a State, had rights; that the Irish people living in what is now called the Republic of Ireland and in Northern Ireland together formed the Irish Nation; that a Nation has a right to unity of territory in some form, be it as a unitary or a federal State; and that the Government of Ireland Act, 1920, though legally binding, was a violation of that national right to unity which was superior to positive [legislative] law. ***This national claim to unity exists not in the legal but in the political order*** and is one of the rights which are envisaged in Article 2; it is expressly saved by Article 3 which states the area to which the laws enacted by the Parliament established by the Constitution apply. The effect of Article 3 is that, until the division of the island of Ireland is ended, the laws enacted by the Parliament established by the Constitution are to apply to the same area and have the same extent of application as the laws of Saorstat Eireann had . . . and the same extra-territorial effect as the laws of Saorstat Eireann."[6] ([1977] *Irish Reports* 129, pp. 147-148; *emphasis ours*.) But the effect of both Articles is, too, as Justice O'Byrne said, "to proclaim that the whole of Ireland is included in the national territory of the State" ([1978] *Irish Reports* 376, p. 380).

In thus explaining the distinction between Nation and State, Chief Justice O'Higgins depicted the Nation-that-Would-Be as being in the political order versus the State-that-Is as being in the legal order and as having (because of Article 3) to acknowledge

6 The possibility of a 32-county Irish State existing under the 1937 Constitution as a juristic person was drawn, in arguments offered in *In the Matter of Article 26 of the Constitution and in the Matter of The Criminal Law (Jurisdiction) Bill, 1975*, from "the Government of Ireland Act, 1920; Articles 11 and 12 of the Anglo-Irish Treaty, 1921; s. 2 of the Constitution of the Irish Free State (Saorstat Eireann) Act, 1922; and Articles 2 and 3 of the Constitution of Ireland," that is, from the historical, 32-county context of the Constitution in which it and Articles 2 and 3 are to be interpreted ([1977] I.R. 129, p. 137).

the legality of the Government of Ireland Act. That is to say, that the territory of the Nation-that-Would-Be (the latter being in the political, national order) is something which the People could do something about reintegrating, but that, at the same time, this same territory the State-that-Is (the latter being in the legal, constitutional order) could do nothing about reintegrating – because that State would have no power over a British statute that it acknowledges to be legally binding to it. The explanation of the learned Chief Justice might be paraphrased as follows: "The 1920 Government of Ireland Act (as amended) is, because of the Constitution Articles 2 and 3 combined, only legally binding for as long as the reintegration of the national territory is pending, which is for as long as the Act (and its amendments) must be acknowledged as legally binding"! This *reductio ad absurdum* of the Articles 2 and 3 might be further spelled out thus: The legally binding nature of the Partition Acts must, as far as the 1937 Constitution is concerned, be factually and constitutionally recognized (it was recognized *de facto* by, as we shall see, the Sunningdale Agreement of 1973 and it was recognized *de jure* by, as we shall also see, the Hillsborough Agreement of 1985) – the legally binding nature of these Acts must be recognized for as long as Ireland awaits reintegration, which Ireland shall have to await for as long as she is constitutionally bound to recognize the contrary British Acts! Such is why, perhaps, Articles 2 and 3 were in the beginning referred to as being "a fiction," "make-believe," "paradoxical" and "contradictory." (See John Bowman, *De Valera and the Ulster Question, 1917-1973*, pp. 147-150.)

The State cannot, then, under the 26-county Constitution, bring about the reintegration of the Irish Nation, but must rather uphold the forces obstructing that reintegration. But should the State for its part institute Irish partition laws more substantially than those it has already created, or should it collaborate positively in fostering or supporting British partition laws in such a way as to make them equally Irish obstacles to reintegration and ***in disregard of the national reintegration mandate of the Constitution*** (the hidden agenda of Articles 2 and 3),[7] as the 1985 Irish-British Agreement appears clearly to have done, then such institution or collaboration would, of course, be in direct conflict with Articles 2 and 3 and, consequently, unconstitutional. That is why the Hillsborough Accord would, to be retained in the face of the Constitution's rein-

7 We shall endeavor to explain the basis of the Constitution's reintegration mandate in the next chapter.

tegration mandate, have to be subjected to legal reformation. (See further the Addendum to this Part.)

Building on the foregoing Supreme Court doctrine of the national-legal distinction, but not alleviating the Catch-22 constitutional obligation to uphold partition while it lasts, Justice D. P. M. Barrington has stated (in "The Constitution and Other Charters") that whatever political or constitutional doctrine Article 2 proclaimed, that doctrine "the State established by the Constitution is pledged to respect for international obligations and the peaceful settlement of international disputes. Article 3 accordingly prohibits it from attempting to legislate for [that area to which the legislative laws of Saorstat Eireann did not apply]. The implication is that the State, with whatever political [national] reservations, accepts the border between North and South in law and in fact until such time as a peaceful[8] solution can be found to the problem." (De Brun Lecture, UCG, November 1981; quoted from C. K. Boyle and D. S. Greer, *The Legal Systems, North and South*, pp. 19-20.)

Justice Barrington's reference to the implication of the Constitution's Article 3 being that the State, with whatever political reservations, accepts partition in law and in fact until a peaceful solution can be found to the problem might likewise be paraphrased as follows: "The implication is that the State, despite the national mandate of the Constitution, must as a quasi nation, and does, accede juridically and factually to the laws instituting and maintaining Northern Ireland until such time as those laws are by judicial or arbitrational or other constitutional means found unconstitutional." In such a sense is it allowed under the present Constitution to recognize and endure the Partition Act, as amended to date, in law and in fact; but it would not be allowed to enact such laws and do such other things (e.g., engage in political extradition) as would lead the Irish State positively to acknowledge

8 It might usefully be noted here that in the Irish constitutional context the term 'peaceful,' that we translate 'judicial,' has a technical meaning. It means, in the words of Article 29, and as Justice Barrington has also pointed out, "the pacific settlement of international disputes by international arbitration or judicial determination." This explanation is an intentional echo of Articles 12 and 13 of the Covenant of the League of Nations, wherein the members of the League agreed that if there should have arisen among them any dispute likely to lead to a rupture they would have submitted the matter either to arbitration or to an inquiry by the Council and accepted the findings of any such arbitration or inquiry. The meaning is also in compliance with Chapter VI of the United Nations Charter, "Pacific Settlement of Disputes," which outlines the procedures for settling disputes - mediation, negotiation, litigation.

a British sovereignty over Northern Ireland ***in disregard of the reintegration mandate*** and for as long as reintegration is officially pending. Conversely, the Constitution mandates the enactment of such laws and the doing of such other things as would enable the Irish ***People-Nation*** to achieve reintegration.

It would appear, in conclusion, from all of the foregoing comments and their implications that there is ample judicial and constitutional opinion to support our contention that, unlike as with the Irish-British Agreement of 1985, neither the Boundary Agreement of 1925 nor its predecessor the Treaty itself (particularly the proviso to Article 12) can be cited to prove or justify the existence of British-Irish land partition; but that Irish national sovereignty was in those Twenties Agreements suspended over Northern Ireland by Great Britain. Neither Agreement in fact intended anything other than an intranational division between two 'states' (not necessarily territorially understood); certainly no international partition was intended, regardless of whether the fateful Agreements were registered with the League of Nations or not (they were). That being the case, it little profits Ian Paisley, Peter Robinson, *et alii* to harp on this latter point when the point they are harping on is not really the point at all. But a proper understanding of what the states of Ireland really import, even since 1937, brings us back to an examination of what Treaty Article 12 actually contains.

The partition plot

To resume our consideration of the Versailles injunction for plebiscites being incorporated in the Anglo-Irish Treaty, what was to determine whether and where boundaries might exist in Ireland was, as the Treaty Article 12 stipulated, ***the wishes of the inhabitants*** insofar as they might be compatible with economic and geographic conditions. This important principle, which was language and thought straight from the Treaty of Versailles, was, as President Cosgrave had stated, the governing factor in the operation of Article 12. Its incorporation in the Treaty was so important that, as Attorney General Hugh Kennedy and Lord Birkenhead declared, without it the Treaty would never have been accepted. The "wishes of the inhabitants" was as integral to Treaty Article 12 as another Versailles principle, "the principle of international limitation of armaments," was integral to Treaty Article 8, because by it the self-determination rights of the two communal traditions in Ireland were assured recognition and fulfillment.

One of the Treaty signatories, Eudhmonn Duggan, referring to the Versailles-type principle in Article 12, wrote: "It has several times been pointed out that the decisive words, 'in accordance with the wishes of the inhabitants so far as may be compatible with economic and geographic conditions,' are almost identical with those employed in the Treaty of Versailles when dealing with the line to be drawn in plebiscite areas such as East Prussia and Upper Silesia. In those cases the words were interpreted to mean no mere rectification in an existing frontier, but the drawing of a completely new frontier." It remained to be seen whether the Boundary Commission was going to so understand its Treaty mandate.

Part of the problem with regard to applying the plebiscite clause of Article 12 was that the Boundary Commission was given complete latitude with interpreting the mandate of that clause, instead of having been given terms of reference by the Governments concerned (as the Versailles Treaty had done). This imprecision in Article 12 left the Commissioners open to being unduly lobbied and influenced from a variety of sources. Given the campaign of press and political pressure undertaken in Britain while the Boundary Commission was being put together, it was extremely unlikely that the British-appointed Commissioners were going to do or think other than the London Government wanted them to. Specifically, they were being told in public how they were to interpret Article 12 of the Treaty. The campaign of advice assumed outrageous proportions as time went on, even with some now-unemployed British signatories to the Treaty jumping in and practically doing the interpreting for the Commission themselves. Chamberlain couldn't believe that the Chairman in his deliberations would prove himself "a fool or a knave." Lord Birkenhead went so far as to declare: "If the Chairman of the Commission does not interpret his functions in the way the British signatories to the Treaty expect him to interpret them, then he can be nothing less than a lunatic." The Chairman, Justice Richard Feetham of the South Africa Supreme Court, was soon to prove in no uncertain way that he was not a fool or a knave – or a lunatic.

The way the Commission Chairman bowed to the British pressure was by railroading partition right through the Treaty itself. How he did this was by taking advantage of the "grave and dangerous ambiguity" of Article 12 that Lord Buckmaster had warned of three months after the Treaty was signed (49 H.L. Deb., ser. 2, col. 757; see also Chapter 9 herein, Note 6). Specifically what Feetham did was to misinterpret the sense in which the first reference to "this instrument" in Article 12 was intended. This he did in such a way as to leave the Treaty requirement regarding the wishes of the inhabitants practically meaningless.[9]

Feetham's notorious gambit was he took the Article 12 phrase "this instrument shall have effect subject to the necessary modifications" to read 'this Treaty shall have effect subject to the necessary modifications.' The fact is, of course, that the instrument first referred to in Article 12 as having effect subject to the necessary modifications was not, could not be, the Treaty. It was, we know, the Government of Ireland Act, 1920, which was duly modified by the Irish Free State (Consequential Provisions) Act on December 5, 1922, and not by either of the Acts which ratified the Treaty (the Irish Free State (Agreement) Act of March 31, 1922 and the Irish Free State Constitution Act of December 5, 1922). Feetham's misinterpretation would amount to a violation of both of these British Acts. The Treaty Article 12 did not take effect until December 8, 1922, before which date the Treaty could not be modified in accordance with the Article and after which date there was no modification save as by mutual consent.

Let Feetham describe his own preposterous interpretation. "The meaning of Article XII is that if the Address therein referred to is presented," he reported, "Northern Ireland shall continue to exist as a province [?] of the United Kingdom in accordance with the provisions of the Government of Ireland Act, 1920, subject to the 'determination' of boundaries . . . and its terms require that once such an Address has been presented the several Articles of Agreement for a Treaty shall be modified, so far as necessary, to give effect to all the consequences which under the provisions of Article XII follow upon such presentation"! Which explanation, particularly with reference to modifying the Treaty, is, in our opinion, pure and unadulterated B.S. (bullheaded stonewalling).

One of the greatest liberties Feetham took with any of the text of the Treaty was in taking the word 'modifications' in Article 12 and having it mean 'interpretations.' But in British jurisprudence the word 'modifications' has traditionally meant 'amendments'

9 It was clear from the plain statement of the Commission Chairman, uttered gratuitously in advance, that the wishes of the inhabitants of Ireland, North or South, were not going to be taken into consideration by the Commission anyway. "They," said Justice Feetham, referring to President Cosgrave and Sir James Craig, "have also concurred in my proposal that I should make a tour on either side of the border in order to familiarise myself with the economic and geographical conditions . . . and they have kindly promised to give me facilities for the purpose of this tour, which will be purely of a private character." H'm.

carried out in Parliament through the ordinary legislative process. No Articles of the Treaty were subjected to that kind of treatment – nor could they have been so modified unilaterally, the Treaty being an international instrument of agreement. Yet, Feetham proceeded to interpret the Treaty Articles as if they were amended already – or as if he had modified them himself, in effect. "To the extent thus indicated," he emphasized, "Article XII necessarily becomes on the presentation of such Address a governing Article in the light of which the other Articles of the Treaty must be read, and to which in case of conflict their provisions must yield"!! Expletive deleted.

The Commission Chairman's misinterpretation takes a lot to stomach. According to him, Treaty Article 12's "this instrument shall have effect subject to the necessary modifications" means "that all the modifications which necessarily follow from the provisions as to Northern Ireland contained in the first part of Article XII shall be made in the other Articles of the instrument. If full effect is given to these words in Article XII, it follows that, once the Address provided for in that Article has been presented, its provisions as to the future of Northern Ireland must be treated as governing the interpretation of the other Articles of the Treaty. It appears to me, therefore, that, once the Address has been presented, the other Articles of the Treaty must be interpreted in the light of Article XII rather than *vice versa*." (Report of the Irish Boundary Commission, pp. 28 and 42.)

What Justice Feetham was trying to say was that the Treaty split Ireland in two – into the Ireland the Treaty recognized now construed as exclusive of Northern Ireland, and Northern Ireland, that is, into Ireland and Northern Ireland. But for it to do this Feetham had to split the Treaty itself in two first. This lame attempt at revisionism was achieved by misinterpreting Article 12 in yet another way as well. Feetham, as we've just seen, stated it appeared to ***him*** (not the Commission) that the provisions of the Address as presented constituted the governing factor in the interpretation of the other Articles of the Treaty. Here was his second major misinterpretation, for it was the provisions of the Address ***as qualified by the proviso to Article 12*** that the Treaty enjoined, not the bare presentation of the Address itself. It would, then, be the proviso to Article 12 that would have governed the other Articles (insofar as Article 12 was a governing Article at all), not the first part of the Article alone. The end result of all this misinterpretation was that the Commission ignored the Treaty requirement that the wishes of the inhabitants of Ireland be considered.

The phrase "the wishes of the inhabitants" meant the wishes of the inhabitants of both states in Ireland now affected, and not, as has been thought, of the inhabitants of the one (the northern) state. At the very least it referred to the inhabitants of all of Ulster. It was intended by Lloyd George at the Treaty Conference that the Boundary Commission, if it were to exist at all, should apply to all nine counties of Ulster, as he normally took the entire province as the logical unit of division (see Thomas Jones, *Whitehall Diary*, pp. 131, 135, 157 and 158). But the phrase might be construed as applying even to both states of all Ireland. The belief that it did was held even by Prime Minister Craig and the Northern Ireland Parliament. " 'I say standing here at this box,' declared Craig, 'on behalf of my colleagues and myself, that there can be no adjustment of the Ulster boundaries without the free consent of both North and South.' – (Hon. Members: Hear, hear)." (N.I. *Parliamentary Debates*, Vol. 2, col. 1154.) Feetham, in fact, agreed that the phrase meant "the inhabitants of the territories [plural] concerned." He even went so far as to concede that the phrase, when qualified by the accompanying phrase "so far as may be compatible with economic and geographic conditions," applied to inhabitants of regions that could be extended one way even to include Belfast, since Belfast depended for its water supply on waterworks situated in southern County Down. By the same token, they could be extended far in the opposite direction if there were inhabitants concerned resident there whose wishes might have to be regarded. "The boundary which had originated as a provincial boundary might under Article XII be converted into a national boundary [between 'a province of the United Kingdom' and 'a Dominion']," the Feetham Commission reported. "A provision that in this event the boundary should be reconsidered, would appear to be a natural provision to insert in the Treaty in the interests of ***the inhabitants of both territories concerned.***" (Report, p. 39; *emphasis ours.*)

Yet, for all his concern for the wishes of the inhabitants of both Irish states, Feetham, as we said, practically ignored the inhabitants, except for a few handfuls along the provisional border. The way Feetham discounted the inhabitants' wishes was by denying the Irish Government's Treaty right to hold the plebiscite that, as we saw earlier, was a right the Dail and Government looked forward to exercising at the opportune moment. John O'Byrne, Attorney General of Saorstat Eireann, when testifying before the Commission in 1924, pointed out that it was his Government's reading of the Treaty that a plebiscite or plebiscites should be held in order to determine the wishes of the inhabitants. He added that there was no other way that wishes of inhabitants could be adequately ascertained. Feetham even agreed, but refused to authorize plebiscites on the grounds that they were unnecessary if, for all practical purposes, Article 12 (privately interpreted and privately amended) partitioned Ireland already and on the grounds that such items as plebiscites were not specifically mentioned in the Treaty document!

Feetham's refusal to hold plebiscites was clearly illegal, unconstitutional and at variance with the 'legislative' intent of Article 12. This intent was, as we saw, derived directly from the Treaty of Versailles, of which the Anglo-Irish Treaty could be said to be an extension. But the plebiscites provided by the Treaty of Versailles were designed for situations similar to the Irish one, especially as Feetham saw this characteristic (as involving international boundaries). It was only natural, therefore, that the Treaty should intend plebiscites. We've seen already that, in fact, it did.

No less a statesman (and insider) than the Marquess of Londonderry, the Leader of the Senate of Northern Ireland, showed in the Senate already on November 29, 1921, that he understood the Boundary Commission proposals to be made in a Treaty of Versailles context, that is, that they were being made in a communal, plebiscite-based, self-determination sense having worldwide effect and influence. "On this occasion," the Marques declared in a speech pitting enormous weight against the Feetham interpretation in advance, "I have no desire to say anything that might endanger the peaceful solution of the problem which fills the minds not only of the people in these islands, but of communities in all parts of the world, a problem which by its successful and peaceful solution will doubtless influence those great worldwide questions . . . In my opinion a temporary or unsatisfactory settlement is worse than no settlement at all. It only means that when all these great questions have advanced a further stage the Irish problem would react with greater and more dangerous force rather than complete an international harmony which all must hope eventually to witness. Therefore it is of paramount importance that the British Government should achieve a settlement consistent with our high Imperial traditions, and on no account . . . pursue any other policy in regard to Ireland." (N.I. *Parliamentary Debates* (Senate), Vol. 1, col. 115.)

The Feetham revisionism revisited

The Feetham Commission's denial of Ireland's right to plebiscites was necessitated by and resulted logically from the Chairman's misinterpretation of the "this instrument" phrase of the first part of Article 12. If a partitioned Treaty were to justify a partitioned Ireland, there would not be much point to holding plebiscites. One would have to go through the motions, of course, of consulting various persons – the wishes of the inhabitants would have to be entertained after all – but if the plan were to maintain partition at all costs, then, of course, one could not risk holding such things as real plebiscites and one would have to find a way of avoiding that calamity through misinterpretation or whatever.

General Richard Mulcahy gave warning in the Dail not to expect plebiscites of the Commission. He, anymore than anyone else in the Ireland of the post-Treaty years, was not so naive as to believe that the wishes of the inhabitants would be respected. "We will know by the manner in which the Boundary Commission sets about its work," Mulcahy said, "whether the intention of England is to set up in the North an Alsace-Lorraine for its own purpose, or to carry definitely into effect what we accepted the Treaty as giving us, that is, the administration of the government of Ireland in accordance with the wishes of the inhabitants." (*Dail Debates*, Vol. 8, cols. 2480, 2524-2527.) Keith Middlemas put the blame squarely on Feetham's misinterpretation of Article 12 for the Commission's failure to hold a plebiscite or plebiscites. The Chairman's "somewhat remote legalistic definition of the terms of reference under Article 12," wrote Middlemas, "precluded [the Commissioners] from considering not merely a general plebiscite, but [even] any large-scale transfers" (*Whitehall Diary*, Vol. III, p. 235).[10]

The Boundary Commission's denial of plebiscites, stemming as it did from misrepresentation of Article 12, was a serious breach of the Treaty mandate to assess the wishes of the inhabitants. The misinterpreting of Article 12, the partitioning of the Treaty, and the denial of plebiscites – all three combined led to the resignation of the Irish Commissioner, to the failure of the Boundary Commission, and ultimately to the stopgap measure, the Boundary Agreement. Explaining his position in the Dail, Eoin MacNeill stated: "I held that the true view and the right interpretation of Article 12 of the Treaty, in the main, was this: that it was to enable the exercise of a franchise to take place which had been denied and withheld in the case of the Act of 1920.... The Chairman held a quite distinct view. He held that the Act of 1920, and the time which had

10 For Feetham's explanation of the principles on which he acted, see his open letter to *The Times* (London), December 18, 1925.

elapsed since then, had created a *status quo* which should only be departed from when every element and every factor would compel us to depart from it. . . .

"The Chairman's point of view," MacNeill continued, "imported, to my mind, a new governing and dominant condition into Article 12, a political condition, a political consideration which was made a dominant consideration, and which did not appear at all within the terms of the Article and could be only read into it by a kind of constructional effort, namely, that if the wishes of the inhabitants were found to indicate a desire on the part of the inhabitants of certain districts to be included under the Free State jurisdiction, and if that inclusion would have the effect of seriously reducing the extent of territory under the jurisdiction of Northern Ireland, so as to produce a political effect on the Government of Northern Ireland, and so as to place the Government of Northern Ireland in a distinctly less advantageous position than it occupied under the Act of 1920, then the political consideration was to override the wishes of the inhabitants. To that position I need not say I never assented. It was not in the Article, I say it was not in the Treaty, and that it was only by what I call a constructional effort it could be brought into play at all." (*Dail Debates*, Vol. 13, cols. 800-801.)

So sorry a story was the Boundary Commission affair that Macardle termed it 'the Boundary Betrayal.' Hard it is to believe that so enormous a debacle could be due to so simple a misinterpretation. A historical parallel comes to mind. Just as the Arian heresy of the ***similarity*** of Christ to the Father (*homoiousion*), as opposed to the accepted doctrine of the ***consubstantiality*** of the two (*homoousion*), dangerously infected early Christianity and just as a diphthong, as Gibbon put it, threatened to destroy the unity of the Church forever, so, too, a 'heretical' misinterpretation of Article 12 of the Treaty dangerously infected the entire Treaty and threatened to divide Ireland forever. The Feetham heresy was so absurd and outrageous that even the British themselves did not all accept it. The para-official interpretation given of Article 12's "this instrument" is, in fact, that it referred to the Government of Ireland Act, 1920, and not, of course, to the Treaty.

Halsbury's Statutes of England, Third Edition, Volume 23, page 901, and *Halsbury's Statutes of England and Wales*, Fourth Edition, Volume 31, page 253, make it clear that Article 12 prescribed that as soon as the Address mentioned in the Article would be presented to the King the Government of Ireland Act of 1920 should be modified and adapted for application to Northern

Ireland instead of it being left for both Northern and Southern Ireland as it stood. The first and main instrument that did this modification and adaptation under the Treaty was the Irish Free State (Consequential Provisions) Act, 1922, an Act that *Halsbury's* describes as having been "passed to provide for the continuance in operation of the 1920 Act subject to the necessary modifications." Which is exactly as the Treaty prescribed: ". . . and this instrument shall have effect subject to the necessary modifications." The language of *Halsbury's* also reflects the Consequential Provisions Act as this stated in its first Section that it was in satisfaction of the Treaty prescription to modify and adapt the 1920 Government of Ireland Act (under certain conditions) that it was modifying and adapting that Act: "Subject to the provisions of the First Schedule to this Act, the Government of Ireland Act, 1920, shall cease to apply to any part of Ireland other than Northern Ireland, and in the event of such an address as is mentioned in Article 12 of the Articles of Agreement for a treaty set forth in the Schedule to the Irish Free State (Agreement) Act, 1922, being presented to His Majesty . . . the Government of Ireland Act, 1920, and the other enactments mentioned in the First Schedule to this Act, shall, as from the date of the presentation of such address, have effect subject to the modifications set out in that Schedule." Concludes *Halsbury's*: "The modifications of the principal Act set out in Sch 1 [the 1920 Act] therefore came into operation." There was no other Constitution or instrument that was, or was to be, modified under Article 12.

We might provide further proof of the Treaty intent. No less eminent an Irish constitutionalist than Sir Arthur S. Quekett not only held that the 1920 Act was what was intended to be modified by the modifications provision of the Treaty when this would be set in motion by the presentation of the Ulster Address (as the Consequential Provisions Act arranged): he took this fact for granted. In *The Constitution of Northern Ireland* (Part I, p. 30, n. 1) Quekett pointed out how the 1920 Act was modified by the Treaty in, for example, its religious liberty clauses, how the religion provisions of Section 5 of the Act were modified by the provisions of Article 16 of the Treaty. An "establishment or endowment" of religion was prohibited by Section 5, while "any endowment" was what was prohibited by Article 16. Obviously here Article 16 predominated.

Again in his magnum opus (Part I, p. 59 n.) Quekett wrote in reference to the presentation of the Ulster Address: "The completion of these proceedings fulfilled the sole condition precedent to the operation of the constitutional changes [of the 1920 Act] provided for by s. 1, etc., of 13 Geo. 5, c. 2 (Session 2) [i.e., by Section 1 (1) (and the First Schedule) of the Consequential Provisions Act, 1922]." What could only have authorized the 1922 Act to provide for any such changes to be made (as soon as the Address would be presented) was, of course, the Treaty Article 12 in its reference to "this instrument" as having effect "subject to the necessary modifications." And since the changes were provided for and made only in the 1920 Act, it follows that the "this instrument" authorization referred exclusively to the 1920 Act, as the CPA controlled.

Quekett went on to describe in Part II of his work (p. 196 n.) how the Treaty would be activated both to modify the 1920 Act and to authorize through its modifications provision such further modifications of that Act as would be necessary (just as, for example, Consequential Provisions in fact initially carried out). Wrote Quekett: "The address was presented to H.M. on 8th December, 1922, and that event set the . . . [Consequential Provisions] Act, and other enactments ['mentioned in the First Schedule'] thereof, in motion." If it did this, it did so only on the authority of and by virtue of Article 12's "this instrument" intending for modification the Act that was in fact duly modified, the Act of 1920.

Another weighty, authoritative conclusion that it was the 1920 Act that was intended by the Treaty to be modified is that of W.C. Costin and J. Steven Watson who, in their *Law and Working of the Constitution* (Vol. II, p. 149), report Article 12 to say just so: ". . . and the provisions of the Government of Ireland Act, 1920 (including those relating to the Council of Ireland), shall so far as they related to Northern Ireland, continue to be of full force and effect, subject to the necessary modifications."

The tricky Treaty provision of Article 12 might possibly be stretched in meaning to apply to Acts later than 1920 and in addition to the 1920 Act, but this would be only insofar as such Acts would be further modifications of the 1920 Act alone. All of such modifications would take place, of course, subject to the Ulster option being exercised in compliance with Treaty-set conditions (which, as Quekett explained, were expressed in the proviso to Article 12). This was not always recognized, and indeed the instrument in which the first modifications were contained, the Consequential Provisions Act itself, was passed three days ***before*** the Ulster option was exercised and almost a week before it was officially reported to have been exercised. So that the constitutionality of any modifications whatsoever being applied to Acts is just as important a consideration as the deciding of what Act or Acts modifications were to be made to at all.

The unconstitutionality of the manner in which these first modifications were made or provided for – and there is no question but that it was unconstitutional – is not what has primarily concerned us here, however. What has concerned us is identification of the ultimate object of the modifications for which authorization was given in the Treaty, and we feel that the identity of that object can quite clearly be demonstrated. Whatever else the object could have been it was not the Treaty itself. To say the least, the very intent and purpose of the Treaty did not allow of such a preposterous notion as that of Treaty self-modification.

In conclusion, the telling argument of an expert constitutionalist in impugning de Valera's misinterpretation of the Treaty regarding the nonobligatoriness of the oath therein could be applied with equal validity to Justice Feetham's misinterpretation that it was obligatory in and of the Treaty that it should modify itself. Both polemecists judged the strict, out-of-context terms of the instrument, a cardinal sin in any exegetical study. Of de Valera's misinterpretation, which was later admitted and corrected, Berriedale Keith declared: "The contention is not wholly impossible of defence as a mere matter of treaty interpretation, but there is not the slightest doubt [about it,] on the basis that treaties are to be interpreted according to their manifest intent and purpose, and in accordance with the agreement really made by the contracting parties, there is not the slightest possibility of accepting his version of the compact" (*The Sovereignty of the British Dominions*, p. 190). Feetham's contention may not be wholly impossible of defense as a mere matter of treaty interpretation, but, by the same token as de Valera is condemned, there is not the slightest possibility of accepting his, Feetham's, version of the compact indeed.

The crowning decision on the interpretation of the Treaty Article 12 was, perhaps, that given by the Judicial Committee of the Privy Council in dealing with the dispute over appointment of a third member to the Boundary Commission. In defining Article 12, the Council adjudicated that the purpose of the Treaty was to ***alter and amend*** the Partition Act: ". . . the Government of Ireland Act, 1920, which Act it is the purpose of the [Irish Free State Agreement] Act of 1922 [i.e., the Treaty] to alter and amend" (Cmd. 2214, 1924). It was precisely in that same Article 12 of the Treaty that specific authorization was made for altering and amending: in the clause "and this instrument shall have effect subject to the necessary modifications." In the Privy Council judgment, accordingly, this "this instrument" provision applies to the 1920 Act alone. (For the text of the CPA see Appendix 6, Note 14, *Supplement.*)

There is no sense, therefore, in which the "this instrument" reference of the Treaty could be to the Treaty itself – the Treaty, any Treaty, could not modify itself – and its misinterpretation by the Boundary Commission can only be seen for what it is – a misinterpretation. (See also Appendix 10, *Supplement.*)

Free State sovereignty is partially suspended

Be it as it may that the Anglo-Irish Boundary Commission's fraudulence commanded legally binding submission, it does not follow that the ensuing Anglo-Irish Boundary Agreement established and confirmed partition in Ireland. To the extent that it might have, this would be absolutely null and void due to undue duress. But because of the fact that the Commission's Report and Award were suppressed and its powers revoked, the Agreement that resulted therefrom did not establish or confirm the kind of partition the flunky Commission had demanded. The Agreement could not confirm what the Treaty had not established, and the Treaty certainly did not establish any *de jure* partition. What the Treaty in fact established was that Saorstat *de jure* sovereignty would be suspended by Britain in the six northeastern counties of Ireland, and what the Boundary Agreement confirmed was that that sovereignty should continue to be suspended in the manner that and for as long as the Treaty indicated.

That the Boundary Agreement did not certainly institute partition, much less a partition set in concrete, is clear from the explanation Prime Minister Chamberlain gave some years later (in 1939) when he declared that to suggest "that Great Britain should say that, if the people of Northern Ireland desire to join the south, that they are not to do so for imperial reasons, is to put the British Government in a position to which they have never aspired and do not aspire" (quoted from John Bowman, *De Valera and the Ulster Question*, p. 197). That is to say, the Agreement was, from the United Kingdom side, to be understood as being at most a British guarantee not to veto Irish unity should the Unionists at any time decide to join in a united Ireland. This British pledge of a non-veto is, as far as the Irish side was concerned, what would likewise at most have been recognized by Ireland in the Agreement. That is, if it were thought by the British that the Unionists needed a breather before unification, the Irish were not going 'to queer their pitch.' The Irish did not go so far as to agree that the nation might be ***partitioned***, much less partitioned for as long as the Unionists might otherwise wish. For the British position itself did not imply that Ireland should be kept divided if the Unionists would ***never*** decide to join in a united Ireland. In other words, all that was agreed to was, as the Treaty had established, that the sovereignty of the Saorstat should for a period be suspended. (In contrast to the stand the Irish took in the 1925 Agreement, in the 1985 Agreement they gave away more: they did not merely offer a negative recognition of Britain's pledge of a non-veto over Irish unity, they made a positive acknowledgment of Britain's support of a Unionist veto over it. However, like the 1939 Chamberlain Declaration, the 1985 Agreement itself, in rendering the continuation of partition to be ***conditional*** (on the wishes of a majority in Northern Ireland), effectively nullified the 1925 Agreement in any ***absolute*** permanence it may have been perceived to have attributed to partition.)

The reality and continuity of Free State jurisdictional suspension in Northern Ireland were to be reflected some twelve years after the Boundary Agreement in the new Irish Constitution. Article 3 states that "pending the re-integration of the national territory, and without prejudice to the right of the Parliament and Government established by this Constitution to exercise jurisdiction over the whole of that territory," the laws of the state "shall have the like area and extent of application [that] the laws of Saorstat Eireann [were *de facto* restricted to]"; that is, with the restricting of the new state's jurisdiction to the area that could but comprise 26 counties of Ireland, the reality of the 1922 Free State *de jure* jurisdiction being suspended in the six other counties would not ever be allowed to be forgotten. It would not be this Constitution's concern, however, that voicing what was at the most a complaint or at the least an aspiration would not bring Ireland any closer than did the 1925 Agreement to a fulfillment of the Treaty and a termination of the suspension the complaint decried or the aspiration desired.[11] It would not be the Constitution's concern,

11 Although the complaint/aspiration was given the appearance of a ***claim***, it "is not a claim by the State established under the Constitution to exercise jurisdiction over the whole of the island," writes Brian Doolan, because the state in voluntarily restricting itself to 26 counties could not at the same time voice a claim to 32 counties. But surrender in one part of the state Article 3 would be redeemed by the mandate in another part of the Article that, together with the nation Article 2, would require that the citizens of the state should strive so that "the Irish nation will one day possess the whole island incorporated into some political structure independent of outside control" (*Constitutional Law*, p. 8).

because the Constitution, in surrendering the Free State's hold on the British suspension of Irish sovereignty over Northern Ireland, did not have it in it to ever reclaim the North and end the derogation from Irish sovereignty. Its framer's greater concern was, if he could not tailor a Constitution to fit Ireland, he would tailor an Ireland to fit it. Did not the Constitution itself describe Ireland as being the 26 counties (Article 4)? Did the Constitution perchance ***constitute*** that new state/nation (Article 3), which it declared 'a sovereign, independent, democratic state' (Article 5)? Was the introduction of a new Constitution at all not a case of changing horses in midstream? Whatever answers can be given to these questions, the fact remains that, despite the introduction of a Constitution with a mandate for national unity in it, the suspension of complete sovereignty continues and the Treaty, as far as Article 12 is concerned, is still unfulfilled – as unfulfilled as it was during the four inglorious years following the Treaty when all Ireland waited for the Boundary Commission to be formed.

However, apart from the fact of the Treaty being unfulfilled, once Article 12 is properly interpreted and understood in its Ulster option provisions, partial and provisional suspension of Free State sovereign jurisdiction is the only rational interpretation to put on the relevant provisions of the Treaty Agreement. Such an interpretation is reinforced by the provision of Article 14, which indicated the exercise of Saorstat jurisdiction to be in the area of the sovereign major powers.

The way the Treaty decreed that Ireland's jurisdiction should be temporarily suspended in six counties of Ireland if Northern Ireland were to opt out of the I. F. S.'s minor powers was by saying that "the powers of the Parliament and the Government of the Irish Free State shall no longer extend to Northern Ireland, and the provisions of the Government of Ireland Act, 1920 . . . shall so far as they relate to Northern Ireland continue to be of full force and effect . . ." Needless to say, this particular interpretation – that Irish jurisdiction should be suspended for the time being in the six counties[12] – has not been agreed with in Britain or the

12 The (Irish) Interpretation Act, 1923 declared, in Section 3 (1), the *de facto* Saorstat Eireann to be for the time being a part of the *de jure* Saorstat, and, in Section 3 (2), Northern Ireland to be also for the time being the remaining part of that *de jure* Saorstat Eireann: "The expression 'Saorstat Eireann' or its equivalent in English 'the Irish Free State' when used for the purpose of defining the application of any law or the extent or incidence of any authority, obligation or imposition shall mean the area for the time being within the jurisdiction of the Parliament and Government of Saorstat Eireann" and "the expression 'Northern Ireland' shall mean such part of Ireland as the powers of the Parliament and

North of Ireland. The British Government's view, following a rationale that even a Feetham could hardly invent, has been that the Treaty references to the Northern Ireland provisions of the 1920 Act as continuing to be of full force and effect meant that the North would be a *province* of Britain. Such a view, since the Treaty, is utterly untenable, since it was the Treaty that excluded Ireland completely – both North and South – from Britain, and this the Treaty did regardless of whether the Ulster option was exercised or not: it did it in the first ten Articles. These, of course, may not be taken in the double sense of Feetham, as we have demonstrated, but have to be understood in their obvious and intended sense – the transfer *en bloc* from Britain of Irish sovereignty to Ireland, the North included.

Britain's formal interpretation put belatedly – after 28 years – on the Treaty reference to the Northern Ireland provisions of the 1920 Act is quite unusual. Actually it is at variance, it must be said, with the intention of the formulators of the Treaty and with the interpretation given to it by such contemporaries as Lord Grey and Kevin O'Higgins. The former saw the Treaty as the complete antithesis of the 1920 Act and the instrument designed to prevent rather than facilitate the partition of the Government of Ireland Act; the latter saw the Treaty as giving to the Irish Government a trusteeship over the Nationalist community in the North of Ireland. If the Feetham misinterpretation can be rejected, as it has indeed been by both Britain and Ireland, the only resort Britain could have by way of justifying her regarding Northern Ireland a British province has, of all things, been to invoke the age-old Act of Union! This, incredibly, is what Britain in fact has done, which is equally preposterous with the Feetham stance. The Treaty, we all know, had the effect of repealing the Act of Union, which in any case was an all-Ireland Act and could in no way be made to

---

Government of Saorstat Eireann shall for the time being not extend to." The closest the Act came to defining the *de jure* Saorstat Eireann was in its definition of the First Dail Eireann of the all-Ireland Republic. Section 2 (7) stated: "The expression 'the First Dail Eireann' shall mean the assembly of members of Parliament elected for constituencies in Ireland at a Parliamentary Election held on the 14th day of December, 1918, who first came together in a Parliament held on the 21st day of January, 1919, in the official residence of the Lord Mayor of Dublin called the Mansion House at Dublin, and there drew up and promulgated a provisional Constitution for the said assembly as Dail Eireann and Government of Saorstat Eireann." The Constitution (Consequential Provisions) Act, 1937, in disregarding the *de jure* Saorstat Eireann, would appear to be undermined by this Section of the Interpretation Act.

apply to Northern Ireland alone. We will discuss this question more fully in Chapter 12. (See also Appendix 14, *Supplement.*) The official British interpretation of the relevant Treaty clause since 1949 is twofold – and, unfortunately, inadmissible.

1. It has been claimed that the Treaty did not decree the suspension of the Irish Free State's jurisdiction over Northern Ireland at all, but arranged that Ulster should if she so chose be subject to the Westminster Parliament for the reserved services instead. In support of this view the Treaty clause 'and the provisions of the Government of Ireland Act . . . shall so far as they relate to Northern Ireland continue to be a full force and effect' would be interpreted to refer to the major powers of jurisdiction and to indicate that they were divisible in their application to Ireland. But such an interpretation is impossible, because either the major powers were to be transferred to all Ireland each *en bloc* or they were not. (They were, of necessity, reserved *en bloc* in the 1920 Act.) Obviously they were by the Treaty transferred *en bloc* to all Ireland, as certain British statesmen of the time explained. The only interpretation to give to the above Treaty clause, then, is that on Ulster's choice in the minor powers area of jurisdiction the exercise of the jurisdiction of the Irish Free State in the major powers area ***would be suspended*** over the Northern area.

2. The second aspect of the claim made for Northern Ireland was that the six-county area should be exempted from Free State jurisdiction for as long as the majority of the inhabitants so desired. The claim, in fact, goes farther and is that Northern Ireland should come under British Government jurisdiction and remain under it for as long as the Loyalists of Ulster so chose. But the Treaty clause 'the powers . . . of the Irish Free State shall no longer extend to Northern Ireland' does not admit of this interpretation at all. The Treaty simply states that the Free State's jurisdiction should no longer extend to Northern Ireland. Although it does not say for how long that jurisdiction is to be suspended, it clearly implies that the suspension should at most last only as long as the 1920 Act was not repealed. It certainly does not say that the duration of the suspension is to depend on the will of the inhabitants of a part of Ireland. Above all, the Treaty clause does not say – nor imply – that Westminster jurisdiction should fill a vacuum after a certain length of time. Britain's claim to Northern Ireland in this vein is groundless, and her filling of the vacuum when it did occur was purely an act of naked aggression, because there is certainly no justification to be found for permanent Westminster jurisdiction

in the Treaty. That is why, when such aggression came to be maintained by armed force after another 20 years (by 1969), that we say the British military presence in Northern Ireland is part of the problem of partition, not independent of it.

Once Britain back in 1921 relinquished the major powers *en bloc*, as she had to, there is no constitutional basis in the Treaty or any of the Agreements signed since for the British claim that Northern Ireland is a part of the United Kingdom. Northern Ireland is constitutionally and in every other sense a part of Ireland, and Britain herself acknowledged as much in the 1914 Home Rule Act, the 1920 Government of Ireland Act, the Treaty, and the 1925 Boundary Agreement; but she began to back away from that position with the 1927 Royal and Parliamentary Titles Act and, more obviously, the 1938 Sovereignty Agreement. It was not until 1949, in reaction to Ireland's leaving the Monarchical Commonwealth (and thus putting the Statute of Westminster into effect), that Britain formally claimed to have an obligation to the Northern Loyalist community and to regard the North as belonging to the United Kingdom. There can be found no constitutional justification for making this claim. And it is interesting to note that as long as the Treaty was correctly interpreted, Britain, at least, did not claim that Ulster was part of the United Kingdom. (We will examine the British claim more fully in Chapter 11.) The 1949 outburst was, however, the climax of Britain's claim to the North of Ireland, because soon enough afterwards (by 1973) the British were again admitting that Ulster was a part of Ireland that was a part of Britain (see Appendix 14, *Supplement*).

As we pointed out at the beginning of this book, because of the Irish people's declaration of independence, their establishment of a Constitution and an Irish Republic in 1919, and their setting up of Dail Eireann, Britain had no constitutional right after two and one half years to claim back any part of Ireland. But here we point out that because of the Anglo-Irish constitutional instruments in which British agreement was secured, Britain has no constitutional right in international law to claim back any part of Ireland. Britain, in fact, would not have dared to reassert a claim to any part of Ireland, and a different kind of Ireland would by now have emerged as well, if all that was constitutionally achieved and agreed on with Britain had been put into effect. A situation that was abandoned to itself did not get better with time – could not get better, because Ireland was on the wrong track – and that from 1949 or so began, in fact, to get worse, has by now become chronic with no real remedies being applied. Certainly the hopes of Dorothy Macardle back in 1926 and 1937 have not been fulfilled.

"Ten years after the Easter Rising, Ireland lay partitioned, impoverished, her people embittered by disappointments, divided and distraught by a half-measure of freedom and exhausted by war. Had the high hopes inspired by the Rising, all the ardour and sacrifice that during 'four glorious years' upheld the Republic, led to no better end than this? The Irish people had created their Republic and sustained it with as much courage and devotion as any people have brought to the defending of the national inheritance . . . Those who refused to surrender . . . were disfranchised and powerless. De Valera was a leader without an army, without a voice in Parliament, without funds.

"Only those who knew the depth, strength, and persistence of the Irish passion for freedom, and had measured the quiet tenacity of de Valera's leadership, could conceive that before another ten years had passed the great majority of the Irish people would find themselves reunited in a steady effort to loosen, without war, the shackles of the Treaty, in a movement with nothing less than Independence as its goal.

"Through four-fifths of Ireland the process goes forward. The stranglehold of the Treaty is being loosened and the imposed clauses of the Constitution removed: every internal function of the King has been eliminated; the Oath, the appeal to the English Privy Council, the Senate, and the Governor-General have disappeared. The economic life of Ireland and the native culture are being, in a large measure, restored. And, while the people are regaining the strength that would enable them, if the need came, to resist coercion, political thought is advancing in Britain: . . . a generation of Englishmen with new ideals of statecraft is taking the reins of power. Perhaps this generation may make anew the opportunity that, in 1921, was so tragically wasted, and may see an Irish Republic make, with the British Commonwealth of Nations, a compact of amity and peace."

Addendum to Part II. If by the Chequers/London Agreement of 1925 the prospect of Irish unification was not exactly forfeited, the same cannot be said of the Chequers/Hillsborough Agreement of 60 years later. In fact, it would seem that, *prima facie*, the 1985 Anglo-Irish Agreement could hardly have been better designed to render unification impossible altogether. The reason for this is that while the earlier Agreement recognized a de facto *exercise* of a provisionally and partially suspended Irish jurisdiction, the recent Agreement treated the de jure *jurisdiction itself* as a full sovereignty and foreign entity.

How the Agreement did this was, as Professor O'Connor, Dean of the Faculty of Law at University College Cork, has put it, by creating "a new international status for Northern Ireland which is quite unique in international law." That status was a twofold one whereby, while the United Kingdom yielded to Ireland on participation in Northern Ireland affairs at the minor powers level of jurisdiction (Articles 2 to 10), Ireland yielded to the United Kingdom (of Great Britain *and* Northern Ireland) on recognition of the permanent status of Northern Ireland in the major powers area of jurisdiction (Article 1, the Addendum to Article 2(b), and Article 12 possibly). "The Irish Government in Article 1 formally affirmed that any change in the status of Northern Ireland would only come about with the consent of a majority of the people of Northern Ireland, thus recognising and legitimising for the first time in an international agreement the virtual veto of Northern Unionists on a United Ireland" (John F. O'Connor, "The Anglo-Irish Agreement 1985," *Annuaire francais de droit international*, 1985). While Northern Ireland may have been internationalized at the domestic level, it was provisionally Briticized at the sovereignty level.

Nothing goes as much to the heart of sovereignty in the Irish context as does the Unionist veto or Loyalist guarantee now institutionalized in an international Treaty. Because so unique an international status as that described above has been accorded to Northern Ireland under the new Treaty, it is not anymore with Britain alone, but with Northern Ireland equally, that the Republic would have to negotiate, internationally, to regain the one-time suspended sovereignty over the North. Since the 1920s, the Treaty Settlement and Boundary Agreement combined had guaranteed a full national sovereignty to be restored to Ireland, by Britain, at the appropriate time, but the 1985 Agreement decreed that it was ultimately with Northern Ireland, now a quasi nation in the international forum, that such a restoration would have to be negotiated. While Britain's position on sovereignty would be that it depends on the North to decide, Ireland's would be that one must destroy the prospects of reunification in order to save them.

The thrust of the 1985 Agreement has been to secure mutual acceptance and cooperation at the domestic political level – devolution – and through that means to engender a willingness among a majority in the statelet to agree to unification with the South. It is not without reason, therefore, that the major portion of the Agreement concerns itself with the minor powers area of jurisdiction. "For the accommodation of the rights and identities of the two traditions which exist in Northern Ireland, and for peace, stability and prosperity throughout the island of Ireland by promoting reconciliation," both the Irish and British Governments declare their willingness to support the policy of devolved government and power-sharing in Northern Ireland "on a basis which would secure widespread acceptance throughout the community" (Article 4). Such desired power-sharing between the Nationalist and Unionist communities would hopefully be initiated by the proxy-type power-sharing of the two sovereign Governments within the framework of the Intergovernmental Conference (Article 2). "Clearly," writes Professor O'Connor, "both Governments hoped to set in motion a process whereby *their* power-sharing might be gradually phased out and replaced by power-sharing directly between the divided communities in Northern Ireland."

Hope and trust that this putting of the cart before the horse will lead to a resolution of the problem at the major powers level of jurisdiction may or may not be misplaced, but certainly such placing of emphasis on devolution and reconciliation at the minor powers level and within the confines of Northern Ireland falls far short of the New Ireland Forum ideal and requirement that a "settlement which recognises the legitimate rights of nationalists and unionists must transcend the context of Northern Ireland" (Paragraph 4.16). Added to that, it would have to be said that the purpose for which the attainment of reconciliation in Northern Ireland was given priority – to achieve peace, stability and prosperity in the entire island of Ireland – was ill-served by Ireland's making the supreme sacrifice of giving *de jure* recognition to partition and abandoning the national position, as enshrined in Articles 2 and 3 of the country's Constitution, which decree the paramountcy of achieving the "re-integration of the national territory."

In 1985, not only were the achievements of the Treaty Agreements of the 1920s unworked and disregarded, but the Constitution of 1937 was not respected and complied with either. That is why we have to say that the entire Agreement of 1985, in the territorial sense in which it was designed, would have to be legally reformed and reinterpreted. Under the constitutional circumstances that exist the Agreement would indeed mandate that it be itself interpreted in an other than territorial sense.

The British-Irish problem, as it focused in the violence of Northern Ireland since 1969, was certainly an international problem requiring an international solution, and that is why the international instruments of the Treaty era should have been resorted to and exploited, instead of having striven for a new interim international Agreement that would give away its own basic aim. But there is hope that the Agreement is not one that cannot still be lived with (if it is not sooner or later to be judicially declared unconstitutional) and that it can yet be interpreted in a mutually helpful manner. For, as John F. O'Connor has again said, "the Irish Government's *de jure* recognition of the position of the Northern Unionists, although this position was achieved originally by the creation of an artificial 'democratic' majority, is a significant acceptance of the international law principle of self-determination in relation to the people of Northern Ireland." We might add that it is a significant acceptance of the international law principle of self-determination in relation to all of the people of all of Ireland – if the Agreement can be legally reformed into conformity with the evolutionary constitutional line it must surely have been intended to be in conformity with.

A forewarning of a national betrayal in the offing, which would have been noted by the FitzGerald Government, was issued in 1981. "The objects of [the Thatcher Government's] policy remain the pacification of the province [of Northern Ireland] and the eventual restoration of its political life within the United Kingdom," stated Peter Jenkins, then policy editor and political columnist of *The Guardian*. "The government's policy is essentially one of containment. For such a policy to be sustainable, periodic attempts must be made – hence the latest proposal for an Advisory [Intergovernmental] Council, a most modest step towards reviving the political life of the province." ("Political Constraints: London," David Watt, ed., *The Constitution of Northern Ireland, Problems and Prospects*, p. 166.)

You cannot go forward with one foot in the Old Order and the other in the New.

PRESIDENT WOODROW WILSON

PART III

RESTORATION

If you have built castles in the air,
your work need not be lost;
that is where they should be.
Now put the foundations under them.

HENRY DAVID THOREAU

The North Is Won

The deed is done! The North is won!
From Derry down to Belfast town!
To Davis, Pearse and brave Wolfe Tone,
All glory be, for Ireland's one!
The Tri is in, the Jack is out,
And we shall raise a rousing shout.
Sing ho, sing hi, my merry men,
The North is won, is won again!
Sing ho, sing hi, my merry men,
The North is won, is won again!

VINCENT J. DELACY RYAN
(With apologies to Thomas Davis)

CHAPTER 11

THE REPUBLIC IS PRESERVED THROUGH DUALITY OF ACTION

A Republican Retrospective

In his book *No Other Law* Florrie O'Donoghue describes the preservation of the Republican Second Dail Eireann throughout the cataclysmic days of the Treaty deliberations as "a master-stroke." And well indeed might it be called a masterstroke, because it meant that in that way, in the face of acceptance of a seemingly overpowering Treaty, the frayed thread of Republican continuity that could so easily have snapped was managed to be maintained. The preservation of the Republican Dail Eireann in spite of the new constitutional status being imposed on Ireland was extremely important, because it meant that the Republic, and with it Irish unity, could be restored in more auspicious times. It was imperative that they not be ***constitutionally*** interrupted now, but be somehow continued. For without Republican continuity there is no restoration of Irish unity.

Such a tremendous effort of life and death had been put into the Republican movement from 1916 on that the preservation and consolidation of what had been achieved in 1919, 1920, and 1921 meant everything to the Irish people. Continuity of Republican independence and national unity was, then, of paramount importance, but it can safely be said that it was touch and go many times during the Treaty deliberations, with the Republic being assaulted by a Treaty that entailed acceptance of the antithesis of Republicanism – Monarchism – and that contained a mechanism for the possible, permanent dismemberment of Ireland. If submission were to be made for the time being, it was doubly important that continuity be preserved for the future when attempts at restoration might be made.

Although preservation of Republican continuity was an achievement in itself, it was difficult to expect the Irish people to be magnanimous just the same and submit to everything that was being thrust upon them. The troubles of the Treaty were not exactly what the people had endured so much for in the Revolutionary War. They were reluctant now to give away under pressure what they had sacrificed so much for and especially what they had some eight months earlier taken precautions to secure. From the moment of the May 1921 elections that were held under the 1920 Government of Ireland Act for a bistate Ireland, with the possibility allowed for the gap between the states to widen in a partitionist sense, the situation had become very tacky. With Britain retaining jurisdiction over Ireland in the major powers area, there was always the danger that the Northern state would be drawn more and more into the British orbit, that she would be drawn in inverse proportion to the degree that the Southern state would be excluded, and that she would ultimately be retained separately as an integral part of the United Kingdom. In other words, partition in the full sense of the term.

Sensing the real danger, Republican Ireland would have nothing to do with the Act that was designed to dismember the country in this fashion. For Republicans the unitary nature of Ireland was an article of faith, although they acknowledged they were at a loss to know how they could put into effect in all of Ireland the Republic that had been declared established. Nevertheless, the last thing they wanted was British bedevilment of their efforts, and they thought their best bet would be to reject the 1920 Act out of hand at the elections that were held with the partition of Ireland as end. The Partition Act would not be worked, Republicans declared, and the Irish electorate told the British so in no uncertain terms. The result of the elections was recognized in Britain as "a sweeping victory for Sinn Fein and a virtually unanimous repudiation of the Government of Ireland Act" (*Annual Register*, 1921).

The result was a clear rejection of partition on a national scale, and as well the right of Britain to legislate for Ireland. By this time, mid-1921, Dail Eireann and the Republic had been two and a half years in place, and Republicans, by making use of the elections North and South to have the Second Dail Eireann elected, made sure to preserve continuity, on an all-Ireland basis, from the Republican beginnings of 1919 and earlier. Nevertheless, from the

British viewpoint the Act of 1920 was now law in Ireland, and so the Irish were to have a problem on their hands. The British dimension that was left out of the Irish calculations in endeavoring to secure the independence of the entire country, North as well as South, was now indeed a force to be reckoned with.

Duality of action preserves Republican continuity

The Irish, for their part, determined as they were to preserve Republican continuity, convened the Second Dail Eireann, the second all-Ireland Parliament, and in the face of this the British, on their side, were determined to maintain their Act of 1920 and to do so by force, if necessary, at least for the North of Ireland. From the moment the Act was given effect in the North, partition in the British view became a fait accompli, and the decision of the electorate in 1921 would come to be treated as a mere protest. "From that moment," Churchill was to write in *The Aftermath* (p. 286), "the position of Ulster became unassailable."

Or so Churchill thought. Presumably he was talking, as most British statesmen of the day were wont to do, of the position of Westminster behind Ulster – that is, of the reservation by Westminster of some major jurisdiction in Ireland, partition itself. And presumably he was not talking about the position of Ulster as a state, which nobody in Ireland wanted to assail and about which Nationalists from as early as 1885 were giving pledges not to coerce into integration with the rest of the country – even though as yet there was no partitioned area of northern Ireland, of course. But if Churchill thought that the Act that created Northern Ireland was going to last and that the British occupation of the six counties was going to endure, he was a little off base. For soon the very Act that was Northern Ireland's partial charter was going to be assailed itself – by the Treaty. In fact, the very day that the Northern Parliament was being opened – June 22, 1921 – preparations were under way for concluding a Treaty between Great Britain and Ireland, a Treaty that would supersede the Partition Act in its entirety.

King George V, as he opened the Belfast Parliament, could not have been unaware of efforts afoot to effect a settlement such as the Treaty was to be, because he was himself a prime mover of developments and in the thick of things at Westminster. His action in opening the Parliament of Northern Ireland appeared to confirm the obstruction to the Irish plan for independence, but ironically the King's upbeat speech on that occasion was the cue for compromise and a breakthrough in the deadlock that had been brought on. As A. J. P. Taylor has written, the King's "initiative was perhaps the greatest service performed by a British monarch in modern times" (*English History, 1914-1945*, p. 157). Seumas MacManus was, however, perplexed that the King should be "calling for union among the people he was dividing" (*The Story of the Irish Race*, p. 710), but there must have been something to his words. He must have had more in mind than the Act under which he was acting. His Belfast speech bears close scrutiny, particularly in view of the fact that the speech was prepared by those who were most concerned with the bringing about of peace negotiations with Dail Eireann, some of whom would be participating in those negotiations themselves. It should also be examined closely because of the fact that King George himself kept Ireland in his thoughts and good wishes and always had the country's best interests at heart. (See Charles Duff, *Six Days to Shake an Empire*, pp. 275-279.)

The King's message went in part as follows: "The eyes of the whole Empire are on Ireland to-day – that Empire in which so many nations and races have come together in spite of ancient feuds, and in which new nations have come to birth within the lifetime of the youngest in this Hall.

"I am emboldened by that thought to look beyond the sorrow and the anxiety which have clouded of late My vision of Irish affairs. I speak from a full heart when I pray that My coming to Ireland to-day may prove to be the first step towards an end of strife amongst her people, whatever their race or creed. In that hope, I appeal to all Irishmen to pause, to stretch out the hand of forbearance and conciliation, to forgive and to forget, and to join in making for the land they love a new era of peace, contentment, and goodwill."

Continuing in this vein of Irish unity, the King said: "It is My earnest desire that in Southern Ireland, too, there may ere long take place a parallel to what is now passing in this Hall; that there a similar occasion may present itself and a similar ceremony performed.

"For this the Parliament of the United Kingdom has in the fullest measure provided the powers; for this the Parliament of Ulster is pointing the way. The future lies in the hands of My Irish people themselves.

"May this historic gathering be the prelude of a day in which the Irish people, North and South, under one Parliament or two, as those Parliaments may themselves decide, shall work together in common love for Ireland upon the sure foundation of mutual justice and respect." (Quoted from Dorothy Macardle, p. 466; Northern Ireland *Parliamentary Debates*, Vol. 1 (1921), cols. 9-15 (House and Senate).)

Now, King George was certainly not an ununderstanding person, nor, as we know, a man unsympathetic towards Ireland, and really not one who would be a party to any suspected duplicity on the part of the London Government. It could not be, then, that he was dividing Ireland in a partitionist sense even as he was seeking to unite it. It can only be that he understood himself, under the Government of Ireland Act of 1920, to be erecting Ireland into two states with minor powers of jurisdiction and that he interpreted the outcome of the impending negotiations to provide for the unity of Ireland. That is, by the transfer to Dublin from London of Irish sovereignty in the major powers area of jurisdiction unity would be ensured and partition as such not instituted. That is what the King would have meant by the observation, "For this the Parliament of the United Kingdom has in the fullest measure provided the powers." By these words he appeared to take the Treaty-to-Be along with the Government of Ireland Act and to intimate that the one would supersede the other and provide Ireland with the unity the other did not.

In the context of partition the King's concluding injunction and call for unity would not make sense. Neither could it be construed to refer to the so-called Council of Ireland envisaged in the Partition Act, because such a proposal as the Council of Ireland one did not itself make sense as formulated and was rightly buried in 1925 (except for a brief resurrection in 1938, 1973, and 1983, but then in the sense of accepting partition and having the minority agree to abolish it).[1] It can only be, then, that the King had in mind the outcome of the impending talks and that a resultant agreement would be made with Dail Eireann on a united, all-Ireland basis. Such an agreement was, of course, the Treaty, an agreement that would lay aside the 1920 Act and that would contain the transfer from the United Kingdom to Ireland of the major powers of

1 The Council of Ireland proposal made of the Partition Act a self-contradiction, because it purported to involve the National Parliament in discussions with the subordinate Belfast Parliament on areas of jurisdiction that might be combined - without reference to Westminster, we were told - areas with which the Belfast Parliament had no competency to deal and which presumably it would first have to arrogate to itself from Westminster - if indeed it would ever have the will to do so.

jurisdiction King George V referred to; it was an agreement that, in the words of Kevin O'Higgins, accorded to the Dail "a position of trusteeship for those [Nationalist] inhabitants of the present area of jurisdiction of the Northern Government, to whom definite rights were secured [to us] by the Treaty . . . [and under which] we regard ourselves as not having the power to do anything to lessen or to alter these rights." (Quoted from Macardle, p. 875; *Dail Debates*, Vol. 7, cols. 1375-1377.)

With the onslaught of a Treaty not only that imposed an alien constitutional status on Ireland, but that also contained a device for the possible dismemberment of the country (although the instrument was mainly designed to preserve the unity of the nation), Republican continuity bade fair not just to be disrupted but indeed to be buried forever as well. With the Treaty came in a host of Imperial and Monarchical forms with which it was next to impossible for Republicans to cope. As we saw, the paramount concern of Republicans was to make sure that all that had so far been achieved by way of independence would be essentially continued. For them continuity of the Republic meant above all preservation of essential Irish unity, since it was for all Ireland that the Republic had been declared. Their job was not going to be easy, however, and we can only marvel at the amount of wafting and weaving that had to be resorted to in Dail Eireann to enable that Assembly to survive the welter of British-inspired forms with which it was beset. Under such harrying conditions the wonder is how continuity of Republican institutions could be and was preserved at all, and certainly in this respect the preservation of Dail Eireann itself as a vehicle of continuity in the face of great odds was nothing short of the masterstroke Florrie O'Donoghue claimed it was.

But preserved it was and with it what looked like being inevitable, the disestablishment of the Republic, was avoided. This was, in fact, further avoided with another stroke of genius,the Collins-de Valera Pact, which led to the election of the Third Dail Eireann and made possible the direct continuity of this Dail from its predecessor. Another plus was the success that was had in getting the British Government and Parliament to agree to the Pact General Election and thus to recognize and support the Third Dail as an all-Ireland Assembly.

Duality of action in response to British pressure

Preservation of the Republic and of Republican Dail Eireann alongside Imperial and Monarchical forms signified, however, something more than Republican continuity. It signified a duality in Irish political life, a duality that translated itself into many forms in the actions the Irish rulers were to take in the post-Treaty months and years. These forms were expressed repeatedly in what George Gavan Duffy aptly called 'an interlocking directorate.' On the one side of the coin there was the British 'legislation' for Ireland, which was being churned out continuously and gave the conservative British the feeling that they were the ones directing Irish political affairs. On the other there was the concomitant Irish legislative direction which was actually what was being followed but which was accompanied by a continuous outward rolling-with-the-punches type of conforming with British directives. This outward show was so impressive at times, couched as it was often in British-derived terminology, that it appeared to observers that the actors had really caved in and were actually doing the British will. But throughout it all the Irish political leaders, in true Irish historical fashion, maintained – perhaps not stoutly at times – the Republican tradition in the internal forum, it could be said. In bending again and again to the British will in the external forum, however, the leaders involved did not quite convince their Republican colleagues that the thread of continuity was not becoming just a bit too frayed at times and that it might easily snap.

This duality of activity, which was a necessity of the times and, as we said, a tradition of Irish history, indicated another important point.[2] It showed in the circumstances that imposition of the Treaty created a situation wherein Republicanism and Monarchism need not necessarily be contradictory to each other. Contraries, yes, but not contradictories, if the one was observed in the internal forum and the other in the external forum. It was only when it came to the oath of allegiance and this was presented as being obligatory that a problem arose, because an oath to Monarchism would certainly conflict with an oath to Republicanism in the internal forum. It was unfortunate that it was not openly

2 The first instance of Irish obeisance to English power in Ireland was in 1171 when the chiefs and princes of Leinster and Munster humbly paid homage to King Henry II as their Lord and liege upon the occasion of his visit to Ireland. But hardly had the King returned to England than the Irish leaders were in open revolt against His Majesty's soldiery left behind. This scene was to repeat itself many times in Irish history, particularly in the lives of Aodh Mor O Neill ('Earl of Tyrone'), Ruairi O Dhomhnaill ('Earl of Tyrconnel' and brother of Aodh Ruadh), and even the great Eoghan Ruadh O Neill himself. Incidentally, and significantly, such submission as this that the Irish rulers and chieftains offered to a foreign overlord was such an act of ignominy to de Valera that he could never understand it. (See Seumas MacManus, *op. cit.*, pp. 326-327, 393-395.)

pointed out, though, that the oath as prescribed by the Treaty was optional because of the freedom of conscience that Article 16 of the Treaty guaranteed, so that those who would have conscientious objections to the oath would not be bound to take it. (Within ten years of the Treaty the oath was held clearly to be optional. "The Oath is not mandatory in the Treaty," stated the High Commissioner for the Irish Free State in a communication to the British Secretary of State for Dominion Affairs dated March 22, 1932; this communication reflected de Valera's thought as well, though later he changed his mind on this.)

But apart from the oath, duality of activity was freely engaged in as a means of political survival for the fledgling Republic. It would be boring to the reader to list all the occasions on which this duality manifested itself throughout the year 1922 especially – from the moment the Treaty was accepted and Griffith, acting in his capacity of former chairman of the ex-delegation of Treaty negotiators, proceeded to summon the 'members' elected to the 'Parliament of Southern Ireland' with a view to electing a 'Provisional Government,' while at the same time agreeing that only the people and not the Treaty could disestablish a Republican Dail Eireann and its Government, the retaining of which made the Provisional Government a mere agency of the Dail for the transmission of power and services from the British Government and for directing the evacuation of the British forces from Ireland – from those initial steps through intervening vicissitudes too numerous to mention to the electing of a Republican Pact Dail Eireann for all Ireland during which there were all the pressures emanating from the British Government and from repeated Acts of Parliament purporting to control and direct Irish affairs that ranged from the calling of elections to the interpreting of the Treaty in the guise of a Westminster-enacted Constitution supposedly suitable for Ireland. On and on the duality of activity went, with sometimes the Irish getting the worse of the trading in punches but all the time preserving precariously direct Republican continuity – up to a point. It is our conviction, as we have shown, that direct Republican continuity in the usurped Third Dail – and with it certainly the hold on Irish unity – was broken off by the submission in late 1922 and throughout 1923 to a British and Monarchical Constitution that eased the Dail out of 32-county jurisdiction. It is our further conviction that the mistake was compounded by the failure to mend the rupture by neglecting to amend favorably a Constitution that rightly applied to all of Ireland

and to make provision in it for expression of the six-county voice (as Alfred O'Rahilly had wanted).

Our examination of duality in Irish affairs leads us onto this sterile path, where the Irish have been sidelined for the past several decades. What happened to bring about this state of affairs? It was that duality in a moment of carelessness broke down. In a moment of oversubmissiveness to the British juggernaut in December 1922 the Irish rulers capitulated in the struggle to maintain Republican continuity and accepted the 26-county jurisdiction that was dished out to them. This was a most disastrous surrender as far as national unity was concerned, of course, because theretofore duality of action had worked well and there was no need for faintheartedness with the goal of success in sight. Was all that had been achieved so far and that had barely survived to be for naught?

In the preceding few years a Republic had been achieved and maintained for all Ireland, the Union of 118 years had been smashed, and the British forces were got out of Ireland. Prior to mid-1921 just about all political action in Ireland had been one-sided – British one-sided. From mid-1921 on a duality of political and constitutional action began to take hold, and it was highly successful because it provided a way to have the British help get themselves out of Ireland. Now it was nearing the time for the Irish to take over completely and to go it alone. Instead, with the promised land in sight, at the end of 1922, duality was abandoned and capitulation was made back to the British on the Constitution, which resulted in partition being well on its way to becoming a fixture. Such was the price the Irish had to pay for having acquiesced so meekly on the Constitution issue (although this acquiescence was perhaps compensated for by their having secured Britain's early recognition of the Pact Dail as being an all-Ireland Parliament[3]).

---

3 The British Parliament recognized the Pact Dail Eireann in its very act of recognizing the Dail as a Constituent Assembly which had adopted the all-Ireland Constitution that the Westminster Parliament now ratified. In the same way, contrary to widespread opinion, Westminster had recognized the Second Dail Eireann insofar as it required the Dail by the Treaty to approve the Treaty so that this could in turn be ratified by the group specified in the Treaty to do this: "By this act of approval it [Dail Eireann]," wrote W.K. Hancock, "sanctioned also the other process of approval which the treaty itself enjoined" (*Survey of British Commonwealth Affairs*, Vol. I, p. 152). (This other process of approval was not, incidentally, effected by the "Parliament of Southern Ireland" proposed by the Act of 1920, since this body never came into being in accordance with the Act: it was not summoned by the Lord Lieutenant, it did not become bicameral, and it never took the oath required by the Act.)

Fortunately, however, there was a strong section of the Irish people who would not be defeated by the breakdown of duality. The fact that it happened did not mean for them that they would have to submit and accept their lot with resignation. These were the few who, led by de Valera for the time being, kept the Republican flag flying through all the difficulties that flowed from acceptance of the Treaty. They would not be overcome by the setbacks of those post-Treaty times, but would themselves as the rightful heirs of the Republican tradition preserve Irish Republicanism with the intention to sally forth when the time would be ripe to restore the all-Ireland Republic. In this way, if Republican continuity was stopped in its tracks in one section of public life, it was preserved in another outside of 'official' politics and a usurped Dail. And, since reunification cannot be achieved without resorting to continuity from the Republican past, it is to this section of political life, these Republicans knew, that Ireland would look for a way out of the national impasse that then arose and that has existed ever since.

The British dimension that still exists demands a return to the 1922 Constitution

The duality of action that worked so wonderfully for Ireland in 1921 and 1922 teaches us another fact, and that is that there is a British side as well as an Irish side to Irish political life. Just as there are more than a million British citizens in Ireland whom since 1917 or before Irish Republicans have pledged not to coerce into subjection to an all-Ireland Parliament, but whom Republicans want to coexist in their own way of life along with the rest of the population, so there is a British side to Irish political life itself. On the one hand the Irish had an all-Ireland Republic proclaimed in 1916 and established in 1919 together with an initial Irish Constitution, while on the other hand they've had an all-Ireland Constitution to which they secured British agreement and support, and over all they've had an international Treaty and other Agreements regulating Anglo-Irish relations. If the Irish could maintain their Republican way of life, they would have no objection to the British side to Irish life. The only reason they objected to the British side before, which was in the form of the Treaty and a Monarchical Constitution, was that it was being imposed on them to ***the exclusion*** of the Irish way of life. With subsequent international agreements, Irish Republicans had no disagreement at all and took them as a matter of course.

There is nothing wrong – in fact there is everything right in the circumstances – with having a British side to Irish life. As soon as reunification is achieved the Irish people will have a sizable British influence right in their midst, and they may as well be ready for it. There is an equally Irish side to British life, with the millions of people of Irish birth or descent who live in Britain itself. Both islands orbit in a Celto-British binary system, and while it would appear that they are by nature meant to be independent of each other they are not meant to be mutually exclusive in their influence on each other. Just as the British sometimes appear to take advantage of their Irish side, so the Irish should utilize to their benefit the British side of Irish life – especially when they have problems with the British themselves. Their main objective should, of course, be to resume their Republican standing – to go back to where they went off course and restore Republican continuity. From that position of strength Ireland should insist with Britain that she honor her Treaty and other obligations and respect Irish national unity. If the Irish once secured Britain's commitment to a united Ireland, as they did with the Treaty and the 1922 Constitution, then that commitment should not be thrown away but should be returned to, taken up again, and exploited to the full. They should with Eamon de Valera be resolved "to get the best out of that Treaty" (*Treaty Debate* (January 9, 1922), p. 38; letter of September 7, 1922 (Dail Eireann, Paper No. 1, p. 8)) or with Willie T. Cosgrave be determined "to get the last ounce out of the Treaty" (*Dail Debates*, Vol. 1 (October 11, 1922), col. 1500). But first the Irish must create the conditions which will make it possible for Britain to cooperate with them, that is, they must establish the all-Ireland Provisional Dail. Ireland keeps saying that Britain should cooperate in solving a problem of her own creation (as, for example, in the New Ireland Forum Report, Chapters 3 and 4), but the country does nothing to provide the framework of action with which Britain could cooperate if she wanted to.

With regard to the reintegrating of Northern Ireland the Irish people face a double problem: (1) the binding over of more than a million unwilling subjects and (2) the getting rid of British hegemony. It ought to be obvious that a three-quarter nation cannot do either thing alone, much less both. The only solution is to secure Britain's cooperation as before, that is, through invoking her 1985 agreement to negotiate in good faith,[4] to tie her to the commitments she made in the past to a united and independent Ireland and, in keeping with those commitments, to have her amend the adversary Acts of the past and to adjust appropriately any other commitments she made to the Loyalist minority in Ireland. That means primarily going back to at least the Republican Third Dail (if not even the Second Dail) and resuming, for all Ireland, the Constitution that that Dail had set up. Britain's hand in the 1922 Constitution might not be seen now for the unhelpful thing it was before, because, as already pointed out, the one redeeming feature the Constitution of 1922 had was that it was for all Ireland and Britain's commitment to upholding it as such was furthermore secured. However, that Constitution before it could be readopted would have to be further restored, by amendment, to its original Republican form and perhaps incorporated into or scheduled to the first Irish Constitution.

The inadequacy of the 1937 Constitution

The Constitution of 1937, by contrast, is of little or no value as far as reunification is concerned. The people of Ireland, in fact, to judge by the cool reception they gave the Constitution when it was proposed in Referendum to them, must have sensed there was something wrong with abandoning a working, all-Ireland Constitution and introducing a new, limited one in its stead. The draft failed to gain the approval of a majority of those registered to vote. Almost half (about 44 percent) of those who participated in the Referendum voted against the de Valera Constitution, more than 72,000 people or 12 percent of those who voted first-preference for Fianna Fail voted against it, a substantial percentage of those who voted second- and third-preference for Fianna Fail voted against the Constitution, and a majority of voters in four constituencies – Cork West, Dublin Townships, Sligo, and Wicklow – turned it down flat. Indeed the measure of support it received was so meager that it was really not sufficient for the Draft to achieve amendment by Referendum under the existing, operative

4 Even if Britain could not be obliged to negotiate in good faith under, for some reason, the Hillsborough Accord, she would be so obliged by virtue of the *pacta sunt servanda* doctrine of international law which, incidentally, was endorsed by the Vienna Convention on the Law of Treaties, to which Britain and Ireland are signatories: "Every treaty in force is binding upon the parties to it and must be performed by them in good faith" (Article 26). She would also be so obliged by the Helsinki Accord of 1975, to which Britain and Ireland also are signatories.

Constitution of 1922 at all. One wonders what might have happened to the Constitution if it had been put to the voters of all of Ireland.

In order for the Constitution of 1937 legitimately to claim to be *capable* of being an all-Ireland, national Constitution, it had to repeal, as it purported to do, the existing all-Ireland Constitution of 1922.[5] This it did not succeed to do. The governing Article of the 1922 Constitution, Article 50, stated that amendments to it, the Constitution, ***might*** be made either by ordinary legislation alone or by Constitutional Referendum up until 1938 but would have to be made by both the Dail and Constitutional Referendum thereafter. Those made by ordinary legislation would have to be *passed*, however, by the Dail (sitting, in effect, as a Constituent Assembly) – they would have to be passed by it ***as amendments***. But the Constitution of 1937, as a repealer amendment of the 1922 Constitution, only claimed (in the Plebiscite (Draft Constitution) Act, 1937) to be *approved* by the Dail – as a ***Draft*** for submittal to the electorate for enactment. It was not intended to be *enacted* by the Dail – as an amendment of the Constitution, and it was not enacted by it. It would be "enacted" by the people in an amendment Referendum; this was the route that would be chosen for it to go as an alternative to the Dail way. And it would be enacted in a Referendum that would have to be conducted in accordance with the requirements the existing Constitution stipulated (in Article 50) for this same Constitution to be amended.

For a Constitutional Referendum to enact an amendment of the Constitution, whether before 1938 or not, Article 50 of the Constitution required that "either the votes of the majority of the voters on the register, or two-thirds of the votes recorded, shall have been cast in favour of such amendment." These figures, as

---

5 The Irish Free State Constitution, it is no exaggeration to say, was indeed the Constitution of all Ireland and recognized the Irish Republic of the people of all Ireland. Justice Hanna, in the case *Carolan* v. *Minister of Defence*, stated that the 1922 Constitution by Article 2 ("All powers of government and all authority, legislative, executive, and judicial in Ireland, are derived from the people of Ireland . . .") "established in law, not for the [*de facto*] Saorstat alone, but for Ireland, and in no metaphorical sense, the sovereignty of the people of Ireland" ([1927] I.R. 62, p. 70). In securing recognition of the all-Ireland character of the Constitution from the British, "the Irish representatives did not, as they would have liked, claim retrospective recognition in the new Constitution of the authority of the revolutionary Dails, but contented themselves with making ratification by the existing Dail under another name a condition precedent to the operation of the Constitution," wrote Richard Latham (*The Law and the Commonwealth*, pp. 535-537).

we have seen, were not met in the election voting. Furthermore, Article 62 (i) of the Constitution-to-Be required that "this Constitution shall come into operation on the day following the expiration of a period of one hundred and eighty days after its approval by the people signified by a majority of the votes cast at a plebiscite thereon held in accordance with law," the law having to be Article 50 of the existing Constitution as invoked by the Draft Constitution Act and that required for such a plebiscite a two-thirds majority (which, of course, was not reached).

The 1937 Constitution, as an amendment of the 1922 Constitution, did not then meet either the Dail or Referendum requirements of the governing Constitution to become even a potentially national Constitution. It would instead have been adopted as the Constitution of a state with a Legislature subordinate to a national Parliament under Article 44 (of the 1922 charter). (Cf. "Twenty-five Years of Irish Constitutional Development," *The Irish Jurist*, Vol. XI (1945), p. 35; Wheare, *The Constitutional Structure of the Commonwealth*, pp. 89-94.)

Ordinarily, a Constitution purporting to be that which it is not would sooner or later have its invalidity exposed by the nation's courts, but a certain theory as to why that has not happened has been advanced by John M. Kelly and it is this: "The possibility that the courts might entertain the point was anticipated by providing [in Article 58 of the Constitution itself] that the judges in office at the moment when the new Constitution came into force would continue in office only subject to taking an oath to uphold the Constitution (none of them declined the oath) . . . But would the judgment of a judge who found against the validity of the Constitution's enactment be invalid by reason simply of his having defied his oath? Such a defiance would presumably be misbehaviour justifying his removal (Art. 35.4); and moreover a pronouncement of invalidity against the Constitution would logically vitiate his own status as a judge appointed thereunder . . ." (*The Irish Constitution*, p. 3.)

But even if the Constitution was arguably not instituted as the charter of a subordinate state, it did *suo proprio vigore* institute a Dail and Government of 26 counties of Ireland alone and, as such, did most to confirm partition. There can be no doubt but that whereas, by admission of the Constitution (Consequential Provisions) Act, 1937, the Saorstat established by the 1922 Constitution extended to more than the 26 counties, the state established by the 1937 Constitution is to be construed as being restricted to the 26-county area. And this was clearly distinguished as a State from the Nation in the Constitution itself (Article 3[6]). The Constitution's Article 10 (Sec. 1) confirms this distinction: "All natural resources . . . within the jurisdiction of the Parliament and Government established by this Constitution" (the formula of Article 3) "belong to the State . . ." Adjudicating the sense of Article 3 in the light of Article 10, the Irish Supreme Court has said: "If the saver contained in Article 3 [i.e., the 'without prejudice' clause] were to be interpreted as entitling the Parliament established by the Constitution to legislate at any time it so decided for [Northern Ireland], then the effect of Article 10 would be that it would apply to the natural resources of the ***national*** territory and [the Article] ***would have been so expressed***" (*In the Matter of Article 26 of the Constitution and in the Matter of The Criminal Law (Jurisdiction) Bill, 1975,* [1977] *Irish Reports* 129, p. 148; *emphasis ours*). The state of the 1937 Constitution is, then, different from, and less than, the (32-county) nation.

Nevertheless, the Constitution the Irish now have may indeed be an excellent Constitution in itself, and no doubt it is. It may be an ideal Constitution for the Republic of the 26 counties, but as a means to securing reunification it is of no more help than would, say, the Constitution of Texas be to that state if Texas should have pretensions to lording it over the entire United States. The Irish Constitution will never be fully acceptable to the Northerners anyway, nor should the Southerners endeavor to amend it, to their own detriment, just to make it more pleasing to the Northern tradition. Besides, if a crusade such as that once contemplated by Garret FitzGerald to delete the Constitution's irredentist claims should ever be launched, the Constitution will be formally made a Constitution of the 26-county state alone[7] – unless it were to be adapted for a Gaelic nation in a mutually accommodative arrange-

6 Article 3 runs: "Pending the re-integration of the national territory ('the whole island of Ireland, its islands and the territorial seas' - Article 2), and without prejudice to ***the right of the Parliament and Government established by this Constitution*** to exercise jurisdiction over the whole of that territory, the laws enacted by that Parliament shall have the like area and extent of application as the laws of Saorstat Eireann and the like extra-territorial effect" as those laws had or were capable of having (*emphasis ours*).

7 Garret FitzGerald's hopes of effecting reunification by nationalist appeasement means were effectively dashed by Cardinal O Fiaich, who bluntly told the then Taoiseach in April of 1986 that "Protestant leaders have made it clear on several occasions - on contraception, on divorce and on moral issues - that no change will influence their political outlook" (quoted from John Cooney, *The Crozier and the Dail*, p. 124).

ment. Which is entirely possible, because: (1) If the Constitution was not instituted as the charter of a subordinate state and still could not become even the potentially national Constitution it was supposed to become, and (2) if it yet is not to be accused of having indirectly established partition (as the decision of the Irish Supreme Court of January 19, 1988 affirming the Constitution to have established the 26-county state effectively said it did), then (3) the only valid view there can be held of the 1937 Constitution is that it was adopted by the Nationalist People as a Communal Constitution for the Gaelic-Irish community with a nonterritorially based Legislature that would be subject to a National Parliament. However, this view of the Constitution becoming what it was instituted as is a view of what the 1937 Constitution would be in a post-unity Ireland, not of what it would, or could, be to bring about that unity. As J.C. Beckett has well said, "the constitution of the Republic, as it now stands, does not provide a framework within which Ireland could be peacefully and permanently united; and a recognition of this fact must be the first step towards unity, whatever form that unity might eventually take" ("Comment on Chapter 2," David Watt, ed., *The Constitution of Northern Ireland, Problems and Prospects*, p. 30).

As far as using a Constitution to achieve reunification is concerned, what should have been done before now would have been to take the 1922 Constitution and amend it in its origin (as we've seen South Africa do with its Constitution), republicanize it fully, and, possibly, graft it onto the 1919 Constitution by further amendment. But de Valera, although he amended the 1922 Constitution in many matters over a period of 15 years, overreacted to its Imperial British taint – and came out for having a brand new Constitution! "New from top to bottom," he vowed it would be, though it was hardly that, it achieving no more than a virtual reenactment of the 1922 Constitution as that stood amended at that time. It was, as John M. Kelly has observed, a putting of new wine into old bottles. As such the new Constitution was not necessary. But de Valera's explanation for presenting a new Constitution was that the existing one was threadbare from amendments, that it was, as his official biographers put it, "no longer a fit document to be regarded as the fundamental law"! The U.S. Constitution, which is now over 200 years old, has by comparison endured about the same number of amendments (one more, in fact: 26 versus 25), with five more pending, and it is still going strong. And the Constitution of California of 1879[8] has hundreds of amendments, additions, and repeals of Articles.

We do not mean to detract from the 1937 Constitution's suitability for the 26-county Republic, but to examine it from the point of view of its usefulness as an instrument of reunification. The de Valera Constitution was brought into existence in a do-or-die effort to bring the Republic to fruition at least for a part of Ireland. The Republican dream, de Valera himself said, had to come to life somehow, even, as he implied in an interview with Michael McInerney in *The Irish Times*, in a partial or defective form, that is, for 26 counties of Ireland only. "The first, the central and supreme purpose of the entire exercise of the new Irish Constitution was to complete the national revolution as far as the 26 Counties were concerned . . ." For these reasons a new even though limited Constitution was seen to be necessary. Besides, a Constitution having its origin in British law was, no matter how much Irishized by amendment, unacceptable to the Republican conscientious objectors and had to be replaced. Unfortunate it was that, 'autochthonous' and all though it might be, only a 26-county Constitution was all that could be had in exchange. And being such it turned out not to be acceptable to Republicans in the end.

The Constitution was furthermore a product of the middle ground that de Valera and Fianna Fail of necessity carved out in order to salvage the salvageable from the wreck of post-Treaty politics. De Valera's effort resembled a balancing act performed between the virile Republicanism of the time and the strong Dominionism that also existed, and for that reason a new Constitution may have been inevitable. Perhaps it was also necessary as an instrument to break the connection of subjection to Britain, and this it achieved by keeping Commonwealth constitutional relations to the barest minimum in it. Unfortunately, it did more than break the connection with Britain. It estranged also the six counties. This was because, as explained by Wheare, (on the Irish view) "the Constitution of 1937 caused a break in Irish constitutional history. There was a gap or break in legal continuity." (*Constitutional Structure*, p. 94.) Ironically, a new Constitution was not necessary for breaking the British connection, because, with the coming to fruition of the provisions of the Statute of Westminster, Common-

8 Although the California Constitution dates from 1879, its Preamble dates from the original Constitution of 1849.

wealth subservience relations disappeared of their own accord anyway and the British connection broke itself.

The obstacle to reunification that the 1937 Constitution is

While preparation and publication of the new Constitution was in progress, the British, rather than show signs of being rebuffed by the whole thing, held their breath and tried to see some good in it for themselves. They appeared to hope that the division between the two parts of Ireland would only be widened by the entire undertaking. Why should they object when de Valera was easing the entire 26 counties out for them and they would not have to pose as being the ones opposed to Irish unity? They were, rather, provided with an ideal opportunity of washing their hands of the 26-county state altogether and of strengthening the position of the Northern state without appearing to do just that. So they set themselves to agonizing over the Irish decision, we have learned, and came up with a novel imperial doctrine – 'Ministerial Responsibility to Commonwealth Parliaments' – that they could use to justify their tolerating in the Commonwealth Ireland's first more obviously Republican Constitution. As a matter of fact, it was the 1937 Constitution itself that was the statute that, by virtue of Section 4 of the Statute of Westminster of 1931 (terminating British Parliamentary supremacy), first enacted this very doctrine, the British theorists said. (See E. C. S. Wade, "Introduction," in A.V. Dicey's *Introduction to the Study of the Law of the Constitution*, p. lxxxviii.)

Five days before the Constitution took effect, December 24, 1937, the Government in London issued a statement declaring that it, the Government (but not the Parliament), and the Governments of Canada, Australia, New Zealand and South Africa were "prepared to treat the new Constitution as not effecting a fundamental alteration in the position of the Irish Free State, in future to be described under the new Constitution as 'Eire' or 'Ireland,' as a member of the British Commonwealth of Nations." But they added the giveaway caveat that they could not recognize the application of the new name to include Northern Ireland, or anything else in the Constitution that might affect what they were now beginning to call "an integral part of the United Kingdom." They went farther, in fact, and formally designated the 26 counties "the Irish Free State" that was thenceforth, they noted, to be called " 'Eire' or 'Ireland,' " and the Irish by Article 4 gave them the opportunity to do so. Such was to be the practical result of changing horses in midstream. (See *Statement* at end of Chapter.)

There was yet another ulterior motive for the British Government's public reaction to the new Constitution being, as Professor Lyons described it, "phlegmatic to a degree that would have excited the envy of Phileas Fogg." That motive was, as most commentators can discern, that since the Statute of Westminster (in the British view) empowered the Dail only, and not the people of Ireland, to alter or amend British legislation affecting Ireland, the London Government saw fit to remedy this omission and conferred what has been termed its 'executive approval' on the Irish Constitution and on the Irish people to enact it. In that way, in the British view, try as de Valera and his colleagues might to ensure that the Constitution was derived from the sovereign Irish people alone, continuity was still preserved for it from British statutory law through the Statute of Westminster. (Cf. V. T. H. Delany, "The Constitution of Ireland: Its Origins and Development," *University of Toronto Law Journal*, Vol. XII, No. 1 (1957), pp. 7-10; *Murray* v. *Parkes*, [1942] 1 All E.R. 558.)

De Valera, by proceeding so persistently with what seemed to many an unneeded Constitution, not only accepted confinement to 26 counties of Ireland, but strengthened the position of the defenders of partition. The logical outcome of all his constitutional efforts would have been to proclaim a Republic – for the 26 counties. He now had a Constitution that was all but Republican in name. The step to proclaiming a Republic would have been a simple matter, requiring nothing more than a mere ceremony, as he had said himself. Yet, he held back from taking the step. Why? Because (1) 'Republic' in the Irish context traditionally meant a united Ireland or 32 counties and was, we were told, "a name which was sacred"; (2) by achieving a 26-county Republic he would only have revealed the inherent worthlessness (for reunification) of the new Constitution and exposed his own inconsistency with his earlier Sinn Fein self; and (3) he realized he had allowed himself by constitutional developments to be led up a creek as far as achieving reunification by then-current constitutional means was concerned. The more he had 'dismantled' the Treaty for the 26 counties and given the area a new constitutionalism, the more he had strengthened partition and played into the hands of the British. He dared not go too far.

What de Valera feared most of all was the effect declaration of a Republic would have on northeastern Ireland, and he admitted as much himself when he refused to participate in ceremonies describing the 26 counties a Republic eventually. He felt increasingly the realization that this step would make partition irrevocable and that it would put paid to all efforts to regain the six counties. Yet, by intentionally not writing a charter that ***would*** be an all-Ireland Constitution, but by writing one that only ***could*** be an all-Ireland Constitution – or, put another way (the way of John J. Hearn, author of the first draft of the Constitution), by intentionally not writing a ***provisionally*** all-Ireland but only a ***potentially*** all-Ireland Constitution, de Valera over-optimistically hoped that he would garner the support of all Republicans and go on to secure the North on that persuasive basis. But it was as vain to trust that Republicans to the left could espouse a partitionist Constitution as it was to expect that Unionists to the right would be persuaded to accept a Republican charter (even though it did not sever the Commonwealth connection). Not visualizing the reunification failures that would eventuate within 50-odd years of the Constitution's adoption, the Irish President in his venture into Constitution making made what with hindsight we see was a grave underestimation and a gross miscalculation. "Here was his one great delusion, the crowning tragedy of his career," concludes Alfred LeRoy Burt (*The Evolution of the British Empire and Commonwealth, From the American Revolution*, p. 775).

Ours is not the only opinion that de Valera by republicanizing the South made reintegration of the North all the more difficult. It is also the opinion of John Bowman at the conclusion of his truly excellent work of research, *De Valera and the Ulster Question, 1917-1973*. It may well be, writes Bowman, that "while securing political stability in the south [he] also stabilized the border." Also, Bowman recounts de Valera's (one might say) deathbed admission of failure in his having neglected to heed Erskine Childers's death-cell advice (of November 1922) not to proceed in the wrong direction. Childers had urged in a long memorandum, daughter-in-law Rita Childers wrote (in a letter to the editor of *The Irish Times* of January 29, 1981), that it was vital "to get to know, understand and tolerate [the Northern majority's] point of view by co-operation in every way possible." De Valera upon reading the memorandum at this point was said to have explained (to Childers's son, President Erskine Childers II) "that because he had been so absorbed in building up the South after Independence he had failed to follow this advice." (Bowman, pp. 337-338; see also editorial "Dev's Admission," *The Irish Times*, February 2, 1981.)

An inkling into what motivated de Valera into writing off the six counties and pursuing a Republic for the twenty-six can be garnered from a speech he made in the Seanad on July 18, 1932, on the occasion of proposing retention of the annuities owing to Britain. In that speech he showed that he completely misread the British mind on the Treaty and the British attitude towards Ireland in concluding a Treaty at all. The Treaty was entered into "between the Twenty-six Counties and Great Britain" (?!), de Valera told his audience, "in order to make the 1920 Act operative" (!). Such thinking can only be judged to be completely askew and if de Valera had reasons for turning the Treaty topsy-turvy in that fashion, those reasons can only have been best known to himself. But the point is that if de Valera could have been possessed of such an incomprehension of the Treaty, that is, if he could believe that the Treaty was concluded with and for Southern Ireland to the exclusion of Northern Ireland, then it is easy to see how he would, at the expense of sealing partition, be inclined to concentrate on saving the South – even if this meant, as Michael Laffan has said, "widening the gap between the two parts of the island." And it is easy to see how such misreading of the real situation could have been responsible for de Valera's setting the country on the mistaken course it pursued in 1937. (See *Seanad Debates*, Vol. 15 (1932), cols. 684 and 1315-1316.)

The relevant part of the President's Seanad speech is as follows:

> We held that position [that we negotiated as the Government of the all-Ireland Republic] and we maintained it up to a certain point. Until the Treaty was actually signed, the position was maintained. But the British did not maintain that position. Mr. Lloyd George's strategy from the beginning was this: "We have the 1920 Act in operation in the North. Theoretically it applies to the South. The people in the South are not coming into the Parliament of Southern Ireland. We will offer them something more in order to get them in." The whole of the Treaty was based, from the British point of view, on the idea of offering more to the people of Southern Ireland in order to make the 1920 Act operative. That was the basis of his whole scheme, and during all that period of negotiation there was nothing done by the British Government which interfered with what Mr. Lloyd George wanted to be the basic position. He wanted partition. He had got it operating in the North. He wanted to complete partition by getting it to operate here in the South. . . . Remember, he was dealing not with people

> who accepted the position as we wanted it here, but dealing with Great Britain whose Government was operating in accordance with British law.

Although this was arguing the case for the British better than they possibly might be able to do it themselves, the President did not explain how, if the Treaty was indeed intended to be negotiated with and for only one part of Ireland, option out would have needed to be offered in it to another part. To have thought that the Treaty was concluded with and for only a part of Ireland was worse than holding that in the negotiations Britain treated Ireland as part of Britain and that she regarded Ireland's declaration of the Republic as being a mere internal or domestic British problem. Such a view is contrary to the facts. It is also at odds with the view of a long list of commentators and authorities, to which we add the name of M. Rynne who claimed State rank to have been acknowledged for all Ireland at the Treaty negotiations (*Die voelkerrechtliche Stellung Irlands*, pp. 44 ff.).

Such was the thinking that led to the tragedy of abandoning the 1919 and 1922 Constitutions, which had been enacted for all Ireland. De Valera had personal reactionary reasons also, however, for devising a new Constitution for the South. As Lord Longford and Thomas P. O'Neill tell us in their official biography, *Eamon de Valera* (p. 290), he reasoned that since the 26-county Dail was tainted in its origin by British Imperialism its product, the old Constitution, was tainted also, and that if he could provide a national charter that would be approved by the people instead ("or that section of the Irish people whom we can consult on the matter," as de Valera himself said) then all state institutions would be more likely to be accepted by extraparliamentary Republicans. But de Valera's reasoning was faulty, because the Constitution was not the product of a tainted Dail, but the antecedent of it. It is true that the Constitution was tainted, particularly in its promulgation, but, as we have seen, this could have been remedied by a simple amendment. All other taint had been purged by de Valera himself.

However, it seemed inevitable that de Valera, if he was to carry out his political program of achieving as much of the Republic as possible, should introduce a new Constitution in keeping with that program. As Professor Lyons asks, how else was he to justify his whole political career? But abandonment of what was already an all-Ireland Constitution in order to fulfill the state's perceived needs was nothing short of the calamitous as far as reunification was concerned. And it was nothing short of the calamitous for Irish nationalism itself, since henceforth that nationalism would be founded on a constitutionally accepted partition. Little wonder that Sinn Fein President Gerry Adams could declare at the 1984 Ard Fheis: "Constitutional nationalism in the Irish context is a contradiction, when the constitutionality involved is British constitutionality." One cannot help feeling that creation of the 1937 Constitution was motivated more by politics than any statesmanlike felt need for a new Constitution, that it was, as Paul Johnson claims, the culmination of de Valera's repudiation of the Cosgrave Government's 1925 supposed recognition of the status of Northern Ireland, as signified by the Chief's 1926 standing for and winning a South Down seat in the Belfast Parliament, which "repudiation of Cosgrave was formalised by a new constitution" (*Ireland: Land of Troubles*, pp. 169-170). But however it was motivated, certain it is that the new Irish Constitution was an instrument that did more to seal partition than the Treaty Amendment – or the Treaty itself – ever did.

The Irish Constitution's reintegration mandate

We have referred (in Chapter 10) to the classic Catch-22 situation which Constitution Articles 2 and 3 present when reintegration is attempted by virtue of them alone and we have alluded to the impossibility, because of this, that there is with regard to bringing about the reintegration of Ireland by means of a Constitution that is vitiated by such Articles (cf. John Bowman, *De Valera and the Ulster Question*, p. 148). We have also said that we would explain, if we could, the basis of the Constitution's mandate to strive for the reintegration of Ireland (by what would have to be other constitutional means). If we can demonstrate that under the 1937 Constitution recognition of Northern Ireland as *de facto* lawfully existing amounts in practice to a recognition of the state as *de jure* existing – and this we will demonstrate more fully in Chapter 12 – and since we can demonstrate that the vicious circle type formula for reintegration cannot (because it is just that) be used to fulfill the reintegration mandate, then we must concede the need for finding the basis of the Constitution's reintegration mandate in other than the Constitution itself and a justification for going outside of the 1937 Constitution to achieve the reunification of Ireland.

To convince ourselves of our correctness in seeing no practical distinction between recognizing Northern Ireland as factually lawfully existing and recognizing it as *de jure* existing, let us consider some further confirmatory arguments on the cul-de-sac nature of Articles 2 and 3 that any pursuance of the unity claim contained therein, by means of those Articles, would lead us into. While the Constitution does not ostensibly acknowledge, as John M. Kelly puts it, "an admission of any *de jure* status of the dispensation under which Northern Ireland exists," it does "allow both the Oireachtas and courts to treat Northern Ireland as lawfully existing." But the Oireachtas or courts cannot do this latter to any great extent without crossing over into the area of the former and acknowledging the *de jure* existence of the Northern province. That, for example, is just what the Oireachtas did in 1985 by its approval of the Hillsborough Agreement. Under the guise of treating Northern Ireland as factually lawfully existing, the Government and Dail, without appearing to be confusing things at all, went on to acknowledge the right of Northern Ireland to exist sovereignly. So that, in effect, the question of whether a *de jure* status for Northern Ireland may constitutionally be acknowledged becomes a question of the degree to which Northern Ireland may be recognized as *de facto* lawfully existing. May this, it may be asked, extend to the *n*th degree, as in Hillsborough?

Obviously, then, it is not the apparent prohibition in the Constitution of acknowledging a *de jure* status for Northern Ireland that prohibits any real acknowledging of a *de jure* status. There is a strong inclination under the Constitution to acknowledge such a *de jure* status, since, on the basis of the fact that the Constitution was established for the 26 counties alone (with the North abandoned to exclusive British rule), there is an in-built compulsion in the Articles 2 and 3 to cross over from acknowledgment of a factually lawfully existing Northern Ireland to acknowledgment of a *de jure* existing Northern Ireland, which, in fact, the Hillsborough Accord virtually did. So that, what really prohibits a constitutional acknowledging of a *de jure* status for Northern Ireland has to be the reintegration mandate ***based on some other foundation than the vicious circle that traditional interpretations of the fateful Articles lead us back into***. The question then becomes, What is this other basis that, in the endeavor to meet the reintegration mandate of the present Constitution, does not lead into the *circulus inextricabilis* that that Constitution does in its practically acknowledging not to be reintegratable that which it claims must be reintegrated? What is this other basis that makes the reintegration mandate to be a real, meaningful mandate? (See also *Postscript*, p. 358.)

We will begin to answer this question by observing that the "Saorstat Eireann" of Article 3[9] is, of necessity, not the Saorstat Eireann that existed under the I.F.S. Constitution, as a realization of this preliminary fact will lead us to an understanding of the point that the basis of the reintegration mandate is not to be found in the Constitution of the one State, but is in that of the other. The "Saorstat Eireann" of the 1937 Constitution has to be but the same former *de facto* (26-county) Saorstat, while the Saorstat Eireann of the 1922 Constitution actually was the *de jure* (32-county) Saorstat. One difference between the two Saorstait (States) lies in the laws of the one being confined to the 26-county State of its own Constitution with Northern extraterritorial effect,[10] and the laws of the other extending to the 32-county State of its Constitution with application in principle (that is, ***more*** than extraterritorially) to the North of Ireland. The laws enacted under the 1937 Constitution were and are, of their Constitution's own designing, restricted to that part of Ireland that was the *de facto* Saorstat Eireann, but the laws enacted under the 1922 Constitution, as conjoined with the Treaty, would apply in principle to all of Ireland, the *de jure* Saorstat of their Constitution's own designing. But there is more than this to the difference between the two States of Ireland.

The major difference between the *de facto* and *de jure* States lies in the fact that the Constitution of the one had a certain set of powers that the Constitution of the other did not. The Constitution of Saorstat Eireann, being the extension of a Treaty that had provisions designed as an alternative to the Partition Act's provisions for 'reserved powers' from ***all*** Ireland, preserved a control mechanism over these powers with Britain to the extent that the powers as reserved (which constituted Britain's suspension of Saorstat rule over the North of Ireland) were, in effect, guaranteed to be restored to Ireland by the Treaty.

9 Article 3: "Pending the re-integration of the national territory . . . the laws enacted by [the Parliament established by this Constitution] shall have the like area and extent of application as the laws of the [*de facto*] Saorstat Eireann . . ." had.

10 See *The State (Devine)* v. *Larkin*, [1977] *Irish Reports* 24, pp. 28-29. It might be noted that extraterritorial jurisdiction extends abroad only to subjects of the state exercising the jurisdiction who live abroad, whereas *de jure* jurisdiction extends in principle to all inhabitants of the state to which the jurisdiction is extended.

It is true that the Treaty guarantee was modified by the Boundary Agreement of 1925. But this did not take anything from the 1922 Constitution that the 1937 Constitution didn't (as we shall see). All the Boundary Agreement amounted to was, as we saw before, the mutual acceptance that, subject to the Boundary Commission's work having been unblunderingly carried out, the border between the six and 26 counties would delineate the extent of the jurisdictions of Northern Ireland and Saorstat Eireann "for the purposes of the Government of Ireland Act, 1920, and of the said Articles of Agreement [the Treaty]." But one of the purposes of the Treaty was that the powers (not laws) of Saorstat Eireann (Irish Free State) that would be equivalent to the 1920 Act's reserved powers,[11] while being applicable to the undelineated Northern Ireland, would not, within the first month from ratification of the Treaty, be "*exercisable*" in the North, and after the 'option out,' would not "*extend*" to Northern Ireland in the same sense. That is to say, that while the major powers of jurisdiction of Saorstat Eireann would apply in principle and *de jure* to Northern Ireland, they would not apply in practice and *de facto*: they would stand suspended – from the Free State of all Ireland. This State, with its sovereignty suspended over a part of Ireland, is the Saorstat Eireann the 1922 Constitution created, whereas the 1937 Constitution, being a *de facto* Free State instrument that set up the 26-county State, concedes thereby that the sovereignty suspended is ***that of the United Kingdom***, that is suspended from Northern Ireland, and not ***that of all Ireland***, that is suspended from Northern Ireland – as the Treaty, the Twenty-two Constitution and the Boundary Agreement had it.

The Saorstat Eireann Constitution had, then, because of its connection with a Treaty that itself contained them, control over some very important powers that the 1937 Constitution does not. It had this control, not only through the Treaty, but also – which is equally important – through the Treaty and Constitution's own counterpart statute in Westminster that was subject to being changed by the Irish Constitution's amendment. These powers, being the reserved powers of the Treaty, represented the area and

11 Another purpose of the Treaty was that the North-to-Be should have preserved all to itself the 1920 Act's provisions for minor powers of jurisdiction. This the 1925 Agreement also confirmed, since "for the purposes of the Government of Ireland Act, 1920, and of this instrument [the Treaty]" the delimiting of the jurisdictions of the North and the Saorstat was to be such as might be determined by the Boundary Commission.

extent of application that the powers of Saorstat Eireann were suspended from. The 1937 Constitution, by its breaking (through Article 48) with the 1922 Constitution, relinquished the control Ireland had over these powers and does not claim them for itself now. It has to be, then, that the basis of the mandate of the present Constitution for the restoration of these powers – that is, of the reintegration mandate – is to be found in that Constitution that does have the power to force a restoration of the powers over that part of Ireland that is outside of the area and extent of application of the current Constitution's laws. If it were otherwise, we would, as we have seen, in an effort to satisfy that mandate, make of Article 3 nothing more than a *reductio ad absurdum* and legal fiction. (That it is only to be expected that there should be fictions to be found in the Constitution is clear from the admission made by de Valera when he told the Dail in 1948 that "our Constitution was intended to be . . . with as few fictions as possible"!) (See *Dail Debates*, Vol. 113, col. 421, Nov. 24, 1948.)

In conclusion, the powers the 1937 Constitution relinquished constituted the hold Ireland always had on Britain to compel her one day to abolish her suspension of Irish rule over Northern Ireland – which is the heart of partition. For, a Constitution that converts what was always only a *de facto* recognition of British rule in the North of Ireland into a *de jure* recognition of it conversely converts what was always a *de jure* recognition of the heart of that rule – Ireland's right to abolition of British suspension of Irish rule over Northern Ireland – into merely a *de facto* recognition of it. That is to say, a Constitution that surrenders Ireland's hold on Britain's suspension of Irish rule and offers *de jure* recognition of sole British rule instead cannot at the same time be a place where a basis of the mandate to rid Ireland of that rule is to be found.

To sum up, when it comes to obeying the reintegration mandate of the 1937 Constitution, the Constitution itself does not empower one to do so. The reasons are: (1) the degree to which the North of Ireland may be factually lawfully recognized under the Constitution can be such that it inevitably and logically becomes a *de jure* recognition, and a Constitution that recognizes a region as virtually foreign to itself cannot at the same time claim that region as its own; and (2) the Constitution recognizes an exclusively British controlled rather than an Irish (1922 Constitution) controlled suspension of powers of jurisdiction over Northern Ireland, the ultimate say in the abolition of which rests with a 70 percent majority there. But (3) there is another reason the 1937 Constitution, when it comes to reintegration, lacks the strength to deliver the coup de grace. That reason is that the 1937 Constitution, unlike as with the 1922 instrument, is, as we saw, bereft of a binding Westminster counterpart. The 1937 Constitution is an Irish Constitution the British – and the Northerners – don't care a fig about. Consequently, with the de Valera Constitution coming to a head in the Hillsborough capitulation, the journey from there must only lead back to the Constitution of Saorstat Eireann and of the all-Ireland Republic.

Statement Issued by the United Kingdom Government, December 24, 1937

> His Majesty's Government in the United Kingdom have considered the position created by the new Constitution which was approved by the Parliament of the Irish Free State in June, 1937, and came into force on December 29. They are prepared to treat the new Constitution as not effecting a fundamental alteration in the position of the Irish Free State, in the future to be described under the new Constitution as 'Eire' or 'Ireland', as a member of the British Commonwealth of Nations.
>
> His Majesty's Government in the United Kingdom have ascertained that His Majesty's Governments in Canada, the Commonwealth of Australia, New Zealand, and the Union of South Africa are also prepared so to treat the new Constitution.
>
> His Majesty's Government in the United Kingdom take note of Articles 2, 3, and 4 of the new Constitution. They cannot recognize that the adoption of the name Eire or Ireland, or any other provisions of those Articles, involves any right to territory or jurisdiction over territory forming part of the United Kingdom of Great Britain and Nothern Ireland, or affects in any way the position of Northern Ireland as an integral part of the United Kingdom of Great Britain and Northern Ireland. They therefore regard the use of the name Eire or Ireland in this connexion as relating only to that area which has hitherto been known as the Irish Free State.

CHAPTER 12

ARE THE IRISH REALLY PRISONERS OF HISTORY?

The Territorial and Communal Claims

When Ireland got her independence in 1921, she got only what Republicans called a half measure of independence, and problems associated with this 'rapine in the sacrifice' obfuscated the basic problem – Northern Ireland's holding out from the jurisdiction of Dail Eireann with the consequent disunity of the nation. Concentration on the myriad peripheral problems in the twenties and thirties served only to cause the central problem to be neglected and put on the back burner, so to speak. In addition, the more the proximate, pressing problems were tackled for solution, the more the basic problem became intractable. There was also the British dimension to the question, and under this aspect the difficulty was compounded, with Britain taking advantage of every opportunity she could. Under those circumstances, it was imperative that Ireland should not miss her step in the scale of consolidated constitutional achievement that was had. But this is exactly what she did do when she decided to abandon her entire Constitution, instead of reconstituting her lost footing in the affected Articles and strengthening and expanding her position there.

From such a position of strength it might have been possible to have a reasonable chance of asserting the nation's right to have her jurisdiction applied to all of Ireland. Instead the country adopted a weak posture in 1937 and enacted a Constitution with only a claim to the extraterritorial North. As might be expected with a nation that lessened its resistance, the British moved in all the more and increased their hold on the six counties. It was from about that time, 1937, that partition really began to become entrenched, in the sense that it was from then on that Britain began to regard Northern Ireland as being 'part' of the United Kingdom (although she did not make any *formal* claim to the territorial North until 12 years later).

Strangely enough, by 1937 Britain's reasons for occupying the North were not as compelling as they had been in prior years. What motivated the British to hold on to six of Ireland's 32 counties to begin with was reasons of prestige and security – prestige, or integrity of the then-existing Empire; security, or protection from foreign attack by way of Ireland. But by 1931 the Empire had been, by the Statute of Westminster, transformed into 'the Commonwealth,' a community of nations coequal with Britain and one another. With that development, one reason for holding Ireland, or part of Ireland, in subjection was removed: prestige was no longer of importance to Britain. The second reason for holding a part of Ireland disappeared with the 1938 Sovereignty, Finance, and Trade Agreements between Ireland and the United Kingdom: security was no longer a worry to Britain from the Irish side.

In the debate in the Dail on the 1938 Agreements, de Valera pledged that Ireland would never be used as a base of attack upon Britain. "I have said that the Irish Government, that this Government anyhow – and that has been our policy and will remain our policy – is not going to permit its territory to be used as a base of attack against Britain," de Valera stated on April 27, 1938. "I have said that for many years now. I indicated the policy which is behind it as long ago as 1920, when, on behalf of the State of that time – of the Republic – I made a request to the Government of the United States for formal recognition. We mean to say that whatever use is made of our territory will be only that use which is agreed to by an Irish Government in the interests of Ireland and in no other interests; and it is in the interests of Ireland to see that our territory is not going to be used as a base of attack upon a neighbouring country." (*Dail Debates*, Vol. 71, cols. 36-37; see also *Seanad Debates*, Vol. 19 (1935), col. 1593.)

But Britain appeared only to tighten her grip on the North, entering into economic agreements with the Stormont Government. All of de Valera's assurances on defense were of no value as far as convincing Britain of the need for Irish reunification was concerned. De Valera had, in fact, argued with the British at the Sovereignty Conference for the return of the six counties, and had reiterated the traditional Sinn Fein pledges of regarding Northern Ireland as a separate state enjoying numerous civil and religious safeguards and privileges. All the British Ministers would say was that it could not be done, lamely putting the blame on Ulster, and de Valera found himself in the difficult political position of not being able to refuse to take no for an answer.

The self-partitioning of Southern Ireland

Great constitutional strides were made in Ireland in the prewar years, all advances being basically applications of the principle of external association *pace* the Statute of Westminster. But the more the 26-county state improved and consolidated its own position, the less hold it had on Northern Ireland and the more the British moved in to secure their hold instead. The growing realization of the dead end to which constitutional progress was leading the Fianna Fail Government caused de Valera to ease off in moving to the logical conclusion towards which he was being inexorably propelled. Constitutional development came virtually to a standstill. Eventually a new, interparty Government could stand the frustration no longer, and posing in a hail-Republican-well-met posture in 1948 it made a bold strike. The External Relations Act of 1936 (but not Article 29(4)(ii) of the Constitution) was repealed, the 26 counties were (virtually) declared a Republic[1], and the state left the Monarchical Commonwealth. This action was to evoke a wholly unconstitutional reaction from Britain – although the British should have known better, because all the departure from the old, Monarchical Commonwealth amounted to was a putting of Britain's own Statute of Westminster of 1931 more fully into effect.

In view of the misunderstanding the Irish action was bound to give rise to, and did, in Britain, it was inevitable that the step taken

1 The Republic of Ireland Act, 1948, in declaring the description of the state to be the Republic of Ireland, had the effect of amending Article 5 of the 1937 Constitution to read Eire is a sovereign, independent, democratic ***republic*** (instead of 'state'). But it did not formally amend the Constitution, nor could it, and it did not alter the name of the state nor provide a new name. (See "A Matter of Nomenclature - 'The Name of the State is Eire . . . ,' " *The Irish Jurist*, Vol. 16 (1950), pp. 5-6.) The 1948 Act did not repeal Article 29 (4)(ii) of the 1937 Constitution, much less did it, even on the British view of the legal basis for Irish Free State constitutionalism, have the effect of repealing either the Treaty of 1921 or the Constitution of 1922, as Sean MacBride claimed in his *Ireland's Right to Sovereignty, Independence and Unity is Inalienable and Indefeasible*. (Article 48 of the 1937 Constitution purported to repeal the 1922 Constitution.)

should result in making the ending of partition even more difficult than before. But Prime Minister Costello, the initiator of the action, claimed that refraining from such a step in the past had not induced a friendly gesture from Northern Ireland and now held that it would be of no use to wait any longer for a reconciliation! (*Dail Debates*, Vol. 113, cols. 347-387.) Costello's action was backed by de Valera, who held that if the arrangement of the External Relations Act that made the British Monarch Head of Ireland in the external forum did not contribute to the removal of partition, then the External Relations Act would have to go[2] (Longford and O'Neill, *Eamon de Valera*, p. 430). But in 1948 such argumentation did not reveal itself as the playing to the gallery that it reveals itself as today. Costello's argument was of very doubtful validity. His Government's action "might not make a bad situation worse, but it surely meant that it would be harder thenceforward to make that bad situation better" (Lyons, *Ireland Since the Famine*, pp. 560-561 hardcover, 567-568 paperback).

The Irish action did, in fact, make the bad situation worse there and then, for Britain's immediate response was to consolidate further her hold on Northern Ireland by passing the Ireland Act of 1949. For the first time the British Government formally guaranteed to the Ulster Loyalists that it would uphold the Northern state as part of the United Kingdom and for as long as the then-existing Stormont Parliament willed it. Thus the British, who "had always justified [their] veto on Irish unity by citing Ulster unionist intransigence," states John Bowman, "were now strengthening the veto by effectively passing it into the custody of the Ulster Unionists themselves" (*De Valera*, p. 271). Here was partition in its most naked form, here was the most flagrant violation of the Treaty Agreement, and the furious protest that was hurled back from 'redeemed' Ireland at Britain was little to be marveled at, but it helped not at all. The price of establishing and proclaiming the 26-county Republic had to be paid – what some considered the locking and bolting of the door against the prospects of ever ending the partition of Ireland.

---

2 De Valera's support for repeal of the External Relations Act was not as real as has generally been supposed. That other official biographer of de Valera, Frank Gallagher, has recorded that repeal of the Act was considered the "height of political folly." It "troubled" de Valera, "for he believed harm would come to the cause of unity from the bridge to the North East being destroyed." (Frank Gallagher Papers, MS 18375 (6), National Library of Ireland; see also John Bowman, p. 273.)

The Resolution of protest aimed at Britain which was adopted unanimously by Dail Eireann in 1949 declared:

> Dail Eireann,
>
> SOLEMNLY re-asserting the indefeasible right of the Irish nation to the unity and integrity of the national territory.
>
> RE-AFFIRMING the sovereign right of the people of Ireland to choose its own form of Government and, through its democratic institutions, to decide all questions of national policy, free from outside interference.
>
> REPUDIATING the claim of the British Parliament to enact legislation affecting Ireland's territorial integrity in violation of those rights, and
>
> PLEDGING the determination of the Irish people to continue the struggle against the unjust and unnatural partition of our country until it is brought to a successful conclusion:
>
> PLACES ON RECORD its indignant protest against the introduction in the British Parliament of legislation purporting to endorse and continue the existing Partition of Ireland, and
>
> CALLS UPON the British Government and people to end the present occupation of our Six North-eastern Counties, and thereby enable the unity of Ireland to be restored and the age-long differences between the two nations brought to an end.

Apart from a consideration of the question in March 1974 and the approval of the Anglo-Irish Accord in November 1985, this Resolution is the only declaration of policy made by the Dail on partition in the more than half a century that the Constitution of the 26 counties has been in existence. One is tempted to believe there is a connection between the two. Was this perchance the last hurrah of Irish Constitutional Nationalism?

But there was a bright side to the 1948-49 Anglo-Irish flap over the 26-county area virtually declaring itself a Republic and departing the Commonwealth. When that happened the United Kingdom and the overseas Realms refused to accept Ireland's resignation from what to them was the ***Commonwealth***. This they did by declaring in their respective Cabinets that Ireland was not to be regarded a foreign country. But they did accept, as King George VI and the Ireland Act had put it, Ireland's resignation from *"His Majesty's Dominions."* In making this distinction they were making history, for in this they were introducing the concepts of what some historians and encyclopedists have since called the Old Commonwealth and the New Commonwealth. For membership in the former allegiance to the British Monarch, whether symbolic or real, was required, while for membership in the latter all that was really required was recognition of the Monarch as head and symbol of the members' free association (or even only free *cooperation*, as Ireland from 1936 had it) and *inter se* nonrecognition of one being a foreign country to the other. In the Old, one was a Commonwealth Realm (with the King/Queen as Head of State); in the New, one was a Commonwealth Republic or other Monarchy (with the King/Queen as Leader). By the Club's refusal to accept Ireland's resignation fully, Ireland was to continue as much as ever it already did from 1936, if not in name, an Associate Member of the Commonwealth, and the situation was, in the phraseology of Kenneth Wheare, that henceforth "include me out" would be changed to "exclude me in."[3] That such is now constitutionally the nature of the situation can be inferred, contrary to Wheare's prior assessment, from the Commonwealth amendment of the Statute of Westminster in 1962 (consequent upon South Africa's departure from the Community) which left the reference to the Irish Free State therein unchanged. But the Westminster Act of 1949 did contradictorily enact, as might have been expected, that eternal Ulster should remain part of "His Majesty's Dominions."

Actually, the "include me out" type of external association achieved in 1936 existed already in 1921-22, though then in less refined form. That is, as de Valera in 1936 said, all that was achieved by Amendment No. 27 and the External Relations Act

---

3 Although Ireland led the way in New Commonwealth membership, she was unwilling to go as far as did India and other countries who accepted the British Monarch as Head of the Commonwealth and symbol of the members' free association with one another. Since this was, in 1949 and subsequently, the minimum requirement for membership and the other members could not agree to forgo it, Ireland, who was unwilling to compliantly apply for reaccession, was obliged to settle for something like Associate Membership of the Commonwealth. Yet she did not ever expressly state in modern times that she could not recognize the King/Queen as sole Head and symbol of her cooperation if not association with the other members, and so her Associate Membership (if that is what it is) has never been formalized or explained. (See K.C. Wheare, *The Constitutional Structure of the Commonwealth*, pp. 27, 114 ff., 138, 150 ff.; Longford and O'Neill, *Eamon de Valera*, pp. 429, 433; also Note 4 referring to Arnold Smith in Chapter 7 herein; and Appendix 11, *Supplement*.)

of that year was the formalization of the functions the King had actually been performing by then anyway. The King was being, de Valera said, utilized for external affairs only. In 1936, due to progressive constitutional amendment and in keeping with the general constitutional development of the Commonwealth (especially after 1931), the shift that was made was to a lesser degree of external association and of utilization of the King than that which existed under the Treaty: to utilization of the Commonwealth Head for diplomatic appointments and treaty signatures only, rather than for *all* foreign affairs (*including* diplomatic appointments and treaty signatures). The 1936 shift did not make any substantial gain, then. (See *Dail Debates*, Dec. 11, 1936, cols. 1279 and 1280.)

The difference between the external association contemplated in the Treaty of 1921 and that which had been reached in practice in the Irish Free State (and formalized legislatively in 1936) has been best explained by Nicholas Mansergh as being "that at the earlier date an indication was given of the matters of common concern in which foreign affairs and defence involving co-operation with the countries of the Commonwealth were specifically included, whilst by 1936 this positive content, not easily to be assimilated with the looser concept of dominion status that had emerged since 1926, was abandoned. The attenuated remainder was more negative both in conception and approach than what had been earlier contemplated." (*Survey of British Commonwealth Affairs, 1931-1939*, p. 290.) One can only surmise what still lesser degree of external association might have been utilized or adopted from 1949 if the present Constitution's Article 29 (2) allowing same (and more) had ever been exploited or put into statutory effect.

Why, it may be asked in passing, if republican status was no longer a bar to Commonwealth membership, did not Ireland after 1949 apply, in accordance with standard procedure, for readmittance to the Commonwealth? It may well be that this question can only be answered, not in constitutional or legal terms, but in the language of political psychology. It may also well be that an Ireland divided, even if the Dail of one of its parts was not angry at all, could not, because it was not Ireland, apply for any such readmittance. The experiment of international equality 'granted' Ireland by the Treaty labored, it has been well said, under three overwhelming liabilities. "The first was that it came too late, the second that it came as the result of violence, and the third that as a result of Partition it was deprived of strong, coherent support." So wrote Mansergh (in *Survey, 1931-1939*, p. 272).

Commenting on the Irish unwillingness or inability due to these handicaps to appreciate the value of Commonwealth membership and seek readmittance, F. S. L. Lyons has written: "Nothing, not even the labours of the pro-Treaty party, not even the sympathy of other dominions, not even the belated generosity of Britain herself, could surmount these fatal defects. Ireland remained deaf to the siren voices of the Commonwealth and in the end heard only the ghosts of Roger Casement and all those other dead men knocking on the door. Equality, it seemed, was no substitute for nationality, and in the case of Ireland too much blood had flowed too often for nationality to be satisfied by any kind of connection or tie with Britain, however widely drawn or however magnanimously conceived." (*Ireland Since the Famine*, p. 570.) It may well be that Ireland needed, after her long unhappy history of subjugation to Britain, to go through the many cathartic experiences through which she was led, but the nagging question remains, where did all these accomplishments leave her with Britain over the six-county question?

The British territorial claim

The intrusion the British committed in 1949 into Irish affairs was quite unwarranted and unjustified both legally and constitutionally. But since this move was something Britain had been working up to and getting away with in the preceding years, she did not think twice before striking in a formal manner this time and in complete disregard of legality or constitutionality. To demonstrate the unwarranted and unjustified nature of the British action, we have to backtrack a moment to the Treaty.

It will be remembered that the device that that international Agreement contained for the possible dismemberment of Ireland was the Boundary Commission proposal with its Ulster option. That was a proposal that was not contingent upon the North's acceptance of it for validity (although the North did accept it). It will be remembered also that Craig and his colleagues created a fuss about not being adequately consulted about the Boundary Commission proposal before accepting it, and wanted to reject the entire idea. Their Parliament did, nevertheless, exercise the Ulster option contained in the proposal.

If we assume, as we may, that the denial of Ulster's right to be consulted about the acceptability to the North of the Boundary

Commission was constitutionally sound, and if we assume further, as we may, that the North's not being a party to the Treaty was likewise constitutional (that is, in terms of the 1920 Act), the question then arises: On what constitutional grounds is the 'Loyalist guarantee' offered? In other words, if the Treaty was consistent with the 1920 Act – and it was, as it was also with the 1914 Act – that is, if in fulfillment of those Acts it went a step beyond them and relinquished to the Irish Free State (all Ireland) those major jurisdictional powers that the 1920 and 1914 Acts had reserved to Westminster, the question is then: On what constitutional grounds does the British Government now begin to withhold to itself jurisdiction in the major powers over a part of Ireland? The question might be, rather: On what constitutional grounds does Britain prevent Irish sovereignty from being extended to the six counties?[4] It may further be asked: What constitutional right does the British Government have to give to a minor powers state in a foreign country the say-so as regards how and for how long the major powers are to be withheld by Britain or the extension of Irish sovereignty to that state to be prevented?

The answer to these questions is plain. There are no constitutional grounds whatsoever for withholding powers that belong to Ireland. There are no constitutional grounds whatsoever for preventing the territorial sovereignty of Ireland from being extended to the six counties. There are no constitutional grounds whatsoever for the United Kingdom to be extending (in a territorial sense) any obligation at all to the Loyalist community in Ireland. And significantly no such obligation was formally acknowledged to Ulster for years after the Treaty was signed.

It is true that Northern Ireland reemerged after the Treaty, but not anymore as the Northern Ireland of the 1920 Act. She reemerged, rather, as the creature of a Treaty that reformed and made its own the 1920 Act – that is, as a state within the Irish Free

4 The question about Britain's right to rule in the North of Ireland ought, of course, to be put in this second form. But, since the present Irish constitutional position vis-a-vis the North is so weak, and has been since the late 1930's at least, the question must also be asked in the first form. Besides, it appears that what is happening is that Britain is withholding to herself the major powers of jurisdiction as they apply to Northern Ireland, instead of preventing Ireland from exercising control over them (which would imply that Ireland possesses those powers already). And Britain, believing since World War II that Ireland is not serious about ending partition, not only thinks she possesses those powers absolutely, but goes ahead and uses them. It is significant that de Valera, in his weak constitutional position, conceded to Britain her mistaken position.

State. That being so, there are no constitutional grounds (in the Treaty) for any guarantee to be offered to Northern Ireland by Britain, and one would have to say that the Ireland Act of 1949 (and, for that matter, the Northern Ireland Constitution Act of 1973 that superseded it) was technically in conflict with the Treaty.

Let us pursue this argument briefly by examining the stand Britain is constrained to take in the matter. Quite a valuable insight into Britain's understanding of the fact that the Treaty took over and modified the Government of Ireland Act, 1920 (especially, as far as we are concerned, in its Ulster option clause [Article 12]) can be gained from a particular 'Order in Council' document of the British Government. The Provisional Government (Council of Ireland) Order, 1922 (No. 316) sheds light on the constitutional status of Northern Ireland once the Treaty would be ratified – or, rather, reratified, as it had to be for the purposes of the 'Ulster month.' That Order, among other things, states: "And whereas the provisions of the Government of Ireland Act, 1920, with respect to the powers of the Council of Ireland have been modified by the said Articles of Agreement [of the Treaty], and the Council of Ireland cannot be reestablished before the Parliament of the Irish Free State has been constituted in pursuance of the said Articles:" A paraphrase of the foregoing with regard to the status of Northern Ireland under the Treaty as reratified might read as follows: "And whereas the provisions of the Government of Ireland Act, 1920 have been modified by the said Articles of Agreement, and the Parliament of Northern Ireland cannot be reestablished before the Parliament of the Irish Free State has been constituted and the Address of Article 12 presented to the King in pursuance of the said Articles:" In other words, just as the Act of 1920 was modified by the Treaty with respect to the Council of Ireland, so also was that same Act modified by the Treaty with respect to the Ulster option and the Parliament of the option could not be established before the option itself had been exercised. All of which is Britain's own understanding of the matter.

Once the Treaty was ratified for the purposes of the Ulster month (which it was on December 5, 1922), notwithstanding the Treaty provision that Irish Free State jurisdiction should not be exercised in the territory of the six counties for one month from the date of such ratification, the Parliament of Northern Ireland would be considered to be inoperative and would remain so until one of two things happened: either an Address as specified would be made to the King or a month from the December 5th date of ratification would expire without such an Address being presented. In the latter case Articles 14 and 15 of the Treaty would come into play, and the jurisdiction of the Free State would no longer be suspended in Northern Ireland. But in the former case, from December 5th to the date of presentation of the Address (December 8th), the Parliament of Northern Ireland would be suspended or rendered a caretaker Parliament and, upon the Address being presented, would be reestablished under the Treaty (Article 12) as modifying the Government of Ireland Act, 1920.

That is to say, the Parliament of Northern Ireland as reestablished in 1922 would be the creature of the Treaty and, insofar as it was allowed to exercise authority only in the minor powers area of jurisdiction, its existence did not at all conflict with the essential Treaty Agreement, since this concerned itself mainly with a wholly other area of rule. The Treaty as a 32-county instrument preserved the Free State's *de jure* jurisdiction in the major powers area – and in so doing it preserved the essential unity of Ireland. That being so, the Ulster option was perforce exercised in a subordinate mode, and any legislation passed since then by Britain in support of the Loyalist guarantee and disruption of Irish *de jure* jurisdiction would have to be in conflict with the Treaty. It certainly finds no basis in the Treaty.

The British themselves were cognizant of this fact, and the alternative course they resorted to was *ipso facto* an admission of the lack of justification for the Loyalist guarantee in Anglo-Irish constitutionalism. For constitutional support of their unconstitutional action they delved back in desperation into history and invoked no less a piece of constituent legislation than that of the repealed Act of Union! This phenomenon bears some exploration on our part, for if the Act of Union can, after the Treaty, be validly construed as applying to Northern Ireland to the exclusion of all Ireland (its subject), and if it can be invoked in constitutional support of the Northern Loyalist veto to the exclusion of any say-so from the people of Ireland as a whole, then there is not much hope of the Irish people ever getting rid of partition – or of the prospect of their ever having any power over it. But it need not necessarily be so if we can belie the British *ex post facto* contention that the Treaty was contracted with one part of Ireland only. The North would be none of the South's business!

The Act of Union resurrected to bolster a claim

In the earlier part of this book we endeavored to trace the wrong turning Ireland took that resulted in the acceptance of partition. Strangely, a correspondingly wrong turning was taken also by Britain which resulted in the consolidation of partition. Where Britain went wrong was in her unwarranted insistence, many years after the event and perhaps inspired by the Boundary Commission misinterpretation, that the Treaty Agreement was concluded with 'Southern Ireland' alone and not with all of Ireland. That is to say, that the Treaty was concluded with that part of Ireland to which the Partition Act of 1920 ostensibly did not apply. That, of course, was begging the question, for under the 1920 Act no such 'Southern Ireland' state existed. As we know, the Act, an all-Ireland instrument that was designed "for the better government of ***Ireland***," was rejected ***nation***wide in the General Election of May 1921. It was proved unworkable, for all of Ireland, and no mandate was given by the Irish people for establishing either a Southern or even a Northern state.

But the British view was that it did not matter that the Act was rendered unworkable or that it was not accepted by the entire nation. All that was needed was that it be accepted by a minority of the voters! After all, Britain had the right, founded in the Act of Union, to legislate for Ireland in any way she thought fit. Never mind what the mandate of the majority was. 'Legislation' to become law did not depend on acceptance by the people. Once the 1920 Act was accepted, by whomever, it became the law of the land simply by the rolling around of "the appointed day" (April 19, 1921 among others) and by the Parliament of the North being willy-nilly opened and assembled. Thus was 'Southern Ireland' created by exclusion as a negative jurisdiction, not as a legal entity. Besides, the Act was going to be forcibly applied in all of Ireland anyway – by having the device of a mythical 'Crown Colony' provided for if any part of the country should not work it – a far cry from asking for the consent of the Ireland that then existed under the Treaty Act of Union. So that if the Partition Act was not going to be imposed in one form, it was in another. With such forced imposition of the Act, the Irish nation would inevitably be divided and the fictional 'Southern Ireland' thrown up. And it was with this legal fiction, existing under the 1920 Act as a separate 'state,' that the Treaty would have been exclusively concluded (which is, actually, what de Valera had thought too).

But this argument, even if it could be taken seriously, does not hold up. It is incapable of being used to bolster the position Britain holds about whom the Treaty was concluded with. The simple fact is that the British could not have entered into Treaty negotiation with such a state as 'Southern Ireland' (or, for that matter, with such a state as 'Northern Ireland'): they would have been prohibited from doing so by their own Act (Sec. 4, subs. (4)). The 1920 Act stated in Section 4: "Subject to the provisions of this Act, the Parliament of Southern Ireland . . . shall not have power to make laws in respect of . . . : Treaties or any relations with foreign states, or relations with other parts of His Majesty's dominions . . ."

In any case, as we have noted, since the Act of 1920 was an all-Ireland instrument, that turned out to be unworkable as such, the Treaty was designed to replace it. As a matter of fact, provision of a constitutional substitute was the reason the Treaty Settlement was negotiated to begin with. The Treaty would, then, have to be negotiated with all of Ireland and be accepted by and for all of Ireland. True, special provision would have to be made in it for an amorphous Northern Ireland, but that fact would not militate against the instrument's being an all-Ireland document. In addition, it would have had to be negotiated on a level that was not at all contemplated by the 1920 Act. The view is untenable, therefore, that the Act was first accepted in Ireland and the Treaty then negotiated under its terms. The opposite, in fact, is the case: the Treaty was first concluded and put into effect, in all of Ireland, and provision was made in it for optionally, after ratification, taking up the Partition Act *as it applied to Northern Ireland* and, "subject to the necessary *modifications*" (of the Irish Free State (Consequential Provisions) Act of December 5, 1922 as this was authorized by and directed so to do by the Treaty itself), working it in the North alone. And if the Act were not going to be tried under the terms of the Treaty in Northern Ireland, then the Treaty, precisely because it was an all-Ireland instrument, provided an alternative scheme for a federal Ireland to be set up – in Articles 14 and 15. So that the very makeup of the Treaty testifies against the view that the instrument was negotiated or concluded on a partitionist basis. The quaint British view that the Treaty was negotiated with Southern Ireland alone would necessitate, as Justice Feetham put it in the Boundary Commission decision (see Chapter 10), that the Ireland with which the Treaty was negotiated be construed as exclusive of *Northern* Ireland. But this theory would be at odds with and nullified by Britain's own Order of the King in Council, given two years earlier, that Ireland be construed as exclusive of *Southern* Ireland (the Irish Free State (Consequential Adaptation of Enactments) Order, 1923, Sec. 2)!

Also, as we have pointed out repeatedly – perhaps over-repeatedly – the Treaty was negotiated with Plenipotentiaries whose credentials as representatives of the all-Ireland Provisional Republic were recognized in London – at least they were not positively disacknowledged – and the Settlement was concluded with those Plenipotentiaries as representatives of all of Ireland, not just part of it. The diplomatic problem the British Government had was that it could not openly recognize a revolutionary, Republican Government until it saw whether that Government would agree to accept the Treaty and stay within the Empire. But it latently recognized that Government as being the Government of all Ireland and it negotiated an all-Ireland agreement with it on that basis.

There is perhaps no more convincing evidence for the truth of the statement that the Treaty was an all-Ireland instrument than that which is on the face of the Treaty itself. As Leo Kohn has pointed out, the document, in referring more than once to "Ireland" in treating its subject, indicated that it was dealing with the entire island of Ireland (which it required to be styled and known as "the Irish Free State"), and it referred to "the rest of Ireland" when it was treating the 26-county part of the island in a Northern Ireland connection.

Further argument to prove the all-Ireland nature of the Treaty Settlement is hardly necessary. The reason we dwell so heavily on this point at all is to highlight the point that, despite the obvious fact that the Treaty applied to all of Ireland and that it ended 121 years of hated union with Britain, in the British view the Act, or rather the Acts, of Union of 1800 still unbelievably hold sway. The U.K. Government must hold this peculiar view if it is to maintain its position of having isolated the 26-county state and concluded the Treaty with it alone. That way if the six-county British province has to be considered instituted by the Partition Act, or by the Consequential Provisions Act, justification has to be found for so legislating for and holding the province. And where outside of the Treaty is such justification to be found if not in the Constituent Acts of 1800? What alternative way is there to undergird the North's constitutional status, especially if the Treaty was concluded outside of it, other than by invoking the only remaining constitutional agreement there is – the Acts of Union? (After all, older Acts than these were dusted off and invoked at times that it was found convenient to do so.)

Incredibly, this is just what Britain has been doing by every few years, even as recently as 1978, revising provisions of these Acts, as if to point out that they still applied. Even if they did, they would apply to all of Ireland: they were never designed for just part of it. Besides, they would have applied as the 'Treaty of Union' they were, which means that they ought not to have been invoked by one side without the consent of the other. Britain's way of invoking the Acts to justify her intervention in Ireland was by amending them – unilaterally. But, as Harry Calvert has pointed out, the Acts of Union were "a bilateral treaty, not subject to unilateral amendment" (p. 24). Britain's amending of them on her own, especially of the Irish Act, has, to say the least, been done since 1931 in violation of the Statute of Westminster.

Britain's error in misapplying the Treaty exclusively to the 26 counties has caused her condescendingly to regard the Acts of Union as being no longer in force with respect to the South of Ireland! But they would be with respect to the North of Ireland! Indeed, states Harry Calvert (in *Constitutional Law in Northern Ireland*, p. 10), "they retain their full vigour so far as Northern Ireland is concerned," an explanation that is frankly beyond us. Calvert describes the strong compulsion Westminster feels for continuing to be bound under the Acts to maintain the union of Northern Ireland with Great Britain. Westminster's passing of the 1949 Ireland Act, for example, caused "a firm seal [to be set] on one of the clearest conventions of the British constitution," he states, which convention "is founded in the Acts of Union." Thus was the 'constitutional' status of Northern Ireland under the Acts first confirmed, and with the passage of the Northern Ireland Constitution Act of 1973 this status was reaffirmed more strongly than ever. (Cf. Roger H. Hull, *The Irish Triangle*, pp. 112-116.)

Halsbury's Statutes of England, Third Edition, in volume 23 at page 832, unabashedly states the British assumed position: "Many of the provisions of the Act [s of 1800] have been virtually repealed by the legislation passed consequent on the establishment of the Irish Free State and the establishment of the Parliament of Northern Ireland, but the Act[s] remains as a statutory warrant for the continued incorporation of Northern Ireland within the United Kingdom." So goes the authoritative statement of the North's forming an integral part of Great Britain, and of the 'constitutional' rationale for forming such a part. *Halsbury's* goes on to point out that that "constitutional status of Northern Ireland has been further confirmed and guaranteed by the Ireland Act 1949, s. 1 (2)." This was the subsection (now replaced by Sec. 1 of the Northern Ireland Constitution Act of 1973) that guaranteed to the Northern Loyalists that the six counties would never have to leave the Monarchical Commonwealth or United Kingdom without the consent of the Northern Ireland Parliament (see Appendix 14, *Supplement*). (In 1973 the British Government substituted a new guarantee that shifted the requirement for consent from the Northern Parliament to "the majority of the people of Northern Ireland," where the term 'majority' is latterly interpreted to mean 70 percent and up.[5]) All of which points up the extent to which a belated, Feetham-traceable misinterpretation of so basic a document as the Treaty could mislead and result in the rigidities that besiege the Irish people today.

But it was not only Treaty misinterpretation and misapplication that was perpetrated. There was also what we've seen that led to it – a certain subterfuge. The way Calvert explains it is that our old acquaintance, the Irish Free State (Consequential Adaptation of Enactments) Order, No. 405 of 1923, generically adapted the Westminster Union with Ireland Act, 1800 to construe Ireland as being exclusive of Southern Ireland, which adaptation would have been allowed by the I.F.S. (Consequential Provisions) Act, 1922 (Sec. 6), a power that would in turn have been authorized by the Treaty Article 12 (subject to certain conditions). But, as we've seen in Chapters 7 and 8, Section 6 of the CPA only allowed amendment of Commonwealth, not British Irish, legislation and, significantly, the 1923 Adaptation Order did amend Commonwealth legislation. Of British Irish legislation, all the Treaty authorized was modification of the Government of Ireland Act, 1920 – and of only a certain five Sections of the Act at that[6] (those listed in Command Paper of 2264 of 1924). Besides, modification of any or all refer-

5 It may indeed be that even 70 percent would not be considered sufficient to constitute a majority. Interpreting the requirement of Cmnd. 7590 of 1980, *The Government of Northern Ireland: Proposals for Further Discussion*, that the minority community must feel able to accept, and identify with, new governmental institutions in Northern Ireland, Claire Palley has said that U.K. Governments "will not proceed with majority community support alone" (David Watt, ed., *The Constitution of Northern Ireland*, p. 191).

6 The five Sections of the 1920 Act containing powers that were to apply to Northern Ireland upon their being modified by Treaty authorization actually contained powers that were not applicable to Northern Ireland at all, those powers being all in the category of reserved powers that were suspended from all Ireland

ences to Ireland in such a partitionist sense as that alleged, in 1923, would have been purely theoretical as long as the Boundary Commission of 1925 had not yet determined the extent, if any, of the Northern Government's jurisdiction and would have been entirely invalid if the required conditions were not to be fulfilled as well. Moreover, such modification exclusive of ***Southern*** Ireland would soon enough be contradicted in any case by the Boundary Commission Chairman's decision that Ireland should be construed as being exclusive of ***Northern*** Ireland. It is entirely unclear to us why Ireland should be construed as being exclusive of either part of Ireland, and not construed as Ireland alone. (See also Appendix 14, *Supplement.*)

One reason we have been so heavily stressing the all-Ireland character of the Treaty Settlement is to illustrate the groundlessness of all of Britain's constitutional legislation for Northern Ireland ever since the post-Treaty period. That groundlessness was established by the Treaty's abrogation of all preceding constitutional arrangements, particularly the one most pertinent, that of 1800. Once Treaty agreement was reached the death knell of the Act or Acts of Union was sounded. Not even were they brought back provisionally in the Treaty (as was the Government of Ireland Act, 1920), nor was any part or parts of them recalled. Not having had a constitutional way of restricting the *de jure* 32-county jurisdiction of the Saorstat to the *de facto* 26-county jurisdiction, that is to say, not having had a constitutional rationale for maintaining a separate Northern state and for subsequently legislating therefor, Britain was obliged to force, through misuse of an Adaptation Order (see Chapter 8), a narrow interpretation retroactively on the Treaty and, by that means, to have recourse back to the Acts of Union for a constitutional base. Such an interpretation, while understandable, cannot of course be sustained. The Treaty marked, in the words of W.C. Costin and J. Steven Watson, "the end of the Irish Union" (*The Law and Working of the Constitution*, Vol. II, p. 145). It ended the Union and began the Commonwealth.

Chief Justice Hugh Kennedy explained clearly in an Irish Supreme Court case how the idea of the British-Irish union endur-

---

by the very provision of the Treaty that affirmed that "so far as they relate to Northern Ireland [they] continue to be of full force and effect" (Article 12)! The five Sections of the Act, as contained in the Command Paper (*Irish Boundary: Extracts . . . relevant to . . . Article XII of the Articles of Agreement . . .*), are: 1 (2), 4 (1), 6 (1), 75 and 76 (2). (See also Appendix 6, Note 14 and Appendix 14, Section 3 in the *Supplement* to this work.)

ing past the Treaty and Ireland's admission into the Commonwealth was entirely unsustainable. "The constitutional position so assumed by Ireland," he wrote, "was quite incompatible with even a notional continuance of the existence of the United Kingdom created by the Act of Union of 1800. It follows that the Union was thereby dissolved, and the political unit theretofore known as 'the United Kingdom of Great Britain and Ireland' came to an end as a matter of constitutional law." (*In re Reade,* [1927] *Irish Reports* 31, p. 48; see also Appendix 14, *Supplement.*) This doctrine is, of course, anathema to Britain, as any notion that the Union did not persist with at least one part of Ireland would undoubtedly undercut the claim that the Treaty was concluded with the other part exclusively – the theory we called the wrong turning of the British.

Where the British began to give official sanction to their wrong turning was, upon having got away with their end-run Adaptation Order in 1923, they proceeded to restrict the Irish Free State's *de jure* jurisdiction with, as we have seen, the Royal and Parliamentary Titles Act of April 1927. In this Act the United Kingdom was defined as being "Great Britain and Northern Ireland." Such an aggressive assertion amounted to a (post-Treaty) revisionist allegation that the six counties were *de jure* part of the United Kingdom. Factually, as per the Treaty and 1925 Boundary Agreements, they were administered by the U.K. while being *de jure* part of the Irish Free State. By such arrangement the North would temporarily be *de facto* part of the U.K. But if Britain could overstep the fine line between *de facto* and *de jure*, she would, and this is what she did by, in 1927 in the RAPTA, (unconstitutionally again) thus defining the United Kingdom to comprise Great Britain and Northern Ireland. By inference the Saorstat would be the rest of Ireland *de jure*, which it had already been obliged to be *de facto*, and this was an inference that was gradually to become hardened into unquestioned fact. Such British revisionism was hardly questioned in those imperialist times.

Section 2 (2) of the Royal and Parliamentary Titles Act read: "In every Act passed and public document issued after the passing of this Act the expression 'United Kingdom' shall, unless the context otherwise requires, mean Great Britain and Northern Ireland." Interestingly, due to Irish uneasiness, the King, George V, bucked Parliament and did not include in his official title the reference to Northern Ireland as being within the United Kingdom. Instead he changed the old phrase 'United Kingdom of Great Britain and Ireland' into 'Great Britain, Ireland,' thus indicating the convention of Northern Ireland being administered by the United Kingdom and not being really an integral part of it.

Section 2 of the Consequential Adaptation of Enactments Order of 1923 is often wrongly cited to justify the audacious definition of 'Ireland' given in the 1927 Act, wrongly because, as we saw, (1) that Order only concerned amendment of Commonwealth legislation (which is all the Consequential Provisions Act, in Section 6, had authorized) and (2) the Order only qualified pre-1922 legislation, whereas the Act related to post-1927 enactments (in the U.K. context). But the change made by the King, though a welcomed if ambiguous gesture, left unimpaired the effect of the RAPTA, which was quite unambiguously a violation of the Treaty Agreement. This latter, in effectively repealing the Acts of Union of 1800 and terminating the integration of Ireland (including Northern Ireland) with Britain, rendered meaningless anymore such a phrase as 'the United Kingdom of Great Britain and Northern Ireland.'

In the Irish Supreme Court decision, Chief Justice Kennedy adjudged that, consequent upon the Treaty of 1921, "the phrase, 'the United Kingdom,' was remitted to its former meaning under the Act of Union of England and Scotland (6 Anne, c. 11), namely, 'the United Kingdom of Great Britain,' though, it is true, in the events that have happened, part of the Province of Ulster has become subject to its authority" (*c. cit.,* p. 48; see also Appendix 14, *Supplement*). However, in 1936 King George VI brought back into the royal title specific mention of Northern Ireland, when he used the phrase 'United Kingdom of Great Britain and Northern Ireland.' On May 28, 1953, Queen Elizabeth II retained this usage when she changed the English, but ***not*** the Latin, version of her title (as the 1953 Royal Titles Act allowed) to: 'Elizabeth II, by the Grace of God of the United Kingdom of Great Britain and Northern Ireland and Her other Realms and Territories Queen, Head of the Commonwealth, Defender of the Faith.' (The Latin version runs: 'Elizabeth II, Dei Gratia Britanniarum Regnorumque Suorum Ceterorum Regina, Consortionis Populorum Princeps, Fidei Defensor.') Finally, in 1962 the Commonwealth Immigrants Act, in Section 21 (2), and in 1978 the Interpretation Act, in Schedule 1, *Definitions*, and Schedule 2, Paragraph 4 (1) (a), confirmed the 1927 Act and reaffirmed that 'the United Kingdom' means the United Kingdom of Great Britain and Northern Ireland. (See also the references to royal titles in Chapter 7 herein; and *Halsbury's Statutory Instruments*, Vol. 5, pp. 2-3.)

In sum, no pre-1922 legislation (Act of Union, etc.) was specifically amended or updated consequentially upon the Free State being established; no 1922-1927 legislation was specifically or generically amended; pre-1922 legislation, that would in reality have been repealed, was generically amended, in 1923, but this was done obliquely through the Order in Council whose scope and effect were never entirely clear.[7] It was only in 1927, with the Royal and Parliamentary Titles Act, that there emerged the first formal inkling of British intentions to define the Irish Free State as if the 1923 generic amendment had really taken effect and was adequate. So that what was practically an amendment of nothing, to the extent that it was a valid amendment at all, came in time to be taken as good and real and to be built into an undoubted fact of law. Then 11 years after RAPTA, in 1938, the British took their restriction of the I.F.S. to 26 counties a step further with the Eire (Confirmation of Agreements) Act, which stated (in now-repealed Sec. 1) that "the territory which, in accordance with the provisions of [the Treaty and the Act ratifying the Treaty] was required to be styled and known as the Irish Free State shall be styled and known as Eire, and accordingly, references in any enactment to the Irish Free State shall be construed as references to Eire." By 'Eire' was to be understood the territory that already also by its own law was to be so known – namely, 26 counties of the Irish Free State.

The truth is, of course, that all Ireland was the territory that was required by the Treaty to be styled and known as the Irish Free

---

7 S.R. & O. 405 of 1923 all the more blatantly excluded the Irish Free State from Ireland when that State had itself passed a similar law the year before, the Adaptation of Enactments Act, 1922, that positively had identified Ireland as the Irish Free State: "For the purpose of the construction of any British Statute the name 'Ireland', whether used alone or in conjunction with the expression 'Great Britain', or by implication as being included in the expression 'United Kingdom', shall mean Saorstat Eireann" (Sec. 3). This adaptation was necessary as a result of the coming into operation of the Constitution of Saorstat Eireann, an event that, as Justice Henchy was to state, "brought to an end the United Kingdom (i.e., of Great Britain and Ireland) which had come into existence with the Act of Union, 1800." Upon the coming into operation of the Constitution of Southern Ireland, however, the State was not so forthright, but passed an adaptation measure, the Constitution (Consequential Provisions) Act, 1937, that obligingly dovetailed with the 405 Order and, in the words again of Justice Henchy, "enacted that the expression 'Saorstat Eireann' in pre-Constitution statutes was thenceforth to be construed as meaning the State brought into existence by the Constitution." (*The State (Joachim Gilsenan)* v. *(District Justice) Peter A. McMorrow*, [1978] I.R. 360, p. 371; see also James O'Reilly and Mary Redmond, *Cases and Materials on the Irish Constitution*, p. 166. For the text of Adaptation Order No. 405, see Appendix 6, Note 14, *Supplement*.)

State, and in corroboration of this fact in the Treaty six counties of that territory were referred to as "Northern Ireland" and 26 as "the rest of Ireland." Now, 17 years later, a new twist would be given to the Treaty Settlement by the Section of the Confirmation of Agreements Act just quoted: the Treaty was made out to say that it was "the rest of Ireland" that was required to be styled and known as "the Irish Free State"! And the Irish Government of the time (which had paved the way by restricting "Eire" to 26 counties in the 1937 Constitution and "Saorstat Eireann" to Eire in the Constitution (Consequential Provisions) Act, 1937) dutifully confirmed the British interpretation by defining in the confirmatory Finance and Capital Sum Agreement Acts of 1938 the United Kingdom as "the United Kingdom of Great Britain and Northern Ireland"! That left "Eire" clearly to be "the rest of Ireland." Any lingering doubt there might be was removed in 1948 by the declaration of this 26-county State to be the Republic of Ireland.[8]

In 1949 Britain threw all imprecision on her part to the winds, and "the territory" referred to in her 1938 Act was forthrightly spelled out and defined. In the Ireland Act, *pace* the Irish 1948 Act, she stated: "It is hereby recognized and declared that ***the part of Ireland*** heretofore known as Eire . . . is hereafter . . . referred to, by the name attributed thereto ***by the law thereof***, that is to say, as the Republic of Ireland" (Sec. 1 (2) & (3); *italics ours*). From there on out there would be no doubt, as far as Britain was concerned, as to what territory the Irish Free State of the Treaty was made to refer to. It was none other than the Republic of Ireland, and the six-county part of the older Ireland would more than ever need the constitutional basis the Acts of Union afforded for its right to exist as part of the United Kingdom. Such is the rationale for the Loyalist/partitionist guarantee.

However, it cannot at the same time be denied that some sort of independent communal Loyalist guarantee was genuinely evolving over the years. But, because of the unwarranted and biased form in which it was expressed, that is to say, because of the way in which the communal was being confused with the territorial,

8 Subsequent recognition was given by Dail Eireann to the *de jure* existence of Northern Ireland in a number of Irish statutes. These were listed to 1974 by T. K. Liston, S.C., in the case *Kevin Boland* v. *An Taoiseach* as: Section 1 of the Erne Drainage and Development Act, 1950; Section 2 of the Foyle Fisheries Act, 1952; Section 2 of the Great Northern Railway Act, 1958; Section 7 of the Irish Nationality and Citizenship Act, 1956; and Section 41 of the Extradition Act, 1965.

we would have to say that the guarantee was being tainted with unconstitutionality (insofar as it was a deviation from the Treaty-established position). It would have been unconstitutional only, however, in its *territorial* aspect, because it was with domestic, communal jurisdiction that the Treaty was concerned in its Northern Ireland (Article 12) clause and not with external territorial jurisdiction. The basic principle the Treaty as a whole affirmed was the territorial integrality of Ireland, while at the same time recognizing the right of dissentient citizens to secede. We are forced to distinguish in the Treaty, then, between territory and those who would secede from that territory – people. Such a territory-people distinction would be required in order to preserve compatibility between the Treaty guarantee of sovereignty and any later-institutionalized Loyalist guarantee of secession, and this distinction must perforce condition the more recent evolution of the guarantee. In this light, we are forced to understand the modern Loyalist guarantee in other than a territorial sense. We are forced, in truth, to return to the Treaty sense.

The sense in which the Treaty was concerned with securing the integrity of the territory of Ireland, while not going counter to the wishes of the *whole* Irish people, was clearly described by Sergeant Henry Hanna (later Chief Justice Hanna) in his submission to the Boundary Commission on behalf of the Government of the Saorstat. "If the Northern Parliament present a petition that the Irish Free State powers should no longer extend to them," he explained, "the position would then be that the Northern Parliament shall continue their powers under the Act of 1920, but they shall not necessarily have the territory of 1920. And why should they not have that territory? Because of the Treaty, and because, on the Treaty basis of Ireland being the unit, there is a portion of the population who desire to secede from that Free State. The wishes of these inhabitants are to be ascertained. . . . The Northern Government, if they put in the petition, were to continue to have the powers under the Act of 1920, but they were not to have the territory, unless it is determined under the Treaty that they are entitled to it." Hanna further suggested to the Commission that it should regard the will of some of the people as acknowledged in the Treaty "from the standpoint of international law as a *secession* of a section of the inhabitants of the Irish Free State from the Free State, and that you should regard yourselves as a tribunal established to determine the extent and method of that secession." (Report of the Irish Boundary Commission, pp. 13 and 16.)

The British communal claim

The 1949 Ireland Act marked the point that Britain was farthest formally from the agreed Treaty position. This Act was formulated on a rebound from the 26-county area leaving 'His Majesty's Dominions' (which technically had not existed since 1931) and declaring itself a Republic. In preparation for the Act the British Government went about formulating its policy on the North of Ireland and recorded it in a secret document that has in recent years been released. "Now that Eire will shortly cease to owe any allegiance to the Crown," the policy statement went, "it has become a matter of first-class strategic importance to this country that the North should continue to form part of His Majesty's Dominions. So far as can be foreseen, it will never be to Great Britain's advantage that Northern Ireland should form part of a territory outside His Majesty's jurisdiction. Indeed, it seems unlikely that Great Britain would ever be able to agree to this even if the people of Northern Ireland desired it. There should therefore be no political difficulty, as circumstances now are, in giving a binding assurance that Northern Ireland shall ever be excluded from the United Kingdom without her full and free consent." (Quoted from Sean Cronin, *Irish Nationalism*, p. 235.)

Having convinced themselves of the necessity to hold on to Northern Ireland and of the rightness of their position, the British proceeded to be equally forthright in the wording of the 1949 Act itself and quite self-assuredly undertook to 'guarantee' to the Irish Loyalists that the territory of the North would remain part of the U.K. for as long as they, the Loyalists, willed it (and, as we know, even if they might not will it at all). "It is hereby declared that Northern Ireland remains part of His Majesty's Dominions and of the United Kingdom," the Act stated, "and it is hereby affirmed that in no event will Northern Ireland or any part thereof cease to be part of His Majesty's Dominions and of the United Kingdom without the consent of the Parliament of Northern Ireland."

Such was the ironclad guarantee of a Parliament that presumed itself to have supremacy over a part of Ireland. The guarantee was not, nevertheless, as absolute as appears at first glance. As F. S. L. Lyons points out (in following Wade and Dicey's explanation of the workings of British constitutional practice), what one statute of the Westminster Parliament could ordain another could repeal. "To say this is merely to emphasise what has been from the beginning a constant element in the link between the two areas – which is that the supremacy of the Westminster parliament carried with it the implication that any radical shift of political attitudes in Britain could have direct and drastic effects upon Northern Ireland" (Lyons, p. 729 hardcover, p. 738 paperback).

Whether the less stringent formulations of the Loyalist guarantee that have occurred since 1949 are due to shifts in British public opinion or to Northern American and European pressures, we don't know, but one thing remains certain and that is that the British Government never did have the constitutional right to make a piece of Ireland part of the United Kingdom at any time. Just as the Statute of Westminster of 1931 made it impossible for Ireland (or any other member country) to belong to His/Her Majesty's Dominions anymore, and just as the Irish Free State, Canada, South Africa, etc., ceased from that time to be Dominions and became technically 'Realms,' so the Treaty of 1921 made it impossible for Northern Ireland to be a part of the United Kingdom anymore also. The 1949 Act and the 1969 Downing Street Declaration, as precursors of the bombastically stark Section 1 of the 1973 Constitution Act, have then, if they are to be taken literally and at face value, to be regarded unconstitutional. But the 1973 Act, even if self-condemningly claiming for the U.K. a Parliamentless Northern Ireland that was never agreed on in the Treaty, illustrated the need to express the constitutional position in a people rather than a territorial sense.

It ought not to be impossible to make this shift in interpretation in the application of the provisions of these instruments. Obviously, for example, the 1949 Act could not be interpreted literally in its provision for "the consent of ***the Parliament*** of Northern Ireland" anymore. This has of necessity had to be translated into "the consent of ***the majority of the people*** of Northern Ireland" in the 1973 Act – and was, incidentally, understood already by Tim Pat Coogan in examining the Ireland Act in *The I.R.A.* (p. 445) in the sense of "the consent of the majority of that state – the Unionists." This is an exegetical liberty Coogan took at the time with the text of the 1949 Act, but it was not out of line with the way in which pledges to the Loyalist community have been formulated by British statesmen (and women) from some twenty years later down to our time. And it pointed the way the relevant section of the Ireland Act has had eventually to be interpreted.

Actually the Downing Street Declaration had progressed a bit in the right direction. It read in part as follows: "The United Kingdom Government reaffirm that nothing which has happened in recent weeks in Northern Ireland derogates from the clear pledges made by successive United Kingdom governments that Northern Ireland should not cease to be a part of the United Kingdom without the consent of ***the people of Northern Ireland*** or from the provision in Section I of the Ireland Act 1949 that in no event will Northern Ireland or any part thereof cease to be part of the United Kingdom without the consent of the Parliament of Northern Ireland" (*italics ours*). (Then the Declaration added pointedly: "The Border is not an issue"!) Note that mention of Northern Ireland as being part of "Her Majesty's Dominions" is dropped, and also that progress is made from "consent of the Parliament of Northern Ireland" to "consent of the people of Northern Ireland."

The Northern Ireland Constitution Act of 1973 guaranteed, as we have seen, that no change would be made in the constitutional status of the North without the consent of the majority of the *people* of Northern Ireland. The Sunningdale Agreement of later that year took the evolutionary process a step further. Mindful of the constitutional restrictions imposed by the Treaty, it did not reiterate the no-change guarantee to the Northern Ireland majority without at the same time recognizing the territorially unitary nature of the island of Ireland. It practically forced itself, then, to admit the distinction between territory and people – although the British still, in their declaration in the Agreement, preserved their 'Northern Ireland is Ours' attitude.

By the 1973 stage of events a new characteristic began to make the official Irish unity scene: the reunification of Ireland by the consent of the minority – an Irish Loyalist guarantee! This was a condition for reunification that would come actually to be expected of the Irish in the post-Sunningdale Anglo-Irish deliberations that were led off by Charles Haughey and Margaret Thatcher, in 1980 (and which we will examine here before returning to a consideration of Sunningdale). The more the condition of unity by minority consent would be conceded by the Irish in these deliberations, the less pronounced the tendency of the British would become to express their constitutional position in terms of Northern Ireland being an integral part of the United Kingdom. The position might be referred to merely, in those same deliberations, as "the constitutional status of Northern Ireland" or, simply, "the status of Northern Ireland." This shift in emphasis by Britain, if it is not to be suspected as masking rather than attempting to resolve the British-Irish conflict of position on the true status of the North, has to be taken as being indicative of three important developments: (1) a willingness to resolve the traditional conflict between the two constitutional positions on the North and to reach a common definition of same; (2) that in return for Irish espousal of the unity by consent principle, Britain was willing to understand her position more in terms of community or people within Ireland rather than of territory or partition without Ireland; and (3) that it was being left up to the majority community in Northern Ireland to decide whether they belonged communally and nonterritorially to the United Kingdom or not.

We might note here that there were seven main Irish-British deliberations succeeding the Sunningdale Agreement that adopted the concept of unity by consent as a trade-off for British indications that the *territory* of Northern Ireland might no longer be regarded an integral part of the United Kingdom (or, to put it in Treaty terms, that the sovereignty of Ireland covering the six counties, might no longer be considered suspended). Six of these deliberations were issued in Joint Communiques and were as follows:

MAY 21, 1980

P.M. Thatcher and Taoiseach Haughey

It was mutually agreed "that a change in the constitutional status of Northern Ireland would only come about with the agreement of a majority there" – an undertaking that was to resonate more than five years later in the Hillsborough Accord.

DECEMBER 8, 1980

P.M. Thatcher and Taoiseach Haughey

The Principals commissioned special Anglo-Irish Joint Studies that would cover "the totality of relationships within these islands" and lead to "possible new institutional structures."

NOVEMBER 6, 1981

P.M. Thatcher and Taoiseach FitzGerald

It was mutually agreed that "any change in the constitutional status of Northern Ireland would require the consent of a majority of the people of Northern Ireland." Giving explicit recognition to the Irish dimension for the first time, the British Prime Minister agreed that "if that consent were to be expressed . . . , the British Government would of course accept their decision and would support legislation in the British Parliament to give effect to it." As an expression of the unique character of the relationship between Britain and Ireland, it was agreed to establish an Anglo-Irish Intergovernmental Council.

NOVEMBER 20, 1983

P.M. Thatcher and Taoiseach FitzGerald

First meeting at the level of Heads of Government of the Anglo-Irish Intergovernmental Council. New Ireland Forum in process (from May 30, 1983 to May 2, 1984).

NOVEMBER 18 & 19, 1984

P.M. Thatcher and Taoiseach FitzGerald

Second meeting at the level of Heads of Government of the Anglo-Irish Intergovernmental Council. After taking into account the position of the British Government as set out in the debate in the House of Commons on July 2, 1984, the principals agreed "that any change in the constitutional status of Northern Ireland as part of the United Kingdom would only come about with the consent of a majority of the people of Northern Ireland." The British Prime Minister confirmed that "if in the future the majority of the people of Northern Ireland clearly wished for and consented to a change in the constitutional status of Northern Ireland, the United Kingdom Government would put forward and support legislation to that end in the British Parliament." It was mutually agreed that the identities of both the majority and minority communities in Northern Ireland should be recognized and respected, and reflected in structures and processes acceptable to both communities.

NOVEMBER 15, 1985

P.M. Thatcher and Taoiseach FitzGerald

Third meeting at the level of Heads of Government of the Anglo-Irish Intergovernmental Council on the occasion of signing the Hillsborough Accord. The Anglo-Irish Agreement of 1985[9] was the crowning deliberation that manifested the unity by consent/territorial integrity trade-off.

---

9 The Agreement of 1985 is usually referred to as such or, at most, as an Accord; not having been formally ratified by Parliament and promulgated by the

But if the British inclination to cede the territory if not the people of Northern Ireland developed in response to Irish yielding on the unity by consent principle, the very idea of such a response was prompted by Ireland itself. (We will explore in the next chapter the evolution of the concept of unity by consent and the nature of the condition (personal self-determination) that is required to resolve the apparent contradiction in the Irish Republican affirmation of that concept.) The first modern-times inkling of the idea that it might be necessary to affirm a personal or communal form of self-determination in order to induce a minority consent to Irish unity came on the Irish side from Taoiseach Liam Cosgrave in Dail Eireann on March 3, 1971: "Any ultimate solution will have to recognise that the political, cultural and religious traditions of the Protestants of Northern Ireland must be given their full weight in the policies and institutions and set-up . . . of a 32-County Ireland." This was quickly followed by a Dail Eireann Resolution that affirmed the corollary of the Cosgrave statement: unity by the consent of the inhabitants of the territory that was to be united. This Resolution was this concept's first official introduction, albeit in veiled form: "That Dail Eireann formally rejects the use of force as an instrument to secure the unity of Ireland, welcomes the steps so far taken and promised to eliminate discrimination in Northern Ireland, and looks forward to the establishment of full fundamental rights and freedoms for everyone, irrespective of religion or political opinion." (See *Dail Debates* for March 9, 1971. It might be noted that it was not too difficult for the Dail to reach the position of affirming the principle of unity by the consent of the minority, the Constitution having by its very act of establishing the 26-county State and abandoning the North inclined the Dail, any Southern Dail, to so require minority consent if the North were ever to be won back. And the Constitution did establish the 26-county State: the Irish Supreme Court has said as much in using this fact to form the basis of its January 19, 1988 decision in the Robert Russell extradition case, to wit, that taking action to attain Irish reunification "without the authority of ***the organs of State***

Queen, it did not become a Treaty in British constitutional law but "is merely the act of private persons" (*Blackstone's Commentaries*, 14th edn., Vol. 1, p. 252). However, "there is no exact list of subjects in respect of which the sanction of Parliament [and the Crown] is required in order to make a treaty binding on British subjects" (*Halsbury's Laws of England*, 3rd ed., Vol. 7, p. 286; see also *ibid.*, Vol. 8, 4th ed., para. 986; *Halsbury's Statutes of England*, 3rd ed., Vol. 6, "Crown"; and *ibid.*, 4th ed., Vol. 10, "Crown").

established by the Constitution is to subvert the Constitution and to usurp the function of Government" (*emphasis ours*; this interpretation of the Constitution was reaffirmed by the Irish High Court on March 16, 1989 in the Paul Kane extradition case).

There followed upon the 1971 initiative, on the 6th-9th of December 1973, the Anglo-Irish Sunningdale Agreed Communique which, for starters, jointly affirmed the Irish constitutional aspiration towards the unity of the nation, North and South. Then, under the pressure of a singly British declaration, that undertook to support the will of the majority of the people of Northern Ireland for only as long as they wished to preserve the North as part of the United Kingdom, a singly Irish declaration, in which no specific mention was made of Northern Ireland as a territorial part of the United Kingdom, formalized the reciprocal Irish acceptance of the unity by minority consent principle: "The Irish Government fully accepted and solemnly declared that there could be no change in the status of Northern Ireland until a majority of the people of Northern Ireland desired a change in that status."

This declaration by the Irish Government was the unity by minority consent concept's first official introduction in explicit form, and nothing, it would seem, particularly in the light of the British Government's Loyalist guarantee in the Communique, could be more calculated to being agreement by the Irish Government to require the consent of the Northern majority before a change in the constitutional status of Northern Ireland could be effected (no matter what that status might yet be defined to be.) Yet the Irish Supreme Court, of all institutions, probably in order not to have to render a definitive decision as to whether the Republic's Constitution contained a *de jure* claim to the North or not, thought differently (in the Kevin Boland case of 1974).

For the Court to decide the issue categorically, it would have had to stake itself on a judicial interpretation of the Constitution's controversial Articles 2 and 3 and to decide either that the Articles contained no *de jure* claim of a 'Nation' to Northern Ireland or that they might have had a mere aspiration of a foreign State in them. The Supreme Court had the golden but unenviable opportunity of deciding this all-important question at that time. But the Court, wisely not wishing to pick up such a hot potato, saw the whole issue under another light and rendered its decision accordingly. In 1974 tensions were so strong between Southern and Northern Ireland, and ran so high in Northern Ireland itself, that the Southern

Supreme Court could hardly have done less than it did. But it could not do less anyway for another reason.

As with the Dail in 1971, so with the Supreme Court in 1974: the truth could not be told, both organs of Government feeling bound not to expose the partitionist Constitution. Ireland, not having even a provisional Constitution for the whole island, does not, can not, unlike as with the United Kingdom, have a constitutional position on (that is, a *de jure* claim to) the extraneous North of Ireland without, as we've seen already, positing an extraconstitutional basis for that position. All the *Nation*-that-Would-Be of Article 3 can have is, as Kevin Boyle wrote in the *Sunday Independent* of November 17, 1985, an aspiration to national unity: the Southern ***State*** that was instituted by the present Constitution can not, does not, claim the territory of Northern Ireland as by right its own.[10] The Constitution of such a State, which can never admit a Saorstat Eireann Oireachtas greater than its own, can do no more than ***aspire*** to a national Oireachtas. But if the Constitution, because of its *de facto* Saorstat Eireann condition, can be shown to lack control over the powers reserved by Britain from Ireland over Northern Ireland, then that Constitution does mandate, through its Articles 2 and 3, that its State and its citizens strive to restore that all-Ireland Constitution that would itself, because of its enjoying that control power (through its British counterpart statute), be a *de jure* Constitution for ***all*** Ireland. Such a Constitution would, of course, be the Saorstat Constitution of a former time. But to expect that an Irish Court operating under the existing Constitution would or could go so far as to make clear that Constitution's mandate for the reactivation of an alternative Constitution to do something the present Constitution could not do is, realistically speaking, to expect too much. The farthest any Court could go in that direction would be the extreme to which the Supreme Court went on January 19, 1988, in *Russell* v. *Fanning*, when (in judging that any activity undertaken to reunite Ireland without the authority of the State established by the Constitution was to subvert the Constitution) it imposed an understanding of

10 The Southern State's Oireachtas can, however, under the present Constitution legislate for Northern Ireland with extraterritorial effect, as it did with the Criminal Law (Jurisdiction) Act, 1976 (which the British Government reciprocated for the Republic with the Criminal Jurisdiction Act 1975), but it cannot, of course, constitutionally claim to legislate for the North in principle (as the 1922 Constitution could), the "Saorstat Eireann" of its Constitution's Article 3 not referring to the *de jure* Saorstat Eireann of 1922.

the present Constitution, if it was not to be considered an obstacle to Irish reunification (since the Constitution itself indirectly established partition), as being the means through which to proceed to institute ***other means*** that ***could*** be made to work to end partition. So advanced a position as this was a big improvement on the position of the Court in the Sunningdale case.

In order for the Supreme Court to skirt the issue of the Republic's Constitution having the type of claim to a reintegrated Ireland that would necessitate recognition of an extra-Constitution basis to be adequately met, what the Court interpreted the Irish undertaking in the Sunningdale Agreement to mean was that the Government fully accepted and solemnly declared that there could be no recognition of the *fact* of a change that might be made in the status of Northern Ireland until a majority of the people of Northern Ireland desired to recognize that fact! The Agreement, said Justice P. O'Keeffe, represented "no more than a reference to the *de facto* position of Northern Ireland coupled with a statement of policy in regard thereto."[11] What's more, the then Taoiseach, Liam Cosgrave, backtracking subsequently in the Dail said that that was indeed what the Government had had in mind: "The factual position of Northern Ireland within the United Kingdom cannot be changed except by a decision of the majority of the people of Northern Ireland"! (See *Dail Debates* for March 13, 1974.)

Although the 'status of Northern Ireland' reference as used in Sunningdale is, under the existing Irish constitutional situation (of Articles 2 and 3), capable of being interpreted as the *factual* status of Northern Ireland, it is important to note that in the post-Sunningdale Irish-British deliberations (of 1980 to 1985) it was the *constitutional* position – rather, positions – that were discussed, and that in the context of these deliberations it was the *de jure* status of Northern Ireland that was intended when the designation 'status of Northern Ireland' would be used alone, not the *de facto* situation. This new development marked a return to the Realpolitik of the conflict between the British and Irish constitutional

11 For an account of the case in which this peculiar decision had to be rendered – *Kevin Boland* v. *An Taoiseach* – a suit in which Kevin Boland challenged the constitutionality of the Sunningdale Agreement in the light mainly of Articles 2 and 3 of the Irish Constitution, see [1974] *Irish Reports* 338, p. 354, and for an analysis of how the Supreme Court arrived at its unavoidably unhelpful interpretation, see also J. M. Kelly, *The Irish Constitution*, pp. 16-17, 130 and 226-242, and Appendix 14, Section VI, *Supplement*.

positions which the 1937 Constitution succeeded only to avoid temporarily but which has to be faced up to in any realistic attempt to solve the Northern problem. But, however much the two mutually contradictory statuses that have since the Treaty era been claimed for Northern Ireland – the one (by the Irish) based on the Treaty and Constitution Settlement, the other (by the British) based on the Acts of Union and statutes from the Adaptation Order of 1923 to the Northern Ireland Constitution Act of 1973 – however much these statuses were once again affirmed in the Sunningdale Agreement by both sides, in Sunningdale and the post-Sunningdale deliberations ***taken together***, there may have been, as we said earlier, intimations of an emergence of a resolution of the conflict between the two positions and arrival at, what Anthony Kenny has called, a common definition of the present constitutional positions on Northern Ireland. (See *The Road to Hillsborough*, p. 101.)

There is nothing legally binding as yet, of course, about such a definition that is only aborning, nor can such a definition *qua* definition be really arrived at without first recognizing the distinctions made in what has been agreed about. If the Sunningdale Agreement could have been contested for constitutionality against the Saorstat Treaty and Constitution and if the conflicting British and Irish constitutional positions could have been recognized for what they really are, then the distinction between people and territory that the Agreement implicitly contained would have been forced out and acknowledged as a pointer to a possible single Anglo-Irish position on Northern Ireland. But, unfortunately, 1974 was too early in the evolutionary process to expect a beset nation to relinquish a pet possession or to expect a beleaguered people to switch jurisdiction from the provincial to the personal, from the territorial to the communal. And so the Irish Supreme Court had to render the decision it did and the switch was not seen for the urgent thing it was. For what that switch entails is a letting go of something that is slipping away in exchange for a grasping of something that would otherwise be slipping away too.

If the switch from the territorial to the communal that went hand-in-hand with the evolution of the unity by minority consent concept – if that switch is at present not seen for the urgent thing it is, given the changed dynamics of the current British-Irish relationship, there is still no way by which the Government of the existing Republic could force the switch to be viewed urgently, because of the weak constitutional basis on which that Government has to depend for its position. By that we mean that if push came to shove on the Unionist front, and if (as they have been) attempts were made to force a judicial interpretation of the 1985 Anglo-Irish Accord as were made with the Sunningdale Agreement, the Accord could be explained by an Irish Court in a sense other than what it had appeared to convey, just as it was found necessary to do with the Sunningdale Agreement. A way out could again be found — if the weak Irish constitutional position could not be fully admitted. That is, the change in the status of Northern Ireland spoken of in the Hillsborough Accord could be interpreted to be merely a change in the *de facto* status of the province, not in the constitutional, *de jure* status. The British Government, for instance, has never stated, and is unwilling to state, whether in fact *de jure* status was not intended in the Accord, and leaves room for *de facto* status to be understood as having been intended. Nor when faced with Unionist *non possumus* is the Irish Government in a constitutional position to force the British Government to admit that a change in *de jure* status was not what was intended. As far as whether *de jure* was not what was intended in the 1985 Agreement is concerned, the British Government takes the position that "Her Majesty's Government would not want to offer interpretations of the wording of treaties in cases like this, even where it believed that the interpretation was shared by the Government of the Republic of Ireland." – Personal communication.

Such is the ageless stalemate, because of the weak 26-county constitutional position Ireland is in, that Agreements like Hillsborough lead the Irish people back into. But if the struggle could be conducted on ***another*** constitutional basis, then progress made since 1973 need not be seen for the ephemeral thing it is now. Meaning could be given to the first small step of the Sunningdale Agreement, for example, meaning that it otherwise cannot be allowed to have. For all the foundering that Sunningdale actually had, it did have the merit of, concomitantly with the shift from Parliament to people that the Agreement did not factually take account of, exhibiting a willingness on the part of the British to begin to modify their constitutional position on Northern Ireland in return for acceptance on the Irish side of the unity by consent concept. It had the merit as well of drawing the connection between the Parliament-to-people shift and the move from territory to communality. It thus indicated it was a communal unity that would have to be consented to.

If all that has happened since Sunningdale is not to be construed as moving the problem onto dead center and leaving it there, it is important to realize that the shift in focus from Parliament to people of necessity also entails, constitutionally speaking, that the *territory* of the Northern Irish Parliament's one-time jurisdiction be lost to the subject Loyalists forever and that for this reason it was in the Parliament and not the territorial inhabitants that the Ulster option of conditional secession[12] was originally vested. This deprivation of territorial jurisdiction is particularly true ever since the 1973 abolition of the Northern Parliament itself – and most particularly since the latest, 1986 (and third) abolition of the Stormont Parliament. It is a Parliament ordinarily that exercises jurisdiction and the Northern Parliament did this – even though its particular existence never did aught but add to the anomaly of the entire setup. Now, at any rate, with the focal point of British attentions being the people,[13] these at best can have control only over their own lives as a separate polity: they can have no control over the territory they inhabit and share with others of a different polity, to whom also a constitutional option of another kind has in any case been guaranteed. So that if one is to shift at the head from Parliament to people, one has also of necessity to shift at the base from territory to personal polity. This is not only what is demanded by the exigencies of later developments, but it is also what is mandated by former constitutional conditions. It is, in fact, the sense in which the Loyalist guarantee was ever extended – and now that there's an Irish-British Agreement saying so (but not why) that guarantee is to be maintained. (Cf. Calvert, pp. 24-25.)

This distinction between territory and people, to which we will return in the next chapter, may provide a way out of the deadlock into which Hillsborough has landed the Irish. We must remember that it was only the *territory* of the North of Ireland that Irish Republicans ever wanted: they never desired to coerce the *people*. Therefore, a compromise is entirely possible, and there is no reason it shouldn't be established along the lines Sean Lemass once suggested of allowing the Loyalist community to have

12 There was no correlative *cession* by the Irish Free State, it is important to note. This was because the subject of the Ulster option was not territory to cede, but people who would secede.

13 Note, for example, former Secretary of State for Northern Ireland Douglas Hurd's emphasis on people in enjoining renewal of the Northern Ireland Act of 1974 in the Northern Assembly on July 2, 1985.

separate laws to preserve its own way of life.[14] (The reason there was so much opposition to the Lemass suggestion when it was first made was that it was misunderstood to apply in a territorial sense, and this would, of course, be an infringement on Irish sovereignty and thus unacceptable.) Such an accommodation is certainly essential by way of providing a safety valve for the Anglo-Irish community when it may suddenly be made to find itself subject to an all-Ireland Parliament – which will be the case as soon as Irish territorial sovereignty is extended to all of Ireland.

The people-territory distinction as a new departure

Though vitally necessary, mutual accommodation must not be taken as the desired end itself, but only as the safety valve type condition for breaking the current impasse. It will be the *conditio sine qua non* to a political solution. It will *not* be the means to the end. We should not use the condition as means, but as what makes working the means possible. We must begin by recognizing the essence of partition and then decide on how to remove it. Partition essentially has two forms, one of which is operative in the present Irish constitutional situation, the other of which would be operative if the constitutional situation of 1919-1922 were to be restored. Under the first form, partition essentially consists in the unwarranted reserving by Westminster to itself of the major powers of jurisdiction as they might apply to Northern Ireland and the guaranteeing to the Loyalists that such reserving will forcibly remain so for as long as they want it so. Under the second form, partition essentially consists in the unwarranted blocking by Westminster of the extension of Irish sovereignty in the major powers area of jurisdiction to Northern Ireland and the guaranteeing to the Loyalists that such blocking will forcibly remain so for as long as they want it so. Whichever the form, insofar as that Loyalist guarantee includes a declaration of occupation by force

---

14 Some forty years after he had thrown them to the winds, Lemass found himself coping with fine distinctions and constitutional abstractions in groping for a solution. Back in 1926 all he wanted was to get moving, it didn't matter how, or where, or whether nowhere. Lemass wrote then in *An Phoblacht*: "We must free ourselves of all the tags and tatters . . . We must forget all the petty conceits and formulae which bedeck us, like rouge on the face of a corpse . . . There are some who would have us sit by the roadside and debate abstruse points about a *de jure* this and a *de facto* that, but the reality we want is away in the distance . . . and we cannot get there unless we move" (quoted from Jeffrey Prager, *Building Democracy in Ireland*, p. 200).

of the *territory* of Northern Ireland, no constitutional basis is to be found for it anywhere; insofar as it offers a support and safeguard to the *people* of Northern Ireland, it is negotiable.

It is difficult, if not impossible, to expect that the Loyalist guarantee, no matter how unwarranted it is, will be withdrawn in its entirety. "The real root of the problem is the guarantee, the flat-footed, unremitting guarantee, which the British Government extends to the Unionist section of the population of Northern Ireland," was the way Taoiseach Haughey put it in an interview with television historian Robert Kee. "I want to, if I can at all, to the British Government and the British public, identify that, isolate that, as the stumbling block, the great, big, immovable object . . ." Nobody would dispute the fact that Haughey had, indeed, identified the root cause of partition – but saying in effect that the problem with partition was partition was no help to explaining how it might be withdrawn. The British surely understand already what the essential partition consists of, as otherwise they would not know how to impose it. Instead of identifying it to them needlessly and pleading with them to remove it, what is needed, rather, is, from a position of constitutional strength, to have pointed out to them their unconstitutional stance, their aggression in the affairs of another nation, and the reasons their creation of a stumbling block and immovable object is legally unjustified. Obviously such a constitutional assault can only be mounted on Great Britain from a position of the restored Provisional all-Ireland Republic.

But Haughey was probably on to something when he said in his concluding remarks, "and until such time as something is done about that, some modification, some way around it is found, there will be no movement." And again he may have pointed the way when, in the Dail on May 29, 1980, he said that he "would like, therefore, to see the British Government modifying the present guarantee by adding a positive element, a new departure, that would open the door to progress." The distinction between territory and people, of which Haughey's own father-in-law was the unwitting precursor, may lead to the hoped-for new departure and action based on that distinction, which the Anglo-Irish deliberations of recent past years have failed to produce, just might be the kind of modification of the Loyalist guarantee Haughey and the rest of the Irish people hope for.

A modification of the Loyalist guarantee that the territory-people distinction would make possible would, of course, have to be beneficial to the Loyalists themselves to be an effective modification of their guarantee. This fact Charles Haughey, too, recognized when in a U.S. speech in April 1988 he highlighted the of-benefit-to-Loyalists condition necessary to any overall solution. "The principal political or constitutional problem that all the people on the island of Ireland face today," Haughey said, "is how to bring about unity or political cohesion while satisfying the minority on the island of Ireland that it would not involve the loss of that part of their tradition which they most dearly cherish and that democratic rule for the whole island could enhance their status and guarantee their rights and their security."

That such a modified Loyalist guarantee as proposed might not be expected to impair the lot of the affected community can be garnered from the Ulster Unionist Party's *The Way Forward* and its 'modest proposal' for interim Administrative Devolution for the Northern Ireland Assembly in the local powers area of jurisdiction. The basic proposal is that so much political power might be exercised as would not be "necessarily inconsistent with the two communities continuing to maintain their diverse constitutional policies." Insofar as it affirms the principle of government by administration, this novel approach represents a very positive step forward in constitutional thinking. It is also of especial interest in that it closely resembles our way of thinking for a personal administration enjoying enabling legislation from Westminster in the minor powers area of jurisdiction, and could well be the forerunner of such an expanded Administrative Devolution. (This idea is also touched on in the New Ireland Forum Report's proposal of Joint Authority (Section 8.3) and in the Subreport – see Appendix 16, *Supplement.*)

Broadly speaking, the proposal of the Official Unionists is that, with the constitutional issue being resolved independently, those functions that had been transferred in the early 1970's from the County Councils and Borough Councils to Stormont and then suspended under direct rule, should now be devolved to the Northern Ireland Assembly, on a territorial basis. The functions would be administered, not legislated. "The proposal is that the Northern Ireland Assembly would be an administrative body for the whole of Northern Ireland. It would not legislate, nor would it exercise its powers through the medium of a Cabinet Government, but rather make its decisions within the area of power granted to it by the enabling legislation and by such legislation as related to the services and functions being administered by it."

Those services and functions, of a Local Government nature, would include: Education and Public Libraries; Personal Health, Welfare and Child Care; Planning, Roads and Traffic Management; Water and Sewerage Systems; Electoral Arrangements; Criminal Injury Compensation; Housing; and, possibly, the Environment. Additionally, an individual's Bill of Rights is proposed in order, presumably, to gain consensus and general agreement on the main proposal – though it is difficult to see how this would be necessary in a local powers situation alone.

This distinction between territory and people is not exactly a new principle. It exists pretty clearly in the Treaty, for example. In that instrument, as we pointed out, (1) provision was made for Ireland to remain a unitary nation (in either federal or unistate form) by guaranteeing to Nationalists their right to enjoy such a unitary Ireland, and (2) the rights of Loyalists to secede and remain subject to Westminster were also guaranteed. As to ***how*** the apparently conflicting rights of both antagonists were to be reconciled, the Treaty did not exactly spell out in great detail. While it dealt with all Ireland as a unitary nation and guaranteed to the Nationalist inhabitants thereof that they should have and hold their national territory, it did not at the same time specify that the secessionists should not take ***their*** territory with them. How the Treaty handled the situation was it provided for an arbitrational determination to be made in accordance with the wishes of the inhabitants insofar as these would be compatible with economic and geographic conditions. Such a determination has never been made, as we know. Consideration of how it might yet be made, involving how the foregoing Treaty formula should be developed and implemented, is what compels us to make the territory-people distinction based on a correct interpretation of relevant Treaty provisions.

Without positing the distinction between territory and people, the Treaty formula is seen to be incapable of being fully applied. Proof of that is the fiasco of the Boundary Commission, which had to resort to misinterpretation when faced with the Treaty mandate to find an equitable solution. That misinterpretation forced an emergency measure in order to prevent a bad situation from becoming worse. But the bad situation was left as bad as ever. All of which can be said to be the root cause of the present confusion and despair in northeastern Ireland. This is what now causes such otherwise well-meaning people as the Californian John Rickerby to conclude that the problem is to know what the problem is, and the historian Richard Rose that the problem is that there is no solution.

Without, in any event, positing the distinction between territory and people, the Treaty formula is impossible of implementation. Put another way, without positing the territory-people distinction, the reunification of Ireland is impossible of implementation. Present-day proof of this is the failure demonstrated by the New Ireland Forum to gain acceptance for any one of its (territory-based) proposals. The territory-people distinction might possibly be the missing key to a breaking of the deadlock. Maybe with this key a variation of all three Forum proposals combined could be formulated which would meet with willing acceptance. Without it the prospects do seem bleak indeed.

However, we cannot accept the gloom of the prophets of doom. We are confident a solution is contained somewhere in Irish history, this properly understood. We hold that it is a matter of understanding that history correctly to gain the mastery over it. If the Irish do not understand their constitutional history correctly, they can only make themselves prisoners of it. It has often been said, ever since Eddie McAteer first voiced the concept, that the Irish are all prisoners of their history. Prisoners of a misinterpreted history, perhaps. Mark J. Hurley, Catholic Bishop of Santa Rosa, California, goes farther and says: "It has been well said that the Irish are prisoners of history and solutions will not be found in history."

The Irish may be prisoners of their history to a large extent, but if it is a properly interpreted history, then to be prisoners of it should be no more detrimental to them than it is to the Pope to be prisoner of the Vatican. It should be to their advantage, in fact. They may be prisoners of a history that contains compelling solutions. Indeed it can hardly be that it should be otherwise. History properly interpreted has a liberating effect – *historia magistra vitae* – and does provide solutions to problems. The Irish people's 'imprisonment' could perhaps force them to accept the very solutions there are in their history – if they are to find a way out. The question no longer is, What way is that? The question at this point is, How might that way be followed on?

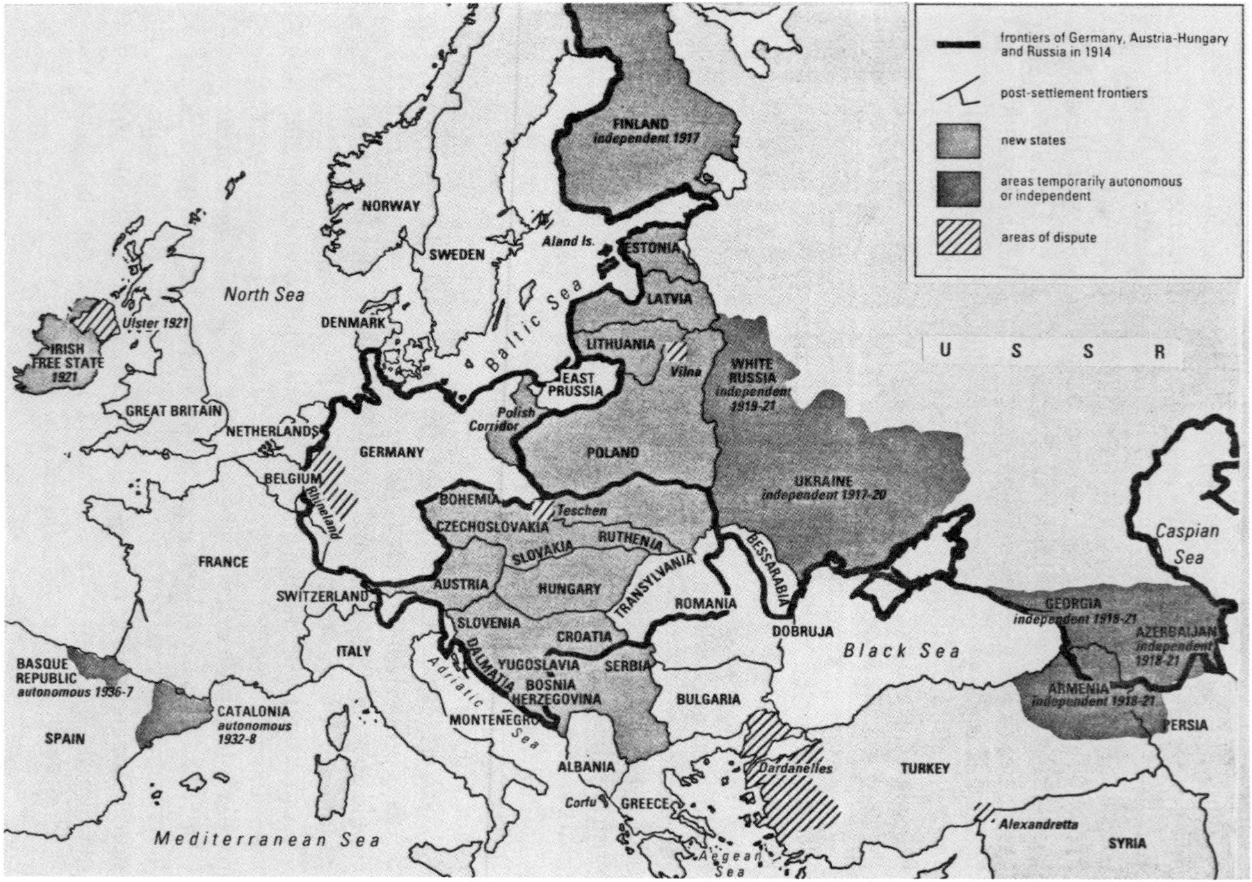

Europe as arranged after the Treaty of Versailles and the application of self-determination to minority nationalities, 1919-1924. (From the *Times Atlas of the World*, courtesy Times Books, London)

CHAPTER 13

THE REUNIFICATION OF IRELAND THROUGH RESTORATION OF THE REPUBLIC

Unity by Consent

The national problem facing Ireland since independence is not only partition, but partitionism as well. This was already identified by Michael Collins back in August of 1922 (in *The Path to Freedom*). The two problems have often been confused as being one and the same problem, so much so in fact that many have been led to believe that the one cannot be solved without the other being solved first. But partition and partitionism are really two distinct entities and at most may be considered to be the obverse and reverse of the same coin. The one, the main constitutional problem, is a purely territorial problem; the other, the correlative of this, is a community, 'people' problem. The one is a national problem that involves the people of all Ireland and is solved on the basis of majority consent alone; the other is not of its nature tied to territory essentially and is solved by allowing special treatment on a community or people basis. These realities being so, the territorial problem, to be solved, does not require the communal problem to be solved *first*. The territorial problem does require the communal problem to be solved – but as the correlative of it, not as the condition to it. They are not one and the same problem.

We know that by resuming the constitutional Republicanism of the past – that is, by restoring the all-Ireland Republic together with the Provisional Dail Eireann of that Republic – and by restoring Anglo-Irish constitutionalism as well, one can solve the territorial problem of partition (in both Irish and Anglo-Irish constitutional law). And one can also solve the communal problem of partitionism (in both Irish and Anglo-Irish constitutional law). Solution of the latter flows from and is dependent on a solution of the former. But not vice versa: the solution to the partition problem is not really dependent on finding a solution to partitionism. A solution to partitionism may make a solution to the partition problem easier to reach (because it could induce a consent to unity), but by reason of its strictly correlative nature it cannot be posited as a precondition to solving partition and achieving reunification. The two problems are of different orders.

Although a solution to the entirely separate and distinct problem of partitionism is not, then, properly made conditional to solving partition, one does need to solve partitionism in order to facilitate a solution to the partition problem. One would need to feel a deep concern about partitionism anyway and, as well, to share the concern of others about it. And since it is inextricably linked to the partition problem, partition in practice is not solved without the ability to give reassurance on a solution to partitionism as well. That is where the concept of unity by consent comes in. Although in the context of territorial reunification unity by consent is not a required condition, nevertheless unity by consent must eventually be attained and in order for this to come about one will need to understand partitionism and know how to solve it.

Along with partition, Irish Republicans have been equally concerned about partitionism or intercommunity relations. There is virtually nobody in Ireland who is unaware of the cultural and religious cleavage that exists between the two main communities that go to make up the island's population. With the problem in mind of bridge building between the two cultural and religious traditions and of welding the two communities together in one pluralistic society, Constitutional Republicans have always insisted that unity must be brought about by consent. A forced unity would not have engendered loyalty or good citizenship. Republicans are ever mindful of their own being forced to join a 'free association of free nations' and with what results. They also remember what Roger Casement said from the dock, "Loyalty is a sentiment, not a law; it rests on love, not on restraint." For that reason, Republican Ireland is prepared to work for Loyalist consent (in the properly understood sense of the term) before unity is finally achieved. And for that reason, Republican Ireland is prepared to face the problem of partitionism and solve it.

How does one solve partitionism? Upon constitutionally solving partition, by accepting partitionism as it is and tolerating it, by meeting its demands and conceding to it a certain autonomy, and by changing one's attitude towards the phenomenon and learning to regard it as an element of a modern-day pluralism. We shall examine more fully later in this and the following chapter the many facets of partitionism. For now let us consider its closely allied principle, unity by consent.

Evolution of the unity by consent concept

The best way to explore the evolution of the concept of unity by consent is, perhaps, to present the idea in terms of de Valera's use of the expression. All his long political life de Valera "laid it down that Irish unity must be restored by peaceful means. He has never wavered in his insistence that unity must come about by consent and not by force" (Longford and O'Neill, pp. 470-471.) Strange words these, in view of the fact that de Valera also always denied the right of northeastern Ireland to secede from the rest of Ireland. The so-called Ulster option he would never concede. He could not, rightly, accord to the Loyalists the right to unity by consent, because he could not accord to them the right to disunity by dissent. He, anymore than Churchill or anyone else, could not acknowledge in a national minority a right to divide the nation in violation of the wishes of the majority, since this is what territorial secession would have amounted to.

In de Valera's attitude does there not lie an apparent contradiction? On the one hand, "he has never wavered in his insistence that unity must come about by consent," while, on the other, he has never wavered in his ***denial*** of the concept of unity by consent (or disunity by dissent). For example, at the outset of his political career, in June 1917, he declared: "Ulster was entitled to justice and she should have it, but she should not be petted and the interests of the majority sacrificed to please her" (*Irish Independent*, June 25, July 2, and July 9, 1917). In other words, the majority in Ireland should not have to surrender their rights to a minority and be forced to accept a partition of their land that they did not want. In an effort to see how the apparent contradiction between de Valera's rigid attitude and that claimed for him by his official biographers might be resolved, let us examine some descriptions and illustrations of the traditional Republican policy on the unity by consent aspect of the Northern problem as evinced mainly by de Valera himself.

During the Treaty negotiations de Valera was adamantly opposed to what was then being called the Ulster option. At the last fateful Cabinet meeting in Dublin before the Plenipotentiaries signed the Treaty, he declared that he "could not sign any document which would give North-East Ulster power to vote itself out of the Irish State" (quoted from Pakenham, *Peace by Ordeal*, p. 209 paperback). This was a reference to the partition clauses of the Treaty, particularly Article 12.

During the Treaty debate de Valera was also adamantly opposed to acceptance of Ulster's secession (although he was not very specific about it, perhaps because the Treaty was not very clear itself on this point). "I am against the Treaty," he said, "because it does not do the fundamental thing." It did not recognize the separate, distinct, all-Ireland Republic, which external association would have done. As the Republic had been declared and established Ireland was indivisible, and it was not only the replacing by the Treaty of Irish constitutionalism with Monarchical and Imperial forms that was unacceptable to de Valera, but also and more particularly the partition that the Treaty smacked of.[1]

The 1925 Boundary Agreement was likewise unacceptable to de Valera. When this was entered into, he issued an angry state-

1 In 1921 Ireland was seeking more than Free State sovereignty, the type of independence towards which the extra-European Dominions were moving and which they achieved in 1931. Ireland was seeking in addition recognition of a separate national identity embodied in the Republic just achieved. The Treaty might give the freedom to achieve freedom and a Republic as well – just as Dominion status gave the overseas Dominions the freedom to become virtual Republics and in some cases actual Republics – but in Ireland Republicans did not want the already acquired Republic to be disestablished so freely, they did not want an international settlement to be incorporated in their Constitution and made the fundamental law of the land, they did not want the Treaty to be anything less than the governor of Anglo-Irish relations it was supposed to be in an international agreement role, and most of all they did not want a Treaty that could be the cause of the partition of their country. Initially the unity of Ireland was epitomized in the Republic, but under the Commonwealth constitutionalism that existed in 1921 a Republic would have been incompatible with membership in the Commonwealth. If push came to shove and the Treaty were rejected, a Republic for 26 counties of Ireland might have been conceded – in the face of which prospect the Treaty backers saw fit to hold tight to a Free State status that at least preserved essential Irish unity (for all 32 counties).

ment: "When Eoin MacNeill resigned [from the Boundary Commission] I had hoped that no Irishman, North or South, would be found prepared to put his hand to an instrument dismembering his country; but now that such Irishmen have been found my only hope is that the people will not consent to it" (quoted from Dorothy Macardle, *The Irish Republic*, pp. 893-894).

"In another place tonight," said de Valera in a speech at the Rotunda, Dublin, on December 10, 1925, "other representatives of the people have met to decide whether or not they will give their consent to the partition of our country. The sanction of our consent that partition could never have." The occasion was the debate in the Republican-boycotted Dail on the Boundary Agreement just signed in London. Then each Sinn Fein Deputy signed a protest: "In the name of the Irish nation and the Irish race, in the name of all who have stood, and will stand, unflinchingly for the Sovereign Independence of Ireland, we, the duly elected representatives of the Irish people, by our names appended hereto, proclaim and record our unalterable opposition to the partitioning of our country" (quoted from Longford and O'Neill, p. 242).

No statements could be more indicative of the fact that a right to secede from the nation would never be recognized by de Valera and his colleagues to exist in a dissenting minority in Ireland. And no such right was for a moment acknowledged by Republicans to inhere in *any* Irish minority. An option to secede, such as the British insisted on for northeastern Ireland, was adamantly opposed and rejected by Republican Sinn Fein, and the right to consent to – or dissent from – national unity could not be accorded in a democracy like Ireland to *any* part of the country. Such a right was not at any time accorded to Northern Ireland also for another reason: the Government of that area never enjoyed anything more than minor powers of jurisdiction and consequently would not have the constitutional competence to consent to or dissent from national unity.

In a democratic society, a dissenting minority would not have the right to secede territorially from the area of the majority. In any democracy there must always be a minority of citizens who are dissatisfied with the way the land is laid out. That does not mean that that minority must dissent and rule itself independently, disregarding completely the existence of those of the majority who are in its midst – the minority within the minority. In any democratic society there must always be a minority of voters who are not satisfied with the results of an election. That does not mean that that minority does not have a voice in Government. The majority's representatives are the minority's representatives equally when it comes to legislating, and a citizen whose candidate loses in any election must wait until the next election before he can have another chance to elect a candidate of his choice. "In the meantime," writes Floyd G. Cullop (*The Constitution of the United States: An Introduction*, p. 14), "it is his duty as a good citizen to accept the wishes of the majority of the voters and cooperate with them. Being a good loser is as important to our democratic republic as being well informed and interested in all activities of our government." But the losing minority in Ireland, with the weight of the British Government behind it, has never done such a thing as accept the wishes of the majority. It has never had the chance to do such a thing even if it wanted to, because before it could decide Britain interfered and partitioned it willy-nilly and forced it to secede territorially as if the right to do so inhered naturally in that same minority. By comparison, during the American War of Independence quite a few Loyalists were concentrated in Vermont and wanted to make that colony a province of Britain! Instead of getting 'special treatment,' they were lucky in those troubled times to escape with their lives!

In Ireland's troubled times the nation was, against all principles of democracy, subjected to tremendous pressure to be divided, pressure that was as wrong as it was strong. Nevertheless, Irish Republicans never did, never could, concede to Northern Ireland the right to secede from Ireland and then at will rejoin it, that is, the right to unqualified unity by consent. Nor could they ever concede to a North that might have already seceded that same right as a condition of reunification. And yet, however contradictory it may seem, noncoercion and voluntary union were at the same time being talked about. It was as if the Loyalists of the North did after all have the right to consent to union – and, by implication, the right to dissent from it, too. Even from as early as 1917, as we have already seen, de Valera favored union by voluntary and peaceful means. Here was an apparent contradiction in Republican policy. But the 'contradiction' was only that – ***apparent***. There was no real contradiction, as is clear from the explanation de Valera gave four years later when the Sinn Fein Government was faced with the challenge of established partition. What de Valera meant was, as his thinking gelled, that an all-round acceptable form of unity might be ***imposed*** on the Ulster Unionists (see Chapter 3 herein). In other words, a qualified unity by consent was what could be conceded. The question was, of course, how could an "acceptable" form of unity be reached, and was it perchance that that the Treaty had managed to secure? We shall see anon.

The predominant Republican doctrine of the noncoercion of Ulster despite denial of a right of secession was reinforced by a Dail Eireann pledge of the same in August of 1921. The attitude of the pro-Treatyites later was based squarely on this official policy of the Dail, since they interpreted the Treaty to have virtually secured the unity of Ireland already. In which case, the consent of the North would not be an essential condition to reunification (but might be encouraged in order to induce willing Loyalist cooperation). Collins himself pointed out in the Treaty debate that in view of Ireland's stated policy of noncoercion, there was no alternative to the Treaty with its implied consent to unity as a way of solving the problem of partition. And Northern Ireland, in what could be called a reciprocative gesture, was to accept the Treaty provisions and subscribe to the essential unity contained therein – the prevision of which is what caused de Valera to be willing even to accept the Treaty, warts and all!

For revelation of the fact that de Valera was willing to accept the Treaty holus-bolus if Northern Ireland were, for its part, to fall into line on the Treaty basis, we have to be thankful to the excellent and original research of John Bowman. It appears that, as Erskine Childers noted in his diary for December 8, 1921, de Valera would willingly accept the entire Treaty, with its abominable oath of allegiance and all, if only Northern Ireland would agree the Treaty's 'Ulster clauses' and thereby the principle of essential Irish unity. "It seems clear," writes Bowman, "that the proposition that de Valera would reject any agreement which contained ***either*** the Treaty's Ulster clauses ***or*** the Oath of Allegiance is no longer sustainable" (*De Valera and the Ulster Question*, pp. 57 and 65).[2]

---

2 John Bowman's account of Childers's recording of de Valera's willingness to accept the whole Treaty if Northern Ireland would agree the Treaty's Ulster clauses is as follows: "Childers, who was present at the decisive cabinet meeting on 8 December, noted in his diary: 'President talked at great length. Vehemently pressed to come into line he refused . . . Someone said (:) "*Supposing Ulster came in* on the treaty basis, would you agree to it [the Treaty]?" he replied that that was the one consideration that might affect his judgment.' Childers added the comment: 'This surprised me.' " (Childers Papers, MS 7814, Manuscripts Department, Trinity College Library, Dublin.)

Given that de Valera could accept the Treaty for the sake of Northern Ireland acceptance of essential unity, it was little wonder that he could, and did, reproduce in essence the Treaty's unity provisions in his counterproposal to the Treaty, Document No. 2. This de Valera did in the face of strong Republican criticism and, in fact, was to go so far at the 1925 Sinn Fein Ard Fheis (which endorsed Document No. 2) as to call his stand "the Republican position." Indeed, de Valera saw the only hope for both preservation of the Republic and restoration of unity as lying in Document No. 2. "I see no programme by which we can secure independence but a revival of the Sinn Fein idea in a new form," he wrote to Joe McGarrity on September 10, 1922. "In fact," he said, "[we would be] acting as if Document No. 2 were the Treaty. Later we could act more independently. ***Whilst the Free State were in supposed existence would be the best time to secure the unity of the country***" (*emphasis ours*). (See McGarrity Papers, MS 17440; Sean Cronin, *The McGarrity Papers*, p. 126; John Bowman, *De Valera and the Ulster Question*, pp. 74-75 and 88.)

A long list of political historians – among them Lyons, Kee, Curran, Wall, Murphy, Laffan, Longford and O'Neill, and this author – hold that in Document No. 2 de Valera did not make proposals on the North differently from the way they were put in the Treaty, that the Document in effect, as its preliminary draft had done literally, duplicated the Treaty's provisions. But in Document No. 2 de Valera very definitely rejected a *de jure* partition of Ireland even though he at the same time allowed what could be a rule of northeastern Ireland from Westminster (see Chapter 3). Therefore, unless all these historians and ourselves are wrong in our understanding of de Valera's position, it has to be held that the Treaty anymore than Document No. 2 did not contain partition as such. Not that the Treaty disregarded the existing partition, but it conceded it no clear ***right*** to exist, and, as we noted in Chapter 3, de Valera saw no partition in the Treaty.

This view is confirmed by the fact that the 'partition clauses' of the Treaty (which really should be called the 'essential unity clauses') were so little discussed in the Treaty debate in the Dail. In the printed reports of the Dail, of 338 pages of debate only nine are devoted to the subject of partition, and of these nine pages Deputies for the Ulster counties of Monaghan and Armagh – Blythe, MacEntee, O'Duffy, and Collins – contributed almost all. Collins insisted that the way the Treaty dealt with Ulster would "lead very rapidly to good-will and the entry of the north-east under the Irish Parliament."[3] It was then that he pointed out that the noncoercion policy as officially adopted compelled the Government to solve the partition problem the Treaty way.

Basically, de Valera agreed with Collins's assessment. In Document No. 2 (Addendum) he, de Valera, expressly refused "to admit the right of any part of Ireland to be excluded from the supreme authority of the Parliament of Ireland," but in this respect he could be said not to have gone beyond the Treaty warrant of essential unity. At the same time, in order to demonstrate the official policy of noncoercion, he offered "privileges and safeguards ***not less substantial*** than those provided for in the . . . Treaty." If such an offer encompassed more than the federal option of the Treaty (Article 14), that is, if, as so many historical and political commentators understand the offer, it encompassed the Ulster option as well (Article 12), then, in view of the fact that a *de jure* partition was denied, some such offer as one importing a form of division that would somehow be compatible with a united Ireland was envisaged (since a division of some sort there was to be anyway). Indeed, if there was, as was contended at the time, only "a shadow of a difference" between Document No. 2 and the Treaty in their provisions on unity (*Treaty Debate*, p. 344), then the Document would amount to being an interpretation of the Treaty in the ineluctable sense we describe. That is to say, Document No. 2 corroborates the sense of the Treaty not to have provisioned a *de jure* partition (but may have provisioned a *de jure* partitionism).

Some years after submission to the post-Treaty skulduggery, when the Irish Free State found itself boxed into the 26-county area and the problem of partition began to be faced up to, the unity by consent idea was in the air again. It was during exchanges prior to the Anglo-Irish Agreements of 1938 that John H. Dulanty, Irish High Commissioner in London, recorded a conversation he had with de Valera. "Do the British really want a settlement that will be satisfactory?" de Valera had asked. "If so, they must face the

3 If Collins's interpretation of the unity clauses of the Treaty were wrong – that is, if those clauses did not import provisional essential unity or Northern Ireland rollback of Free State sovereignty, but did infer partition or Westminster usurpation of Free State sovereignty, surely then more Deputies than the few there were, de Valera among them, would have come out swinging more strongly and more explicitly against the Treaty than they did. When they did not, their reticence – notably Griffith's – must be attributed to their unwillingness to upset the Ulster applecart or cause the Northerners to change their mind on Treaty acceptance, and to a desire to see a Treaty go through on all fronts that would commit the Ulsterites to the principle of essential Irish unity.

issue of a united Ireland. No agreement on the basis of partition would be acceptable to the Irish people and no such agreement could bring active goodwill and co-operation."

Dulanty's record continues: "In the absence of any proposal for an all-Ireland settlement, President proposes to proceed with the [1937] Constitution on which he has already made unequivocal statements in public. The President's aim in this Constitution is to establish now such a relationship with the members of the British Commonwealth of Nations that, in the event of the Six Counties ***voluntarily accepting union with the rest of Ireland***, the Constitution would not require amendment" (quoted from Longford and O'Neill, p. 307; *italics ours*; the relationship referred to was to have provision made for it in Article 29 of the Constitution).

Dulanty's record was written in 1936. Two years later de Valera made a proposal on Ulster, as he had done in 1922 in Document No. 2. He had then proposed in effect that, while allowing a possible six-county rule from Westminster in the minor powers area of jurisdiction, the United Kingdom should cease from reserving to herself the major powers of Government in the North that rightly belonged to Ireland. That is to say, he was urging that the Treaty be strictly observed, because nowhere in the Treaty was it apparent that Westminster should do more than hold the reserved powers in trust for Ireland. Now, in late 1938, de Valera was proposing something along the same lines, but he was more specific about it this time.

"I would say to Belfast," he proposed, "keep all your present powers. We ask only one thing of you. We think the area you control is not the area which in justice you could claim, even for a local parliament, but we make the concession if you guarantee fair play for the minority and consent to the transfer to an All-Ireland Parliament of the powers now reserved to the Parliament at Westminster." (Quoted from Longford and O'Neill, p. 341; William D. Griffin, comp. and ed., *Ireland, 6000 B.C.-1972,* p. 127.)

In terms of the unity by consent principle being posited as a pre-unity condition, de Valera's proposal would actually be misdirected. He would have wrongly recognized in the Loyalist community a right to control what might be called the Westminster option (an option that was not authorized by the Treaty). He would have no constitutional right to ask Belfast to act in a matter outside of its own jurisdiction, and neither could he propose to London that it get Belfast's permission to act in an area of London's own competence. Insofar as he was not at liberty to ask the Northern

Government to act *ultra vires*, he could not concede to them the constitutional right to a prior unity by consent that involved action by Westminster. Much less could he concede to them that same right as authorizing them possibly to secede on their own, because in point of fact Northern Ireland did not of its own accord secede and go independent (since most of its autonomy was withheld from it), but Britain it was that excluded the North from the rest of the country.[4]

What then did de Valera, constrained by constitutional bounds as he was, mean by his offer of a consent on the part of the Loyalists to unity? If it was an outright offer of consent as a precondition to reunion he was making, to say the least he mistakenly couched his offer in terms that authorized the Northerners to allow Westminster to relinquish the powers of jurisdiction it was reserving from Ireland. It was not like de Valera to make such a constitutional mistake and he would have realized that, as we have seen, Belfast had no jurisdictional competence to authorize London to do anything. It could not be, then, that it was an offer of consent as a pre-unity condition he was making. Nor would de Valera, who was himself the man in a hurry, have been content to wait indefinitely for the Northerners' consent to be forthcoming so that partition might be ended – which is what he would have had to do if he was conceding to the Loyalist minority the right to consent to unity before partition could be ended. It may be that by his offer de Valera ***seemed*** to be acknowledging in the Loyalists a natural right to consent to reunion with the 'South' as a precondition of that reunion – even though it was a federal or bistate form of unity he talked about – but constitutionally speaking he was not really acknowledging any such right. Nor could he be in contradiction with his own and Republican long-held policy of denial of the right to consent, in fact.

---

4 By going ahead with the 1937 Constitution, because of "the absence of any proposal for an all-Ireland settlement," de Valera, perhaps unwittingly, helped only to cut himself and his area (26 counties) off from the North. It was perhaps because of his weak constitutional position that he made the rather overgenerous offer that he did to the Northerners. He certainly had no ***constitutional*** obligation to make it, but he could not perhaps insist on enforcement of a Treaty that he was at the same time rejecting. In all other respects we would have to say he was observing the unbroken continuity from the beginning of the concept of the indivisible unity of Ireland and, as a corollary to this concept, the resolve to deny the right of territorial secession to any part of Ireland and hence the right to consent to unity as a condition of reunification.

The only sense in which de Valera could have meant his offer to be understood then, we feel – especially as he spoke of the Loyalists "voluntarily accepting union with the rest of Ireland" and had made provision in his Constitution for just such an eventuality (Article 29) – would have to be as an offer of a consent that would be forthcoming simultaneously with an imposed acceptable national unity. Such a consent would probably be engendered by the concession of a form of personal or popular autonomy designed to lead to an intercommunity rapprochement or mutual acceptance of each side's position.

This interpretation of de Valera's thought is reinforced by the fact that he also in his offer expressed concern for the Nationalist community of the North, and this is, of course, an extension of the like community in the South that does not recognize a geographic division of Ireland. Could it be then that, in addition to offering what was already agreed upon – a separate northeastern state – de Valera, with partitionism in mind, was groping towards the idea of an external association of the Northern Loyalists as a community with the Republic? He would have meant that the Irish people would be patient and would wait for the Loyalists to come to terms with the Republic under such a formula, but he could not have intended that for territorial unity to come about it should or could be made to depend on this form of rapprochement to develop first. In the meantime he would make the Northerners such concessions as he had already offered them in the past, consisting of certain safeguards that would accompany the grant of a separate state. This would have resulted in a bijurisdictional arrangement for Ireland, an idea that was to be propounded more explicitly later by Sean Lemass and later still, in more developed form, by Charles Haughey.

Unity by consent properly understood translates to multinational self-determination

In view of the fact that a frustrated partitionism is, along with an entrenched partition, the problem with Northern Ireland, Constitutional Republicans, as de Valera did, have had to hold the policy of unity by consent. And, as we've seen in the previous chapter, Constitutional Nationalists have, to the present day, had to hold the policy too. But it is important to understand the sense in which that policy is meant. It has never been meant in a partitionist or territorial sense. That is, as citizens of a naturally unitary nation and democratic state, the Irish people could not concede the right to a dissenting minority to secede territorially or to dissent from territorial unity. If ever they admitted the principle of unity by consent, they have intended it in an entirely different and qualified sense. Hence, there has been no real contradiction in Republican policy – but there certainly has been a lot of confusion of the senses in which the unity by consent concept has been understood, and this confusion has not particularly helped the reunification cause. Let us explain the true sense of the concept further.

The effort to resolve the apparent contradiction in the Republican policy on unity by consent has forced us to rethink the concept in its various ramifications and to restate Republican thought on the subject. We may formulate the evolution of the unity by consent principle essentially in the following terms. Unity by consent to Republicans does not mean, cannot mean, territorial reunion that is conditional upon the consent of the minority. It has to mean that a way would be worked out (such as adopting partitionism) which would induce consent to a unity that would, independently of the consent, have to be put in place in fulfillment of the demands of Irish and Anglo-Irish constitutionalism. More specifically, unity by consent to Irish Republicans means an initially implicit consent that is accompanied by a viable, intercommunity quasi-pluralism or certain partitionism that in turn will facilitate the gradual acceptance of mandatory territorial unity. That consent, we noted, is not an antecedent to or precondition of territorial unity. The concept as it exists in Irish Republicanism involves, rather, a co-unity affirmation which is engendered by an autonomy exercised on a correlatively constitutional community or personal rights basis. That is to say, it consists of an affirmation that is based on communal, cultural, educational, or religious grounds – in short, a 'personal autonomy' or, more properly, a 'communal autonomy' – of a necessarily 'interaffiliated' nature.

As for guaranteeing to the Loyalists of Northern Ireland self-determination in this and any other related sense there may be of the unity by consent principle, we anticipate a separate system of legislating – on a nonterritorial basis – being adopted and made acceptable to all sides. What we would acknowledge to the Loyalist community is something analogous to what the Irish once desired for themselves vis-a-vis the British Commonwealth – external association, with the Republic. While before it was territorial and territorially external (to the Commonwealth), now it would be personal and personally external (to Ireland). Under such a formula the Loyalists of the North – of Ireland – while they would be subject to an all-Ireland Parliament in national matters, would be subject to Westminster for enabling legislation in limited matters (as before) and could remain British subjects; they would be regarded as resident aliens in Ireland – unless they wished otherwise, as well some might. (It should be noted that the concept of personal autonomy is not entirely novel in jurisdictional arrangements: the idea exists in ecclesiastical jurisdictions as 'personal prelatures' and 'identity parishes,' that is, as nonterritorially based self-governing communities. These are new juridical forms that were introduced into the law of the Catholic Church by the Second Vatican Council. The concept is also given implementation in the present-day Parliament of South Africa which, under the new Constitution, is composed of three separate Houses for the three main groupings of non-Black people in that country – see Appendix 15, *Supplement*.)

We have arrived at the foregoing conclusions by virtue of our acceptance of the fact that ultimately the Loyalists of Ireland have (since 1922) a Treaty-guaranteed right to be awarded separate treatment and the continuance of their political allegiance to Westminster. They now also (since 1985) have an Accord-guaranteed right to a personal unity by consent. These conclusions are also derived from the fact that Irish Loyalists have always regarded themselves as a people set apart. The idea of having their community governed on a people rather than a territorial basis has, then, suggested itself naturally to many minds besides ourselves. One such, we have seen, is Sean Lemass. Another is Harry Calvert, who does not go beyond claiming for the Loyalists "a separate polity" on the basis of existing constitutional arrangements. For Calvert these latter do not, impliedly, extend to territory. In attributing completion of the Boundary Agreement of 1925 and the Ireland Act of 1949 to "a rare single-mindedness on the part of the government of Northern Ireland" and in querying whether this attitude ought to be described as one of "mature statesmanship or monumental intransigence," he states that "the fact that [such an attitude] existed at all is the substance of the North's claim to treatment as a separate polity." The North's claim to treatment as a separate ***polity***, be it noted, not as a separate ***territory***. (Calvert, *Constitutional Law in Northern Ireland*, pp. 47-48.)

The distinction between people and territory in Ireland has suggested itself also to Judge William Newsom, one-time President of the Irish Forum in the U.S. In treating the causes of the violence in Northern Ireland, Newsom referred to the existence of "a separate Loyalist peoplehood." Perhaps no one in recent history has better described the deadlocked society in which both the Loyalists and the Nationalists of Northern Ireland find themselves than has Judge Newsom and perhaps no one has put the case better for urging a just constitutional solution rather than falling back on increased and continuing violence. The California Judge's comments are as follows:

"Some Nationalists bitterly view themselves as victims of institutionalized violence, while some Loyalists anticipate living as victims of institutionalized violence if forced into what they perceive as the Catholic theocracy of a united, 32-county Ireland.

"The Nationalist in arms draws upon a long historical tradition ... which claims a political legitimacy to the present day. The Loyalist extremist feels himself to be part of a centuries-long refusal to be submerged in a Gaelic Catholic Ireland, and subject to laws which incorporate hated precepts of Roman Catholicism. The Republic is seen as theocratic and the British link [as] essential to the preservation of ***a separate Loyalist peoplehood***" (*italics ours*).

The idea of a people rather than a territorial jurisdiction for Unionists has suggested itself as well to none other than a former Secretary of State for Northern Ireland, James Prior. Speaking during the debate on the New Ireland Forum proposals at Westminster on July 2, 1984, he interpreted the Loyalist veto to be a veto applicable to the position of the Loyalists personally within the United Kingdom, and not a veto applicable to the territorial status of the North of Ireland constitutionally within the U.K. And it may even have suggested itself in a manner to de Valera himself, who held that the bond in Ireland with the King was merely personal, that it was not based on any national allegiance, and that it could be compared to the personal union that existed until 1837 between Hanover and the British Monarchy.

In conclusion, while we 'sovereigntywise' deny to Loyalists a right to unity by consent, we 'externally' or pluralistically quite concede such a right. A way to resolve the apparent contradiction in our position, we have seen, is to make a distinction between a consent based on territorial integrity and a consent based on intercommunity pluralism. Our attitudes to both kinds of consent are taken on different levels. To a consent based on undeniable territorial integrity we never admitted a constitutional right; to a consent based on intercommunity partitionism or externally associated personal autonomy we never denied a pluralistic right.

In the context of reunification the position might be restated as follows: On the basis of the unitary nature of Ireland, the right of a minority to dissent (or consent) could not be admitted; on the basis of partitionism or a working pluralism, the right of a minority to consent (or dissent) could not be denied. Holding that distinction, we would proceed to restore the Provisional Republic of Ireland and, in the process, reunite Ireland territorially and provisionally. This territorial reunification, if coupled with a concession of external association of the Loyalist community on a nonterritorial or partitionism basis, would we believe lead to at least an implicit consent to unity (which, after all, is only what was given already in their Treaty acceptance). Our theory is that as soon as the Provisional Republic is restored on the one hand, and an acceptable partitionism is developed on the other, then the explicit consent to unity would not be long forthcoming. The solution inevitably demands, it seems to us, that within the Provisional Republic framework a virtual unity be introduced and proposed on a nonoptional basis so that consent based on popular external association could reasonably be expected to be forthcoming and to come about by degrees.

Our idea that a virtual unity of Ireland be proposed on a nonoptional basis is very akin to the policy of Charles Haughey and Fianna Fail that the consent of the Northern majority is not required for the establishment of a unitary, sovereign nation, but only for the form such unitariness should take. Indeed it is akin to the thinking of Garret FitzGerald of Fine Gael as well, who is reported to have described the unitary nation proposal as the traditional demand of Irish Nationalists and to have referred to it in June 1982 as what he would aspire to instinctively. But to give effect to the unitary nation concept in harsh reality, Haughey appeared able to foresee in December 1980 that other factors (such as federalism or joint authority) might be required also to be brought into play (though neither of these is the particular factor we would favor).

Declaring that some degree of autonomy might have to be considered for the Northern people, Haughey at that time said: "I don't set any limits to what [new institutional structures] might or might not involve and I think the fact that they are structures, or institutional structures, means the possibilities are very wide indeed, and it would be our wish and our intention that no possibility would be ruled out, but that different concepts would be considered solely on the basis of whether or not they can contribute to political development, to successful forward movement."

Reiterating this plea at the opening session of the New Ireland Forum on May 30, 1983, Haughey said: "We readily and willingly concede that the establishment of a new political order in Ireland and a new social contract can only come about through a major revision of existing structures.... That [all-Ireland] Republic could develop structures, relationships and associations of a bilateral or multilateral kind with Britain that would not compromise our sovereignty and independence, but would give recognition to the long-established links with Britain of those who adhere to the Unionist tradition in Ireland."

And Garret FitzGerald, too, has appeared to imply that more than reaffirmation of the unitary nation principle is necessary to achieve full independence when he and Prime Minister Thatcher, in November 1984, agreed that the identities of both the majority and minority communities in Northern Ireland should be recognized and respected and reflected in structures and processes of a kind acceptable to both communities. This was in confirmation of the Forum Report in Section 5.2 (3) which stated that agreement means the political arrangements for a new and sovereign Ireland would have to be freely negotiated and agreed to by the Irish people North and South. That is, of course, what has been done already and is what issued incipiently in the Treaty formula. Agreement has already been achieved in principle. What remains to be done is to apply the agreed-on formula in the concrete of present-day realities. (See also the view of some Northern Nationalists in the Addendum to this Part.)

The two-nation theory of Ireland

What has led to a confusion of the senses (territorial and pluralistic) in which the concept of unity by consent has been understood is probably the mistake that has occurred since partition of judging Ireland *territorially* to consist of the equivalent of two 'nation-states,' corresponding loosely with the two cultural 'nations' in Ireland.[5] But the two-nation theory was never meant to be taken as intending this much, and the confusion that arose

5 A preliminary reading of Dennis Pringle's *One Island, Two Nations*?, although broadly confusing national self-determination with nationalism and nation with nation-state, will be extremely helpful to an introductory understanding of our treatment in the following pages of the two Irish nations and their affirmation as such without a necessity for partition.

was probably due to the widespread misunderstanding that surrounded the way a related concept, that of self-determination, was applied after World War I at the Versailles Peace Conference (which bears some examination by us) and that resulted in the creation of 'nation-states' for "the little nationalities of Europe."

As with the concept of unity by consent in its territorial and personal ramifications, and now as with the way the two Irish nations (nationalities) have been interpreted, there has been a similar confusion of the senses in which the concept of self-determination was understood and applied on the continent of Europe after the Treaty of Versailles, and this misunderstanding has affected Irish thinking on and understanding of the concept's application too. Once the unity by consent principle is understood correctly, however, and once we are clear on the nature of the two nations in Ireland, that is, once unity by consent is understood as not being conditional to unity of (historically united) territory, but as only being conditional to unity of (historically divided) nations or nationalities (and therefore, implicitly, as being concessionary to secession of a nation or nationality), then the principle so understood opens up, in the Irish context, the whole new question of the subject of application of self-determination.

The question centers on the 'self' of self-determination – to what or to whom is self-determination to be applied? Is it the *majority* demanding a united island nation that is to be 'determined,' and so the 'nation-state' to be created (much as nationalism would achieve)? Or is it *all* the people in their nationality communities that are to be 'determined,' and so the 'multinational state' to be created? Is it, accordingly, national self-determination that is the demand, or is it multinational self-determination? More fundamentally, can self-determination only be made operative when a distinction is made between the major and minor powers of government, and only be made possible of practical application on the basis of that distinction? These are the kinds of questions that faced the architects of the New Europe after World War I, and they are the kinds of questions that now face those of us who would set ourselves to fashioning the New Ireland.

Since, with regard to Ireland, unity by consent is not considered conditional to territorial unity, self-determination cannot be invoked, and historically has not been invoked, to justify the majority achieving an independent united territory *as a nation-state*. It can only be invoked, then, on behalf of all of the people inhabiting that territory in their efforts to achieve self-rule in the territory ***as a multinational state***, and this is particularly true since a unity by consent ***is*** admitted. Unity of territory would have to, and as a fact of history has been, demanded (albeit by the majority) on other grounds (on the grounds, for example, of 'the historic Irish nation'), but, because a hard-to-achieve consent to unity is conceded, unity could only be gained by the application of self-determination to people, that is, to the nationality communities comprising the people. This is all the more so since unity by consent can be understood as being concessionary to a secession of people and their right to be ruled by others, an expression of self-determination that, like the expression affirming the right of people to be ruled by themselves, is of the highest order of the principle.

Self-determination has, however, been applied in Europe in such a way as to achieve the nationalist nation-state only. It was applied more to the nation formed of the majority nationality than to the nationalities forming any existing state. And in Ireland, the way self-determination was applied – or misapplied – there resulted, as we know, a pair of partitioned fictitious European-type nation-states. On the other hand, if self-determination were to have been applied discriminately to the traditional Irish communities, it is obvious that a unitary nation-state that would be accommodative of only one of the communities/nationalities, the majority, would not be allowed to ensue. (This would not happen if the self-determination in its application were to be kept distinct from nationalism in its purposes.) In other words, the demand ought not to have been for national, but for multinational, self-determination. What would have ensued then, would have been the communal multinational state, and this we might regard as a unitary territory the nationalities of which would be united (at the sovereign level) but would separately choose either to be self-governed (at the nonsovereign level) or to secede and be governed by another power (also at the nonsovereign level). (We might define 'multinational state' as a politically organized and integrated territorial state the inhabitants of which comprise multiple self-determined politicocultural communities who, at the sovereign level, enjoy a unity of self-rule and who, at the nonsovereign level, enjoy the right singly to be governed either by themselves or by another power with which the state is confederated.)

The demand of the Irish communities to have their particular form of self-determination applied to them – the Unionists to have union with Britain and the Nationalists to have a rule from within Ireland – must be balanced over against the longstanding demand of the native majority to have their historical island nation restored to them.[6] It is from such a necessary balance that the multinational state with its dual rule would emerge (cf. Lee C. Buchheit, *Secession: The Legitimacy of Self-Determination*, pp. 224-228). But, for reasons that we shall further see, in Europe the multinational state was not accommodated at the Versailles Peace Conference, and the fact that it was not was due mainly to the confusion that existed between the forms of application of self-determination at that time. This confusion we shall examine more fully so that we will be clear on the multinational form self-determination should take when its application to Ireland is completed. But first we ought to look more closely at the communities that would comprise the multinational state in order better to understand how such an entity as the multinational state could emerge unhindered from those communities in Ireland.

The Dutch political geographer, Marcus Heslinga, studied in depth the geographic, historical, religious, cultural, and political aspects of the Irish problem to determine whether partition represented a territorial or cultural divide. While he found strong arguments to support a unity in Ireland, and even an overall unity in the Celto-British Isles, he nevertheless concluded in his work, *The Irish Border as a Cultural Divide*, that Ireland consists of 'two nations.' Heslinga understands his findings, of course, in a cultural rather than territorial sense, but he emphasizes that a territorial division can intensify cultural differences when he says that "the two parts [of Ireland] . . . demonstrate that a so-called artificial frontier (line) can be a greater cultural divide than a so-called natural frontier (zone)." In other words, the division into Northern and Southern Ireland is symptomatic of – and contributory to –

6 Georges Scelle, in favoring under self-determination the right of secession for minorities, has argued, nevertheless, in the light of the Versailles Peace Treaty's Article 10 on the rights of the state, that the application of self-determination must strike a balance between the aspirations of secessionist minorities and the needs of the 'statal' majority. The existence of the state is itself one form of the right of peoples to self-determination and it would be a curious application of this right, he has written, if one should attempt to satisfy in all cases the aspirations of, sometimes tiny, dissident groups at the risk of sacrificing the conditions necessary to the existence of the state, which are those of serving the vital needs of the more numerous majority. (*Precis de Droit des Gens,* Vol. 2, pp. 268-269; cf. Lee C. Buchheit, *Secession: The Legitimacy of Self-Determination*, p. 133.)

Irish cultural differences, but these do not for that reason warrant the creation of Irish nation-states.

Or, as the Australian Patrick O'Farrell points out, Britain's mistake was in applying territorially political solutions to politically cultural problems. The two ***politicocultural*** nations did not have to be translated into two ***politicoterritorial*** nations. This was the 'abomination and blasphemy' of John Redmond for sure.

From the seventeenth century on, nobody denies, two politicocultural traditions existed in Ireland. Both of these traditions, Nationalist and Unionist, equally regarded Ireland as a territorial unit themselves. When the term 'two nations' arose, as it did in 1912 with the publication of *The Two Irish Nations* by W. F. Moneypenny, the expression was used to denote the bicultural nature of Ireland and the conflicting stands the two cultures took on the status-to-be of the one nation. Moneypenny wrote thus: "The Home Rule struggle is a struggle between two nations, the Protestant and the Roman Catholic, or as, to avoid the semblance of ministering to religious bigotry, they had better perhaps be called, the Unionist and the Nationalist."[7]

Irish Nationalism has a singularly Gaelicist quality – "Ireland, not free only but Gaelic as well, not Gaelic only but free as well" – and Irish Unionism has a distinctly British orientation; but Irish Republicanism quite freely admits the two-nation theory (in a bicultural or pluralistic sense, of course) and accommodates the members of both nations in their respective political positions. Irish Republicanism goes so far, in fact, as to realize that the two component communities of Ireland, after some seventy years of partition in addition to their historical origins and separate developments, are polarized – if not indeed fossilized – in their respective positions. The political aspirations of the one community are anathema to the other, and this dichotomy of allegiance is what in fact constitutes a main part of the problem in Ireland – the identity crisis with which the nation is afflicted under the present constitutional conditions. That being so, the controversy is likely to go on. But we believe that the framework of the

7 As far back as 1886 Joseph Chamberlain and Lord Salisbury had argued for the existence of two nations in Ireland. But it appears these were understood in a purely territorial sense, the impossibility of integrating which led to the concept of 'special treatment for Ulster,' which in turn facilitated the theory of the two communal nations in Ireland. (See Nicholas Mansergh, "The Influence of the Past," David Watt, ed., *The Constitution of Northern Ireland, Problems and Prospects*, pp. 7-8.)

Provisional Republic is the only forum in which a solution to the controversy can be found, because, as we have shown, the mutual antipathy of the communities does not necessarily militate against a unity by consent being achieved in a popular, nonsovereign and nonterritorial sense. That is to say, a reunification through restoration of the Provisional Republic does not ***depend*** on a rapprochement on territorial sovereignty between Republicans and Loyalists,[8] but within the Republican framework coupled with popular external association a unity by consent at the nonsovereign level can gradually come about.

The customary confusion that exists between territorial jurisdiction and popular jurisdiction, between national sovereignty and personal autonomy, and between territorial unity by consent and communal unity by consent, is paralleled to a degree by a common confusion between the conflicting ways in which self-determination has been simultaneously applied to both territory and people, by a confusion between what we may call national self-determination (or indeed nationalism) and multinational self-determination (or self-determination proper[9]). For example, at the 4 October 1983 Public Session of the New Ireland Forum, when Sean MacBride was asked by Frank Prendergast "Would you accept that Ulster Unionists as a large minority within the whole of Ireland have a right to self-determination?" Mr. MacBride's response was "No, not to self-determination." Here it is obvious both Prendergast and MacBride were confusing self-determination proper with nation-state/national self-determination, because MacBride we know meant national self-determination and besides the Ulster Unionists do, under the Treaty Settlement, have a right to self-determination proper (that is, multinational self-determination) – as anyone who has read the Dail and Emyvale speeches by President Cosgrave on the subject (reproduced in Chapter 10 herein) will agree. That MacBride meant national self-determination (and was not distinguishing between the nation-state and multinational forms of the application of self-determination) is clear from his immediately following words: "At the outset I pointed out there are four principles to be satisfied," and when we

8 Or as, to avoid the semblance of ministering to political polarity, they had better perhaps be called, 'Gaelic-Irish' and 'Anglo-Irish.'

9 Our regarding multinational self-determination to be self-determination proper is explained in the following section headed "The historical course of self-determination." This form of self-determination is composed, essentially, of nationality self-determinations.

look up what he said about those four principles we see there that MacBride said (in response to a question from Brian Lenihan): "There are four well-recognised principles which determine what constitutes a 'national entity' for the purposes of ***national*** self-determination" (*italics ours*). Then he went on to enunciate the four principles of qualification of a nationality for national self-determination as this was employed to create the unsatisfactory nation-states of Europe. First of all, he said, there must be a well-defined territorial unit with clearly defined frontiers. Secondly, the 'national unit' claiming self-determination must have a longstanding history as a national unit. Thirdly, the 'national unit' must have a reasonably homogeneous population. And fourthly, there has to be the expressed will of the majority of the inhabitants of the territorial unit which claims to be recognized as a national entity. (See the Report of the New Ireland Forum, Public Session, No. 3, 4 October 1983, pp. 1-2, 10.)

The enunciation of these four requirements for national self-determination, which the large minority Unionist community in Ireland would not, understandably, meet, confirms the point that what MacBride had in mind was the national self-determination of the nation-state and that what he was denying to the Ulster Unionists, was, naturally, this same national or nation-state self-determination. But he was not, and could not be, denying to them, at the same time, self-determination itself – even though that is what he called it. The reason he referred to national self-determination as self-determination was that he, anymore than others, did not ordinarily make the distinction between the two forms of its application – national and multinational. But this distinction has to be made for Ireland, it being in the Anglo-Irish constitutionalism: it was made in the original Treaty, when both opposing communities – the majority and the minority – were guaranteed self-determination proper within the broader context of the multinational state, and we are not at liberty to disregard it.

The historical course of self-determination

It is little wonder that the two forms of the historical application of self-determination – that having as object of the 'determination' the homogeneous (or near-homogeneous) nation-state with the exclusive (or almost exclusive) majority and that having as object of the 'determination' the heterogeneous communities that would constitute the multinational state – it is little wonder that the two forms should have been confused at the Forum for a

New Ireland when they have not been successfully separated apart by the political philosophers ever since self-determination was hurriedly dealt with at its inception at the Peace Conference of Versailles. And self-determination was, just when it was for the first time being formulated into a practical principle of international politics, hurriedly dealt with at Versailles, because the function of the Peace Conference was as much to draw the boundaries of the new smaller nations as it was to bring self-government to the oppressed nationalities of the former larger nations and empires of Europe. Since the Conference had to attend so much to the task of nation building, it was only to be expected in a way that it should generally neglect to apply self-determination proper, what might be called the 'Wilsonian self-determination' that had been fought for in World War I and that was demanded by countless (European and Asian) nationality communities in Paris as having been promised them.

The principle of self-determination that President Wilson had intended to have applied in Europe is most nearly defined in Principle Four of his Speech of 11th February 1918: "That all well-defined national aspirations shall be accorded the utmost satisfaction that can be accorded them without introducing new or perpetuating old elements of discord and antagonism that would be likely in time to break up the peace of Europe, and consequently of the world." But Wilson himself it was that had self-determination (as it was being understood) hurriedly dealt with at the Peace Conference, and he rushed its mistaken application through so fast that he was, in the opinion of Lee Buchheit, guilty of abandoning after the war the principles that had furthered the Allied effort during the war. "In an almost pathetic tone," writes Buchheit, "Wilson explained the circumstances of this inconsistency [through Frank P. Walsh of the Friends of Irish Freedom] in the 1919 hearings before the United States Senate Committee on Foreign Relations":

> You have touched on the great metaphysical tragedy of to-day. My words ["that all nationalities had a right to self-determination"] have raised hopes in the hearts of millions of people. . . . When I gave utterance to those words, I said them without the knowledge that nationalities existed, which are coming to us day after day. Of course, Ireland's case, from the point of view of population, from the point of view of the struggle it has made, from the point of [view of the] interest it has excited in the world, and especially among our own people,

> whom I am anxious to serve, is the outstanding case of a small nationality. You do not know and can not appreciate the anxieties that I have experienced as the result of these many millions of people having their hopes raised by what I have said....
>
> No one knows the feelings that are inside of me while I am meeting with these people and discussing these things, and as these things that have been said here go over and over in my mind I feel it most profoundly. It distresses me. But I believe, as you gentlemen do, in Divine Providence, and I am in His hands, and I don't care what happens me individually. I believe these things and I know that countless millions of other people believe them.[10]

But even of those communities that were accommodated within nation-states, not all had had granted them in the postwar settlement the form of self-determination that had been promised them. This was due, in part, to the confusion, as we've seen, of self-determination with nationalism that still persisted and out of which self-determination grew. But it was also due to the fact that communities that did not or could not be made to constitute sovereign states were not for practical purposes regarded at the Conference as being viable political nationalities. This was due, in turn, to the failure of the Conferees to distinguish between the major and the minor powers of government, for, if they had, they would have realized that the inability of a nationality to acquire 'statal' sovereignty does not obviate the possibility for that nationality to achieve self-government. (To admit that 'statally' nondeterminable communities could be considered viable political nationalities was deemed dangerous and destructive of the Conference's main work of forming nation-states as coterminously as possible with the dominant nationality's territory. "This principle, if once adopted," explained Harold Temperley, "could have been interpreted in such a way as to bring the negroes in the Southern States of America under the protection of the League; it could have been applied to the Basques of Spain, to the Welsh and to the Irish"! (*A History of the Peace Conference of Paris*, Vol. V, p. 142).)

10 Buchheit, *Secession*, p. 115; *Treaty of Peace with Germany*, Hearings before the Committee on Foreign Relations, U.S. Senate, 66th Congress, First Session, *Senate Documents*, Vol. 10, No. 106 (Aug. 30, 1919), p. 838; Macardle, *The Irish Republic*, p. 297; Harold W. V. Temperley, *A History of the Peace Conference of Paris*, p. 429.

The Peace Conference's application of self-determination for the achievement of nation-states corresponding as closely as possible to the territory of the majority nationalities, other necessary factors having been taken into consideration also, had the effect that many nationalities found themselves split among the new states, while others found themselves disregarded altogether. Such imprecise application, if not indeed misapplication, that came in time to be uneasily lived with, gave rise to the idea among some that the achieving of independent nation-states for majority communities was all there was to self-determination – that the principle meant virtually no more than nationalism had but that since it should be applied more with regard to the satisfaction of the nationalities, therefore as many nation-states as feasible should be set up.

But many political authorities – such as Lord Acton, Proudhon, Lloyd George, Le Play, Bakunin, Macartney, Cobban, Carr – held, insofar as they regarded nationalism the antithesis of nationality, that self-determination (although that may not have been what they all called it) intendedly applied to nationalities regardless of their ability to form themselves into sovereign states. For example, in the Irish Treaty negotiations, Lloyd George held that self-determination applied equally as much to Northern Irish people in noncontiguous areas with Southern Ireland as it did to those who could have the separate states set up coextensively with their regions of habitation. Like as with Lloyd George, the others of these authorities held in effect that the principle of self-determination was of a communal rather than 'statal'/national nature, and that accordingly it should issue in multinational rather than national states. In no other sense but this could self-determination meaningfully be applied to remote communities or to people in regions where their communities were inextricably intermingled. "No power on earth," wrote Temperley in not unfamiliar terms, "could disentangle the Germans and Poles in Posen and West Prussia, Poles and Ruthenians in Galicia, Magyars and Rumanians in Transylvania, Serbs and Rumanians in the Banat" (*op. cit.*, p. 121).

Self-determination cannot logically but apply to people rather than territory (with reservations) when those people constitute the populations of communally mixed regions. We readily see the correctness of this once we realize that the right a would-be ***multinational*** state may have to existing in satisfaction of its majority's demands based on independent (e.g., geographic, historical, ethnographic) grounds cannot be met unless the right of its communities to be governed as they please is also satisfied (which right in each case is exercised in different orders of Government and on different bases of rule). All the more reason is there then, if such a state must come into being, that its inhabitants be governed on a people basis and that the state be of a multinational nature.

When we say that government in a multinational state has to be based on people we must, of necessity, apply only the minor powers of Government to the communities comprising those people, while we would reserve the major powers for the sovereign multinational state itself. The reason that, under a practical self-determination, only the minor powers of Government can be applied to the people and the major powers to the state arises from the necessary concession of secession as a right of self-determination inhering in the communities of the multinational state, while sovereignty as a right of the same self-determination must be recognized for the state. That secession must be conceded as a right under self-determination (contrary to the way many see it) is demanded by reason of the fact that there may be no forced unity of the state under the sovereignty that is equally conceded as a right. The conflict that would otherwise arise between sovereignty and secession is resolved by, as Alfred Cobban put it, "allowing each [principle] to operate within its own proper field."[11] This of necessity means that sovereignty must be confined to the territory-based major powers of jurisdiction (the state), while secession may apply only to the minor powers (the people).

Because of the fact under self-determination of the right to secession there is no obligation to submit to a forced union, but, on the other hand, because of the equal right under self-determination to a unitary state (which may be imperative anyway for historical and other reasons) there would be no right to resist a

11 Cobban in the conclusion of his concise work on nationality self-determination, states the case as follows for what he calls "the new self-determination": "The truth seems to be that if we take the right of sovereignty on the one hand, and the right of secession on the other, as absolute rights, no solution is possible. Further, if we build only on sovereignty, we rule out any thought of self-determination, and erect a principle of tyranny without measure and without end, and if we confine ourselves to self-determination in the form of secessionism, we introduce a principle of hopeless anarchy into the social order. The only hope, it seems, must be in a combination of the two principles, allowing each to operate within its own proper field, and recognizing neither as an absolute right, superior to the rights of individuals, which are the true end of society." (*The Nation-State and National Self-Determination*, p. 138.)

forced union. However, a forced union could only be put into effect if, at the same time, the right of secession (in its own special way) were to be given effect. In the case of Ireland and Northern Ireland, for example, we would wholeheartedly agree with the declaration of Frank Aiken, given at the United Nations in 1957, that the Irish right of self-determination meant the right of the historic unitary state to be restored as a unit. But this right, if it meant anything in practice, surely meant that the communities making up the state of Ireland had the right singly (at the non-sovereign level) to be governed by themselves or by others, as they individually wished, even as they would jointly (at the sovereign level) be governed by themselves in confederation with those others (if they had chosen to be ruled by them at the nonsovereign level). And it meant also that it would be recognition of this latter right that would make possible fulfillment of the right of Ireland to be a restored united Irish nation, or rather, Irish multinational state.[12]

That such has not, of course, happened in Ireland, nor its equivalent on the continent of Europe, is due among other reasons, as we have said, to the confusion of self-determination with nationalism, of 'nation' with nation-state, and of communal (or, as it might more rightly be called, 'national') self-determination with 'statal' (or, as it is commonly called, national) self-determination. That is, the misapplication of self-determination, and consequently the misunderstanding about the principle, is due to the confusion of ***national*** (i.e., nationality) self-determination (community) with ***national*** (i.e., nationwide) self-determination (nation-state). And perhaps because of the confusion of terminology too, the demand for multinational self-determination (which is what was mainly intended in the first place) was not clearly voiced. The sorting out of all of this requires, on our part, some inspection of what the experts on the subject think and some recapitulation, if this be permitted, of what we've so far seen the experts to think. This will enable us particularly to understand the actual form of self-determination put in the Treaty of 1921 for Ireland.

12 Frank Aiken's argument was as follows: "When, as in Ireland, the case concerned a historic nation which had always been united in the same territory despite an outside rule which it had never ceased to resist, its right to self-determination could not be withheld without denying the principle of the right of self-determination and the concept of democratic freedom and justice on which the principle was based." (Gen. Ass., 12th Sess., 1st Cmte., 911th Mtg., 26 Nov. 1957, para 43.)

In former times the term 'nation' meant the cultural, linguistic, religious or tribal community that was political to the extent of needing to preserve its own nationality or communal identity. This was the *Kulturnationen* of Meinecke, the nation within a nation that was defined by Cobban as "any territorial community, the members of which are conscious of themselves *as* members of a community, and wish to maintain the identity of their community" (*The Nation-State and National Self-Determination*, p. 107). Gradually in many instances this (as we may call it) politicocultural nation, under the influence of a misguided nationalism and the impetus of a misapplied self-determination, strove so vigorously to maintain its national identity that it did so at the expense of another or other nations (nationalities) within the same general territory. It became the exclusive 'nation-state.' This was the *Staatsnationen* of Meinecke, the sovereign nation-state that, due to the failure to distinguish between the nonsovereign or personal powers of government (of the nation) and the sovereign or territorial powers of government (of the state), came unfortunately to be identified with the nation that strove the hardest to prevail or that enjoyed a numerical majority in the formative state. After all, to accommodate territorially the minuscule nation or fraction of a nation, the sovereign nation-state was not, as Angustias Moreno Lopez puts it, going suicidally to break itself up after having struggled to come into being (*Igualdad de Derechos y Libre Determinacion*, pp. 191 ff.)

The identification of the sovereign state with the dominant politicocultural nation was unfortunate, because it resulted either in the uninational state that disregarded the interests and aspirations of other coinhabitant nationalities, or in the partitioned state that constituted a problem in itself. It meant in its results that, as Cobban said, "satisfaction cannot be given to diverse national communities within the same state by any measures short of complete political separation" (*op. cit.*, p. 146). Identification of the state with the nation was denounced too by Carlile Macartney, who decried its results as manifested in the nation-states of central and eastern Europe: "So long as the majority of nations which have assumed command of the different states persist in their theoretically absurd and practically unattainable endeavour to make of those states the exclusive instruments of their own national ideals and aspirations, so long will the minorities be placed in a position which no system of international protection can render tolerable" (*National States and National Minorities*, p. 421).

But it was not only the identification of the sovereign state with the political nation that, in issuing in the uninational nation-state, prevented the emergence of the multinational state – it was also the mind-set that held that to grant nationalities or fractions of nationalities self-determination it was necessary to do so only on a territorially demarcated basis. That is, that the territory nationalities inhabited or shared would need to be fractured along the lines of habitation or sharing of those nationalities – if such could be physically done. If it could not, then the unlucky nationalities had to make do with being guaranteed by the state civil, religious, economic, and other protection ***as individuals***, not as communal groups. But the point is that the false assumption that self-determination could not be applied except on a territorially demarcated basis was but a false assumption.

If it is only on the basis of territorial fracture that self-determination could adequately be effectuated, then it is little wonder that the pressure should be felt to identify national (communal) self-determination with statal (nationwide) self-determination and to bring about the uninational rather than the multinational state. But this is not what self-determination was conceptually intended to achieve. Macartney has criticized the unintended uninational sovereign-cum-politicocultural state in terms that have a familiar ring. "The troubles of our day," he wrote, "arise out of the modern conception of the national state: out of the identification of the political ideals of all the inhabitants of the state with the national-cultural ideals of the majority in it. If once this confusion between two things which are fundamentally different can be abandoned, there is no reason why the members of a score of different nationalities should not live together in perfect harmony in the same state, and not even the smallest of them need suffer from the moral degradation which to-day attends the lot of the 'national minority' " (*op. cit.*, pp. 99-140, 450).

Elaborating on Macartney's condemnation of self-determination being used to create the nation-state, except in rare cases in which both nation and state would fully coincide, Cobban went so far as to label the idea a self-contradiction. "The two tendencies we have described," he wrote (that is, of the sovereign state seeking, in its own defense, to be a single and united politicocultural nation, and of the politicocultural nation, or fraction of a nation, seeking to be a sovereign state) – these two tendencies "moving in contrary directions, are bound to come into conflict.

They have been the source of endless domestic disputes and international strife" (*op. cit.*, pp. 110-111).

Even as long ago as 1862 Lord Acton condemned the uninational state the institution of which he blamed on nationalism, which he called "the greatest adversary of the rights of nationality." "By making the state and the nation commensurate with each other," he wrote, "it [nationalism] reduces practically to a subject condition all other nationalities that may be within the boundary." Of the multinational state, on the other hand, Acton wrote: "A state which is incompetent to satisfy different races condemns itself; a state which labours to neutralize, to absorb or to expel them, destroys its own vitality; a state which does not include them is destitute of the chief basis of self-government." (*History of Freedom and Other Essays*, Vol. IX, *Nationality*, pp. 297 and 298.) Reechoing Acton's plea for the multinational state, Alfred Cobban has written: "The multi-national state must re-enter the political canon, from which, as Acton many years ago declared, it should never have been expelled" (*op. cit.*, pp. 127-128).

The multinational state would never have been expelled from the political canon had a formula been found whereby the demands of both those advocating a territorially bound national self-determination and those advocating what Frederick Hertz has called 'the ethnic personality principle' could have been met. The bogey has always been the necessity of a certain territory (and hence partition) for the demarcation of people. But it doesn't have to be so, we know. The proposals made by Otto Bauer and Karl Renner for a nonterritorial federalism of nationality communities forming the Austro-Hungarian Empire went unheeded. Basically, these proposals were, as Carl Friedrich and Arend Lijphart have, separately, described, were that every individual should be enabled to declare to which nationality he or she wished to belong, and that the various nationalities so formed should be allowed to rule themselves as autonomous politicocultural communities on a nonterritorial basis.

This idea was first given practical effect in Estonia in 1925. Minority groups there were given virtual independence in certain jurisdictional fields which were not territorially based. The experiment was so successful, Georg von Rausch noted, that "the Estonian Government was able to claim, with every justification, that it had found an exemplary solution to the problem of its minorities" (*The Baltic States, the Years of Independence, 1917-1940*, p. 142). Cyprus adopted a similar system of government in 1960, and

Belgium in 1970. (See Carl J. Friedrich, *Trends of Federalism*, p. 124, and Arend Lijphart, *Democracies*, pp. 183-185.)

The key to the solution of the problem in all of these cases has been, simply, nonterritoriality. "The demarcation of a nation can be founded on either the territorial or the ethnic principle," writes Frederick Hertz. "It can either identify the nation with the inhabitants of a given territory, or with a group irrespective of territory." "Ulster, of course," adds Hertz (in what might be regarded a vindication of our thesis), "rejects [the statal self-determination principle and] claims that the principle of ethnic personality should be applied." (*Nationality in History and Politics*, pp. 241, 243.)

The claim of Ulster can be met, without any derogation from the claim of Republicans, under the principle of the multinational state, which depends itself on one necessary condition. Once the distinction between the major/sovereign powers and minor/nonsovereign powers of governmental rule is made, with the major powers being shared by the nationalities at the sovereign level of the territorial state and the minor powers being exclusively exercised by the individual nationalities at the personal/communal level of the nonterritorial nation – once this distinction is made, territorial boundaries can be dispensed with in the installation of the multinational system of government under essential self-determination. In fact, once such a distinction is carried through to its logical conclusion, and under certain conditions, as argued by Macartney from similar premises, then "there is no need for national communities to be organized by states at all. If nation and state are recognized for the separate things which they in fact are, then just as each state exercises political sovereignty within its own territorial limits, so each nation may form a cultural community, independent of territorial considerations, which would organize the cultural life of all its members throughout the world" (*op. cit.*, p. 469).

By way of comment on this very desirable end, we would have to note that it is only an assumption that politicocultural communities would desire to organize themselves internationally; in practice it would not be very likely to happen. The fact is that such communities, as those in Ireland, only have nationality problems within their own political states; in their international dimension, to the extent that they exist indeed as nationalities abroad, they would have no such problems at all. Moreover, the countries with which such communities would 'interfiliate' would not only have also to confederate with the home state, but they would have to confederate with each other – something that while not being impossible, would not be very probable in practice.[13] The one possibility we see of Macartney's vision being fulfilled would be the case in which only one other country would be involved with the home state, both of which would have to confederate with each other anyway. In that way, to take an example, the Irish Government would rule the Hiberno-British in Britain (as James Molyneaux has happened, in fact, to suggest), while the British Government would rule the Anglo-Irish in Ireland, both Governments being, of course, confederated with each other.

Outside of that scenario, however, it would be difficult enough to establish multinational self-determination in home countries alone, and the example of Ireland itself is sufficient evidence of this. That it would be difficult is understandable, in a way, because of a nationality's particular attachment to the homeland and of its desire for a certain local autonomy. This fact of life is what, in truth, makes the breakout from a territorybound to a people-oriented self-government to be all the more difficult. As a matter of fact, political thinkers on the subject have not themselves before recently broken away from territory-based conceptions of possible systems of government, and Cobban, perhaps the foremost of the thinkers, only goes so far as to suggest a reworked region-based system of self-determination. If we may substitute "*peoples*" for "regions" in his thought, we would with Cobban hold as follows: "Where *peoples* with a separate national consciousness exist, even if they are smaller than the communities we are accustomed to regard as nations, they must be treated as the basic elements in the pattern of European society. This is the first principle of the new self-determination. It is only the beginning, of course, and not the end of international reunion." Mikhail Bakunin too, Cobban's

13 We do not share Alfred Cobban's fears for the potential danger to national security and international peace that would ensue from an international interfiliation. The reason is that politicocultural nations would be restricted to operating in the nonterritorial minor powers areas of government and thus, even if organized on a worldwide basis, would present no danger of "overriding all state frontiers." We agree that national communities have a particular sentiment for territory, but, as long as we do not confuse the personally political nation with the territorially political state, this does not translate into the territorial major powers area of jurisdiction of the Governments concerned and so the question of any infringement of sovereignty by one state against another would not arise. (See Macartney, *op. cit*, p. 469 and Cobban, *op. cit.*, p. 265; for a treatment of the relationship between nation and territory, see Frederick Hertz's above-cited work, pp. 146-151.

"prophet of the future," could only think of minority peoples in terms of "communes": "Universal peace will be impossible so long as the present centralised States [of 1867] exist. We must desire their destruction in order that, on the ruins of these forced unions organised from above by right of authority and conquest, there may arise free unions organised from below by the free federation of communes into provinces, of provinces into the nation[-state], and of nations into the United States of Europe." Confirming this view, incidentally, Cobban wrote: "The principle of building from below is both more democratic and more realistic than the nation state theory of 1918." (*The Nation State*, p. 264.)

Defining the new self-determination for Ireland

The foregoing discursive exploration of self-determination as an evolving concept, issuing in Cobban's encouraging call for a new self-determination, bids us examine, in the light of the four MacBride principles of national (nation-state) self-determination, what the principles of that new self-determination ought to be for Ireland.

Actually there is only one self-determination, the old self-determination, but, as used in the past it serves no present purpose. Formerly, as we have seen, the concept has been so applied to nationalities as to achieve their communal independence through territorial determination and thus to succeed in achieving more or less homogeneous independent nation-states. But, by virtue of this very event, as we have also seen, the doctrine failed to achieve independence for the nationalities that happened not to be co-extensive habitationwise with the nation-states that came into being. The emphasis was so much on nation-state building, in fact, that the self-determination that achieved it all has to this day been taken by many to be a ***national***, that is, a statal self-determination of the majority. So true is this that the demand in such a communally mixed country as Ireland is still for nothing more than a national self-determination of the state of the majority and not the minority rather than a multinational self-determination of the majority and the minority of the state.

What is required today is a new definition of the old self-determination, "that re-definition of national self-determination which," as Edward Hallett Carr stated, "is so badly needed" (*Conditions of Peace*, pp. 39-69), for, as we've seen too, there is more to self-determination than self-determination of the state. It has largely been forgotten that the principle was intended primarily for people and only secondarily for states, and the call of such authorities as Alfred Cobban for a new self-determination is really a call for a new application of the old self-determination, that is, for a fuller application of an inadequately applied theory. It is a call for moving self-determination away from an international protection for groups against discrimination in their exclusive majority nationality states on to a positive, forthright self-rule of the groups in their inclusive majority and minority nationality states. It is a call for a self-determination that is people oriented and community based, that is personal, communal and multinational, and that is enjoyed within – and even without – the territory of the inclusive majority and minority nationality state. Such is a self-determination that is, in a word, and in the Irish context, the self-determination that was affirmed in the 1921 Anglo-Irish Treaty Settlement, that was reaffirmed in the 1985 Anglo-Irish Agreement (constitutionally interpreted), and that must now be put into effect in Ireland and Northern Ireland, in all Ireland, that is.

The task to hand is, then, it reinterpret the four principles of national self-determination as formulated by Sean MacBride in terms of what would fit the peculiar people-structured Irish political society. By this we mean that a self-determination that would fit only the exclusive majority-based system of rule, that is, a national self-determination, has obviously to be abandoned. The system adopted must fit the facts of the situation – ***and***, we say, the Treaty provisions for it.

The four principles of national self-determination apply without qualifications to nations that are of a generally homogeneous character and in which such a thing as the swing vote exists between the majority and the minority. But in Ireland, where the population is not exactly homogeneous and the swing vote is unheard of and where the majority and the minority comprise mutually exclusive communal and politico-socio-economic entities, the four national self-determination principles cannot be applied without their being qualified by and interpreted in the light of the existing people-structured situation that demands the self-determination the Treaty provided. The four MacBride principles must be reformulated in such a way as workably to determine a particular group's qualifications for claiming a communally oriented multinational self-determination when that group exists within the frontiers of an otherwise determined nation whose ethos the group cannot share. That is, when such a nonparticipatory opposition group exists within a nation formed on historical grounds or on the basis of the way self-determination was used to create nation-states, that group has the right to have the four reformulated principles of self-determination applied to it to test its qualifications for separateness in the multinational state.

With the four MacBride principles in mind, the four principles of the new self-determination may be expressed as follows: First of all, there must be a particular community or separate group sufficiently visible and sufficiently different in character, culture, values and outlook from the nationally determined population as to merit separate treatment and distinction from the national citizenry (e.g., in Ireland the Anglo-Irish). Secondly, the unique group claiming separate treatment must have a longstanding tradition as an identifiably distinct and (to a degree) separately ruled community or nationality in the history of the nation of which it forms a part (e.g., in the U.S. the Amish, in Iran the Jews). Thirdly, the communal group must have a reasonably homogeneous and cohesive membership claiming the same form of self-determination for all who belong to it (e.g., in Ireland the British-subject condition). And fourthly, it has to be the expressed intention of a majority of the members of the communal group that the particular group is unable to share the ethos of the national population under any circumstances (e.g., in New Caledonia the French, in the Soviet Union the Jews, in Israel the Palestinians).

We would have to say that the Loyalist community of Ireland meets these four requirements and should accordingly be accorded self-determination, but, by the same token and to preserve national unity, the Nationalist community should be accorded a similar self-determination. However, in view of the fact that such self-determination would be enjoyed in a territorially unitary state, with which the majority community would be happy (as if it were their own nation-state attained by national self-determination) but with which the minority community would be perfectly unhappy, the self-determination acquired by the minority must of necessity be conferred in an other than territorial sense. What that sense is exactly we pretty well know already, but how it will be applied and what precise form or forms it will take is what has now to be worked out. Certain it is that, in a general way, it will call for nothing less than a complete restructuring of Irish society and a conversion of the nation into a multinational state. What can safely be said at this stage, perhaps, is that the proposed societal restructuring might best be described an 'interfiliation' of subject groups, since basically two communities would be subject to diverse authorities (Dublin and Westminster) in the minor powers area of jurisdiction and simultaneously to a single, central but confederated authority (Dublin) in the major powers area, without either community's rights being compromised in the process.

In the light of all the foregoing historical analysis of self-determination and of its form that was intended for nationalities that could not be formed into nation-states but that could be formed into multinational states, and particularly in the light of the application of such a self-determination to Ireland, we may define the new self-determination or interfiliation as follows:

- The right of a sovereign state's politicocultural community, the members of which are conscious of themselves as members of a community, and wish to maintain the identity of their community, to determine whether, at the nonsovereign, personal and minor powers level of Government, the community shall: (1) be governed by the multinational state of which its area of habitation forms a constitutionally integral part; (2) be governed by itself within the multinational state whose sovereign, territorial and major powers jurisdiction extends to the community's area of habitation; or (3) be governed from within the multinational state by another sovereign state with which it may have a politicocultural affinity and with which its own state would confederate – provided that, if this third choice is made, it is accepted under international agreement or treaty by the two sovereign states concerned.

Actualizing the provisional in the New Ireland

If Irish reunification is ever to be brought about, Irish Republicans must stand firm on the Republican – and Gladstonian and Lincolnian and Churchillian – constitutional doctrine that there can be no dissent from long-established territorial unity. The basic principle is that the island of Ireland is a geopolitical unit, and in the light of that principle no minority in Ireland may enjoy the option of dissenting from unity or indeed of consenting to it. In other words, the concept of territorial unity by consent *in a constitutional sense* does not exist. But how do the Irish restore that territorial unity (epitomized in the Republic) in spite of the opposition of those who still insist that reunion must be achieved either by consent or by force? How do Irish Republicans convince their opponents that they may, even as those Republicans are reuniting Ireland, yet enjoy unity by consent? How do they offer reunion on a nonoptional basis without evoking the gravest of repercussions (let alone get it accepted)?

Actually, restoration of the Provisional Republic of all Ireland is an event that need have no repercussions at all, so imperceptible would the changeover be. As Republicans are proceeding to restore the Republic, they might assure the Loyalist majority of the North that the six-county area would be preserved for the time being as the equivalent of a separate state in a federal Ireland. Although the Northerners have already refused the offer of a state (in 1922 and 1984), within the framework of a Provisional Republic they would very likely want to hold the North as a distinct region in some form. This would not be a problem. The separate identity of the six counties would have to be preserved indefinitely anyway for certain functions of Government, and at the very least the area would have to be treated as a distinct School District for educational purposes. In whatever way one would proceed, in other words, the act of restoration would be very gradual.

However, no matter how one may proceed, the very first step and *sine qua non* condition of Irish reunification is restoration of the Provisional all-Ireland Republic. From within that broad framework, anything can be achieved. Without it, the same old stalemate goes on. Any lesser arrangement might provide a forum for the same old controversy to go on in, but it could not possibly provide a constitutional solution to the actual problem. Any other forum would be of as much value towards achieving reunification as was the Lloyd Georgian Irish Convention of 1917-18 towards achieving independence. It was the establishment of the Provisional Republic of 1919 that brought Ireland independence and it will be the reestablishment of that Republic that will bring her reunification. Once the Provisional Republic is restored, and the mandate of Irish constitutional law is satisfied, steps might be taken right away to secure the situation in corresponding Anglo-Irish constitutional law. To that end negotiations would be undertaken with Britain to have her withdraw her administration and to relinquish the powers of Government she would then more obviously be unconstitutionally withholding from Ireland.

By first restoring the Provisional Republic in Irish constitutional law and then settling and finalizing in Anglo-Irish constitutional law the totality of legal relations existing between Britain and Ireland, the Irish would be converting the Provisional Irish

Republic into the actual Irish Republic. And since 'Irish Republic' means all Ireland, they would at the same time be restoring Irish unity. In the meantime, discussions would be undertaken within Ireland with a view to achieving rapprochement between the two main Irish traditions. These, as stated, would center on the possibility of having autonomy arranged on a people or community basis. The long-term goal of the discussions would be to arrive at a consensus of opinion so that a new, all-Ireland Constitution might be formulated.

Ordinarily, such a thing as an all-Ireland Constitution might be considered a dream, and agreement on it impossible of attainment, but it will never be agreed on, and never reached, unless and until the right conditions for its formulation are created. Likewise, since the cooperation of the United Kingdom is required for our plan of reunification to be effectuated, that is more likely to be secured in a situation in which the Irish are already helping themselves than in one in which they would be asking the British to help them in spite of their not helping themselves at all. By the same token, as things stand, Republicans cannot realistically expect the Northerners to consent to final unity and take the plunge into the unknown. They should first provide the provisional framework and allow for a gradual unity by consent to take effect.

The important thing to realize is, then, that without restoration of the all-Ireland Provisional Republic, none of the above-described process of rapprochement or consensus can be undertaken. Without restoration there is no progress to be made on either the partition or partitionism front. Hence, restoration is the very first step. As soon as that breakthrough is achieved, members of the Anglo-Irish comunity would be assured that they have nothing to fear from constitutional progress. The Provisional Republic would not be actualized in a hurry. Loyalists could take as long as they liked to consider options open to them. They would be welcome to enter the all-Ireland Dail to express their opinions and desires; they could state whether they wanted dual British and Irish citizenship and nationality or wished to continue being British citizens and/or British subjects alone (provided this were all right with Britain), or whether they desired the one form for some and the other for others.

By having a provisional framework to actualize, instead of trying (perhaps hopelessly) to introduce change directly, the conditions are created that would make it apparent to those concerned that the more things change, the more they remain the same. At first an all-Ireland Judiciary may be set up, for example. Evolving this within the framework of the all-Ireland Republic is much better than trying to establish an all-Ireland Court under present conditions. The reason it is better is that it would be less likely to arouse opposition or to give rise to suspicions of a sudden sellout or irreversible takeover. On the gradual actualization principle all involved can feel their way in a participatory manner, and nobody need have fears of such a thing as a noose tightening inexorably around his or her neck.

Also, the possibility of establishing an all-Ireland police force – if such is to be recommended – can best be discussed and achieved in the more favorable climate of a Provisional Republic. Then, too, other goals may or may not be reached as desired, such as establishment of an all-Ireland Economic Development Council and consolidation of Health and Social Services on an all-Ireland basis. At present such issues are so many proposed steps in the path to hoped-for Irish unity, which remains as chimerical as ever. But, in the context of the Provisional Republic they would be so many real steps taken in the rapprochement process. Also, they would have a better chance of attainment, because they would be discussed more meaningfully and with better reference to reality. And there would be no grounds for suspicions of anyone's having ulterior motives, because with a provisional framework established the intended ultimate goal would be quite clear to everyone and with regard to it a serious stand could be taken by each individual sooner or later.

It ought not to be beyond the wit of (Irish) man to work out in practice the details of the interfiliation system of government. This might be conducted broadly along the lines of the Subreport of the New Ireland Forum Report of 1984. We say "broadly," because interfiliation would actually go beyond the scope of the Subreport, as it would be based on an all-Ireland rather than a Northern Ireland foundation. The working out would, too, be done in such a way as to be acceptable to Nationalists and Republicans in all of Ireland without at the same time being objectionable to Loyalists and Unionists in the whole of Ireland. The Subreport is so important and relevant to our model that we have reproduced it in Appendix 16, *Supplement*.

The way to tackle the unification problem is, then, to adopt a gradual approach. First, the Provisional Republic is established, or restored. Then, after some time, it is actualized. The Provisional Republic would be the skeleton of which the actualization would be the fleshing out. The actualization of the Republic may, as we said, also be very gradual. It may be so gradual and undisturbing, in fact, as to be almost imperceptible, and no move is made without first having secured a consensus of opinion. In that way is unity achieved by degrees, and everybody sees up ahead what the end result is going to be. Unity that is achieved by agreement, unity by consensus and rapprochement, unity by degrees – in short, unity by consent – is a unity that is more likely to be accepted by all and to be of the lasting kind. This will especially be true if a formula for rapprochement is found in conferring autonomy on a community basis rather than a territory basis, and if that interfiliation formula were to meet with widespread agreement (although it would not depend on this for emplacement), then both the Anglo-Irish and the Gaelic-Irish communities could each get what it wants without the other being denied what it wants in the process. Nothing, it seems, could be more democratic than that.

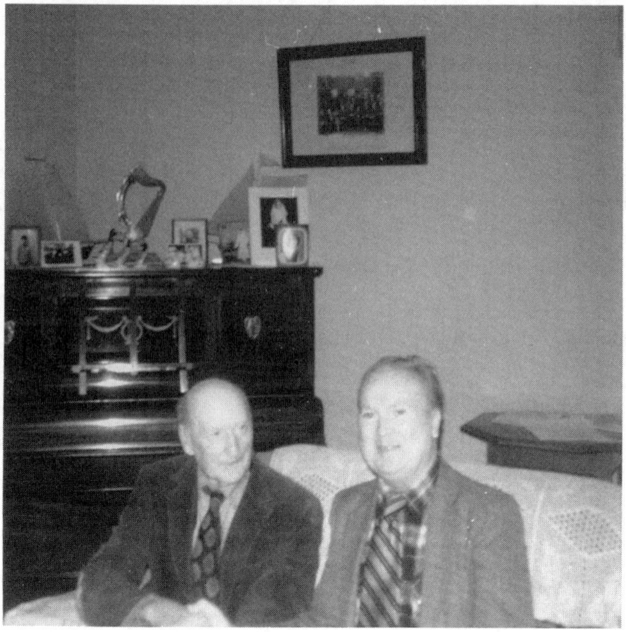

Commandant-General Tom Maguire, last surviving member of the Second Dail Eireann, with the author, at age 95 in 1987.

President Sean T. O Ceallaigh at St. Isidore's Irish Church, Rome, St. Patrick's Day, 1956, with Mrs. O Ceallaigh in background.

CHAPTER 14

REUNIFICATION THROUGH THE RESTORATION OF CONSTITUTIONAL POWER

The Search for the Key

In preceding chapters we have endeavored to present the principles and practice of Republican continuity and succession that it is necessary to observe if the early Irish Republic is to be restored and reunification to be achieved. We have also taken the 'British dimension' into consideration, and from that standpoint we have examined the Anglo-Irish constitutionalism that was formed and established on an all-Ireland basis. We have endeavored as well to show how from a restoration of Irish Republicanism and a reactivation of Anglo-Irish constitutionalism the unity of Ireland that once existed and was acknowledged by all sides can be reinstituted and partition effectively ended.

In treating Irish Republicanism, it might be noted, we have not taken the term 'Republic' in the literal, territorial, all-Ireland unity sense alone. We have also understood it in the more spiritual or people sense of Wolfe Tone, Davis and Pearse, that is, in the sense of a unity of the people expressed in a working interrelationship of the traditional Irish communities and in a guaranteeing of the preservation of each group's rights in a united Ireland – and so that that united Ireland might be made possible. In other words, we have also understood Republic in the Tonian sense of 'Catholic, Protestant and Dissenter under the common name of Irishman,' in the Davisean sense of 'a nationality of the spirit as well as of the letter,' and in the Pearsean sense of guaranteeing 'religious and civil liberty, equal rights and equal opportunities to all its citizens.' It is just such an all-embracing Republic that ever was the instinctive national demand of the Irish and it is just such an all-embracing Republic that is intended to be restored.

Crucial though all-Ireland Republicanism may be to the national effort, Anglo-Irish constitutionalism cannot be neglected and we remain convinced that the cooperation of Britain also is absolutely essential. As a matter of fact, in view of the existence of the British dimension Britain bears a major responsibility for the situation in Ireland today, a fact that has been brought out well in the Report of the New Ireland Forum of 1984. Britain, under all-Ireland compulsion, will have to discharge her responsibility fully to Ireland and to guarantee her cooperation, not on a Northern Ireland but an all-Ireland basis. She will have to do better than pledge, as Prime Minister Margaret Thatcher did to Taoiseach Garret FitzGerald on November 6, 1981, that if a consent to unity were to be expressed by a Northern majority in a poll conducted in accordance with the Northern Ireland Constitution Act of 1973, then the British Government would introduce legislation in Parliament to give effect to that national minority "decision." Britain will have to do still better than pledge, as Thatcher did again to FitzGerald on November 19, 1984, that "if in the future the majority of the people of Northern Ireland clearly wished for and consented to a change in the constitutional status of Northern Ireland, the United Kingdom Government would put forward and support legislation to that end in the British Parliament." And Britain will have to do even better than she did in the latest Irish-British Agreement when, in concert with the Irish Government, she declared that "if in the future a majority of the people of Northern Ireland clearly wish for and formally consent to the establishment of a united Ireland, [the two Governments] will introduce and support in the respective Parliaments legislation to give effect to that wish" (Article 1). (For the essential Articles of the Anglo-Irish Agreement of 1985 see Appendix 17, *Supplement.*)

Britain will, indeed, have to do better than she has done heretofore – and Ireland will have to be in a position to see that she does it. For if Ireland is not in a position to compel cooperation, she is surely not going to get it. The 1985 commitment to the Republic ought to give Ireland the needed leverage. When we say 'Ireland' we mean, of course, all Ireland, and that means that it is the Provisional Dail and Government of the all-Ireland Republic that will have to be in place to compel Britain's cooperation through the medium of fulfilling Anglo-Irish constitutionalism. A Republican Government will have to have Britain start from 1914 and fulfill the pledge of unity she gave in the all-Ireland Home Rule Act at that time (see Appendix 14, *Supplement*). The Government would then have Britain proceed in the same vein through the Treaty, the 1922 Constitution, the subsequent Agreements, and the totality of relations between the two islands until Irish unity would be accomplished in Anglo-Irish law. Such a process is a far cry from irredentist collaboration with Britain in taking umbrage in partition-conditioned promises based on a visionary and foredoomed six-county poll that would itself be based on the partitionist Northern Ireland Constitution Act of 1973 and that would, according to the 1982 Northern Ireland Act, have to reach a 70 percent majority in a Belfast Assembly to be even considered.

There need not be much fear that the proper contribution cannot successfully be extracted from Britain. There are signs of hope, in fact, from among the British people. The Episcopal Bishop of Salisbury in England, John Austin Baker, Chaplain to the Speaker of the House of Commons, spoke encouragingly to the consciences of his fellow Britons during the hunger strikes of 1981. "No British Government ought ever to forget that this perilous moment, like many before it," he warned, "is the outworking of a history for which our country is primarily responsible. England seized Ireland for its own military benefit. It planted Protestant settlers there to make it strategically secure. It humiliated and penalized the native Irish and their Catholic religion. And then, when it could no longer hold on to the whole island, it kept back a part of it to be a home for the settlers' descendants, a nonviable solution from which the Protestant population has suffered as much as anyone else. Our injustice created the situation, and by constantly repeating that ***we will maintain it so long as the majority wish it, we actively inhibit Protestants and Catholics from working out a new future together.*** This is the root cause of the violence which has taken place" (*italics ours*).

No British Government ought, indeed, to forget the historical roots of its ill-starred involvement with Ireland that has issued in the current problems. And no British Government ought ever to forget, we might add, that in the long, tortuous history of that involvement Ireland never sought to achieve an absolute and complete separation from the neighboring island. Irish Republicanism, or Separatism, never meant a wall of separation between Britain and Ireland. All it ever meant was that the excessive involvement by one nation in the affairs of the other should stop, and that what involvement there might be would be controllable, reciprocal, and restricted to the level indispensable for ordinary interisland relations.

It is unfortunate that the Irish effort to set right the irregularity in relations between Britain and Ireland should have been misunderstood by the British in the past. It was so misunderstood, in fact, as to be termed "secession" by Lloyd George – of one part of Britain from the rest! So extreme a break in ages past was unthinkable to the British and for them to concede it, for *all* of Ireland, was, as H. G. Wells has written in his *Outline of History*, "a thing almost as agreeable to thoughtful Englishmen as it would have been to an American in 1863 to have seen Jefferson Davis treating with Abraham Lincoln in Washington upon the future status of the cotton states. For the complete separation of Ireland from Britain promised to be not a merely inconvenient thing, but a very dangerous and, it may be, a disastrous thing, for both countries."

The politics of persuasion

Well, indeed, might the break have been disastrous to both sides were it not the lesser degree of separation as described that was sought. The British, though they yielded, overreacted to the event, and in their inability to collaborate held on to a portion of Ireland. And they have managed to hold on to that portion these many years mainly through the device of the Loyalist veto. This is the great stumbling block that has baffled Irish statesmen and politicians and defied all efforts at removal. As inducements to removing it, various proposals have been put forward – particularly to the Forum for a New Ireland – for various British-Irish alignments or models – for example, that an arrangement on the lines of the Nordic Council be set up, or that a model on the Benelux Economic Union (a subdivision of the EEC) be established, or even that an arrangement based on the European Economic Community be introduced. And even the Forum itself put forward some three proposals of its own. But all these proposals, known as the politics of persuasion, have come to naught. And they have come to naught particularly because they are acts of persuasion or inducement, and not legal acts of compulsion or enforcement. They are political, not constitutional.

Not only did it prove impossible, by constitutional Nationalist means, to shove off the Loyalist veto or to have it interpreted in any other than the traditional way, but the exact opposite was had for Irish efforts. The veto was reaffirmed in no uncertain terms, as we know, and this event, as Austin Baker of England would have warned and as Elizabeth Crighton of Los Angeles has observed, only served to increase rather than decrease the mutual polarization of the communities in Northern Ireland, with the prospects of a reciprocally agreeable solution on province-transcending lines being made more remote than ever.

It is not just because the Loyalist veto is so intractable and formidable, and because it needs to be reinterpreted rather than confronted, that we have proposed the particular model of this work, but also – and primarily – because the framework of an interfiliational Republic is what is latent in both Republican and Anglo-Irish constitutionalism. To propose models not contained in Ireland's constitutional equipment, and to propose them as *means* to reunification, is nothing, it seems to us, but a putting of the cart before the horse and an exercise in ultimate futility. They are this, because they do not lead to unity, but follow after it. Such 'extraconstitutional' models, if any of them is ever going to come about, belong in the long-distant future. It may well indeed be that, after reunification, both Ireland and Great Britain will end up even as a confederation between them (as was once envisaged by none less than Thomas Davis). *After* reunification, however, some such association may come about; certainly not as a means to it.

To understand the uselessness of positing extraconstitutional models as means to achieving Irish unity it may be helpful to put these models in their proper perspective. There are three possible approaches to solving the problem of reunification – or, rather, to attaining independence and self-determination for all Ireland and the entire Irish people. These three approaches – or forces – have been or are being worked out in three corresponding stages of recent Irish history:

- The first approach was represented by revolutionary force or the War of Independence, and was espoused by Sinn Fein Republicans. This stage closed on July 11, 1921 and issued in the Treaty Settlement of 1921-1925. (Violence is still, of course, espoused by some as a means to regaining the six counties, but at this stage it is popularly unsupported, futile and counterproductive. One reason it is futile is that its stated aim – to bring the British to the negotiating table – has already been achieved. The problem now is not one of negotiation, but of implementation of what has been already negotiated – and agreed.)

- The second approach constituted mainly moral and political force, and was espoused by the discretionist Nationalists of the twenty-six and six counties in Ireland. The models people of the Nationalist persuasion had to offer were derived wholly from partition politics and presented purely as appeasing proposals. They amounted mainly to persuasion, pleading and plausibleness. The epoch of this constitutional approach came to an end with the holding of the New Ireland Forum in 1983 and 1984 when Constitutional Nationalism just about died as a force that could reunite Ireland. (A counterforce, Unionism, existing as long as Nationalism, has failed as a political system and, with the Anglo-Irish Agreement of 1985, likewise died as a force that could keep any part of Ireland subject thenceforth to Great Britain.)

- The third approach is that of constitutional strength and enforcement, and is espoused by Republicans in all of Ireland and propounded on an all-Ireland basis.[1] The era of this third force is the present, with roots dating from the period of the First Republic and the Treaty/Document No. 2 event. With the 1984 Chequers event Constitutional Republicanism appeared to have been vindicated and bids fair to be the way of the future. (The 1985 Hillsborough event may have greatly hindered and has hardly helped this movement.)

The third of these approaches, that of constitutional force, is the model we have presented in this work. It is the only viable model, we believe, because it is what is contained in Irish constitutionalism, not something manufactured outside of it. Any 'solution' coming from the outside is of its nature doomed to be rejected even in advance. The reason it is foredoomed is that it is not only heavily reliant on hope and persuasion for acceptance, but also because it lacks one essential ingredient: a commonly agreed-upon basis or accepted formula, an already agreed-upon ground upon which to base the solution or constitutional system.

---

1 The fact that some Irish Republicans rather than others, upon thinking through their Republicanism, have of late come to the conclusion that their position ultimately rests on persuasion (and thus do not differentiate themselves from Nationalists), is perhaps due to their fighting shy of the Treaty Settlement, though this was endorsed by Sinn Fein in 1925 in effect as Document No. 2 and has, sooner or later, to be faced up to as containing the only true basis of force. (See Gerry Adams, *Sinn Fein Statement*, September 5, 1988.)

In Ireland, as we know, proposals put forward for a constitutional compromise have never attained their common objective of providing a solution that would be acceptable to both North and South, to both Loyalists and Republicans, because the mutually exclusive aims of the opposing sides prevented efforts at going beyond those aims to find a common formula upon which to base a mutually acceptable system or solution. Proposals and guarantees that have been so painstakingly worked out ever since 1914 and before, and that have been so earnestly put forward on numerous occasions over the years, may be regarded by the one side as steps to eventual reunification, but by the other as British capitulations which must be resisted by all means, if necessary by the use of force. Such is the peculiar Irish political difficulty, which has always been more complex than the experiences of most other countries with mixed populations. As for understanding why there never has been a resolution of the problem, Alfred Gaston Donaldson has put the matter quite succinctly. "The core of the Irish question was not the difficulty of devising a form of Constitution," he has written, "the chief difficulty was to discover a basis on which any constitutional system could be founded" (*Some Comparative Aspects of Irish Law*, p. 72). Archimedes could hardly have put it better!

The politics of force

Just about the only viable basis discernible for the purpose is that which was discovered once in the Versailles-oriented Treaty, and if the problem is still not one of devising an acceptable constitutional system, but of discovering a basis upon which to found one such, then it behooves the Irish to look to their past constitutionalism and to derive from it to the full what has been achieved by agreement there already. That is the basis that has to be discovered, or rather rediscovered, and maybe – just maybe – a new constitutional system can be erected on it. Certain it is, at any rate, that a new constitutional system – a New Ireland – cannot be erected on any but a basis that has already been, but never again will be, agreed upon.

Without some such solution, or key to a solution, as the basis latent in our interfiliational model of constitutional force, not even Britain could, if she wanted to, end partition under existing conditions. The reason is that Ireland would not likely be able to live with the kind of reunification Britain could deliver – even if the Northerners would agree in advance to accept it (?!).

When in 1940 and 1941, Britain's hour of greatest difficulty, an apparently golden opportunity to end partition arose, it was not seized by Ireland, because, as de Valera chiefly felt, within an Ireland forcibly united by Britain the Unionist community could not be contained. The group would never give in and concessions would have to be made that would be "opposed to the sentiments and aspirations of the great majority of the Irish people," explained de Valera in rejecting the offer of Prime Minister Chamberlain on the 4th of July, 1940. Then, on December 8th, 1941, de Valera responded to Churchill's "A Nation once again" overture by saying "I did not see the thing in that light . . . I didn't see any basis of agreement." In other words, unity under conditions other than those the Northerners would agree to was impossible, and Britain's generous offer of "categorical reunification" had to be refused. (See Longford and O'Neill, pp. 364-368, 392-395, and T. Ryle Dwyer, *Irish Neutrality*.)

It is not only, then, that some such basis as an interfiliational model capable of making Irish unity workable must be found; it is not just that a basic formula capable of engendering a form of unity that Ireland could live with must be made known; it is not only that a constitutional basis drawn from a system of already existing agreement, a basis which reasonable minds would judge acceptable, must be offered – it is not just that such a basis must be found and made known and offered as a possible key to a solution, but it is also, since such a basis *was* educed from the Irish-cum-Anglo-Irish mandatory constitutional agreement, that its acceptance must be compelled even as it is offered. For it is in the very act of educing and deriving this formulary and reasonable basis from such mandatory agreement that we are at once compelling its acceptance as the firm foundation of a constitutional system to be constructed.

It is precisely because the constitutional equipment one would be working with contains so much bipartite and tripartite agreement that a fundamental basis of unity derived from it would be of a nonoptionally offerable nature. The interfiliational basis would, furthermore, be such as to make workable Irish reunification. On that sure basis the edifice of reunification, designed to be acceptable to all, would be built. And since the work as it proceeded would be the implementation of already existing agreement, it could leave no room for political persuasion: it would command all-round cooperation and acceptance. The process would be one of constitutional force, not gentle persuasion. One must forge ahead statutory step by statutory step and compel Britain and the

Unionists to cooperate as fully and as seriously as they are by Treaty bound so to do. All of which ought not to be impossible to achieve once the proper basis for action is found and adopted.

The imperative to restore the Irish Republic

The failure until the present post-1985 era to establish the basis of mutual accommodation between the traditional Irish communities as a foundation upon which to build an independent, united Ireland only serves to bear out the truth of Padraic Pearse's observation that more than political independence is required for independence. There is also required a ***basis*** for such independence. Just two months before the Easter Rising Pearse expressed this fundamental truth thus: "True political independence requires spiritual and intellectual independence as its basis, or it tends to become unstable, a thing resting merely on interests which change with time and circumstances" (*Political Writings and Speeches*, p. 299).

Establishment, or, rather, implementation of the hitherto elusive and missing basis entails as a minimum having the Provisional Republic in place. This is where a beginning must be made. All that has ever been said or done for Irish reunification is for naught if sound Republican principles based on continuity from the past are not exercised in concrete action to achieve the goal of a Provisional Dail Eireann of the all-Ireland Republic. All the urgings for consensus and pluralism, all the proposals for rapprochement and external association, all the strivings to provide a key to the solution of the partition problem – all are for naught if the very first step of fulfilling the *sine qua non* condition of them all, that of restoring the Provisional Republic, is not taken.

All, too, is for naught if there is not a spearhead political movement that will lead the national and constitutional struggle in the right direction to reach the clear goal of Restoration. As de Valera once said, "We realize the difficulties of uniting in the cause of freedom. We know that in such a fight there has to be a vanguard, and we know that very often it is only a few choice spirits who can form that vanguard." It is time for those Republicans in Ireland who have maintained continuity and succession from the 1919-1922 period to provide this spearhead. As the vanguard composed of choice spirits, they must play a leading part in bringing the Irish people, North and South, into a united Ireland and into full and final freedom and peace. The journey of a million miles begins with a single step.

Addendum to Part III. A model of possible reunification that goes a step beyond the 1985 Agreement is the "Irish dimension option" briefly described by Tom Collins in *The Centre Cannot Hold* (pp. 177-179). As with the Agreement, this model approaches the partition problem irredentistically from within the 26/six-county division of Ireland and, as does the Agreement, surrenders the South's Constitutional claim to annex the six counties so as to remove the threat of an ulterior-motived takeover by the Republic. Thus, it can only be a model of *possible* reunification, because, like the Agreement, it has to concede that maybe the Northern majority's wish might be *not* to reunite with the South.

But the more appealing aspect of the model is, whether the North would reunite or not, that the administration of affairs in the North should be conducted on a popular or communal basis. It does not attempt a territorially based solution, but concentrates on a people-based one. "It is not a matter," writes Collins, "of looking at territories and borders and divisions of land, but of considering the people involved – the individual human beings – and letting them decide what allegiance they prefer. . . . The right of Catholics to be Irish, and the right of Protestants to be British, have to be guaranteed institutionally and constitutionally." The administrative system proposed would be similar to that of the Northern Irish education system, in which schools are run on a separate but equal basis, Collins explains.

In its aspect of an allegiance-based administration the model is similar to our interfiliation model, but it differs in that it would treat its forms of self-determination as means to an end, as inducements to the acceptance of an eventual reunification. In addition, its self-determination would be for the communities in the North alone and not in all of Ireland. The interfiliation model, by comparison, would not treat its self-determination forms as means to an end, but as the conditions essential to the achievement of the end, which would be reached by quite other means – the institutionalizing of existing constitutional dictates. And for this reason the interfiliation model would approach the problem from within the all-Ireland context.

Another model of political accommodation in Ireland that is closer to the interfiliation model is that of a "federation" described by Desmond Fennell which would give the "Ulster British" and Irish Nationalists separate recognitions by distinguishing legally, between citizenship and nationality, as is done in Yugoslavia (where there is a republic for all and nationality subrepublics for the Serbs, Croats, Slovenes, Bosnians, Macedonians and others), and in the Soviet Union (where there are more than 100 nationalities). "Thus there could be an Irish *citizenship* shared by all (leaving it open to those who so wished to have British citizenship also) and two recognised *nationalities*, Irish and British" (*The State of the Nation*, pp. 116-117). It would help, observed

Fennell, if there were a distinct name for the citizenship ('Eirish'? 'Brirish'?) embracing the two nationalities, in the manner of 'Yugoslav' or 'Soviet' that embrace many nationalities. There is, it should be noted, a distinction made already in the British Nationality Acts between British citizenship and British nationality in Britain and the other Commonwealth countries. By these Acts (of 1948, 1965 and 1981) British national/subject status is, within limits, applicable to Irish citizens also.

It might also be added here that it would not take all that much, from the British side, to put such a system of government as the interfiliation model into action, since the machinery for doing so practically exists already – and has in fact existed for the past century or more. It exists in the form of a law that was designed, through successive versions, to protect British subjects in non-Commonwealth countries: the Foreign Jurisdiction Act of 1890 (amended to 1913).

Under this law, "within divers foreign countries" in which the Crown "by treaty, capitulation, grant, usage, sufferance, and other lawful means" (Preamble) has jurisdiction, or "may at any time hereafter have jurisdiction," over British nationals, "it is and shall be lawful for Her Majesty the Queen to hold, exercise, and enjoy" such jurisdiction "in the same and as ample a manner as if Her Majesty had acquired that jurisdiction by the cession or conquest of territory" (Section 1). "Every act and thing done in pursuance of any jurisdiction of Her Majesty in a foreign country shall be as valid as if it had been done according to the local law then in force in that country" (Section 3). (See *Halsbury's Laws of England and Wales*, Fourth Ed., Vol. 7, pp. 239-246 and 249-250, and *Halsbury's Laws of England*, Fourth Ed., Vol. 18, Para. 1545.)

The Foreign Jurisdiction Act, by its very existence, would appear to deprive Britain of any capability she might imagine herself to have of refusing to solve the Anglo-Irish problem. The Act seems to be tailor-made to fit the Irish situation that is marked with its need for British enabling legislation transmitted through the technique of Orders of Her Majesty in Council. All it would take for the British to activate the interfiliation principle would, we feel, by treaty or other lawful means, be to adapt this Act to accommodate the interests and protect the rights of Irish Loyalists.

Give me whereon to stand
and I will move the world.

ARCHIMEDES

EPILOGUE

When one man has reduced a fact of the imagination
to be a fact of his understanding,
I foresee that all men
will at length establish their lives on that basis.

HENRY DAVID THOREAU

Harmony

Moonbeams glow with their shimmering glare,
Illuminating all the darkness of the night,
Piercing too the stillness of the silent air,
In the forest dark where shadows now turn bright.

The clean and pure beams coming from above
Disperse the evil lurking in the dark,
Replacing it with comfort, warmth and love
Which guard 'gainst sin 'til singing of the lark.

And now as the sun rises in the east,
And the moon fades and sets into the trees,
A new justice comes to rule man and beast,
Ending night's chaos with a morning breeze.

Nature's course o'erseen by these two lights,
One to rule the days, one to rule the nights.

FINTAN D. RYAN

EPILOGUE

Interfiliation – The Irish Constitutional Mandate

It is perhaps not a little coincidental that the solutional constitutional model that is found in and evolved from past Irish and Anglo-Irish constitutionalism, that of 'interfiliation' (as we have called it), is paralleled closely by the model of 'confiliation' newly proposed by Albert P. Blaustein and J. Singler of Rutgers University, New Jersey. Confiliation is not a federation of areas based on a geographic foundation, but concerns itself primarily with personal jurisdictions based on 'group rights.' It is defined as "a new constitutional form which recognizes the human dimension of government by preserving the right of groups to be different while remaining part of the common union." That is to say, it is a restructuring of society that affords a maximum recognition of group rights, without abridging individual freedoms and identities, while still maintaining the unity of the pluralistic society in which those group and individual rights are recognized.

The Blaustein-Singler model of confiliation (which was not made public until 1985 and so, unfortunately, not available to us until after our theory was developed) was arrived at by an entirely different route than the one by which we arrived at our model of interfiliation. The 'East Coast' model was derived from a study of modern developments and trends away from an ill-fitting integration (in certain areas of the world) in which groups' rights, if not also individuals' rights, can be totally disregarded; it was also derived from a study of modern UN rights documents and the Constitutions of new nations of the world that reflect the principles of these documents. Our 'West Coast' model was derived strictly from a study of Republican Irish and Anglo-Irish (including Treaties of Versailles and Commonwealth) constitutionalism and of the ways by which the principles contained therein might be legally and constitutionally implemented and the evolved model put into effect. Both routes led essentially to very similar results.

The Blaustein-Singler model and ours resemble each other closely, but they have distinctive differences too. Both are concerned with the acknowledgment of (major powers) allegiance to the central, sovereign authority in the multinational, multicultural or pluralistic state. After that, confiliation is concerned with the coexistence of personal jurisdictions owing (minor powers) allegiance to lower-level authorities within one and the same sovereign country; while interfiliation is concerned with the coexistence of personal jurisdictions owing (minor powers) allegiance to lower-level authorities also which would be some inside, some outside the domestic sovereign area. The one model is *intra*filiational; the other *inter*filiational.

While we may, in referring to either the confiliation or interfiliation model, use the term "personal jurisdiction," we only do so to make clear the idea that the communal jurisdiction that either model is is the mode of expression of the personal rights the people who make up the community have. Personal jurisdiction itself is not a new idea. For that reason it may be what will convince us of the workability of communal jurisdiction, since the two systems of government have so much in common.

In the evolution of law personal jurisdiction preceded territorial jurisdiction. Personal jurisdiction was the authority asserted over individuals in response to fidelity and loyalty to the sovereign. With personal jurisdiction the subject of the sovereign was considered to remain under the sovereign's authority wherever the subject might go. The trend in law, however, was away from personal jurisdiction and towards territorial jurisdiction. Sovereigns insisted on exclusive jurisdiction not only over every person and every thing within their borders (excluding diplomats), but over every person and every thing that moved into their territory – and lost it over every person and every thing that moved out of their territory. Thus did territorial jurisdiction (and diplomatic immunity) evolve, and it is by no means the only form of jurisdiction that ever did or that could now exist. The modern-day affirmation of communal jurisdiction is a re-evocation of personal jurisdiction, but is due in the main to the success had with the affirmation of individual human and civil rights.

Heretofore in the evolution of (national and international) law, from the end of the seventeenth century on, the emphasis in Constitution writing has been on the rights of individuals ***as individuals***. Locke (*The Treatises on Government*), Rousseau (*The Social Contract*), Jefferson (The Bill of Rights), Paine (*The Rights of Man*), the American and Irish Declarations of Independence, to name some of the main sources, all supported individual human rights over against those of the authoritarian state. But with the Treaty of Versailles and the Covenant of the League of Nations the pendulum began to swing away from a consideration of individual rights as such (though the person came to be regarded as 'sovereign' in international law) onto the (international) consideration and ***protection*** of the rights of 'national minorities,' communities, groups ***as groups*** – in a word, to the self-determination of World War I for minority nationalities. However, the Charter of the United Nations of 1945, the UN's Universal Declaration of Human Rights of 1948, and the OAS's American Convention on Human Rights of 1969, all endeavored to protect (from discrimination) ***both*** individual and minority group rights, though they did not further develop the theory of nationality self-determination. They were more negative, therefore, in their formulation than positive.

This swing away from protection of the rights of individuals in an integrated national society towards concentration on the rights of groups that are not themselves coterminous with governmentally manageable territorial regions of the nation is a swing that relies presently for impetus on the work of individual scholars more so than on that of organizations, though ultimate justification for the work of either arises from a reversion to the Treaties of Versailles. The novelty, too, of the idea of regarding individuals as being 'sovereign' and enjoying benefits in international law is perhaps something that impedes the group-determination idea's progress. But, the notion of catering to the rights of groups as groups and to their being ruled on a nonterritorial basis is really only an instance of history repeating itself. Group rights can be traced back to the Magna Charta of 1215 when the barons were guaranteed rights as barons, and even back to biblical times when the family was guaranteed rights as a group in the Old Testament. In the New Testament the Christian community is regarded a nation. In I Peter 2:9 the Apostle addresses new Christians in these terms: "But you are a chosen race, a royal priesthood, a holy ***nation***, a people set apart." And from time immemorial Indian tribes in the United States have been regarded Indian nations and treatied with as such.

Although the nonterritorial communal self-determination concept is not, then, exactly new, it was only at the time of the Treaties of Versailles and the Anglo-Irish Treaty that the principle made its debut on the international arena as a legal concept. The "Minorities Treaties" (as the latter Treaties of Versailles were called) by coming into being as instruments that affirmed communal self-determination introduced the concept into international law. According to Alfred Zimmern, there was to be an Article in the Covenant of the League of Nations (that became part of the Treaty of Versailles) which would have required "that there should be 'exacted' of all [member states of] the League of Nations a promise of equal treatment 'to all racial or national minorities' within their jurisdiction." This requirement was taken out of the Draft Covenant, explains Zimmern, "and provided for in the individual treaties with the states concerned" (*The League of Nations and the Rule of Law, 1918-1935*, pp. 241-242).

The States Treaties into which this principle was incorporated were, apart from the Treaty of Versailles itself (Articles 86 and 93), the Treaty concluded between the Allied and Associated Powers with Austria, Bulgaria, Hungary and Turkey; the Treaties concluded with Czechoslovakia, Greece, Poland and Romania; the Treaties concluded by Poland with Danzig and, in particular, with Germany (the Treaty of May 15, 1922 concerning Upper Silesia); and, though not formally so, the Treaty concluded by Great Britain with Ireland in 1921. Each of these Minorities Treaties guaranteed the following rights, with the emphasis given here being that of N. A. Maryan Green, from whose work, *International Law*, the listing is reproduced (pp. 114-115).

> (1) life, liberty and free exercise of religion to all *inhabitants* of the territory;
>
> (2) equal treatment before the law and the same civil and political rights to *all nationals*;
>
> (3) the same treatment and security in law and in fact to all linguistic, religious or ethnic *minority groups of nationals*;
>
> (4) the rights of such *minority groups* to establish schools and religious institutions, and to use their own language for publications, at public meetings and before the courts.

All of the Versailles Treaties, and as well the Anglo-Irish Treaty, made history in identifying the self-determination rights of communities and, more importantly, in identifying peoples, communities as the bodies in which those rights inhere. But the Treaty with Ireland went ahead of the European Treaties in affirming those rights for communities that were not exclusively coextensive or coterminous with the regions they inhabited, that is, the areas of habitation overlapped. (The Versailles Treaties accommodated peoples whose regional boundaries ***could*** to a reasonable extent be adjusted in order for the groups' rights to self-determination to be suitably satisfied.) The Versailles and Irish Treaties made history also in that ***international*** protection (European and Commonwealth) for nationality minority rights was for the first time provided. Concludes Maryan Green: "The recognition by states that all human beings regardless of nationality possess rights deserving international recognition and protection marked a revolution in international law."

Although the Treaties of Versailles and the Anglo-Irish Treaty broke ground in recognizing the rights of minorities and peoples as communities, attention continued to be paid in succeeding years to individual civil rights territorially/integrationally but in a manner that contributed to and strengthened the concept of group rights not necessarily territorially/integrationally. Eschel Rhoodie, in his avant-garde, thought-provoking and question-raising study, *Discrimination in the Constitutions of the World*, makes the statement that "group rights are really more important than individual rights when it comes to causing or preventing human conflict and in settling significant political or ideological disputes" (p. 35). In treating (along with his own) the work of Blaustein and Singler, Rhoodie points to the fact of movement away from concentration on individual rights and onto examination of group rights. This is exemplified in the multidimensional documents that have issued of late from the United Nations on minorities, communalism, ethnic groups, religious groups, cultural groups and so forth. Some such documents, formulated chiefly because of the need felt to improve on the overly civil rights/integration oriented Universal Declaration and American Convention (although these, by designating the ***community*** as the entity to which civil ***duties*** are owed, pointed the way), are the International Covenant on Economic, Social and Cultural Rights[1] (1966), the International Covenant on

1 Article 1.1. All peoples have the right of self-determination. By virtue of that right they freely determine their political status and freely pursue their economic, social and cultural development.

Civil and Political Rights (1966), and the Declaration on Friendly Relations (the Principle of Equal Rights and Self-Determination of Peoples)[2] (1970). The shifting of attention to group human rights is also expressed in the Helsinki Accord of 1975[3] and the follow-up Madrid Accord of 1983, agreements that, combined, complement the UN documents particularly for the self-determination of national minorities. (See Appendices 19 and 20, *Supplement.*) The developing concern for group or people's rights found reflection in most of the world's modern Constitutions, particularly those of Nigeria, Ghana and India (which owe so much to Ireland's Constitution[4]) in which the emphasis is strongly on the rights of groups as groups.

However, the rights of groups as groups in these Constitutions, even though inspired by some UN documents, were not exactly put down in a way in which they could be made meaningfully operational. The reason is that, although the concept of groups' rights has been around since "the right of peoples to self-determination" of World War I, the satisfaction of these rights has not been conceptually disconnected from an identification with territorial independence and, leading to this, a generally agreed-on definition of the concept has not yet, in fact, entered the realm of international law. Not even has precise terminology to indicate the subject of those rights been agreed on, although the term 'national minorities' (following the lead given by UNESCO in its Convention against Discrimination in Education) is gaining currency

2 Article 1. By virtue of the principle of equal rights and self-determination of peoples enshrined in the Charter of the United Nations, all peoples have the right freely to determine, without external interference, their political status . . .

3 Principle VIII, Para. 2. By virtue of the principle of equal rights and self-determination of peoples, all peoples [and, as per the Madrid Accord, Principle 11, national minorities] always have the right, in full freedom, to determine, when and as they wish, their internal and external political status, without external interference, and to pursue as they wish their political, economic, social and cultural development.

4 The Irish Constitution of 1937 led the way in the evolution of group or communal rights, according to a recently published sourcebook of human rights. "Group rights protections had their pioneer constitutional manifestation in Ireland in 1937," wrote the editors. "The Irish Constitution recognized the family group as the natural, primary and fundamental unit of society, possessing inalienable and imprescriptive rights, antecedent and superior to all positive law [Article 41]. . . . Principles of human rights social policy, intended for the general guidance of Parliament but not cognizable by the courts, may also be found in Article 45 of this Constitution." (Albert P. Blaustein, Roger S. Clark, and Jay A. Sigler, eds., *Human Rights Sourcebook*, p. 759.) A complete list of international documents on group human rights since the United Nations Charter (1945) is to be found in Appendices 19 and 20, *Supplement*.

(even though a *'people'* is not necessarily a ***minority***). And even the question of what precisely constitutes a minority group has not as yet been satisfactorily settled, although the following descriptors adapted from the UN's "Definition and Classification of Minorities" (1950) have generally been found helpful.[5]

> 1. The group may formerly have constituted an independent State with its own tribal organization.
>
> 2. The group may formerly have been part of a State living broadly within its own territory, which was later segregated from the jurisdiction of the State and annexed to another State.
>
> 3. The group may formerly have been, or may still be, a regional or scattered group which, although bound to the predominant group by certain feelings of solidarity, has not reached even a minimum degree of assimilation into the predominant group.

The problem of defining national minorities and what the rights of those minorities should precisely be, much more, ***how*** those rights should be given constitutional and legal effect – that is, the problem of legislating self-determination – these are matters that are still subject to study. Not even has there been, as Maryan Green points out, any definition of a 'people': "This fact, plus the absence of any body capable of deciding the question with authority, renders the existence of these rights somewhat subject to hazard" (*International Law*, p. 123). But, as Satish Chandra has said in his informative compilation, *Minorities in National and International Laws*, the United Nations "did not wait for an exhaustive and universal definition of the notion of the 'right of peoples to self-

5 It is likely that it was the lack of a definition of national minorities and a knowledge of handling the administration of minority rights that impeded de Valera from moving seriously on the abolition of partition throughout his life. In 1934 he acknowledged to the League of Nations that "the greatest difficulty was to agree upon the problem, 'What is a minority?' " John Bowman tells us. Seeing some years later that the Irish problem "was not the division of territory but the separation of the people," he held that it was one of a group now a majority "fearing to become a minority inside a temperamentally different state," Frank Gallagher recorded. "That was the essence of the persistence of Partition," de Valera said, "and it should be approached from that point of view." (Frank Gallagher Papers, Note December 20, 1939, MS 18375, National Library of Ireland; see also Bowman, pp. 136 and 316, and Warwick McKean, *Equality and Discrimination under International Law*, pp. 44-45, for an account of de Valera's contribution to debates on minorities at the League of Nations.)

determination' before proclaiming the application of the principle" (p. 13). That is one reason, it is hoped, the present work on interfiliation and that of Blaustein and Singler on confiliation, which not only offer a definition of minority rights in specific situations but also, and correlatively, a model for their effectuation in the real world, may prove a watershed for the recognition and settlement of the rights of national minorities in Ireland and throughout the world. And it might be added that, as regards Ireland in particular, this working out in practice of peoples' rights will for her be nothing more than a return to the custom of her own Brehon Laws as these existed in the Ancient Gaelic State.

It ought to be noted here that, with regard to the giving of constitutional expression and effect to national minority rights for Ireland, the Forum for a New Ireland was the first attempt since the Treaty era to give these rights, as such, explicit affirmation and recognition. Taoiseach Garret FitzGerald pointed out this advance when he stated that the central operational conclusion of the Forum Report was encapsulated in the principle identified by the Forum convention, namely, that "the validity of both the Nationalist and Unionist identities in Ireland . . . must be accepted; both of these identities must have equally satisfactory, secure and durable political, administrative and symbolic expression and protection." The 1985 Anglo-Irish Accord would, in conjunction with this Report, and if it were to be judicially interpreted in accordance with the 1922 *de jure* all-Ireland Constitution, be the first constitutional instrument since 1922 that formally reflected and acknowledged the existence of national minority rights in Ireland and that made their being given governmental expression and protection to be incumbent upon the Irish and British Governments.

An Irish Nationalist scholar and author (who must remain unnamed) goes farther still and says that interfiliation even, that is, the actual form that the political, administrative and symbolic expression and protection of the two Irish identities would take in reality, was included in the Irish Forum deliberations: "The idea that Unionists could if they wished retain a personal allegiance to Britain for some time after the creation of a 32-county Ireland was put forward at the New Ireland Forum." – Personal communication. If this is so, then, if we were to invoke (as we do) Section 5.10 of the Forum Report for that purpose,[6] the political Parties to the

6 Section 5.10 of the New Ireland Forum Report states: "The Parties in the Forum also remain open to discuss other views which may contribute to political development."

Forum would be required formally to consider interfiliation and the ***way*** we propose that it might be put into effect in Ireland and between Ireland and Britain.

The marks by which interfiliation might be identified are, *mutatis mutandis*, the same as those of confiliation. The following are the essential marks of the Blaustein-Singler concept of confiliation, which are adapted from a summary given in Rhoodie's comparative study of the 144 most recent of the world's 166 Constitutions.

"Ethnic consciousness and ethnic identification are on the increase throughout the world. So is ethnic-oriented aggressiveness and aggression. And so is the determination to oppose balkanization – to resist the breakup of existing nationalistic sovereignties to meet the demands of ethnicity.

"If ethnic (and multicultural, pluralistic) rights are to be recognized (and protected) within the boundaries of today's internationally recognized state entities, there must be compromise. And it must be in the form of a new type of governmental structure. A ***confiliation*** (or an ***interfiliation***).

"Under a confiliation, each ethnic 'child' (the personal jurisdiction) pursues its own cultural rights, with the 'parent' (the central authority of the state) being responsible for rights common to all. Each ethnic entity, for example, might choose to follow certain religious practices, or speak a particular language, or operate its own schools, or maintain customary courts, etc. The parent would be charged with national security, foreign affairs, etc.

"A confiliation (or interfiliation) is not merely a federation based on a geographic foundation. It is a new constitutional form which recognizes the human dimension of government by preserving the right of groups to be different while remaining part of the common union.

"Other scholars, groping for adequate terms to explain constitutional forms designed to preserve group rights, have added a variety of new words and phrases to law and political science lexicons. Such terms as 'segmented pluralism,' 'consociational democracy' and 'subcultural segmentation' have now been invented. But none of these fully explain either the form or process of recognizing the rights or accommodating the demands of divergent groups within a particular society.

"Ethnic rights are group rights. For the most part they are also minority rights. They are rights based on race, religion, language and culture. And to the people concerned with such rights they are far more pervasive and more important than the rights to a public trial or even freedom of the press, according to Blaustein. They are rights too fundamental (and too precious) to be determined by majority rule. Language and religion cannot be subject to majoritarian determination.

" 'The right of everyone . . . to take part in cultural life' is guaranteed by Article 15 of the International Covenant on Economic, Social and Cultural Rights. . . .

"Belgium is an excellent example of this. . . . Article 3c of its Constitution acknowledges that Belgium comprises three cultural communities. Appendix 1 of the Constitution calls for splitting the members of the Lower House into a French linguistic group and a Dutch linguistic group, each with legislative powers over its own group. Its Constitution also provides for equal representation of the two language groups in the cabinet. . . .

"Article 27 of the International Covenant on Civil and Political Rights emphasizes the importance of ethnic and communal rights. 'In those states in which ethnic, religious or linguistic minorities exist, persons belonging to such minorities shall not be denied the right, in community with the other members of their group, to enjoy their own culture, to profess and practise their own religion, or to use their own language.'

"But to give effect to such a manifesto requires the recognition and establishment of confiliations (or interfiliations).

"According to Blaustein, one can apply the confiliation concept to the rights of Palestinian Arabs in Israel, to the rights of Jews in the Egyptian Sinai, to the white minority in Zimbabwe, to South African blacks both in and out of the so-called Homelands, to French-speaking Canadians who do not live in Quebec, to the Kurds in Iraq, to the Asian Indians in Guyana and Fiji, to the ethnic Chinese in Thailand and Vietnam, to all the diverse peoples of Indonesia, to Moslems in the two-dozen countries where they constitute a substantial minority, to Jews, Armenians, Estonians, Latvians, Lithuanians, etc., etc., in the Soviet Union, to Gypsies in various countries, and to the rights of every other communal minority every place.

"This type of institutional arrangement, of course, is not applicable in the separate homogeneous society. Nor does it serve the melting pot or integrationist state. It is applicable to multiethnic plural states, particularly those which can no longer be geographically divided on the basis of group rights, e.g. South Africa, Zimbabwe, Namibia, Israel (and Ireland). It is an institutional arrangement consistent with and in the spirit of Article 27 of the International Covenant.

"Those who would argue against Blaustein's confiliation concept might find words of criticism phrased in terms of neocolonialism, extraterritoriality, or settlers' rights. This would be unfair. Consistent with the principles of individual rights and consistent with a sense of international morality, the confiliation plan is designed to afford maximum accommodation between or among the various groups comprising any type of plural society."

Blaustein himself adds: "Group rights is legal-constitutional terminology for the new ethnicity of which the world has become increasingly conscious. Where there was once a universal plea to treat each individual alike, ***regardless*** of sex, race, religion, language and culture, there now exist constitutional mandates to treat groups of people in special ways – precisely ***because*** of their sex, race, religion, language and culture.

"Studying the legal-constitutional response to the new nationalism – the manifestation of the new ethnicity – is essential in understanding the evolution of modern human rights. For there is an inherent conflict between individual human rights and the rights demanded by, for and on the basis of special groups. The era ahead will become increasingly concerned with this problem, and our responses will dictate the scope of human rights in our future."

The fact that there is "an inherent conflict between individual human rights and the rights demanded by, for and on the basis of special groups" may be an eye-opener to the reason Northern Ireland Unionists never accepted Irish unity that had offers of bills of rights and other guarantees of individual rights attached ever since 1914 and beyond. Because guarantees of individual rights, in whatever form, are designed to facilitate acceptance of the integrationist state, traditional Northern leeriness of them can begin to be understood. Guarantees of group rights, on the contrary, have no such integrationist designs, but are devised to create a state of an entirely different character. Such a state would preserve the component groups as separate – but equal – entities, which is what the groups in the Irish case have always wanted to be. What is now required, therefore, is a complete rethinking of Ireland's standard response to the longstanding national demands, a rethinking that perhaps will lead to a restructuring of Government and society accommodative of native and domestic groups' rights. That, we would argue, is in the Irish binational context the interfiliation model. That is the Irish Constitutional Mandate.

POSTSCRIPT

On March 1, 1990, in the case *McGimpsey and McGimpsey* v. *Ireland and Others*, the Irish Supreme Court rendered a rather avant-garde and brave interpretation of the enigmatic Articles 2 and 3 of the 1937 Irish Constitution — and in the process subjected the 1985 Anglo-Irish Agreement to a form of legal reformation that rendered it in Article 1 merely recognizable of the *de facto* position of Northern Ireland. In this the Court agreed with the decision of the High Court of 1988 in the same case ([1989] ILRM, 209).

In its interpretation of the Constitution Articles the Court raised the Articles out of the *reductio ad absurdum* to which traditional interpretations stressing their *de facto* character had lowered them. At the same time, however, the Court failed to extricate these Articles from the *circulus inextricabilis* in which interpretations emphasizing their *de jure* nature have trapped them. Whereas formerly a political aspiration to national reintegration was held to exist in the Articles in the face of a factually lawful recognition of Northern Ireland, now a legal and *de jure* claim to Northern jurisdiction is seen to exist in them which is at the same time prohibited by them from being exercised while national reintegration is pending. The Articles in effect prohibit a reintegration of the national territory for as long as reintegration of the national territory is pending! And this, from the British view, would be for as long as the Northern Unionists so wish it.

Still, the Court stated that reintegration of the national territory is a constitutional imperative. But if Articles 2 and 3 have no real power in them to make good the *de jure* claim they contain, that is, if they are powerless to force a termination of the British (***not the Irish***) suspension of Irish jurisdiction over Northern Ireland, a suspension that has to be recognized for as long as a majority in Northern Ireland does not consent to its termination, then it is difficult to see how the imperative to reintegrate the national territory under the Constitution of the Republic could ever be fulfilled.

This conclusion from the Supreme Court's interpretation would be in keeping with traditional views that Articles 2 and 3 contained no *de jure* claim to the North at all. (One exception to these views was that rendered as far back as 1947, in the maverick case *The People* v. *Ruttledge* ([1978] IR, 376), which held that Articles 2 and 3 contained the claim that "the whole of Ireland is included in the national territory of the State" and to which the Court in the 1990 case arched back in its argumentation.) But now that it has been judicially stated that the Articles do contain a *de jure* claim, and that reintegration of the national territory is accordingly a constitutional imperative, it has to be concluded that it is only under a Constitution already binding on Northern Ireland that a breakout could be made and the constitutional imperative fulfilled. Such a Constitution is the Saorstat Eireann Constitution of 1922. Restoration of that all-Ireland Constitution as an instrument to free the present Constitution's entrapment and to serve its legal claim to unity is the real Irish constitutional imperative.

LITERATURE CITED AND CONSULTED

You need not expect the Kingdom of God
to appear in a highly visible manner.
Neither need anybody say,
'lo, it is here,' or, 'lo, it is there.'
For the Kingdom of the Father
Is spread throughout the earth,
And no man recognizes it.

THOMAS

There must be a beginning
of any great matter,
but the continuing unto the end
until it be thoroughly finished
yields the true glory.

SIR FRANCIS DRAKE

LITERATURE CITED AND CONSULTED

Those items marked with an asterisk contain comprehensive bibliographies pertinent to our thesis. Of particular usefulness are John Darby's **Conflict in Northern Ireland** *(1976), which lists and evaluates much of the vast and fast-growing mass of literature on the British-Irish constitutional problem, and his* **"Logistics of Enquiry: A Guide for Researchers"** *(1983). Also very useful to the constitutionalist are the listings in J. L. McCracken's* **Representative Government in Ireland** *(1958, 1977) and Alfred Gaston Donaldson's* **Some Comparative Aspects of Irish Law** *(1957). The most recent American or Commonwealth edition, in either cloth or paperback, is the edition that is cited for most of the titles here, since very often it is this edition that will be most readily accessible to the reader.*

Adams, Gerry. *The Politics of Irish Freedom.* Brandon Book Publishers, Dingle, Ireland and Wolfeboro, N.H., 1986.

Agreement between the Government of Ireland and the Government of the United Kingdom. *Anglo-Irish Agreement 1985,* The Stationery Office, Dublin, 1985; Cmnd. 9657; *The Times* (London), November 18, 1985; *Ireland Today,* November 1985, special edition, Department of Foreign Affairs, Dublin. See also *Anglo-Irish Studies;* Articles of Agreement; Gerken, Karl Heim, *The Anglo-Irish Agreement of 1985;* O'Connor, John F., "L'accord Anglo-Irlandais de 1985".

Agreements between the Government of the United Kingdom and the Government of Eire Signed at London on 25 April 1938. Cmd. 5728; H.C. XXX (1937-38), 1003; *British and Foreign State Papers,* Vol. 142 (1938), pp. 14-30; also in Appendix 12, *Supplement* (1st Agreement).

See also Articles of Agreement; Goldberg, Donald M., *The Anglo-Irish Agreements.*

Akinson, D. H., and J. F. Fallin. "The Irish Civil War and the Drafting of the Free State Constitution", Parts I, II and III, *Eire-Ireland* (St. Paul, Minn.), Vol. V, Nos. 1, 2 and 4 (Spring, Summer and Winter, 1970), pp. 10-26, 42-93 and 28-70 respectively. *See also* Constitution of the Free State of Ireland; Draft Constitution of the Irish Free State; O'Rahilly, Alfred.

Anglo-Irish Studies. Department of Foreign Affairs, Dublin, 1981. *See also* Agreement between the Government of Ireland and the Government of the United Kingdom; Articles of Agreement; Joint Communique; New Ireland Forum.

Annual Register (Longmans, London), Vols. CLXIII-CLXV, 1921-1923.

Anson, Sir William R. *The Law and Custom of the Constitution.* Vol. II. *The Crown.* Part I and Part II. Fourth edition, by A. Berriedale Keith. Clarendon Press, Oxford, 1935.

Appeal Cases. *The Law Reports.* Incorporated Council of Law Reporting, London, 1935. See also *The Irish Reports.*

Articles of Agreement for a Treaty between Great Britain and Ireland, 1921. Cmd. 1560. H. M. Stationery Office, London, [1941?]; also in Appendix 6, *Supplement. See also* Agreement between the Government of Ireland and the Government of the United Kingdom; Agreements between the Government of the United Kingdom and the Government of Eire; Cabinet Papers; Cabinet Registered Files; Constitution of the Free State of Ireland; Curtis, Edmund, and R. B. McDowell, eds., *Irish Historical Documents;* Dail Eireann, *Debate on the Treaty;* Financial Agreements; *Halsbury's; Index; Irish Boundary;* Records of Anglo-Irish Negotiations; Records of the Treaty Negotiations; Report of the Irish Boundary Commission; Statute of Westminister; Treaty; Treaty (Confirmation of Supplemental Agreement) Act; Treaty (Confirmation of Amending Agreement) Act.

Ayearst, Morley. *The Republic of Ireland. Its Government and Politics.* New York University Press, New York, 1970; University of London Press, Ltd., London, 1970.

Banba (Dublin), 1921-1922.

Beckett, J. C. *The Making of Modern Ireland, 1603-1923.* Faber and Faber, London, 1966; Alfred A. Knopf, Inc., New York, 1966; pbck. ed., Faber and Faber, London, 1969.

A Short History of Ireland. 3rd ed., Hutchinson's University Library, New York, 1966; 6th, revd. hrdbck. and pbck. eds., Hutchinson, London, 1979.

The Ulster Debate. The Bodley Head, London, 1972.

The Anglo-Irish Tradition. Cornell University Press, Ithaca, New York, 1977.

Belfast Telegraph (Belfast), 1919-1922.

Bell, J. Bowyer. *See* Bowyer Bell, J.

Bertelsen, Judy S., ed. *Nonstate Nations in International Politics. Compartive System Analyses.* Praeger Publishers, New York, Washington, London, 1977. *See also* Cobban, Alfred; Henkin, Louis; Macartney, C. A.; Maryan Green, N. A.; Prager, Jeffrey; Pringle, D. G.; Rigo Sureda, A.; and Rhoodie, Eschel.

Bettey, J. H., ed. *English Historical Documents, 1906-1939. A Selection.* Routledge & Kegan Paul, London, 1967.

Blaustein, Albert P., and Gisbert H. Flanz, eds. *Constitutions of the Countries of the World.* 19 vols. (Vol. XVII: *United Kingdom*, by Michael Curtis.) Oceana Publications, Dobbs Ferry, N.Y., 1971-1986.

Blaustein, Albert P., and Eric B. Blaustein, eds. *Constitutions of Dependencies and Special Sovereignties.* 6 vols. (Vol. IV: *Northern Ireland,* by Leslie Phillips.) Oceana Publications, Dobbs Ferry, N.Y., 1975-1986.

Blaustein, Albert P., Roger S. Clark and Jay A. Sigler. *Human Rights Sourcebook.* Paragon House Publishers, New York, 1987.

See also Rhoodie, Eschel, *Discrimination in the Constitutions of the World.*

Boland, Kevin. *The Rise and Decline of Fianna Fail.* The Mercier Press, Dublin and Cork, 1982.

Bolton, G. C. *The Passing of the Irish Act of Union. A Study in Parliamentary Politics.* Oxford University Press, London, 1966.

Bonar Law Papers, 103, 107, Correspondence, 1920-21. Beaverbrook Library, London; House of Lords Record Office, London.

Boundary Commission. *See* Report of the Irish Boundary Commission, 1925; *see also* North-Eastern Boundary Bureau; *Irish Boundary;* Wambaugh, Sarah.

*Bowman, John. *De Valera and the Ulster Question, 1917-1973.* Clarendon Press, Oxford, 1982, 1983, 1984.

Bowyer Bell, J. *The Secret Army. A History of the IRA, 1916-1970.* A. Blond, London, 1970; Sphere Books, London, 1972; idem, *1916-1974,* MIT Press, Cambridge, Mass., 1974; idem, *1916-1979,* Academy Press, Dublin, 1979.

Boyle, Kevin, and Tom Hadden. *Ireland. A Positive Proposal.* Penguin Books, Harmondsworth, Mdlsx., Eng., 1985.

Braden, W. H. *The Irish Free State.* Chicago Daily News, Chicago, 1925.

Breen, Dan. *My Fight for Irish Freedom.* The Talbot Press, Dublin, 1924; 1st, revd. pbck. ed., Anvil Books, Tralee, 1964; 3rd pbck. ed., Anvil Books, Dublin and Tralee, 1981; 3rd hrdbck. ed., Anvil Books, Dublin, 1983.

British *Parliamentary Debates. See* United Kingdom *Parliamentary Debates.*

Bromage, A.W. "Constitutional Development in Saorstat Eireann and the Constitution of Eire", *American Political Science Review,* Vol. XXXI (1937), pp. 842-861 and 1050-1070.

Bromage, Mary C. *De Valera and the March of a Nation.* Hutchinson, London, 1956; pbck. ed., 1967.

Churchill and Ireland. University of Notre Dame Press, Notre Dame, Ind., 1964.

Buchheit, Lee C. *Secession. The Legitimacy of Self-Determination.* Yale University Press, New Haven and London, 1978. *See also* Cobban, Alfred.

*Buckland, Patrick. *A History of Northern Ireland.* Holmes & Meier Publishers, Inc., New York, 1981.

*Buergenthal, Thomas. *International Human Rights in a Nutshell.* West Publishing Co., St. Paul, Minn., 1988. *See also* Helsinki Accord; Sohn, Louis B., and Thomas Buergenthal.

Bunreacht na hEireann (Constitution of Ireland), 1937. Government Publications Sale Office, Dublin, 1937. *See also* Casey, James; Chubb, Basil; Delany, V. T. H.; Doolan, Brian; Finlay, Thomas A.; Forde, Michael; Grogan, Vincent; Hearn, John J.; *Irish Jurist*; Kelly, J. M.; Kennedy, Brian P.; and Morgan, David Gwynn.

Burt, Alfred LeRoy. *The Evolution of the British Empire and Commonwealth. From the American Revolution.* D. C. Heath and Company, Boston, 1956.

Busteed, M. A. *Northern Ireland.* Problem Regions of Europe Series. Oxford University Press, London, 1974.

Cabinet Committee on Ireland, 1919-22. Cab. 23. Cabinet Office Records, Public Record Office, London.

Cabinet Papers, 1921-22. Cab. 24. Cabinet Office Records, Public Record Office, London. *See also* Records.

Cabinet Registered Files, 1921-22. Cab. 21. Cabinet Office Records, Public Record Office, London. *See also* Records.

Calvert, Harry. *Constitutional Law in Northern Ireland. A Study in Regional Government.* Stevens & Sons Ltd., London and Belfast, and Northern Ireland Legal Quarterly, Inc., 1968.

The Canadian Constitution 1981 [1982]. Publications Canada, Ottawa, Ont., 1982.

Capotorti, Francesco. *Study on the Rights of Persons Belonging to Ethnic, Religious and Linguistic Minorities.* UN Doc. E/CN.4 Sub. 2/384 (Revd. 1/1979); UN Pub. E.78.XIV.1. *See also* Henkin, Louis.

Carr, Edward Hallett. "The Crisis of Self-Determination", *Conditions of Peace,* The Macmillan Company, New York, 1944, pp. 39-69.

*Carroll, F. M. *American Opinion and the Irish Question, 1910-23. A Study in Opinion and Policy.* Gill and Macmillan, Dublin, 1978; St. Martin's Press, New York, 1978.

Carty, James. *Ireland, a Documentary Record.* 3 vols. C. J. Fallon, Dublin, 1949-1951.

Bibliography of Irish History, 1911-1921. Dublin, 1936.

Casey, James. *Constitutional Law in Ireland.* Sweet & Maxwell, London, 1987.

Cassese, Antonio. "The Self-Determination of Peoples", Louis Henkin, ed., *The International Bill of Rights* (q.v.), pp. 92-113.

"The Helsinki Declaration and Self-Determination", Thomas Buergenthal, ed. and Judith R. Hall, asst., *Human Rights, International Law and the Helsinki Accord,* Allanheld, Osmun/Universe Books, Montclair, N.J. and New York, 1977, pp. 83-110.

Cassidy, Janet. "An Interview with Sean MacBride", *Sign* (Union City, N.J.), November 1981, pp. 15-18.

Caulfield, Max. *The Easter Rebellion.* London, 1964; pbck. ed., London, 1965.

Austen Chamberlain Papers, AC 5-6, 30-31, Correspondence, 1921-22. University of Birmingham Library, England.

*Chandra, Dr. Satish, ed. *Minorities in National and International Laws.* Deep & Deep Publications, New Delhi, [1986]. *See also* Bertelsen, Judy S.

Chubb, Basil. *The Government and Politics of Ireland.* Stanford University Press, Stanford, Calif., 1970; Oxford University Press, London, 1970; 2nd ed., Stanford University Press, Stanford, Calif., 1982; Longman, London and New York, 1982.

Churchill, Winston S. *The Aftermath,* new ed. *The World Crisis, 1911-18.* 2 vols. Signet Classics Books, London, 1968; New American Library, New York, 1968.

Cobban, Alfred. *The Nation State and National Self-Determination.* 2nd ed. Collins, London and Crowell, New York, 1969. *See also* Bertelsen, Judy S.; Henkin, Louis; Lillich, Richard B.; Ofuatey-Kodjoe, A.; and Pomerance, Michla.

Collins, Michael. *The Path to Freedom.* Talbot Press, Dublin, 1922; 2nd pr., The Mercier Press, Cork, 1968; Dublin, 1982.

Arguments for the Treaty. Lester, Dublin, 1922.

Collins Assorted Papers, MS 5845. National Library of Ireland, Dublin.

Collins Assorted Papers. Liam Collins, Clonakilty, County Cork.

Collins, Tom. *The Centre Cannot Hold. Britain's Failure in Northern Ireland.* Bookworks Ireland, Dublin and Belfast, 1983.

Colonial Office Records. Public Record Office, London.

Colum, Padraic. *Ourselves Alone. The Story of Arthur Griffith and the Origin of the Irish Free State.* Crown Publishers Inc., New York, 1959.

Comerford, Maire. *The First Dail.* Dublin, 1971. *See also* Dail Eireann; "History of the Dail"; "Meeting of the First Dail".

Committee of Imperial Defence, Sub-committee on Ireland, 1922. Cab. 16/42. Cabinet Office Records, Public Record Office, London.

Conclusions of Cabinet Meetings, 1919-22. Cab. 23. *See* Cabinet Committee on Ireland.

Connolly, Robert Emmet. *Armalite and Ballot Box. An Irish-American Republican Primer.* Cuchullain Publications, Forth Wayne, Ind., 1985.

Constitution of the Free State of Ireland (Saorstat Eireann) [the Constituent Act]. The Stationery Office, Dublin, 1922, 1982; also in Appendix 8, *Supplement. See also* Akinson, D. H., and J. F. Fallin, "The Irish Civil War and the Drafting of the Irish Free State Constitution"; Articles of Agreement; Cabinet Papers; Cabinet Registered Files; Constitution of the Irish Free State (Saorstat Eireann) Act, 1922; Curran, Joseph M., *The Birth of the Irish Free State;* Curtis, Edmund, and R. B. McDowell, eds., *Irish Historical Documents;* Dail Eireann, *Dail Debates;* Draft Constitution of the Irish Free State; Farrell, Brian, "The Drafting of the Irish Free State Constitution"; Figgis, Darrell, *The Irish Constitution Explained; Halsbury's Statutes; Index;* Irish Free State Constitution Act; *The Irish Jurist,* "Twenty-five Years . . ."; Kohn, Leo, *The Constitution of the Irish Free State;* Lyons, F. S. L., *Ireland Since the Famine;* O'Brian, Barra, *The Irish Constitution;* Provisional Government, *Select Constitutions of the World; Public General Acts;* Records of Anglo-Irish Negotiations; Statute of Westminister; *Statutes in Force;* Swift MacNeill, J. G., *Studies in the Constitution of the Irish Free State.*

Constitution of the Irish Free State (Saorstat Eireann) Act, 1922 embodying the Constitution as amended by subsequent enactments. Edited in the Office of the Clerk of the Dail. Presented to Dail Eireann by the Ceann Comhairle. (P No. 2538; PP 44/1.) Government Publications Sale Office, Dublin, 1936. *See also* Constitution of the Free State of Ireland (Saorstat Eireann).

Constitution of Ireland. *See* Bunreacht na hEireann.

The Constitution of Northern Ireland: Being the Government of Ireland Act, 1920, as amended to 31 December 1968. H. M. Stationery Office, Belfast, 1968. *See also* Government of Ireland Act, 1920.

*Coogan, Tim Pat. *Ireland Since the Rising.* Pall Mall Press Ltd., London, 1966; Praeger Publishers, Inc., New York, 1966; repr., Greenwood Press, Westport, Conn., 1976.

The I.R.A. Pall Mall Press Ltd., London, 1970; Praeger Publishers, Inc., New York, 1970; 10th imp., Fontana Paperbacks, London, 1987.

Corish, Brendan. *The New Republic.* Abbey Printing Service, Dublin, 1969.

Cork Examiner (Cork), 1919 - Present.

Correspondence relating to Article 12 of the Treaty. See *Irish Free State; Irish Free State and Northern Ireland* (bis).

Costello, John A. "Ireland in International Affairs", *The Canadian Bar Review,* Vol. XXVI (1948), pp. 1195-1211. *See also* Mulvey, Helen F.

Costigan, Giovanni. *A History of Modern Ireland. With a Sketch of Earlier Times.* Pegasus, New York, 1969; pbck. ed., Macmillan, New York, 1970.

Coughlan, Anthony. *Fooled Again. The Anglo-Irish Agreement and After.* The Mercier Press Ltd., Cork and Dublin, 1986. *See also* O'Connor, John F.

Creed, George. *Ireland's Fight for Freedom.* Dublin, 1919.

Crighton, Elizabeth. *Political Leadership in Northern Ireland* (in preparation).

Cronin, Sean. *Ireland Since the Treaty. Fifty Years After.* Irish Freedom Press, Dublin, 1971.

The McGarrity Papers. Revelations of the Irish Revolutionary in Ireland and America, 1900-40. 1st pbck. ed., Anvil Books, Tralee, 1972.

Irish Nationalism. A History of Its Roots and Ideology. Continuum, New York, 1981.

Cross, Colin. *The Fall of the British Empire, 1918-1968.* Coward-McCann, Inc., New York, 1969.

Cullop, Floyd G. *The Constitution of the United States. An Introduction.* A Signet Book. New American Library, New York, 1969.

*Curran, Joseph M. *The Birth of the Irish Free State, 1921-1923.* University of Alabama Press, University, Ala., 1980. *See also* O'Brien, William, "The Irish Free State . . ."; Treaty.

Currey, C. H. *The British Commonwealth Since 1815.* Vol. I. *The United Kingdom, the Countries of the Commonwealth, and the Republic of Ireland.* Angus and Robertson, Sydney and London, 1950; Anglobooks, London, New York and Toronto, 1952.

Curtis, Edmund, and R. B. McDowell, eds. *Irish Historical Documents, 1172-1922.* 3rd ed. Methuen & Co., Ltd., London, 1977; Methuen, Inc., New York, 1977.

Curtis, Edmund. *A History of Ireland.* 6th ed., London, 1950; pbck. ed., Methuen, London, 1961; repr. 1968; University pbck. ed., Methuen, Inc., New York, 1961; repr. 1978.

Curtis, Michael. *See* Blaustein, Albert P., and Gisbert H. Flanz, eds.

Dail Eireann Cabinet Minutes. State Paper Office, Dublin.

Dail Eireann Files. R Series and S Series. State Paper Office, Dublin.

Dail Eireann Papers D.E. 2/471. State Paper Office, Dublin. *See also* Records.

Dail Eireann. Papers relating to the First Dail Eireann. P. O'Keeffe (private possession).

Miontuairisc an Chead Dala, 1919-1921. Minutes of Proceedings of the First Parliament of the Republic of Ireland, 1919-1921. Official Record. The Stationery Office, Dublin, 1922.

Private Sessions of [the] Second Dail, 1921-1922 (August - September 1921 and December 1921 - January 1922). The Stationery Office, Dublin, 1922.

Iris Dhail Eireann. Diosboireacht ar an gConnradh idir Eire agus Sasana do signigheadh i Lundain ar an 6adh la de mhi na Nodlag 1921. Debate on the Treaty Between Great Britain and Ireland Signed in London on 6 December 1921 (December 1921 - January 1922). Tuairisg Oifigiuil. Official Report. [*Treaty Debate.*] The Stationery Office, Dublin, 1922.

[*Dail Debates*] *For the Periods 16-26 August 1921 and 28 February to 8 June 1922.* Tuairisg Oifigiuil. Official Report. The Stationery Office, Dublin, 1922.

Returns Made Annually for the Years 1923-38 of Private Bills, Questions in the Dail, Sittings of Dail Eireann, Committees, Closure of Debate, and Public Bills in the Dail. The Stationery Office, Dublin, 1923-38.

Diosboireachtai Parlaiminte (Parliamentary Debates.) Tuairisc Oifigiuil (Official Report). [*Dail Debates.*] Vols. I - (September 1922 - Present). The Stationery Office, Dublin, 1922 - Present.

See also Northern Ireland; Seanad Eireann; United Kingdom.

Daily Bulletin, 1922 (typewritten sheets). Gavan Duffy Papers (q.v.).

Dale, Sir William. *The Modern Commonwealth.* Butterworths, London, 1983.

Dangerfield, George. *The Damnable Question. A Study in Anglo-Irish Relations.* Atlantic Monthly Press, Little, Brown and Company, Boston, 1976; Constable & Co., Ltd., London, 1977; pbck. ed., Little, Brown and Company, Boston, 1976; Quartet Books, Ltd., London, 1979.

*Darby, John. *Conflict in Northern Ireland: The Development of a Polarised Community.* Gill and Macmillan, Dublin, 1976; Barnes & Noble Books, New York, 1976.

"The Historical Background", John Darby, ed., *Northern Ireland. The Background to the Conflict* (q.v.), pp. 13-31.

*"The Logistics of Enquiry: A Guide for Researchers", John Darby, ed., *Northern Ireland. The Background to the Conflict* (q.v.), pp. 225-243.

*ed. *Northern Ireland. The Background to the Conflict.* Appletree Press, Belfast, 1983; Syracuse University Press, Syracuse, N.Y., 1983.

David, Arie E. *The Strategy of Treaty Termination. Lawful Breaches and Retaliations.* Yale University Press, New Haven, Conn., and London, 1975.

Davis, Richard. *Arthur Griffith and Non-Violent Sinn Fein.* Anvil Books, Dublin, 1974.

Deasy, Liam. *Towards Ireland Free.* The Mercier Press, Cork, 1973.

De Burca, Padraig. *Free State or Republic? Pen Pictures of the Historic Treaty Session of Dail Eireann.* The Talbot Press Limited, Dublin, 1922; T. Fisher Unwin Limited, London, 1922.

"Declaration by the Commonwealth Prime Ministers at the London Conference, 27 April 1949", compd. by Frederick Madden, *Imperial Constitutional Documents, 1765-1952: A Supplement,* p. 54. Basil Blackwell, Oxford, Eng., 1953. (Supplement to Arthur Berriedale Keith, ed., *Speeches and Documents on the British Dominions, 1918-1931.)*

"The Declaration of Commonwealth Principles", Appendix C., A. J. R. Groom and Paul Taylor, eds., *The Commonwealth in the 1980's* (q.v.), pp. 346-347.

Delany, V. T. H. "The Constitution of Ireland: Its Origins and Development", *University of Toronto Law Journal,* Vol. XII, No. 1 (1957), pp. 1-26.

Democratic Unionist Party. *Ulster - The Future Answered.* Belfast, 1984. *Task Force Report.* Belfast, 1987. See also *The Way Forward.*

De Paor, Liam. *Divided Ulster.* Penguin Books, Harmondsworth, Mdlsx., 1970.

*Deutsch, R. R. *Northern Ireland 1921-1974: A Select Bibliography.* Garland Publishing, Inc., New York, 1975.

De Valera, Eamon. Letter of September 7, 1922, No. 13, *Correspondence of Mr. Eamon de Valera and Others.* Dail Eireann, P.P. [Parliamentary Papers], 1. The Stationery Office, Dublin, 1922.

The Alternative to 'The Treaty': 'Document No. 2'. Dublin, 1923.

"Preface", Dorothy Macardle, *The Irish Republic* (q.v.), pp. 19-21.

Peace and War: Speeches by Mr. de Valera on International Affairs. Dublin, 1944. *See also* Moynihan, Maurice, ed., *Speeches and Statements.*

Ireland's Stand. M. H. Gill & Son, Dublin, 1946.

Eamon de Valera Papers. Franciscan Institute of Celtic Studies and Historical Research, Dublin.

Devlin, Bernadette. *The Price of My Soul.* A. Deutsch, London, 1969; Vintage Books, New York, 1969.

Dicey, A.V. *Introduction to the Study of the Law of the Constitution.* Ed. by E. C. S. Wade. 10th ed., St. Martin's Press, New York, 1959; Macmillan, London, 1974. *See also* Wade, E. C. S., "Introduction".

The Digest. Annotated British, Commonwealth and European Cases. (Formerly the English and Empire Digest). Butterworths, London, etc., 1919 – Present.

Documents on British Foreign Policy, 1919-1939. First Series. Vol. XIV. London, 1966.

Documents Relative to the Sinn Fein Movement. Cmd. 1108. H.C., XXIX (1921), 429.

*Donaldson, Alfred Gaston. *Some Comparative Aspects of Irish Law.* Duke University Press, Durham, N.C., and Cambridge University Press, London, 1957.

"The Constitution of Northern Ireland: Its Origins and Development", *University of Toronto Law Journal,* Vol. XI (1955-56), pp. 1-42.

Doolan, Brian. *Constitutional Law and Constitutional Rights in Ireland.* Gill and Macmillan, Dublin, 1984.

Draft Constitution of the Irish Free State [the British-revised version]. The Stationery Office, Dublin, 1922; also in Darrell Figgis, *The Irish*

Constitution Explained (q.v.), and in Appendix 8, *Supplement*. *See also* Constitution of the Free State of Ireland.

Draft Standing Orders of the First Dail. Gavan Duffy Papers (q.v.).

Dudley Edwards, R. *A New History of Ireland.* Gill and Macmillan, Ltd., Dublin, 1972; University of Toronto Press, Toronto and Buffalo, 1972.

Duff, Charles. *Six Days To Shake an Empire.* A. S. Barnes and Company., Inc., South Brunswick, N.J. and New York, 1966.

Duffy, George Gavan. *See* Gavan Duffy, George.

Durant, Will and Ariel. *The Lessons of History.* Simon and Schuster, New York, 1968.

Dwyer, T. Ryle. *Michael Collins and the Treaty. His Differences with de Valera.* The Mercier Press, Dublin and Cork, 1981; 2nd imp., 1982.

Irish Neutrality and the U.S.A., 1939-1947. Rowman, Totowa, N.J., 1977.

De Valera's Darkest Hour, 1919-1932. Mercier Press, Cork, 1982.

De Valera's Finest Hour, 1932-1952. Mercier Press, Cork, 1982.

Charlie. The Political Biography of Charles J. Haughey. Gill and Macmillan, Dublin, [1987].

*Eager, A. R. *A Guide to Irish Bibliographical Material.* Library Association, London, 1980.

Eire (Dublin), 1923.

Eire-Ireland (St. Paul, Minn.), Vol. 1 - , 1966 - Present.

Eire Nua. The Social and Economic Programme of Sinn Fein. Sinn Fein, Dublin, 1971.

Elliott, Sydney. *Northern Ireland Parliamentary Election Results, 1921-72.* Political Reference Publications, Chichester, West Sussex, 1973.

Fallin, J. F. *See* Akinson, D. H.

Farrell, Brian. "The Drafting of the Irish Free State Constitution: I, II, III and IV", *The Irish Jurist* (Dublin), Vol. V n.s. Part 1 (Summer, 1970), pp. 115-140; Vol. V n.s. Part 2 (Winter, 1970), pp. 343-356; Vol. VI n.s. Part 1 (Summer, 1971), pp. 111-135; Vol. VI n.s. Part 2 (Winter, 1971), pp. 345-359. *See also* Constitution of the Free State of Ireland; Draft Constitution of the Irish Free State.

The Founding of Dail Eireann. Parliament and Nation Building. Studies in Irish Political Culture, 2. Gill and Macmillan, Dublin, 1971.

The Irish Parliamentary Tradition. Dublin, 1973.

Farrell, Michael. *Northern Ireland. The Orange State.* Pluto Press, London, 1973 and 1976.

Fennell, Desmond. *The State of the Nation. Ireland Since the Sixties.* Ward River Press, Dublin, 1983, 1984.

Figgis, Darrell. *The Irish Constitution Explained.* Mellifont Press, Dublin, [1922]. *See also* Constitution of the Free State of Ireland; Draft Constitution of the Irish Free State.

Recollections of the Irish War. Doubleday, Doran & Company, Inc., Garden City, N.Y. [1927?].

Financial Agreements between the British Government and the Irish Free State Government, 17 February 1923. Cmd. 4061. H.C., XIV (1931-32), 239. *See also* Articles of Agreement.

Finlay, Thomas A. *The Constitution Fifty Years On.* Round Hall Press, Dublin, 1988.

FitzGerald, Garret. *Towards a New Ireland.* Charles Knight & Co. Ltd., London, 1972; 2nd ed., Gill & Macmillan, Dublin, 1973.

"Irish Identities", Richard Dimbleby Lecture, BBC, May 20, 1982 (*The Irish Times,* May 21, 1982).

Flackes, W. D. *Northern Ireland: A Political Directory, 1968-79.* Gill and Macmillan, Dublin, 1980; St. Martin's Press, New York, 1980.

Ford, P. and G. *A Select List of Reports of Inquiries of the Irish Dail and Senate, 1922-72.* Irish University Press, Dublin, 1974.

Forde, Michael. *Constitutional Law of Ireland.* Mercier Press, Cork and Dublin, 1987.

Forester, Margery. *Michael Collins. The Lost Leader.* Sidgwick & Jackson, London, 1971; 2nd ed., Sphere Books, London, 1972.

Freeman's Journal (Dublin), 1919-1924.

Friedrich, Carl J. *Trends of Federalism in Theory and Practice.* Praeger Publishers, New York, 1968.

Gallagher, Frank. *The Indivisible Island. The History of the Partition of Ireland.* Victor Gollancz, London, 1957; repr., Greenwood Press, Westport, Conn., 1974.

The Anglo-Irish Treaty. Ed. with an Intro. by Thomas P. O'Neill. Hutchinson, London, 1965.

Frank Gallagher Papers. National Library of Ireland, Dublin.

See also Hogan, David (pseud.).

Gallagher, Michael. "The Pact General Election of 1922", *Irish Historical Studies* (Dublin), Vol. XXI, No. 84 (Sept. 1979), pp. 404-421.

Garnier, Charles-M. *Eire: Histoire d'Irlande.* Aubier, Editions Montaigne, Paris; *A Popular History of Ireland,* transd. and adptd. by Hedley McCay. The Mercier Press, Cork, 1961.

Garvin, Tom. *The Evolution of Irish Nationalist Politics.* Gill and Macmillan, Dublin, 1981. *See also* Prager, Jeffrey, *Building Democracy in Ireland;* Pringle, D. G., *One Island, Two Nations?*

Gavan Duffy, George, and A. O'Connor, eds. *A Register of Administrative Law in Saorstat Eireann, Including the Statutory Rules and Orders from 6 December 1921 to 31 December 1933.* Dublin, 1935.

Gavan Duffy, George. *A Calendar of the Statute Roll for 21 Years Now in Force [from December 6, 1922 to January 1, 1944].* At the Sign of the Three Candles, Ltd., Dublin, 1944.

Article on the Constitution of the Free State of Ireland. *L'annuaire de legislation comparee.* Volume for 1922. Societe de Legislation Comparee, Paris.

George Gavan Duffy Papers. National Library of Ireland, Dublin.

Gerken, Karl Heim. *The Anglo-Irish Agreement of 1985.* Ph.D. thesis. University of Frankfurt, [1988].

Goldberg, Donald M. *The Anglo-Irish Agreements of 1938.* M.A. thesis. University of California, Los Angeles, June 1949. *See also* Agreements between the Government of the United Kingdom and the Government of Eire.

Gorbachev, Mikhail. *Gorbachev: Mandate for Peace.* PaperJacks Ltd., Toronto and New York, 1987.

Perestroika: New Thinking for Our Country and the World. Harper & Row, Publishers, New York, etc., 1987.

Government of Ireland Act, 1914. *Public General Acts,* 4 & 5 Geo. V, ch. 90. H. M. Stationery Office, London, 1914; also in Edmund Curtis and R. B. McDowell, eds., *Irish Historical Records, 1172-1922* (q.v.); in *Butterworth's Twentieth Century Statutes (Annotated).* Vol. X. Butterworth & Co., London, etc., 1915; and in Appendix 14, *Supplement.* See also *Halsbury's Statutes.*

Goverment of Ireland Act, 1920. *Public General Acts,* 10 & 11 Geo. V, ch. 67. H. M. Stationery Office, London, 1920; also in Edmund Curtis and R. B. McDowell, eds., *Irish Historical Records, 1172-1922* (q.v.); in *Halsbury's*; and in Appendix 14, *Supplement. See also* Donaldson, Alfred Gaston; Quekett, Sir Arthur S.

Greaves, Desmond. *The Irish Crisis.* Lawrence & Wishand, London, 1972.

Green, N. A. Maryan. *See* Maryan Green, N. A.

Greenspan, David J. "Bridging the Irish Sea: The Anglo-Irish Treaty of 1985", *Syracuse, Journal of International Law and Commerce,* Vol. 12 (Spring 1986), pp. 585-599. *See also* Gerken, Karl Heim.

Griffin, William D., comp. and ed. *Ireland. 6000 B.C.-1972. A Chronology and Fact Book.* Oceana Publications, Inc., Dobbs Ferry, N.Y., 1973.

Grogan, Vincent. "Irish Constitutional Development", *Studies* (Dublin), Vol. XL (1951), pp. 383-398.

Groom, A. J. R. "The Commonwealth as an International Organisation", A. J. R. Groom and Paul Taylor, eds., *The Commonwealth in the 1980's, Challenges and Opportunities,* Macmillan, London, 1984, pp. 293-304.

Groom, A. J. R., and Paul Taylor. "The Continuing Commonwealth: Its Origins and Characteristics", A. J. R. Groom and Paul Taylor, eds., *The Commonwealth in the 1980's* (q.v.), pp. 3-14.

Guernsey Books. *Ireland – Union to Free State: A Collection of 3000 Original Pamphlets, etc.* Intro. by F. S. L. Lyons. Guernsey Books, St. Peter Port, Guernsey, 1973.

Guide to Government Orders, 1951-1960. [Continuation of *Index to Statutory Rules and Orders.*] H. M. Stationery Office, London. See also *Index to Government Orders.*

Gwynn, Denis. *The Irish Free State, 1922-7.* London, 1928.

The History of Partition (1912-1925), Browne & Nolan, Dublin, 1950.

Hachey, Thomas E. *Britain and Irish Separatism. From the Fenians to the Free State, 1867/1922.* With Revised Epilogue. 2nd ed. The Catholic University of America Press, Washington, D.C., 1984.

Hall, H. Duncan. *Commonwealth. A History of the British Commonwealth of Nations.* Van Nostrand Reinhold Company, London, etc., 1971.

"What is Dominion Status?" *The Nation* (London), November 27, 1920, pp. 306-307.

Halsbury's Laws of England. Fourth Edition. Vol. 3: Bankruptcy and Insolvency (1973); Vol. 4: British Nationality, Alienage, Immigration and Race Relations (1973); Vol. 6: Commonwealth and Dependencies (1974); Vol. 8: Constitutional Law (1974); Vol. 18: Foreign Relations Law (1977); Cumulative Supplement, Part 1 (1986). Butterworths, London, 1973-1984. [1st edition: 1907-1917; 2nd edition: 1931-1942; 3rd edition: 1952-1964.] Also: *A User's Guide.*

Halsbury's Laws of England. Annual Abridgment. Butterworths, London, 1974 - Present.

Halsbury's Statutes of England. Third Edition. Vol. 4 (1968); Vol. 23 (1970); Continuation Vols. 43 (1973), 44 (1974), 52 (1982); Cumulative Supplement, Part I (1985); Current Status Service – Noter-up, 1985. Butterworths, London, 1968-1985. [1st edition: 1929-1931; 2nd edition: 1948-1952.] Also: *A User's Guide.*

Halsbury's Statutes of England and Wales. Fourth Edition. Vol. 7: Commonwealth and Other Territories (1986); Vol. 31: Northern Ireland (1987); Current Status Service, Noter-up (current year). [Continuation of *Halsbury's Statutes of England.*] Butterworths, London, 1985-1989. Also: *A User's Guide.*

Halsbury's Statutory Instruments. Being a Companion Work to Halsbury's Statutes of England. Vol. 6. Fourth Re-Issue. "India and Ireland", pp. 170-174. Butterworths, London, 1982. Also: *A User's Guide.*

See also *Index to Government Orders; Index to Statutory Rules and Orders; Index to the Statutes; Northern Ireland Measures; Northern Ireland Public General Acts; Public General Acts; Statutes in Force; Statutory Rules & Orders.*

Hancock, W. K. *Survey of British Commonwealth Affairs.* Vol. I. *Problems of Nationality, 1918-1936.* Oxford University Press, London, 1937. 2nd ed., 1964. *See also* Latham, R. T. E., *The Law and the Commonwealth.*

Hand, Geoffrey J. "MacNeill and the Boundary Commission", F. X. Martin and F. J. Byrne, eds., *The Scholar Revolutionary: Eoin MacNeill, 1867-1945, and the Making of the New Ireland,* Irish University Press, 1973, pp. 199-275.

"Introduction", Report of the Irish Boundary Commission, 1925 (q.v.).

Hanna, Henry, and A. Denis Pringle. *The Statute Law of the Irish Free State (Saorstat Eireann), 1922 to 1928.* Alex Thom & Company, Limited, Dublin, 1929.

Hansard. *Parliamentary Debates.* Fifth Series (House of Commons), London, [1909 - Present].

Harkness, D. W. *The Restless Dominion. The Irish Free State and the British Commonwealth of Nations, 1921-1931.* Macmillan, London, Melbourne and Toronto, and Gill and Macmillan, Dublin and London, 1969; New York University Press, New York, 1970.

Northern Ireland Since 1920. Educational Company of Ireland, Dublin, 1983.

"Britain and the independence of the dominions: the 1921 crossroads", *Historical Studies,* Vol. XI, *Nationality and the Pursuit of National Independence,* The Appletree Press, Belfast, 1978, pp. 141-159.

Hearn, John J. *The Constitution of Ireland of 1937.* Lecture delivered at the Catholic University of America, Washington, D.C., 1960. (Private possession.) *See also* Kennedy, Brian P.

Preliminary Draft of Heads of a Constitution, "First Draft Tackled Role of King", by Joe Carroll, *Irish Times,* July 1, 1987.

Helsinki Accord. Igor J. Kavass, Jacqueline Paquin Granier and Mary Frances Dominick, eds. *Human Rights, European Politics, and the Helsinki Accord: The Documentary Evolution of the Conference on Security and Co-operation in Europe 1973-1975.* 6 vols. William S. Hein

& Co., Inc., Buffalo, N.Y., 1981. Thomas Buergenthal, ed. and Judy R. Hall, asst. ed. *Human Rights, International Law and the Helsinki Accord.* Allanheld, Osmun, Montclair, N.J., and New York, 1977.

Henkin, Louis. "Preface" and "Introduction", Louis Henkin, ed., *The International Bill of Rights, The Covenant on Civil and Political Rights,* Columbia University Press, New York, 1981, pp. ix-x and 1-31. *See also* Bertelsen, Judy S.; Capotorti, Francesco; Cassese, Antonio; Lillich, Richard B.; and Sohn, Louis B.

Henry, Robert M. *The Evolution of Sinn Fein.* 2nd pr., Talbot Press, Ltd., Dublin, 1970; reprints of 1920 ed., Arno Press Inc., New York, 1970, and Kennikat Press Inc., Port Washington, N.Y., 1970.

Hepburn, A. C., ed. *The Conflict of Nationality in Modern Ireland.* Edward Arnold, London and St. Martin's Press, New York, 1980.

Heslinga, M. W. *The Irish Border as a Cultural Divide. A Contribution to the Study of Regionalism in the British Isles.* 2nd ed., Van Gorcum, Assen, 1971; Humanities Press, New York, 1962.

"History of the Dail", *Freeman's Journal,* August 16, 1921.

Hogan, David. *The Four Glorious Years.* Irish Press, Ltd., Dublin, 1953; repr., Johnson Reprint Corporation, New York and London, 1971.

See also Gallagher, Frank.

Hogan, J. "Ireland and the British Commonwealth, 1931-7", *Ireland Today,* Vol. II (1937), pp. 11-26.

Holt, Edgar. *Protest in Arms. The Irish Troubles, 1916-1923.* Putnam, London, 1960; Coward, McCann, Inc., New York, 1961.

Hull, Roger H. *The Irish Triangle. Conflict in Northern Ireland.* Princeton University Press, Princeton, N.J., 1976.

Hurley, Mark J. *Northern Ireland Today. An Irish-American Preview.* Lecture. Irish Forum, San Francisco, Calif., 1982.

Index to Government Orders in Force, 1961 - Present. Subordinate Legislation. The Powers and their Exercise. [Continuation of *Guide to Government Orders.*] H. M. Stationery Office, London. See also *Table of Government Orders.*

Index to Statutory Rules and Orders, 1922-47 [Ir.] 3 Vols. The Stationery Office, Dublin, 1944-1955.

Index to Statutory Rules and Orders in Force, 1891-1950 [Br.]. H. M. Stationery Office, London. See also *Guide to Government Orders*.

Index to the Statutes, 1922-1968. The Stationery Office, Dublin, [1970].

Inglis, Brian. *The Story of Ireland.* Roy Publishers, New York, 1958; 2nd pbck. ed., London, 1965.

Irish Boundary. Extracts from Parliamentary Debates, Command Papers, etc., relevant to Questions arising out of Article XII of the Articles of Agreement for a Treaty between Great Britain and Ireland, dated 6th December, 1921. Cmd. 2264. September 1924. H. M. Stationery Office, London, 1924. *See also* Report of the Irish Boundary Commission, 1925; North-Eastern Boundary Bureau; *Irish Free State; Irish Free State and Northern Ireland;* Wambaugh, Sarah.

Irish Bulletin. Official Organ of Dail Eireann (Dublin), 1919-1921.

Irish Forum. *See* Hurley, Mark J.; New Ireland Forum.

Irish Freedom (Dublin), 1910-1914.

Irish Free State (Agreement) Act, 1922. *Public General Acts,* 12 & 13 Geo. V, ch. 4. H. M. Stationery Office, London, 1922; also in Chapter 5 (partly); in Appendix 9, *Supplement;* and in *Halsbury's. See also* Articles of Agreement.

Irish Free State (Consequential Provisions) Act, 1922. *Public General Acts,* 13 Geo. V, ch. 2. H. M. Stationery Office, London, 1922 [o.p.]; also in Appendix 6, *Supplement,* and in *Halsbury's. See also* Articles of Agreement.

Irish Free State Constitution Act, 1922 (Session 2). *Public General Acts,* 13 Geo. V, ch. 1. H. M. Stationery Office, London, 1922 [o.p.]; also in Appendix 9, *Supplement,* and in *Halsbury's. See also* Articles of Agreement; Constitution of the Free State of Ireland.

Irish Free State. Correspondence between His Majesty's Government and the Government of the Irish Free State relating to Article 12 of the Articles of Agreement for a Treaty between Great Britian and Ireland. July 1923. Cmd. 1928. H. M. Stationery Office, London, 1923. *See also* Articles of Agreement; *Irish Boundary.*

Irish Free State and Northern Ireland. Correspondence between His Majesty's Government and the Governments of the Irish Free State and Northern Ireland relating to Article 12 of the Articles of Agreement for a Treaty between Great Britain and Ireland. June 1924. Cmd. 2155. H. M. Stationery Office, London, 1924. *See also* Articles of Agreement; *Irish Boundary.*

Irish Free State and Northern Ireland. Further correspondence relating to Article 12 of the Articles of Agreement for a Treaty between Great Britain and Ireland. (In continuation of Cmd. 2155.) June 1924. Cmd. 2166. H. M. Stationery Office, London, 1924. *See also* Articles of Agreement; *Irish Boundary.*

Irish Free State v. *Guaranty Safe Deposit Company. The Miscellaneous Reports,* State of New York. Austin B. Griffin, Reporter, pp. 551 ff. Vol. 129 (1927). J. B. Lyon Company, Albany, N.Y.

Irish Historical Studies. Hodges, Figgis, Dublin; Vols. 1-4 (1958-1963), Dufour Editions, Inc., Chester Springs, Pa.; Vol. 5 (1965), Arno, New York, N.Y.

Irish Independent (Dublin), 1919 - Present.

Irish Independent's Supplement Jubilee Week, 1916-1966. Irish Independent, Dublin, 1966.

The Irish Jurist (Dublin). "Repeals and Amendments of the Treaty to 1935", Vol. I (1935), pp. 28 ff.

"Twenty-five Years of Irish Constitutional Development", Vol. XI (1945), pp. 31 ff.

"The Republic of Ireland Act, 1948", Vol. XIV (1948), pp. 55 ff.

"A Matter of Nomenclature – The Name of the State is Eire . . .", Vol. XVI (1950), pp. 5-6.

See also Farrell, Brian, "The Drafting of the Irish Free State Constitution".

Irish News (Belfast), 1921-1922.

Irish Political Miscellany, 1916-1923 (miscellaneous documents and illustrations). National Library of Ireland, Dublin.

Irish Press (Dublin), 1931 - Present.

The Irish Reports. Cases Determined in the Irish Free State. Edited by Albert D. Bolton, K.C. Incorporated Council of Law Reporting for Ireland, Dublin. *See also* Appeal Cases.

Irish Statesman (Dublin), 1923-1930.

The Irish Times (Dublin), 1919 - Present.

The Irish Uprising, 1916-1922. A CBS Legacy Collection Book. New York, 1966.

Iris Oifigiuil (Official Gazette). Dublin.

Jain, M. P. "Safeguards to Minorities: Constitutional Principles, Policies and Framework", Mohammed Imam, ed., *Minorities and the Law.* Tripathi Publishers, Bombay, 1972.

Johnson, Paul. *Ireland: Land of Troubles. A History from the Twelfth Century to the Present Day.* Eyre Methuen, London, 1980; Holmes & Meier, New York, 1980; pbck. ed., Panther, London, 1981; Academy Chicago Publishers, Chicago, 1984.

*Johnston, E. *Irish History: A Selected Bibliography.* Historical Association Pamphlet No. 73, 1969.

Joint Communique. May 21, 1980. Meeting between Taoiseach Charles J. Haughey and British Prime Minister Margaret Thatcher. Bulletin of the Department of Foreign Affairs, Dublin. (Sequel: *Northern*

Ireland: Speech by the Taoiseach, Mr Charles J Haughey, TD, in Dail Eireann on 29 May 1980, following discussions with the British Prime Minister, Mrs Margaret Thatcher, MP, on 21 May. Statements and Speeches, 3/80, Bulletin of the Department of Foreign Affairs, Dublin.)

December 8, 1980. Meeting between Taoiseach Charles J. Haughey and British Prime Minister Margaret Thatcher. Bulletin of the Department of Foreign Affairs, No. 972, December 1980/January 1981, Dublin. (Sequel: *Meeting of Heads of Government: Statement by the Taoiseach, Mr Charles J Haughey, TD, in Dail Eireann on 11 December 1980, following talks with the British Prime Minister, Mrs Margaret Thatcher, MP, in Dublin on 8 December.* Statements and Speeches, 7/80, Bulletin of the Department of Foreign Affairs, Dublin.)

November 6, 1981. Meeting between Taoiseach Garret FitzGerald and British Prime Minister Margaret Thatcher, together with a Joint Report on Anglo-Irish Studies. Government Information Services, Dublin.

November 19, 1984. Anglo-Irish Summit, on the Report of the New Ireland Forum, between Taoiseach Garret FitzGerald and British Prime Minister Margaret Thatcher. Government Information Services, Dublin.

November 15, 1985. Anglo-Irish Summit Meeting, on the Anglo-Irish Agreement of 1985, between Taoiseach Garret FitzGerald and British Prime Minister Margaret Thatcher. Government Information Services, Dublin.

Jones, F. P. *History of the Sinn Fein Movement and the Irish Rebellion of 1916.* New York, 1919.

Jones, Thomas. *Whitehall Diary.* Edited by Keith Middlemas. Volume III. *Ireland, 1918-1925.* Oxford University Press, London, New York, Toronto, 1971.

Kamanda, Alfred M. "Law of the Commonwealth", A. J. R. Groom and Paul Taylor, eds., *The Commonwealth of the 1980's* (q.v.), pp. 125-139.

*Kee, Robert. *Ourselves Alone.* Vol. 3 of *The Green Flag.* 2nd pr., Quartet Books, London, Melbourne and New York, 1980.

**The Green Flag. A History of Irish Nationalism.* The Delacorte Press, New York, 1972; pbck. ed., Quartet Books, London, Melboure and New York, 1976-1980.

**Ireland. A History.* Weidenfeld and Nicolson, London, 1980; Little, Brown and Company, Boston and Toronto, 1982.

Keith, Arthur Berriedale. *Responsible Government in the Dominions.* 2nd ed., rewritten and revised to 1927. 2 vols. Oxford, at the Clarendon Press, 1928.

The King, the Constitution, the Empire and Foreign Affairs. Letters and Essays, 1936-1937. Oxford University Press, London, 1938.

The Sovereignty of the British Dominions. Macmillan and Co., Limited, London, 1929.

ed. *Speeches and Documents on the British Dominions, 1918-31. From Self-Government to National Sovereignty.* Oxford University Press, London, 1932; repr., 1938 and 1948; AMS Press, Inc., New York, 1975; facsim. of 1932 ed., Greenwood Press, Westport, Conn., 1976; London, 1977. For Supplement to this work, see "Declaration by the Commonwealth Prime Ministers".

The Constitutional Law of the British Dominions. Macmillan and Co., Limited, London, 1933.

On Certain Legal and Constitutional Aspects of the Anglo-Irish Dispute. Irish News & Information Bureau, London, 1934.

Letters on Imperial Relations, Indian Reform, Constitutional and International Law, 1916-1935. Oxford University Press, London, 1935.

Letters on Current Imperial and International Problems, 1935-1936.

The Dominions as Sovereign States. Their Constitutions and Governments. Macmillan and Co., Limited, London, 1938.

See also Anson, Sir William R., *The Law and Custom of the Constitution*; Kohn, Leo, *The Constitution of the Irish Free State*.

Kelley, Kevin. *The Longest War. Northern Ireland and the IRA.* Brandon Book Publishers, Dingle, Kerry, 1982; Lawrence Hill & Co., Westport, Conn., 1982; Zed Press, London, 1982.

Kelly, J. M. *The Irish Constitution.* 2nd ed., Jurist Publishing Co. Ltd., University College, Dublin, 1984.

Kennedy, Brian P. "John Hearn and the Irish Constitution", *The Irish Times,* April 8, 1987, p. 13.

Kennedy, Hugh. "Character and Sources of the Constitution of the Irish Free State", *American Bar Association Journal,* Vol. XIV (1928), pp. 437-445.

"The Association of Canada with the Constitution of the Irish Free State", *Canadian Bar Review,* Vol. VI (1928). *See also* Costello, John A.

Hugh Kennedy Papers. University College Archives, Dublin.

Kenny, Anthony. *The Road to Hillsborough. The Shaping of the Anglo-Irish Agreement.* Pergamon Press, Oxford, New York, etc., 1986.

Kohn, Leo. *The Constitution of the Irish Free State.* George Allen & Unwin, Ltd., London, and W. W. Norton & Company, Inc., New York, 1932. *See also* Constitution of the Free State of Ireland.

*Laffan, Michael. *The Partition of Ireland, 1911-25.* Dublin Historical Association Student Paperbacks. Dundalgan Press, Dundalk, 1983.

Latham, R. T. E. *The Law and the Commonwealth.* Oxford University Press, London, New York and Toronto, 1949. Publd. also as suppl. to W. K. Hancock, *Survey of British Commonwealth Affairs,* Vol. I (q.v.).

Lawlor, Sheila. *Britain and Ireland, 1914-23.* Gill and Macmillan, Dublin, and Barnes & Noble Books, Totowa, N.J., 1983.

Lawrence, R. J. *The Government of Northern Ireland: Public Finance and Public Services.* Oxford University Press, London and New York, 1965.

The Law Reports. The Public General Statutes. Vol. LX (1922). Council of Law Reporting, London, 1923. *See also* Appeal Cases; *Public General Acts.*

The Leader (San Francisco), ed. Peter Yorke, 1882-1942. Copies perusable at University of San Francisco McKenna Library, San Francisco, and University of California Library, Berkeley, Calif.

Lee, Joseph. *Irish Historiography, 1970-1979.* Cork University Press, Cork, 1981.

and Gearoid O Tuathaigh. *The Age of de Valera.* Ward River Press, in Association with Radio Telefis Eireann, Dublin, 1982.

Lemass, Sean. "The Need of Sinn Fein: A Fighting Policy", *An Phoblacht* (Dublin), January 22, 1926.

"The Will To Win", *An Phoblacht*, February 5, 1926.

"Lemass and His Two Partnerships", by J. J. Lee, *Irish Times*, May 19, 1976.

Lijphart, Arend, and Diane R. Stanton. "A Democratic Blueprint for South Africa", S. Prakash Sethi, *The South African Quagmire, In Search Of a Peaceful Path to Democratic Pluralism*, Ballinger Publishing Company, Cambridge, Mass., 1987, pp. 89-98.

Lijphart, Arend. *Democracies. Patterns of Majoritarian and Consensus Government in Twenty-One Countries*. Yale University Press, New Haven and London, 1984.

Democracy in Plural Societies. Yale University Press, London, 1977.

Lillich, Richard B., ed. *International Human Rights Instruments.* William S. Hein Company, Buffalo, N.Y., 1983, 1986 and continuing.

Lillich, Richard B. *The Human Rights of Aliens in Contemporary International Law.* Manchester University Press, Manchester, Eng. and Dover, N.H., 1984.

and Stephen C. Neff. *The Treatment of Aliens in Contemporary International Law* (in prep.).

Lloyd George Papers, Series F, Prime Minister, 1916-1922. Beaverbrook Library, London; House of Lords Record Office, London.

Lloyd George, Earl. *My Father, Lloyd George.* Crown Publishers, Inc., New York, 1961.

Longford, Earl of, and Thomas P. O'Neill. *Eamon de Valera.* Hutchinson of London, 1970; Houghton Mifflin Co., Boston, 1971; Arrow Books, London, 1974; *see also* O Neill, Tomas.

Longford, Lord, and Anne McHardy. "The Unwanted Solution, 1914-1921", *Ulster,* Weidenfeld and Nicolson, London, 1981, pp. 60-73.

Longford, Lord. *See also* Pakenham, Frank.

Lynch, John M. ''The Anglo-Irish Problem'', *Foreign Affairs* (New York), Vol. 50, No. 4 (July 1972), pp. 601-617.

*Lyons, F. S. L. *Ireland Since the Famine.* Weidenfeld and Nicolson, London, 1971; Charles Scribner's Sons, New York, 1971; revd., pbck. ed., 10th imp., Collins/Fontana, London, 1986.

Charles Stewart Parnell. Oxford University Press, London, 1977; Oxford University Press, New York, 1977.

McAllister, Ian. *See* Pollock, Laurence.

Mac Aonghusa, Proinsias, and Liam O Reagain, eds. *The Best of Tone.* Mercier Press, Cork, 1972.

Macardle, Dorothy. *The Irish Republic.* Victor Gollancz, London, 1937; 2nd revd. ed., Irish Press, Dublin, 1951; Farrar, Straus & Giroux, New York, 1965; Ambassador Books, Ltd., Toronto, 1965; pbck. ed., Corgi Books, London, 1968. *See also* O'Brien, William.

Macartney, C. A. *National States and National Minorities.* Oxford University Press, London, 1934. *See also* Bertelsen, Judy S.; Cobban, Alfred; Henkin, Louis.

MacBride, Sean. *Civil Liberty.* Dublin, [1947].

Our People - Our Money. Dublin, [1949].

"Anglo-Irish Relations", *International Affairs,* XXV (July 1949), pp. 257-273.

Ireland's Right to Sovereignty, Independence and Unity is Inalienable and Indefeasible. Brendan Hyland, Dublin, [1984].

See also Cassidy, Janet.

McCaffrey, Lawrence. *The Irish Question, 1800-1922.* University of Kentucky Press, Lexington, Ky., 1968.

Ireland. From Colony to Nation State. Prentice-Hall, Inc., Englewood Cliffs, N.J., 1979.

McCormick, Malachi, ed. *Provisional Government of Ireland. The Proclamation of the Republic: Easter 1916.* The Stone Street Press, New York, 1984.

*McCracken, J. L. *Representative Government in Ireland. A Study of Dail Eireann, 1919-48.* Oxford University Press, London, New York, and Toronto, 1958; 2nd ed., Greenwood Press, London, 1977.

"Northern Ireland, 1921-66", T. W. Moody and F. X. Martin, eds., *The Course of Irish History* (q.v.), pp. 313-323.

MacDonagh, Oliver. *Ireland.* Prentice-Hall, Inc., Englewood Cliffs, N.J., 1968; Spectrum, NewYork, 1968; as *Ireland. The Union and Its Aftermath,* revd. and enlgd. ed., George Allen & Unwin Ltd., London, 1977; pbck. ed., George Allen & Unwin Ltd., London, 1977.

McDowell, R. B. *See* Curtis, Edmund.

*MacEoin, Gary. *Northern Ireland: Captive of History.* Holt, Rinehart and Winston, New York, Chicago, San Francisco, 1974.

Joseph McGarrity Papers. National Library of Ireland, Dublin; also in Cronin, Sean, *The McGarrity Papers* (q.v.).

MacManus, Francis, ed. *The Years of the Great Test, 1926-1939.* Mercier Press, Cork, 1967.

MacManus, Seumas. *The Story of the Irish Race. A Popular History of Ireland;* revd. ed., 38th pr. The Devin-Adair Company, Old Greenwich, Conn., 1988; repr. of 22nd ed., Darby Books, Darby, Pa.

MacMillan, Mary Gretchen Michelle. *Legislative Authority, Sovereignty, Legitimacy and Political Development. The Constitutional Basis of the Irish Free State.* Ph.D. Thesis. University College, Dublin, 1986.

MacNeill, J. G. Swift. *See* Swift MacNeill, J. G.

Madgewick, P., and Richard Rose, eds. *The Territorial Dimension in United Kingdom Politics.* Macmillan, London, 1982.

Manchester, William. *The Last Lion: Winston Spencer Churchill; Visions of Glory: 1874-1932.* Little, Brown and Company, Boston-Toronto, 1983.

Manning, Maurice. *Irish Political Parties.* Gill and Macmillan, Dublin, 1972.

Mansergh, Nicholas. *The Irish Free State. Its Government and Politics.* George Allen & Unwin Ltd., London, 1934.

The Government of Northern Ireland. A Study of Devolution. Allen & Unwin, Ltd., London, 1936.

The Irish Question, 1840-1921; revd. ed., Allen & Unwin, London, 1965; pbck. ed., Allen & Unwin, London, 1975; pbck. ed., University of Toronto Press, Toronto, 1976; originally published (1940) as *Ireland in the Age of Reform and Revolution.*

"Ireland and the British Commonwealth of Nations: The Dominion Settlement", T. Desmond Williams, ed., *The Irish Struggle* (q.v.), pp. 129-139.

The Commonwealth Experience. Weidenfeld & Nicolson, London, 1969; Praeger, New York, 1970; 2nd ed., 2 vols., The Macmillan Press, London, 1982; revd. ed., 2 vols., University of Toronto Press, Toronto and Buffalo, N.Y., 1983.

Marshall, Tyler. "Protestant Backlash in Ulster May Lack Target", Los Angeles Times, November 18, 1985.

"Rhetoric, Legacy of Strife Mark Ulster's Bible Belt", Los Angeles Times, November 25, 1985.

"Drumbeats of Tension Set Cadence in Ulster Marches", Los Angeles Times, July 9, 1986.

"The Commonwealth. Legacy of Empire – A World 'Club' ", Los Angeles Times, August 9, 1986.

Martin, F. X., ed. *Leaders and Men of the Easter Rising. Dublin 1916.* London, 1967; Cornell University Press, Ithaca, N.Y., 1967.

"The Origins of the Irish Rising of 1916", T. Desmond Williams, ed., *The Irish Struggle* (q.v.), pp. 1-17.

See also Moody, T. W.

Maryan Green, N. A. *International Law.* 3rd ed. Pitman Publishing, London, 1987. *See also* Zimmern, Alfred E.

"Meeting of the First Dail", *Irish Press,* January 21, 1944.

Middlemas, Keith, ed. *See* Jones, Thomas, *Whitehall Diary.*

Mitchell, Arthur, and Padraig O Snodaigh. *Irish Political Documents, 1919-1949.* Irish Academic Press, Dublin, 1983; Biblio Distribution Centre, Totowa, N.J., 1983.

Moneypenny, W. F. *The Two Irish Nations.* London, 1912.

*Moody, T. W., ed. *Irish Historiography, 1936-70.* Irish Committee of Historical Sciences, Dublin, 1971.

**The Ulster Question, 1603-1973.* Mercier Press, Dublin and Cork, 1974.

ed. *The Fenian Movement.* Mercier Press, Cork, 1978.

Moody, T. W., and F. X. Martin, eds. *The Course of Irish History.* 11th pr., The Mercier Press, Cork, 1978; Weybright and Talley, Inc., New York, 1967.

Morgan, David Gwynn. *Constitutional Law of Ireland. The Law of the Executive, Legislature and Judicature.* The Round Hall Press in association with Irish Academic Press, Blackrock, Dublin, [1985].

Mowat, Charles Loch. *Britain Between the Wars, 1918-1940.* 2nd ed. The University of Chicago Press, Chicago, Ill., 1958.

"The Irish Question in British Politics (1916-1922)", T. Desmond Williams, ed., *The Irish Struggle* (q.v.), pp. 141-152.

Moynihan, Maurice, ed. *Speeches and Statements by Eamon de Valera, 1917-1973.* Gill and Macmillan, Dublin and St. Martin's Press, New York, 1980.

Richard Mulcahy Papers. University College Archives, Dublin.

Mulvey, Helen F. "Ireland's Commonwealth Years, 1922-1949", Robin W. Winks, ed., *The Historiography of the British Empire-Commonwealth, Trends, Interpretations, and Resources,* Duke University Press, Durham, N.C., 1966, pp. 326-343.

Murphy, John A. *Ireland in the Twentieth Century.* The Gill History of Ireland, 11. Gill and Macmillan, Dublin, 1975.

Nationality (Dublin), 1915-16; n.s., 1917-1919.

Neeson, Eoin. *The Life and Death of Michael Collins.* Mercier Press, Cork, 1968.

New Ireland (Dublin), 1915-1919.

New Ireland Forum. *Report.* Vol. No. 1. The Stationery Office, Dublin, 1984. *See also* Agreement between the Government of Ireland and the Government of the United Kingdom; *Anglo-Irish Studies;* Articles of Agreement; Joint Communique.

Reports of Proceedings. Vols. Nos. 2-11. The Stationery Office, Dublin, 1983-84.

The Legal Systems, North and South. The Stationery Office, Dublin, [1984].

Newspaper clippings, 1919-1923 (articles from *The Times* and the *Observer).* National Library of Ireland, Dublin.

Norman, Edward. *A History of Modern Ireland.* Allen Lane, London, 1971; University of Miami Press, Coral Gables, Fla., 1971; pbck. ed., Pelican Books, Harmondsworth, Mdlsx., 1973.

North-Eastern Boundary Bureau. *Handbook of the Ulster Question.* The Stationery Office, Dublin, 1923.

Northern Ireland: Agreed Communique Issued following the Conference between the Irish & British Governments and the Parties Involved in the Northern Ireland Executive (Designate) on 6th, 7th, 8th, and 9th

December, 1973. H. M. Stationery Office, Belfast, 1973; Government Information Services, Dublin, 1973.

Northern Ireland *Assembly Debates.* Official Report. Vols. 1-3, 1973-74. H. M. Stationery Office, Belfast, 1973-74.

Northern Ireland Constitutional Convention. *Report of Debates.* 8 May 1975 to 7 November 1975. H. M. Stationery Office, Belfast, 1975.

Northern Ireland Measures and Orders in Council. H. M. Stationery Office, Belfast.

Northern Ireland *Parliamentary Debates.* Official Report. First Series. Vols. 1-84 (House of Commons) and Vols. 1-56 (Senate), 1921-1972. H. M. Stationery Office, Belfast, 1921-1972.

Northern Ireland Public General Acts (var.). H. M. Stationery Office, London and Belfast; see also *Halsbury's.*

Northern Ireland Supplement to the United Kingdom Index of the Statutes. Being an Index to the Imperial Statutes in Force Relating to Northern Ireland. To the End of the Session 13 Geo. 5, Sess. 2, 31st December, 1922. H. M. Stationery Office, Belfast, 1925.

Oath of Allegiance. *See* Papers Relating to; *see also* Treaty.

O'Ballance, Edgar. *Terror in Ireland. The Heritage of Hate.* Presidio Press, Novato, Calif., 1981.

O Briain, Barra. *The Irish Constitution.* The Talbot Press, Dublin and Cork, 1929. *See also* Constitution of the Free State of Ireland.

O'Brien, William. "The Irish Free State. Secret History of Its Foundation". MS 4210. William O'Brien Papers (q.v.).

"Corrections and Notes on Macardle's *Irish Republic".* MS 13972. William O'Brien Papers (q.v.).

William O'Brien Papers. National Library of Ireland, Dublin.

O'Cahan, T. S. *Owen Roe O'Neill.* T. Joseph Keane & Co., London, 1968.

Sean T. O Ceallaigh Memoirs (unpublished). National Library of Ireland, Dublin. *See also* O'Kelly, Sean, *et al.*

O'Connor, John F. "L'accord Anglo-Irlandais de 1985", *Annuaire francais de droit international,* 1985, Vol. XXXVI (1986), pp. 191-203. *See also* Greenspan, David J.

O'Donnell, James D. *How Ireland Is Governed;* 5th ed. An Foras Riarachain, Institute of Public Administration, Dublin, 1974.

O'Donnell, Peadar. *There Will Be Another Day.* Dolmen Press, Dublin, 1963.

O'Donnell, Terence. *The Case for American-Irish Unity.* American Council on Public Affairs, Washington, D.C., 1941.

O'Donoghue, Florence. *No Other Law. The Story of Liam Lynch and the Irish Republican Army, 1916-1923.* Irish Press Ltd., Dublin, 1954.

Florence O'Donoghue Papers. National Library of Ireland, Dublin.

*O'Dowd, Liam, Bill Rolston, and Mike Tomlinson. *Northern Ireland: Between Civil Rights and Civil War.* CSE Books, London, 1980.

O'Farrell, Patrick J. *Ireland's English Question. Anglo-Irish Relations, 1534-1970.* London, 1971; Schocken Books, New York, 1971.

England and Ireland since 1800. Oxford University Press, New York, 1975.

Ofuatey-Kodjoe, A. *The Principle of Self-Determination in International Law.* Nellen Publishing Company, Inc., New York, 1977. *See also* Rhoodie, Eschel.

An t-Oglach, Official Organ of the Irish Volunteers (Dublin), 1918-1922.

O'Hegarty, P. S. *The Victory of Sinn Fein. How It Won It, and How It Used It.* The Talbot Press Ltd., Dublin, 1924.

A History of Ireland under the Union, 1801 to 1922. With an Epilogue carrying the story down to the acceptance in 1927 by de Valera of the Anglo-Irish Treaty of 1921. Methuen & Co. Ltd., London, 1952.

O'Higgins, Brian. "The Story of the Republic of Ireland from 1791 to the Present Day", *Silver Jubilee Wolfe Tone Annual,* 1957.

O'Kelly, J. J. *The Republic of Ireland Vindicated.* Dublin, 1931.

O'Kelly, Sean T., *et al. The Irish Republic and the Peace Conference.* Dublin, 1921

O'Kelly, Sean T. *See also* O Ceallaigh.

O'Neill, David. *The Partition of Ireland.* M. J. Gill and Son, Dublin, 1946.

O Neill, Tomas, agus Padraig O Fiannachta. *De Valera,* I & II. Clo Morainn, Baile atha Cliath, 1968, 1970; *see also* Longford, Earl of.

O'Rahilly, Alfred. "The Constitution and Senate", *Studies* (Dublin), Vol. 25 (March 1936), pp. 1-19. *See also* Akinson, D. H., and J. J. Fallin.

Thoughts on the Constitution. Dublin, 1937.

Alfred O'Rahilly MSS, University College Archives, Cork.

O'Reilly, James, and Mary Redmond. *Cases and Materials on the Irish Constitution.* The Incorporated Law Society of Ireland, Dublin, 1980.

O'Shannon, Cathal. "The 1919 Democratic Programme", *Irish Times,* January 31 and February 1, 1944.

O'Snodaigh, Padraig. *See* Mitchell, Arthur.

O'Sullivan, Donal Joseph. *The Irish Free State and Its Senate. A Study in Contemporary Politics.* Faber and Faber, London, 1940.

Owen, Frank. *Tempestuous Journey. Lloyd George, His Life and Times.* Hutchinson, London, 1954.

Pakenham, Frank (Lord Longford). *Peace by Ordeal.* Jonathan Cape Ltd., London, 1935; Mercier Press Ltd., Cork, 1951; 3rd, revd. ed., Geoffrey Chapman, London, 1962; Mentor pbck. ed., The New English Library Limited, London, 1967; Sidgwick & Jackson, London, 1972.

"The Treaty Negotiations", T. Desmond Williams, ed., *The Irish Struggle* (q.v.), pp. 107-115.

See also Longford, Lord.

Papers Relating to the Parliamentary Oath of Allegiance in the Irish Free State and the Land Purchase Annuities. Cmd. 4056. H.C. XIV (1931-32), 273. H. M. Stationery Office, London, 1932. *See also* Articles of Agreement; Treaty.

Papers Relating to a Conference Held in London, 14-15 October, 1932. Cmd. 4184. H.C. XIV (1931-32), 285. H. M. Stationery Office, London, 1932.

Papers of individuals. *See* Bowman, John, "Private Papers", *De Valera,* pp. 343-347; Michael Collins; Eamon de Valera; Frank Gallagher; George Gavan Duffy; Hugh Kennedy; David Lloyd George; Joseph McGarrity; William O'Brien; Sean T. O Ceallaigh; Florence O'-Donoghue; and Alfred O'Rahilly. *See also* Dail Eireann.

Parliamentary Debates. See Dail Eireann; Northern Ireland; Seanad Eireann; United Kingdom.

Pearse, Padraic H. *Political Writings and Speeches.* The Talbot Press Ltd., Dublin, 1922.

Collected Works of Padraic H. Pearse. Repr. of 1917 ed. AMS Press, Inc., New York, 1975.

Peck, Sir John. *Dublin from Downing Street.* Gill & Macmillan, London and Dublin, 1978.

Poblacht na hEireann: War News (Dublin), 1919-1921.

*Pollock, Laurence, and Ian McAllister. *A Bibliography of United Kingdom Politics: Scotland, Wales and Northern Ireland.* University of Strathclyde, Glasgow, 1980.

Pomerance, Michla. *Self-Determination in Law and Practice. The New Doctrine in the United Nations.* Martinus Nijhoff Publishers, The Hague/Boston/London, 1982. *See also* Buchheit, Lee C.; Rhoodie, Eschel.

Prager, Jeffrey. *Building Democracy in Ireland. Political Order and Cultural Integration in a Newly Independent Nation.* Cambridge University Press, Cambridge, Eng., etc., 1986.

*Pringle, D. G. *One Island, Two Nations? A Political Geographical Analysis of the National Conflict in Ireland.* Research Studies Press Ltd., Letchworth, Herts., Eng. and John Wiley & Sons Inc., New York, etc., 1985. *See also* Bertelsen, Judy S.; Garvin, Tom; and Prager, Jeffrey.

Provisional Government. *Select Constitutions of the World.* Prepared for Presentation to Dail Eireann ("the Third Dail Eireann, Which Was To Act as a Constituent Assembly for Saorstat Eireann") by Order of the Irish Provisional Government, 1922. The Stationery Office, Dublin, 1922.

Public General Acts Passed by the Oireachtas. The Stationery Office, Dublin, 1922 - Present.

Public General Acts. H. M. Stationery Office, London. See also *Halsbury's; Index; Law Reports; Statutes in Force.*

Quekett, Sir Arthur S. *The Constitution of Northern Ireland.* Part I: The Origin and Development of the Constitution. H. M. Stationery Office, Belfast, 1928. Part II: The Government of Ireland Act, 1920, and Subsequent Enactments. H. M. Stationery Office, Belfast, 1933. Part III: A Review of the Operations under the Government of Ireland Act, 1920. H. M. Stationery Office, Belfast, 1946.

*Ranelagh, John. *Ireland. An Illustrated History.* Collins, London, 1981.

Records of Anglo-Irish Negotiations, 1921-22. Cab. 43. Cabinet Office Records, Public Record Office, London.

Records of the Treaty Negotiations, 1921. DE 2/304. Dail Eireann Files, State Paper Office, Dublin Castle, Dublin.

Redmond-Howard, Louis G. *The New Birth of Ireland.* Collins, London, [1914].

Six Days of the Irish Republic. A Narrative and Critical Account. London, 1916 and Dublin, 1916.

Ireland, the Peace Conference and the League of Nations. T. Kiersey, Dublin, [1919].

Report of the Irish Boundary Commission, 1925. Intro. by Geoffrey Hand. Irish University Press, Shannon, Ireland, 1969. *See also* Articles of Agreement; *Irish Boundary;* North-Eastern Boundary Bureau; Saorstat Eireann; Treaty.

Republic of Ireland (Dublin), 1922.

*Rhoodie, Eschel. *Discrimination in the Constitutions of the World. A Study of the Group Rights Problem.* Brentwood Communications Group, Columbus, Ga., 1985. *See also* Chandra, Dr. Satish, *Minorities in National and International Laws.*

Rhoodie, Nic., ed. *Intergroup Accommodations in Plural Societies.* Macmillan Press, London, 1978; St. Martin's Press, New York, 1979.

*Rigo Sureda, A. *The Evolution of the Right of Self-Determination. A Study of United Nations Practice.* A. W. Sijthoff, Leiden, 1973. *See also* Cobban, Alfred; Lillich, Richard B.; Macartney, C. A.

Robertson, C. Grant. *Select Statutes, Cases, and Documents To Illustrate English Constitutional History, 1660-1832.* 2nd revd. and enlgd. ed. Methuen & Co. Ltd., London, 1913.

Rolston, Bill. *See* O'Dowd, Liam.

Rose, Richard. *Governing without Consensus. An Irish Perspective.* Faber & Faber, London, 1971; Beacon Press, Boston, Mass., 1971

*"Ulster Politics: A Select Bibliography of Political Discord", *Political Studies,* Vol. XX (June 1972).

The United Kingdom as a Multi-National State. Occasional Paper No. 6. Survey Research Centre, University of Strathclyde, Glasgow, 1970.

See also Madgewick, P.

Ryan, Desmond. "Sinn Fein Policy and Practice (1916-1926)", T. Desmond Williams, ed., *The Irish Struggle* (q.v.), pp. 31-40.

Ryan, Vincent J. D. *Towards the Restoration of the Irish Republic.* QED Literary Agency, Los Angeles, Calif., 1980.

A Political Initiative for the Reunification of Ireland. QED Literary Agency, Los Angeles, Calif., 1981.

What We Have, We Hold. Unity Claims of the Constitution Must Not Be Changed. QED Literary Agency, Los Angeles, Calif., 1982.

Rynne, M. *Die voelkerrechtliche Stellung Irlands.* Munich, 1930.

Saorstat Eireann, Irish Free State. Official Handbook. Talbot Press, Dublin, 1932; Ernest Benn Limited, London, 1932.

Sarbaugh, Timothy J. "Irish Republicanism vs. 'Pure Americanism': California's Reaction to Eamon de Valera's Visits", *California History, The Magazine of the California Historical Society,* Volume LX (Summer 1981), No. 2, pp. 172-185.

Satish Chandra. *See* Chandra, Dr. Satish.

Saunders, A. E. "The Irish Constitution", *American Political Science Review,* Vol. XVIII (1924).

Savage, D. C. "The Origins of the Ulster Unionist Party, 1885-1886", *Irish Historical Studies* (Dublin), Vol. 12 (1961), pp. 185-208.

Seanad Eireann. *Diosboireachtai Parlaiminte (Parliamentary Debates).* Tuairisc Oifigiuil (Official Report). [*Seanad Debates.*] Vols. I - (December 1922 - Present). The Stationery Office, Dublin, 1922 -

Present. *See also* Dail Eireann; Northern Ireland; United Kingdom.

*Shannon, Michael Owen. *Modern Ireland: A Bibliography on Politics, Planning, Research, and Development.* Library Association, London, 1982; Greenwood Press, Westport, Conn., [1982].

Sinn Fein (Dublin), 1906-1914.

Sinn Fein. *Ireland: The Facts.* Sinn Fein, Dublin, 1971.

Where Sinn Fein Stands. Sinn Fein, Dublin, 1972.

Smith, Arnold, with Clyde Sanger. *Stitches in Time. The Commonwealth in World Politics.* General Publishing Co. Limited, Don Mills, Ontario, 1981; Andre Deutsch, London, 1981.

Sohn, Louis B., and Thomas Buergenthal. *International Protection of Human Rights.* The Bobbs-Merrill Company, Inc., Indianapolis, Kansas City, New York, 1973.

Sohn, Louis B. "The Rights of Minorities", Louis Henkin, ed., *The International Bill of Rights* (q.v.), pp. 270-289.

Statute of Westminster, 1931. *Public General Acts,* 22 Geo. V, ch. 4. H. M. Stationery Office, London, 1931; also in Bettey, J. H., ed., *English Historical Documents* (q.v.), and in Appendix 11, *Supplement.*

Statutes at Large Passed in the Parliaments Held in Ireland, 1310-1800. Dublin, 1786-1801.

Statutes in Force. Official Revised Edition. Constitutional Law, Vol. 3, "Northern Ireland". Commonwealth and Other Territories, Vol. 32, "Republic of Ireland". H. M. Stationery Office, London, 1978-1982. See also *Halsbury's; Public General Acts.*

Statutory Rules & Orders and Statutory Instruments. Revised to December 31, 1948. Vols. X and XVI, pp. 297 and 933 respectively. H. M. Stationery Office, London, 1951.

Stewart, Robert Burgess. *Treaty Relations of the British Commonwealth of Nations.* New York, 1939. Cf. R. Y. Jennings, "The Commonwealth and International Law", *British Year Book of International Law,* Vol. XXX (1953), pp. 320-351.

Stewart, A. T. Q. *The Ulster Crisis. Resistance to Home Rule.* 2nd ed. Faber and Faber, London, 1972.

The Narrow Ground. Patterns of Ulster History, 1609-1969. Faber and Faber, London, 1977; pbck. ed., Pretani Press, Belfast, 1986.

Studies (Dublin), Vol. I - , 1912 - Present.

The Sunday Times (London), 1919 - Present.

Sunningdale Agreement. 886 H. of C. Official Report (5th ser.), 10th December 1973, cols. 37-41.

Sureda, A. Rigo. *See* Rigo Sureda, A.

Swift MacNeill, J. G. *Studies in the Constitution of the Irish Free State.* The Talbot Press Limited, Dublin and Cork, 1925. *See also* Constitution of the Free State of Ireland.

Table of Government Orders. Covering the general instruments to 31 December 1984. H. M. Stationery Office, London, 1985. See also *Index.*

An Tan Bo. Official Irish Government's Jubilee Celebration Publication, 1916-1966. The Stationery Office, Dublin, 1966.

Taylor, A. J. P. *English History, 1914-1945.* At the Clarendon Press, Oxford, 1965.

Taylor, Paul. "The Commonwealth in the 1980's: Challenges and Opportunities", A. J. R. Groom and Paul Taylor, eds., *The Commonwealth in the 1980's* (q.v.), pp. 305-323.

Taylor, Rex. *Michael Collins.* Hutchinson, London, 1961; pbck. ed., Four Square Books, London, 1961.

The Times (London), 1919 - Present.

Tomlinson, Mike. *See* O'Dowd, Liam.

Treaty. *See* Articles of Agreement. *See also* Bromage, Mary C., *De Valera and the March of a Nation;* Collins, Michael, *The Path to Freedom;* Curran, Joseph M., *The Birth of the Irish Free State;* De Burca, Padraig, *Free State or Republic?;* Gallagher, Frank, *The Anglo-Irish Treaty;* Lyons, F. S. L., *Ireland Since the Famine;* Pakenham, Frank, *Peace by Ordeal* and "The Treaty Negotiations".

Treaty (Confirmation of Supplemental Agreement) Act, 1924 (No. 51). The Stationery Office, Dublin, 1924; also in Appendix 10, *Supplement. See also* Articles of Agreement; *Irish Boundary;* Treaty (Confirmation of Amending Agreement) Act.

Treaty (Confirmation of Amending Agreement) Act, 1925 (No. 40). The Sationery Office, Dublin, 1925; also partly in Appendix 10, *Supplement. See also* Articles of Agreement; Report of the Irish Boundary Commission; Treaty (Confirmation of Supplemental Agreement); Wambaugh, Sarah.

Treaty Debate. *See* Dail Eireann, *Debate on the Treaty.*

Ulster Year Book. H. M. Stationery Office, Belfast, 1926 et seq.

Unionist Party. See *The Way Forward; see also* Democratic Unionist Party.

United Irishman (Belfast), 1931 - Present.

United Kingdom *Parliamentary Debates.* Official Report. Fifth Series. Vols. 147-159 (House of Commons) and Vols. 45-52 (House of

Lords), 1921-1922. H. M. Stationery Office, London, 1921 and 1922. *See also* Dail Eireann; Northern Ireland; Seanad Eireann.

United Nations Actions, Conventions, Covenants, Declarations, Studies, etc. in the fields of National Minorities and Human Rights. United Nations Publications, New York. *See also* Blaustein, Albert P., *et al., Human Rights Sourcebook;* Chandra, Satish; Maryan Green, N. A.; and Rhoodie, Eschel.

University Review (Dublin), Vol. I - , 1964 - Present.

Uris, Leon and Jill. *Ireland. A Terrible Beauty.* Doubleday, New York, 1975; Andre Deutsch, London, 1976; pbck. ed., Corgi, London, 1977; pbck. ed., Bantam Books, Toronto, New York, London, 1978.

Wade, E. C. S. "Introduction", A. V. Dicey, *Introduction to the Study of the Law of the Constitution* (q.v.), pp. ix-cxcviii.

Walker, Brian M. *Parliamentary Election Results in Ireland, 1921-1976.* Royal Irish Academy, Dublin, [in press].

Wall, Maureen. "Partition: the Ulster Question (1916-1926)", T. Desmond Williams, ed., *The Irish Struggle* (q.v.), pp. 79-93.

Wallace, M. *Drums and Guns: Revolution in Ulster.* Geoffrey Chapman, London, 1970.

Wambaugh, Sarah. *A Monograph on Plebiscites.* Oxford University Press, London and New York, 1920.

Ward, Alan J. *Ireland and Anglo-American Relations, 1899-1921.* University of Toronto Press, Toronto, 1969; Weidenfeld and Nicolson, Ltd., London, and the London School of Economics, 1969.

Watt, David, ed. *The Constitution of Northern Ireland. Problems and Prospects.* Heinemann, London, 1981.

The Way Forward. Devolution and the Northern Ireland Assembly. A discussion paper presented by the Ulster Unionist Assembly Party's Report Committee. Ulster Unionist Council, Belfast, [1984].

Wells, H. G. *The Outline of History.* 7th ed. Doubleday & Company, Inc., Garden City, N.Y., 1971.

Westminster *Parliamentary Debates. See* United Kingdom *Parliamentary Debates.*

Wheare, Kenneth C. *The Statute of Westminster and Dominion Status.* 5th ed. Oxford University Press, London, 1953.

The Constitutional Structure of the Commonwealth. Clarendon Press, Oxford, 1960; repr., Greenwood Press, London and Westport, Conn., 1982.

Modern Constitutions. Oxford University Press, London, 1966.

Williams, Desmond. "The Summing Up", T. Desmond Williams, ed., *The Irish Struggle* (q.v.), pp. 183-193.

ed. *The Irish Struggle, 1916-1926.* Routledge & Kegan Paul, London, 1966; University of Toronto Press, Toronto, 1966.

Wolf-Phillips, Leslie. *See* Blaustein, Albert P., and Eric B. Blaustein, eds.

Younger, Calton. *Ireland's Civil War.* Frederick Muller, London, 1968; 2nd, pbck. ed. Fontana Books, London, 1970.

Arthur Griffith. Irish Lives Series. Gill and Macmillan, Dublin, 1981; Irish Book Center, New York, 1981.

Zimmern, Alfred E. *The League of Nations and the Rule of Law, 1918-1935.* 2nd ed. London, 1939; Russell & Russell, New York, 1969.

ADDENDA

Adams, Gerry. *A Pathway to Peace.* Mercier Press, Cork, 1989.

Etchegaray, Roger Cardinal, and Jorge Mejia: Pontifical Commission for Justice and Peace. *The Church and Racism. Towards a More Fraternal Society.* Vatican, 1989; Origins, NC, Washington, D.C., 1989.

Foster, R. F. *Modern Ireland 1600-1972.* Allen Lane/The Penguin Press, London, 1989; Viking Press, New York, 1989.

John Paul II, Pope. *To Build Peace, Respect Minorities.* Vatican, 1989; Origins, NC, Washington, D.C., 1989.

Keeton, George W., and Dennis Lloyd. *The British Commonwealth: The Development of Its Laws and Constitutions.* Vol. I, *The United Kingdom.* Stevens & Sons Limited, London, 1955.

Kmiec, Douglas W. "The Separation of Powers", *Catholic University Law Review* (Washington, D.C.), Vol. 37 (Fall 1987), No. 1, pp. 73-84.

Lieberman, Mark. *Is Northern Ireland Free? An Inquiry.* Freedom House, New York, 1990.

Lynch, John M. "The Anglo-Irish Problem", *Foreign Affairs* (New York), Vol. 50, No. 4 (July 1972), pp. 601-617.

McInerney, "Mr John A. Costello Remembers", *The Irish Times,* Sept. 8, 1967.

Mansergh, Nicholas. *Survey of British Commonwealth Affairs: Problems of External Policy, 1931-1939.* Oxford, 1952.

ed., *Documents and Speeches on British Commonwealth Affairs, 1931-1952* (2 vols.). Oxford, 1953.

Merrills, J. G. *The Development of International Law by the European Court of Human Rights.* Manchester University Press, Manchester, Eng., [1988]. Distrd. St. Martin's Press, New York.

GLOSSARY, TABLES AND INDEXES

Another hand than ours weaves the pattern from the tangled threads, I believe . . .

CATHY CASH SPELLMAN
(*An Excess of Love*)

Hymn of the Nations

God of the ages, be with us always;
Guide the nations in the path of unity.
Your inspiration, Lord, we crave;
Strengthen our spirit, freedom to save;
Building a land of liberty.
God of the ages, uplift your mighty hand;
Love and protection give to ev'ry noble land.
Let all the nations as one stand brave;
Freedom's banner over all shall wave;
Freedom's banner evermore shall wave.

RICHARD KEYS BIGGS, 1986
Based on American Hymn

New Thinking on Northern Ireland

The Holy See expresses ready support for those steps being taken by the Governments involved to bring about the conditions required for peace . . .

We can only hope that the people of Northern Ireland themselves will urge their representatives to engage in dialogue about the situation as it really is, a dialogue without partisan, constitutional or political prejudice and without exclusions.

There, too, new ways of thinking are needed, more fully centered on achieving the integral well-being of all sectors of the population.

POPE JOHN PAUL II
January 27, 1990

GLOSSARY OF TERMS

Clann na Poblachta: Gaelic for the "Clan (or Party) of the Republic." Founded in 1947 by Sean MacBride, the Party was probably the most Republican oriented of the Constitutional Nationalist Parties while it lasted (until 1951). The Clann formed part of the Coalition Government with Fine Gael and Labour from 1948 to 1951.

Commonwealth, The (formerly British Commonwealth of Nations): A voluntary association of independent states and their dependencies (currently numbering 47), whose association is inspired by a common interest based on their having once been members of the British Empire, who accept Queen Elizabeth II of Britain as the symbolic head of their association, and who meet and consult on a regular basis to foster common links and achieve a more equitable world society. General activities are conducted by a Permanent Secretariat, however. Ireland became a member of the Commonwealth by the Anglo-Irish Treaty of 1921, but Southern Ireland left the Commonwealth in 1949 – though it may, as a Republic, be an Associate Member.

Cumann na mBan: Gaelic for the "League (or Society) of Women." Formed in 1914 as the Women's Auxiliary of the Irish Volunteers. The group now sides with Republican Sinn Fein.

Cumann na nGaedheal: Gaelic for the "Irish League" or the "Irish Society." The Party was formed in 1923 of the pro-Treaty members of Sinn Fein. It developed in 1933 into Fine Gael.

Dail Eireann: The Irish National Assembly or House of Parliament. The First Dail Eireann and Constituent Assembly was founded on January 21, 1919, the Second Dail Eireann came into existence in mid-1921, and the Third Dail Eireann, which was also a Constituent Assembly, was convened in September 1922. Constitutional Republicans regard the Third (all-Ireland) Dail Eireann as having been usurped by its later self as a partitionist, 26-county Dail of Southern Ireland, and regard the present Dail Eireann as being the collateral successor of the early Third Dail. Members of the Dail are referred to as "Deputies" or "Teachta Dala" (as abbreviated, TD), the Gaelic for "Parliamentary Deputy."

Democratic Unionist Party: The Party founded by Ian Paisley in 1971 and closely associated with the fundamentalist Free Presbyterian Church founded also by Paisley, in the 1950's. As a split-off from the traditional Unionist Party in Ireland, the DUP is generally considered an extreme right-wing, pro-union-with-Britain group, which is supported mainly by working-class Loyalists.

Document No. 2: The instrument devised by Eamon de Valera that bridged the gap between the position of Nationalists who espoused the Anglo-Irish Treaty of 1921 and that of Republicans who rejected it.

Eire: The name in Gaelic by which the island of Ireland has traditionally been known, but since 1937 (by reason of Article 4 of the current Irish Constitution) it is the name (as is "Ireland") by which the 26-county area of Southern Ireland is known. Traditional Ireland has 4 provinces and 32 counties, but present-day Ireland has 3 1/3 provinces and 26 counties, while Northern Ireland has 2/3 province and 6 counties. Provinces are former administrative areas of regional government, but today only counties mainly are used as adminstrative districts of local government. With Tipperary County having two such districts, "ridings," North Tipperary and South Tipperary, Southern Ireland has 27 administrative districts. However, it is only in the South that county administrative districts now exist, county councils having been abolished in Northern Ireland in 1972 and replaced with 26 administrative districts.

Fianna Fail: Gaelic for "Soldiers of Destiny." Largest political Party in the South of Ireland. Formed as a split-off from Sinn Fein by de Valera in 1926. Self-styled "The Republican Party," it is viewed as the most Republican oriented of the Constitutional Nationalist Parties in modern Ireland. The Party bases its national policy on unity by consent (of a majority in Northern Ireland) and political persuasionism.

Fine Gael: Gaelic for the "Irish Family." Formed in 1933 from a merger of Cumann na nGaedheal, the National Centre Party and the Army Comrades Association or National Guard ("the Blueshirts"). The National Centre Party was a group with agricultural interests that came together in 1933 to oppose the Anglo-Irish Economic War brought on by the decision of Fianna Fail to withhold payment of land annuities to the British Exchequer. The Blueshirts received the name when they adopted a blue uniform, modeled on that of Mussolini's Blackshirts, and used the Fascist salute. Fine Gael is generally considered the most conservative of the Constitutional Nationalist Parties in Ireland and bases its Irish unity policy on mutual consent and persuasionist politics. The Party has only been able to form a Government when in coalition with other Parties.

Irish Citizen Army: Group organized by James Larkin in 1913 as a workers' defense force and fashioned by James Connolly into a revolutionary socialist force. The Plough and the Stars was the flag of the Army and flew alongside the flag of the Republic in the 1916 Rising, in which the Irish Citizen Army took part with the Irish Volunteers.

Irish Free State: The name by which Ireland was known under the 1921 Treaty as a member of the Commonwealth. The name was used officially (e.g., in the 1922 Constitution) as a synonym with "Saorstat Eireann" ("Irish Repulic"), of which it is the literal and etymological translation. The Irish Free State *de jure* comprised all of Ireland, while the Irish Free State *de facto* comprised the 26 counties of Southern Ireland. Usage of the term was restricted in practice to the 26 counties until 1949, when Southern Ireland departed from the Commonwealth and became the "Republic of Ireland."

Irish Republican Army: The name given to the Irish Volunteers, the guerilla army which fought the British in the War of Independence of 1919-1921. After the signing of the 1921 Treaty, the I.R.A. split into two factions, with those opposed to the Treaty going "irregular" and retaining the name "I.R.A." and those supporting the Treaty forming part of the newly founded National Army. The failure to retain popular support for its campaigns of physical force as a solution to the British-Irish problem led to a decision by the IRA in the 1960's to discontinue the armed struggle in favor of concentrating on political action and, in keeping with this purpose, to drop its policy of abstention from the partitionist Dail Eireann. This departure from traditional policy resulted in a split in 1970, with the dissenting minority forming the "Provisional Irish Republican Army" and the majority the "Official Irish Republican Army." The closely associated Sinn Fein Party split correspondingly into "Provisional Sinn Fein" and "Official Sinn Fein". The Official IRA eventually faded away and Official Sinn Fein became known as "Sinn Fein the Workers Party" and later only as "The Workers Party," while the Provisional IRA went back to being called "IRA," and Provisional Sinn Fein to "Sinn Fein." In 1986 the IRA voted to recognize the existing Dail Eireann and in 1987 a majority in Sinn Fein followed suit.

Irish Volunteers: Defense force founded in 1913 by Eoin MacNeill, the section of which that did not participate in World War I becoming the Irish Republican Army.

Labour Party, Irish: Founded in 1912 by James Larkin and James Connolly as a trade unionist Party, with membership limited to trade unionists. This restriction was removed in 1930 in order to widen the Party's power base. The Party has formed Coalition Governments with Fine Gael off and on since 1948.

Labour Party, Northern Ireland: A trade union based Party, established in 1924. The Party abandoned its neutral position on Irish unity in 1949, when it endorsed union with Britain.

Loyalists: The term applied to individuals or groups in Ireland favoring retention of the British connection. Synonymous with "Unionists."

MEP: Member of the European Parliament.

MP: Member of Parliament (British).

Nationalists: The term applied to individuals or groups in Ireland who favor a united and independent state that would be achieved by persuasion and peaceful, political means. Sometimes called "Constitutional Nationalists" because of the members' one-time efforts to liberate Ireland by means of the British constitutional system and their more recent efforts to unite and liberate Ireland by means of the British-oriented partitionist Irish constitutional system.

Northern Ireland: The name given by the Government of Ireland Act of 1920 to the portion of northeastern Ireland comprising the "counties of Antrim, Armagh, Down, Fermanagh, Londonderry and Tyrone, and the parliamentary boroughs of Belfast and Londonderry." *See also* Eire; Stormont.

Official Unionist Party: The branch of the traditional Unionists in Ireland that survived the split of 1971 and that is descended from the Party formed during the era of the Union of Britain and Ireland. The group advocates continuance of the British connection with Ireland.

Oireachtas: The Dail and Seanad of Ireland combined.

Republicans, Constitutional: The term applied to individuals or groups in Ireland who advocate a reunited and independent multinational state to be achieved by restoration of the original Irish Republic and reactivation of the de Valera Document No. 2 constitutionalism.

Republican Sinn Fein: The name by which the Irish Republican Party, Sinn Fein, was known in the 1920's after the Cumann na nGaedheal and Fianna Fail split-offs. Currently it is the name by which the dissenting minority in Sinn Fein is known since the decision taken in 1987 to recognize the present, 26-county Dail (that in turn recognizes the six-county setup). Under the leadership of Ruairi O Bradaigh, the group would recognize the Dail only as a means to restoring the original, all-Ireland Dail Eireann as the Assembly of a reunited Ireland (though this policy has not been formalized).

Royal Ulster Constabulary: The official police force of Northern Ireland, set up in 1922 to replace the Royal Irish Constabulary in the North; the latter was theretofore the police force of all Ireland.

Saorstat Eireann: The official name given to the Republic of Ireland in 1919. Translated officially into Latin as "Respublica hibernica," into French as "Republique irlandaise," into Spanish as "Republica irlandese," and into English (since 1918) as "Irish Republic" and (since 1921) as "Irish Free State."

Seanad Eireann: The Irish Senate. Members are known as "Seanadoiri."

Sinn Fein: Gaelic for "Ourselves," though the two words have often been mistranslated "Ourselves Alone." The name "Sinn Fein" was first given to an umbrella organization formed by Arthur Griffith (who was assisted by William Rooney) in 1905-1908, with a policy designed to bring together Nationalists and Republicans. Having succeeded to make practicable this policy in 1917 and having been victorious in the General Election of 1918, the organization proceeded in 1919 to set up the first Dail Eireann of all Ireland. The Dail ratified the Republic proclaimed in 1916, issued a Declaration of Independence, and promulgated the first Constitution of Ireland. The Dail also decreed that the Irish Volunteers, now to be known as the Irish Republican Army, should take an oath of allegiance to Dail Eireann, though many of the officers and men continued to be independent. The relationship between modern Sinn Fein and the IRA is practically the same as that of 1919. In 1987 a majority of Sinn Fein, under the leadership of Gerry Adams, and following the precedent set by the IRA in 1986, decided to recognize the present Dail of Southern Ireland, and in 1988 the Party adopted a policy of political persuasionism on the Irish unity question, thus making itself virtually indistinguishable from all other Constitutional Nationalist Parties in Ireland.

Social, Democratic and Labour Party: Formed in 1970 by Gerry Fitt (Republican Labour), John Hume (Independent), Ivan Cooper (Independent), Paddy O'Hanlon (Northern Ireland Labour), Austin Currie (Nationalist), Paddy Devlin (Nationalist) and Paddy Wilson (Republican Labour), with Fitt as Party leader (and later, to the present, Hume). The SDLP "slides uneasily between, on the one hand, measures to bring nearer the reunification of Ireland and, on the other, methods to advance a consociational system of power-sharing in Northern Ireland. In so far as it is offered real prospects of getting the power-sharing, it is willing to play down united Ireland. It resumes lusty advocacy of united Ireland when its efforts over power-sharing are proving so futile that it is in danger of losing all political support." (Keith Kyle, Executive Committee, British-Irish Association.) The Party is a member of the Socialist International and the Confederation of Socialist Parties of the European Community.

Stormont: Seat of the former Assembly of Northern Ireland. It was dissolved in mid-1986.

TD: Teachta Dala (Parliamentary Deputy) of Dail Eireann.

Treaty Settlement: The overall Settlement consists of an unprescribed number of agreements and statutory instruments, but it could be said to consist mainly of the following: the Treaty itself – the "Articles of Agreement for a Treaty between Great Britain and Ireland" – that was signed in London on December 6, 1921; the Irish Free State (Consequential Provisions) Act of 1922; the Irish Free State/Saorstat Eireann Constitution of 1922; and the British-Irish agreements amending the Treaty, particularly the Boundary and Financial Agreement of 1925. The Treaty – and Constitution – applied to all of Ireland and, particularly as amended by the 1925 Boundary Agreement, enshrined the principle of essential Irish unity.

Unionists: Those individuals or groups in Ireland who, stemming from the era of the British-Irish Union, favor continued union with Britain and loyalty to the Crown. Forming a majority in present-day Northern Ireland, they are represented by two main Parties, the Official Unionist Party and the Democratic Unionist Party.

Westminster: Seat of the British Parliament.

TABLE OF CASES

The State (Ryan and Others) v. *Lennon and Others,* 1935: 77-78, 129, 143, 145-146, 151

The State (Joachim Gilsenan) v. *(District Justice) Peter A. McMorrow,* 1978: 270 n.

TABLE OF STATUTES, ORDERS, TREATIES, CONSTITUTIONS, COVENANTS, AND OTHER INSTRUMENTS

NOTE. *Those items that are marked with an asterisk are treated also, analitically, in the Index of Subjects.*

Sunset Over Grand Canyon

(If the 2 billion years of geologic time that the Grand Canyon represents were to be encapsulated in a 24-hour time frame, only the last fifth of the last second would represent historic man's time on earth.)

I stand transfix'd above the awesome sweep,
As sands' sun sinks and red gloom bathes thy domes.
Thy purpled temples settle down to sleep,
While I, alone, do contemplate thy tomes.

Awake, O Canyon Grand, and speak to me!
On bended knee I list to hear thy lay.
From aeons past what can thy story be?
In slumber wrapt must thou lie mute for aye?

Some mighty hand hath carved this vast profound,
One long day stands loud symbol of his power,
With sun and moon and stars his praises sound,
While man hears but one moment of one hour.

VINCENT J. DELACY RYAN

INDEX OF AUTHORS

NOTE: *Those names that are marked with an asterisk are listed also in the Index of Names.*

INDEX OF NAMES

NOTE. *Those names that are marked with an asterisk are treated also, analytically, in the Index of Subjects.*

INDEX OF SUBJECTS

NOTE: *Those items of the Table of Statutes and names of the Index of Names that are treated here also, as subjects, are marked with an asterisk. Cross-references are not made from here to that Table or Index.*

Focus on Issues

Big Story: How the American Press and Television Reported and Interpreted the Crisis of Tet-1968 in Vietnam and Washington,
Peter Braestrup; Two volumes 1977;
One volume paperback abridged 1978, 1983

Afghanistan: The Great Game Revisited,
edited by Rossane Klass; 1988

Nicaragua's Continuing Struggle: In Search of Democracy,
Arturo J. Cruz; 1988

La Prensa: The Republic of Paper,
Jaime Chamorro Cardenal; 1988

The World Council of Churches & Politics, 1975-1986,
J.A. Emerson Vermaat; 1989

South Africa: Diary of Troubled Times,
Nomavenda Mathiane; 1989

The Unknown War: The Miskito Nation, Nicaragua, and the United States,
Bernard Nietschmann; 1989

Power, the Press and the Technology of Freedom The Coming Age of ISDN,
Leonard R. Sussman; 1989

Ethiopia: The Politics of Famine; 1989

The Imperative of Freedom: A Philosophy of Journalistic Autonomy
John. C. Merrill; 1990

Racing With Catastrophe: Rescuing America's Higher Education,
Richard Gambino; 1990

Soviet Propaganda As A Foreign Policy Tool,
Marian Leighton; 1990

Ireland Restored: The New Self-Determination
Vincent J. Delacy Ryan; 1991

After the Velvet Revolution: Václav Havel and the New Leaders of Czechoslovakia Speak Out
Tim Whipple, editor; 1991

An Occasional Paper

General Editor: R. Bruce McColm

Glasnost and Social & Economic Rights
Valery Chalidze, Richard Schifter; 1988

Peace and Human Rights in Cambodia: Exploring From Within
Kassie Neou with Al Santoli; 1990

Freedom House Books

General Editor: James Finn

Yearbooks

Freedom in the World: Political Rights and Civil Liberties,
annuals from 1978-1991

Studies in Freedom

Escape to Freedom: The Story of the International Rescue Committee,
Aaron Levenstein; 1983

Forty Years: A Third World Soldier at the UN,
Carlos P. Romulo (with Beth Day Romulo); 1986. (*Romulo: A Third World Soldier at the UN*, paperback edition, 1987)

Today's American: How Free?
edited by James Finn & Leonard R. Sussman, 1986

Will of the People: Original Democracies in Non-Western Societies,
Raul S. Manglapus; 1987

Perspectives on Freedom

Three Years at the East-West Divide,
Max M. Kampelman; (Introductions by Ronald Reagan and Jimmy Carter; edited by Leonard R. Sussman); 1983

The Democratic Mask: The Consolidation of the Sandinista Revolution,
Douglas W. Payne; 1985

The Heresy of Words in Cuba: Freedom of Expression & Information,
Carlos Ripoll; 1985

Human Rights & the New Realism: Strategic Thinking in a New Age,
Michael Novak; 1986

To License A Journalist?,
Inter-American Court of Human Rights; 1986.

The Catholic Church in China,
L. Ladany; 1987

Glasnost: How Open? Soviet & Eastern European Dissidents; 1987

Yugoslavia: The Failure of "Democratic" Communism; 1987

The Prague Spring: A Mixed Legacy,
edited by Jiri Pehe, 1988

Romania: A Case of "Dynastic" Communism; 1989